GOVERNING THE SOCIETY OF COMPETITION

This book considers the manner in which the making and implementation of law and governance is changing in the global context. It explores this through a study of the deployment of the global anti-doping apparatus including the World Anti-Doping Code and its institutions with specific reference to professional cycling, a sport that has been at the forefront of some of the most famous doping cases and controversies in recent years. Critically, it argues that the changes to law and governance are not restricted to sport and anti-doping, but are actually inherent in broader processes associated with neoliberalism and social and behavioural surveillance and affect all aspects of society and its political institutions.

The author engages with concepts and arguments in contemporary social theory, including: Dardot and Laval on neoliberalism; Agamben on sovereignty; Hardt and Negri on globalisation; and others including Foucault, Deleuze and Guattari and Louis Dumont. The work seeks to answer a question posed by both Foucault and Agamben; that is, given the growing primacy of the arts of government, what is the juridical form and theory of sovereignty that is able to sustain and found this primacy? It is argued that this question can be understood by reference to the shift from a social or public contract that was understood to be the foundation of society, to a society that is constituted by consent, private agreement and contract.

In addition, the book examines the juridical concepts of the rule of law and sovereignty. Commencing with the Festina scandal of 1998, the Spanish case of Operación Puerto and concluding with the fall from grace of the American cyclist Lance Armstrong in 2012, the principal processes examined include:

- The increasing crossing of the borders between different legal regimes (whether supranational or simply particularised) and with it the erosion of what we knew as state sovereignty and constitutionalism;
- The increasing use of judgment achieved through the media and how this arrives at new configurations of moral panic and scapegoating;
- The creation of a need for rapid outcomes at the expense of the modernist value or version of the rule of law;
- The increasing use of new and alternative methods of guilt, proof and ultra-legal detection.

Governing the Society of Competition

Cycling, Doping and the Law

Martin Hardie

·HART·

OXFORD · LONDON · NEW YORK · NEW DELHI · SYDNEY

HART PUBLISHING

Bloomsbury Publishing Plc

Kemp House, Chawley Park, Cumnor Hill, Oxford, OX2 9PH, UK

1385 Broadway, New York, NY 10018, USA

HART PUBLISHING, the Hart/Stag logo, BLOOMSBURY and the Diana logo are
trademarks of Bloomsbury Publishing Plc

First published in Great Britain 2020

A catalogue record for this book is available from the British Library.

Library of Congress Cataloging-in-Publication data

Names: Hardie, Martin, author.

Title: Governing the society of competition : cycling, doping, and the law / Martin Hardie.

Description: Oxford, UK ; New York, NY : Hart Publishing, an imprint
of Bloomsbury Publishing, 2020. | Includes bibliographical references and index.

Identifiers: LCCN 2020025317 (print) | LCCN 2020025318 (ebook) | ISBN 9781509936564
(hardback) | ISBN 9781509936588 (ePDF) | ISBN 9781509936571 (Epub)

Subjects: LCSH: Doping in sports—Law and legislation. | Cyclists—Drug use. | Cycling—Law
and legislation. | World Anti-Doping Agency. World Anti-Doping Code.

Classification: LCC K3702 .H37 2020 (print) | LCC K3702 (ebook) | DDC 344/.099—dc23

LC record available at https://lccn.loc.gov/2020025317

LC ebook record available at https://lccn.loc.gov/2020025318

ISBN: HB: 978-1-50993-656-4
       ePDF: 978-1-50993-658-8
       ePub: 978-1-50993-657-1

Typeset by Compuscript Ltd, Shannon

To find out more about our authors and books visit www.hartpublishing.co.uk.
Here you will find extracts, author information, details of forthcoming events
and the option to sign up for our newsletters.

... However, I already had in my head a sketch of an article, in which I thought demonstrated the place where human greatness may be displayed at its fullest, that is, in sport, the scum also enter, unscrupulous, without ever lifting their head to take a serious view of the hero. They only seek their own gain, caring solely for their own interest, and at its best, they seek to justify their position by saying that they do it for the general good.

Franz Kafka

In the history of cycle sport, fabrications crowded out facts from the very outset.

Benjo Maso

This is the west, sir. When the legend becomes fact, print the legend.

The Man Who Shot Liberty Valance.

If we want things to stay as they are, things will have to change.

Il Gatopardo or The Leopard.

Nobody starts out wanting to dope, but to survive in this system you must.

Floyd Landis

Macrobius assimilates *homo sacer* to the statues (Zanes) in Greece that were consecrated to Jove with the proceeds from the fees imposed on oath-breaking athletes, statues that were in fact nothing other than the colossi of those that had broken their word and had therefore been vicariously consigned to divine justice ... Insofar as he incarnates in his own person the elements that are usually distinguished from death, *homo sacer* is, so to speak, a living statute, the double or colossus of himself.

Giorgio Agamben

Led like a lamb into this gloom
Yeah Freud is in the back room with his goons
Now they've got new experiments, the metal groans, the limbs are rent
The anti-heroes' mock dissent, we market now by mass consent
We swing for the crime everyone in double time ...
They swing for the crime everyone in double time
And we hope that you had a good time
Yeah smile as you sign on the line
Because life on your knees can be fun
Are you glad that you're not the only one?

Edmund Kuepper, Chris Bailey.

4Eva – for without her this would never have been written.
Eva Teresa Gonzalez Garcia
4 October 1972, Bilbao – 24 January 2017, Geelong
Always remember: what would Eva do?

TABLE OF CONTENTS

Prologue: Before and after *Festina*

The *Festina Tour*

The day before the 1998 *Tour de France* was set to start in Dublin, Willy Voet, a *soigneur* (or masseur) for the *Festina* team, was stopped on a back-road border crossing between Belgium and France. A search of the team car he was driving revealed syringes, a few hundred grammes and capsules of anabolic steroids, as well as 400 bottles and ampules of various products, which included 250 bottles of EPO that had come from three laboratories in Germany and Switzerland. By the time the race had reached France a few days later Voet had already confessed to smuggling offences, admitting that it was not the first time and that he was acting under team instructions. Voet's admission caused the team manager Bruno Roussel to publicly state that he was 'stunned' and 'shocked'. The next day both Roussel and the team doctor Eric Rijckaert were held for questioning by French police. Gendarmes subsequently searched the team hotel and Voet was formally charged with drug smuggling. Up until this point, the team management had continued to deny being involved and the *Tour de France* director, Jean-Marie Leblanc, publicly confirmed that he would not expel the *Festina* team from the *Tour*.

By the following morning things started to change as the Union Cycliste Internationale (UCI) suspended Roussel. Later, that night, following a tearful press conference by members of the team, the *Tour de France* decided to expel the entire *Festina* team from the race. That decision followed Roussel's admission that banned substances were used to maximise the team's performance. Roussel's lawyer said that the doping was organised by the team; a practice of 'a deliberate management' of doping products organised by the team officials, doctors, support staff and cyclists in order to avoid their dangerous use outside medical supervision. The revelations appeared to upset the *Tour* director who was reported as saying: 'These few sentences seemed awful to us, the organisers of the Tour de France, the greatest cycling challenge in the world, because they constituted a confession.'[1]

Within days other teams, such as the Dutch *TVM* team, were also implicated in doping with their team manager and doctor also arrested. By the second week of the *Tour*, as the race came out of its annual passage through the Pyrenees, and where the Italian Marco Pantani had all but destroyed Jan Ullrich's defence of his title, the riders were holding stop work meetings. The start of Stage 12 was delayed

---

[1] cyclingnews.com, Tour de France, Grand Tour July 11–August 2, 1998, Stage 6, La Chatre – Brive-la-Gaillarde, available at autobus.cyclingnews.com/results/1998.

by two hours with the subsequent go-slow forcing the race organisers to annul the day's results. Following the delayed start, the stage had progressed very slowly and after only 32 kilometres the peloton came to a halt at the first intermediate sprint. Sitting on the bitumen, the riders held another stop work meeting and only after their own internal deliberations were complete and their representatives had spoken to the *Tour* Director, who himself was in discussion with the French Sports Minister, did the riders start to ride again, but still only at pedestrian speed. The peloton decided to ride to the finish line in Aix-les-Bains without their race numbers on their backs. Even before the arrival at the 'finish', the Spanish *ONCE*[2] team had decided to quit the race altogether. Shortly after the go-slow recommenced, the *ONCE* riders fell behind the convoy of team cars and abandoned their race. Their manager Manolo Saiz (whom we shall meet again) said: 'The Tour is over.' The team leader Laurent Jalabert told reporters: 'I stop. I made this decision knowingly. I was too depressed …'[3]

* * * *

During the late 1990s, for the average antipodean cycling fan, as I was then, sitting at home in Darwin, the *Tour*, and pro cycling generally (if we were really lucky), could only be watched by way of daily 30-minute TV highlights broadcast the following evening. Mostly, we followed the race by live updates and coverage on the nascent internet. The drama of the *Festina* Tour became a part of the daily mix and rise of, amongst other things, post-Cold War globalisation, the internet and a more aggressive global sports marketing and broadcasting machine. For the fan of the daily chronicles of Bill's cyclingnews.com,[4] the spectacle brought with it another aspect, namely, sport being the subject of a police operation, an operation that had become as exciting to watch as the race itself. Cycling's path out of Europe and the problematisation of doping coincided with the emergence of the new global 'consciousness' that had been brought into existence by the new conditions. As the English cycling journalist William Fotheringham wrote in his forward to Willy Voet's confessionary and classic cycling text, *Breaking the Chain*, 'in future cycling might come to be seen in two eras: before and after … Festina.'[5]

---

[2] The *ONCE* team, sponsored by the Spanish association for the blind, was later to be rebranded to become *Liberty Seguros*.

[3] Cyclingnews.com, Tour de France, Grand Tour 11 July–2 August 1998, Stage 17, Albertville – Aix-les-Bains, available at autobus.cyclingnews.com/results/1998/tour98/stage17.html.

[4] Professor Bill Mitchell ran cyclingnews.com in those days from his home near Newcastle, Australia, coordinating in the early hours of the morning with his network of informants. In 1999, he decided to focus full time on his academic work at the Centre for Full Employment and Equity (e1.newcastle. edu.au/coffee/) where he has developed Modern Monetary Theory. He sold cyclingnews.com for what would now be considered a meagre sum. The website went on to become the largest global source of news for the sport. But it was never the same beast after Bill, losing its irreverence and incisiveness to become part of the mainstream media.

[5] W Voet, *Breaking the Chain, Drugs and Cycling – The True Story* (Yellow Jersey Press, 2001) ix.

In many ways *Festina* marked the beginning of the future for all sport and, as we will see, quite possibly for us all.

For our immediate purposes, the importance of *Festina* was not the spectacle that played out, nor the subsequent trial of members of the team and its management, but it is that the *Festina* 'scandal' has been characterised as one of the principal catalysts for the inception of the World Anti-Doping Agency (WADA). Danish sports scientist Verner Møller sees the action of the French police, acting on the orders of the French Minister for Youth and Sport Marie-George Buffet, to raid the *Tour* as signalling the end of the time-honoured tradition of self-administration of sport. For Møller, these events led to the establishment of the new global anti-doping agency, which compromised sport's special autonomy and thus opened up sport and sporting institutions to political pressure and vulnerability.[6] One of the things we will start to encounter, as we move on in our story, is that to promote such a position isn't really an adequate response to the manner in which Government and governance is structured in the twenty-first century, nor does it take account of sport's place in that system of governance.

Nevertheless, questions abound as to why cycling and why that time? In 1998 the *Tour* started later than its normal first weekend in July, for the reason that the football (soccer) World Cup was also being held in France at that time. As one former member of the *Festina* team told me:

> Who knows, the apocryphal tale, the sort of the legendary background is that the French minister for sport wanted to go after soccer in '98 but it was the year of the World Cup in France and the powers have said no way you are not going to, these are the tales from history, so she went after cycling, whatever sport in Europe, the French minister of Sport went after ...: rugby, absolutely soccer, absolutely, they could have gone and raided any club, any cycling team, any rugby or football club at that era and would have had a similar impact ... cycling seems to have been leading the way on doping throughout its history ... [But cycling] is different because of the difficulty of the sport itself, this means that pharmacological intervention maybe has a greater impact, I suspect, because it is so long and so hard, and recovery so difficult, I suspect that cycling potentially benefits more than other shorter, faster sports.[7]

Whatever the reason for the raid, after *Festina* things would indeed be different. *Festina* provided the catalyst for a new network of technicians and scientists (or in some cases the same ones who doped the riders), funded by the State and sport and coordinated by the new global agency, WADA, to develop new testing

[6] V Møller, 'The Anti-Doping Campaign – Farewell to the Ideals of Modernity?' in J Hoberman and V Møller (eds), *Doping and Public Policy* (University Press of Southern Denmark, 2004) 145, 146. See also U Wagner, 'The World Anti-Doping Agency, Power and Law beyond the State' in U Wagner, RK Storm and J Hoberman (eds), *Observing Sport, Modern System Theoretical Approaches* (Hofmann, 2010) 77; and DV Hanstad, A Smith and I Waddington, 'The Establishment of the World Anti-Doping Agency: A Study of the Management of Organizational Change and Unplanned Outcome' (2008) 43 *International Review for the Sociology of Sport* 227.

[7] Martin Hardie, and Ianto Ware, unpublished interview 2010.

procedures to counter the EPO-driven practices of blood doping and its derivatives. Post-*Festina*, cycling was no longer simply a place populated by the sport's governing bodies, the European-based teams, entourages and riders and the fans. Cycling became a point of intersection between the sport's traditional stakeholders and government, transnational agencies, scientists and technicians. It is this post-*Festina* difference that we seek to interrogate here.

An Incomplete History of the Origins of Cycle Sport

Cycling is certainly different to other sports in many ways and it may be this difference that gave rise to its vulnerability. Although professional road cycling has its origins back in the nineteenth century, it has never developed the power base of other sports. Unlike other sports, or for that matter track racing held on an enclosed velodrome, you can't enclose a road race and hence you cannot sell admission tickets. Until the advent of television, cycling could not be completely seen: it could only be spoken or written. Cycling is neither a team sport nor an individual sport. Cycling teams are nomadic, itinerant, changeable (unstable) bands of gypsies. They have no home ground or place. Road cyclists are like wolves in so far as they both hunt or move solo or in packs. In contrast to a football player in a football team, who must necessarily live near his or her team mates to train together on nearly a daily basis, a cyclist might not see another team mate between races, often training and spending time with their 'opposition' and coming together with each other only from race to race or within a race. Cyclists thus tend more to be lone wolves pursuing a line of flight or a chasing, hunting pack. Because of its lack of enclosure, cycling has always had to sell something other than itself – newspapers, sponsors' products, nationalism, or simply dreams. From the very beginning, cycling was work. Its amateur side developed later than its professional side. It also developed in a different context outside of Continental Europe. It was as much work and sport as it was a show, a moving advertising hoarding. It was always linked to medical or physiological experimentation.[8] The links between nationalism, the media, money and later the dissolution of national borders all were dominant in cycling well before other sports (save possibly Rugby League[9]). Because of the manner in which it lives, no one organisation is able to exert complete control over the sport. There is no one dominant sovereign power, rather a network of the international union, national federations, professional teams, riders, race organisers and sponsors; all of them cooperating and competing, albeit, with no single group able to exert total dominance.[10]

---

[8] J Hoberman, *Mortal Engines: The Science of Performance and the Dehumanization of Sport* (The Free Press, 1992), where he chronicles the early links between cycling and medical research.

[9] T Collins, *Rugby League in Twentieth Century Britain, A Social and Cultural History* (Routledge, 2006).

[10] Cycling, in this respect, is a long way from Australian or American Football, sports with one peak competition, one governing body and, in many ways, one media voice. In these sports, one group appears to exert total control and dominance.

From the very beginning, the professional peloton has always existed within a nexus of commerce, media, athleticism and nation building. The European tradition of cycling is a product of the Industrial Revolution and as such bears the marks of an era in which nations reformed, mass audiences came into being and the daily social and economic life of individuals shifted from primarily localised to nationalised and, finally, globalised. The birth of professional cycling and its relationship with the press was in itself part and parcel of what Benedict Anderson describes in *Imagined Communities* as the production of nations in modernity. For our purposes, the newspaper and the myth of the early professional cyclist were two forms that provided the technical means for representing the kind of imagined community that is the nation.[11] Accordingly, professional cycling was never not just a sporting endeavour or a competition amongst individuals, it was a process of making, and selling, a product – a product of industry and the nation itself.

From the beginning it was impossible to separate cycling and the media. Benjo Maso notes the presence of at least three magazines devoted to the bicycle by April 1868, with the Paris-based *Le Velocipede Illustre* gaining dominance in the market by organising a 135-kilometre race from Paris to Rouen.[12] This was merely one year after Pierre Michaux began producing pedal velocipedes for a growing French market.[13] Notably, though, the race was won by the Englishman James Moore. Maso, however, draws attention to the fact that Moore in fact came second. The actual winner seems to have been lost in the mythology that quickly surrounded a race that was, at that point, unique. *Le Velocipede Illustre* funded the race through sponsorship from bicycle manufacturers, for whom the spectacle of a long-distance race was prime advertising (Moore rode a machine built by Jules Suriray, the prime competitor of the Michaux-owned *Compagnie Parisienne*). It was possible to gamble on the race outcome, with Moore billed as the favourite, and the entire foray was specifically designed to attract attention to *Le Velocipede Illustre* and increase its capacity to attract advertisers. Maso's suggestion is that, somewhere in between those various factors, the actual sporting outcome got lost amidst the hubbub of who the paper, the bookies, the bike companies and, indeed, the wider audience wanted to win. As Maso notes: 'In the history of cycle sport, fabrications crowded out facts from the very outset.'[14] The fact that Moore's 'victory' is still cited as fact a century and a half later says something special about myth and truth in professional sport. Moreover, it complicates our understanding of it: from commerce as merely a side effect of sporting competition towards something that actively shapes it; something that goes against the desire to see sport as 'pure' by lodging it firmly within a social, historical and economic context.

---

[11] B Anderson, *Imagined Communities: Reflections on the Origin and Spread of Nationalism*, (Verso, 1991) 30.

[12] B Maso, *The Sweat of the Gods* (Mousehold Press, 2005) 3. Much of the following history is drawn from the work of Maso and that of H Dauncey and G Hare, 'The Tour de France: A Pre-Modern Contest in a Post-Modern Context' (2003) 20(2) *The International Journal of the History of Sport* 1.

[13] DV Herlihy, *Bicycle: The History* (Yale University Press, 2004).

[14] Maso, The Sweat of the Gods (n 12) 2.

Paris-Rouen was a relatively short-lived venture, but its historical impact was immense. It proved that there was public interest, and a commercial market, in bicycle racing. In its wake, two things happened. Firstly, the bicycle flourished. The early velocipedes, with the pedal crank attached directly to the front wheel underwent substantial technological development, with the use of lighter steel frames and wire spoke wheels. To increase speed, the front wheel continued to grow until it reached penny-farthing proportions. In 1885, John Starley produced the first widely successful 'safety' bicycle – the Rover – which replaced the direct connection between the pedal crank and the front wheel hub with the chain and gear system that has since become dominant. On top of making it possible to attain high speeds without a large front wheel, the Rover made cycling far safer and, combined with the cheaper production of steel machinery, much more affordable. Between 1885 and the turn of the century the bicycle gained what remains essentially its modern form. The pneumatic tyre was on the market by 1890, around the same time that most manufacturers began to focus on the diamond frame that remains standard. Fuelled by the technological and manufacturing improvements of the Industrial Revolution, the bicycle continued to drop in price until, by the start of the twentieth century, there existed a mass market and a nascent sport with a mass audience. It was also around this time that the term '*peloton*' was employed to describe the mass of riders taking advantage of the lead riders' slipstream.

The second impact of *Paris-Rouen* was a recognition that cycling was a sport that could be used to sell newspapers. This was the fundamental means through which the sport reached an audience right up until the coming of television in the 1950s and 1960s. From the 1840s and the early part of the twentieth century, readership of newspapers, journals and similar periodicals rose into the millions. This growth thus occurred alongside the birth the bicycle. Between 1860 and 1900, both the printed word and the bicycle became affordable and accessible to a mass audience and both became engaged in the production of mass national identities, one by allowing ordinary people to traverse distances previously seen as insurmountable without a horse and one by rapidly speeding the flow of information. It was a shift that was particularly conducive to road racing. While track racing came into competition with other stadium sports, most notably soccer, the only way to keep track of a 300km road race was to read about it.

The final decade of the nineteenth century marked a distinct separation between the rise of professional cycling in Europe and Britain. That division drifted out across the Anglophone world and has only been bridged in the last decade and a half. Unlike cycling in Europe, which garnered an increasingly working-class following, the British National Cycling Union retained a conservative, 'respectable middle class' ethic, focusing on touring and track racing. Thus, prior to the first *Tour de France* in 1903, a major divergence had already taken place between cycling in Britain and cycling in Europe. The Commonwealth and the United States roughly followed suit, with road racing suffering a further decline in the face of increased rates of automobile ownership from the1930s onwards, particularly in the United States. Road racing, accordingly, became almost exclusively a European sport until it was rediscovered by the Anglophone world in the 1990s.

The rise of cycling in Europe and the rise of the *Tour de France* are inseparable. As the Anglophone world effectively removed itself from cycling as a professional sport, the *Tour* marks the point at which the Continent began to perfect the formula that remains in place today. The popular story of the *Tour's* origins hinges on an anti-Semitic publisher, Count Philippe de Dion, falling out with his editor over the Dreyfus Affair and starting a new paper, employing the equally anti-Semitic Henri Desgrange as its editor. Desgrange specified in the first edition of *L'Auto Velo* (later renamed *L'Auto* for legal reasons) that the paper had no interest in politics and its investors reveal as much about its economic, as well as its political, interests. Dion, as well as Baron Etienne de Zuyen de Nyevelt, and Count Gaston de Chasseloup-Laubat were car manufacturers seeking to gain publicity within the newly developed field of motor racing. The other investors included Adolphe Clement, a bicycle manufacturer, and Edmond Michelin, co-owner of the tyre company, who had already used road races to promote his brand, dating back to the 1891 *Paris-Brest*.

As editor of *L'Auto*, and with the considerable help of his assistant Géo Lefèvre, Desgrange had the job of both placing his publication into the market as quickly as possible and producing an event which attracted sponsorship and rewarded the interests of investors. He already had a successful record of organising races, and reviving *Paris-Brest* in 1901 had been one of his first acts as editor. The quest now was to run something so spectacular that it completely dominated the market. Initially the project seemed so far-fetched it had trouble attracting serious attention: a three-week race, with six stages lasting for around 400kms each. Desgrange, mindful of his own reputation, placed Lefèvre in the position of 'race director' and on the first day, with only a few hundred spectators in attendance for the stage start, *L'Auto* gave over its front page to coverage of motor racing. That said, by the end of the first week, it was obvious the formula was working. The circulation of *L'Auto* had risen from 20,000 to 65,000. *Tour* historian Geoffrey Wheatcroft remarks:

> The first winner of the *Tour* was a wiry little 32-year old of Italian parents, but the true winner may have been Desgrange. His race had succeeded far beyond his or Dion's expectations, with great numbers turning out to watch, even when their enthusiasm had been tested by the absurdity of the race passing through their town or village in the small hours. When the twenty-one riders who completed the race reached Ville d'Avray south west of Paris, a crowd of 100,000 greeted them, with another 20,000 at the Parc des Princes for the Arrivée.[15]

---

[15] G Wheatcroft, *Le Tour: A History of the Tour de France* (Simon & Schuster, 2007).

One of the major reasons for the race's success is that both Lefèvre and Desgrange knew how to present it. Stage racing itself still lacked any real uniform set of rules and Desgrange would spend the next decade altering regulations wildly, experimenting with national versus trade teams, banning teams altogether, allowing and disallowing the use of different makes of bicycle and so on and so forth. However, as Benjo Maso concludes, Lefèvre had quickly figured out that to make the race popular he had to turn the competitors into heroes. Desgrange, a master of bombastic, dramatic turns of phrase, took this to new heights. Maso cites a passage from *L'Auto* penned by Desgrange:

> The steepest mountains, the coldest and blackest nights, the sharpest and most violent winds, constant and unjust reverses, the most difficult routes, never-ending slopes and roads that just keep going on and on – nothing has been able to break the determination and willpower of these men.[16]

The Convicts of the Route

By the 1920s, the heroic image of the *Tour* was already being exposed as something quite different. The investigative journalist Albert Londres chronicled the 1924 edition of the *Tour*. Londres was a correspondent of the hells of his world.[17] Previously Londres had, in 1920, found his way into the USSR where he profiled both VI Lenin and Leon Trotsky for the French press. He later travelled to China and India where he covered Jawaharlal Nehru, Mohandas Gandhi and Rabindranath Tagore. After joining *Le Petit Parisien* he went to the penal colony of Cayenne, in French Guyana and North Africa, where he chronicled the horrors of forced convict labour. Following his coverage of the *Tour* he wrote about the abuse in lunatic asylums in France and the abuse of African workers in Senegal and French Congo.[18]

Londres dubbed the race the *Tour of Suffering* and its participants, in keeping with his other exposés, the 'the convicts of the route'. It was in his interview with the cyclist Henri Pélissier, following the 405km stage from Cherbourg to Brest, that Londres exposed the harsh reality of the lives of Desgrange's heroes. His chronicle[19] of that day is worthy of complete reproduction as it introduces in stark terms the antithesis of Desgrange's hero; the convict or athletic worker and the place of drugs in assisting them to maintain their job and to put on the show.

---

[16] Maso, The Sweat of the Gods (n 12) 21.
[17] A Londres, *Los forzados de la carretera Tour de Francia 1924* (Editorial Melusina SL, 2009) 5.
[18] ibid 5–8; see also at en.wikipedia.org/wiki/Albert_Londres.
[19] This is my translation of the Spanish reprint of Londres.

Henri Pélissier, 1912.

Coutances, June 27, 1924

This morning, we set out before the peloton …

We reached Granville as the bells chimed 6.00am. In front of us the riders marched. As soon as they appeared, the crowd, sure that they had recognised them, shouted "Henri! Francis!" Henri and Francis were not in the bunch. Everybody waited. Both categories of riders went by – first-category professionals and the 'shadow men'. The shadow men are the tourists of the road touriste-routiers, a bunch of independent gutsy guys, not under contract to the wealthy bike manufacturers. They have a hard life but they've got plenty of fight in them. Neither Henri nor Francis appeared. The news came through: the Pélissier brothers have abandoned. We climbed into the Renault and, without a thought for the tyres, drove back up to Cherbourg. The Pélissiers are well worth a set of tyres.

Coutances: a mob of boys chattering about the scoop.

"Have you seen the Pélissiers?"

"I even touched them," says one of the grubby little urchins.

"Do you know where they are?"

"In the Café de la Gare. Everybody's there."

Everyone was there. I had to push through to get into the bistro. The crowd stood in silence, just staring open-mouthed towards the back of the room where three jerseys were installed in front of three bowls of chocolate. It was Henri, Francis and the third was none other than the second, I mean Ville, who came second at Le Havre and Cherbourg. "Did you throw a tantrum?" I asked.

"No," said Henri, "but we're not dogs."

"What happened?"

"It was a problem with some scum, or rather, over a jersey. This morning in Cherbourg, a commissaire came up to me and, without saying a word, pulled up my jersey. He was checking I hadn't got two jerseys on. What would you say if I just pulled up your waistcoat to see if you really were wearing a white shirt? I don't like their manners, that's all."

"Why was he bothered about you wearing two jerseys?"

"I could be wearing 15, but I can't leave with two and arrive with just one."

"Why?"

'It's the rules. We not only have to ride like animals, we also have to either freeze or suffocate. It's all part of the sport, apparently. Anyway, I went and found Desgrange. 'I'm not allowed to ditch my jerseys on the road, is that it?'

'No. You must not throw away any material belonging to the organisation.'

'It doesn't belong to the organisation, it belongs to me.'

'I'm not discussing it in the street.'

'If you won't discuss it in the street, I'm going back to bed.'

'We'll sort it out in Brest.'

"'It all will be completely sorted out in Brest because I will slap you in the face before then.' And I did."

"And your brother?"

"My brother's my brother, is that right, Francis?" And they kissed over their hot chocolate.

"Francis was already on the road with the bunch. I caught up with him and said 'Francis, let's chuck it in.'"

"It was like fresh butter on hot toast," said Francis. "Just this morning I'd got a stomach ache. I didn't feel at all good."

"And you, Ville?"

"Me?" replied Ville, laughing like a baby. "They found me in bad trouble on the side of the road. Both my knees were seized up, dead, like the bones of the relics of a saint."

The Pélissiers not only have legs, they have a head. And in that head they've got good sense.

"You have no idea what the Tour de France is," said Henri. "It's an ordeal, a Calvary. Worse still, because there were only fourteen stations of the Cross while ours has fifteen. We suffer from start to finish. Do you want to know how we keep going? Here …" He pulled out a vial from his bag. "That's cocaine for the eyes. This is chloroform for the gums."

"This," said Ville, emptying his musette, "is liniment to put some warmth in our knees."

"And the pills? You want to see the pills? Take a look, here are the pills." Each one of them pulled out 3 bottles.

"Fact is," said Francis, "we fly."

Henri continued: "You haven't seen us in the bath after the finish. You should buy a ticket for the show. After we get rid of the mud, we're white as a funeral shroud, drained empty by diarrhoea; we pass out in the water. At night in the bedroom, we can't sleep, we twitch and dance and jig about like St. Vitus. Look at our shoelaces, they're made of leather. Well, they sometimes give out, they break, and that's tanned hide. Just think what's happening to our skin."

"There's less flesh on our bodies than you'd see on a skeleton," said Francis.

"And our toenails," said Henri. "I've lost six out of ten, they get worn away bit by bit every stage."

"They grow back for next year," said his brother. The brothers kissed once more over the chocolate.

"So, that's it. And you've seen nothing yet; you wait till the Pyrenees, that's 'hard labour' [in English]. We put up with everything, even with what we wouldn't make a mule do. We're not work-shy, but in God's name we won't be kicked around. We can take physical torment, but we won't tolerate abuse. My name's Pélissier, not Atlas. If I put a newspaper over my stomach and set out with it, I have to arrive with it. If I throw it away – penalty. When we're dying of thirst, before we put our can under the running water, we have to make sure there isn't somebody fifty metres away working the pump, otherwise – penalty. You need a drink, you do your own pumping. The day will come when they'll put lead in our pockets because someone reckons that God made men too light. It's all going down the chute – soon there'll only be tramps left, no more artists. The sport has gone haywire, out of control."

"Yes," said Ville, "mad, haywire."

A young boy came up. "What do you want, lad?"

"Er, well, Monsieur Pélissier, seeing as you don't want to, who's going to win now?"

A Few Brief Words about the Role of the Grand Tours

Originally the Grand Tours (the *Tour de France*, the *Giro d'Italia* and the *Vuelta a España*) played a role in marking out and defining the territory, the nation and the people. Dauncey and Hare note the ways in which the 'mythically heroic'[20] *Tour* both maps out and interprets France as a nation and a Republic.[21] The *Tour*, from its inception, was a 'self-consciously modern project in which sport was to become a gigantic crusade, a herald of progress and discovery' where 'modern concerns with the instrumental role of sport and technology coalesced with the fundamentally "pre-modern" gladiatorial contest' and which is 'increasingly a "pre-modern" contest conveying "modern" values in a "post-modern" context'.[22]

Unlike any other sporting events, the three Tours of the year embody the dramatics of life played out over a full three weeks. To those involved they seem to be a lifetime. These races embody all the aspects of life in such a way that they are so much more than sporting events. They are, above all, human dramas of an intense, immense stature. Each is part and parcel of the consciousness of societies, and a search for some truth and meaning to the human condition. All are built upon an idea of moulding the individual, the land, and people through a spectacle involving superhuman figures that seek to mark out their own territories and conquer the boundaries of their precarious existence.

In their marking out of a territory, of a nation and of a people, the Tours were as much a part of creating the Europe of the twentieth century as was the documentation and administration of life as Foucault so very well describes in his lectures entitled 'Society Must be Defended' – the people, customs, fêtes, fairs and fiestas, each day complete with the local version of cheese, chorizo and champagne. The Tours were created and maintained by an alliance of the State, industrial capital and the media. In France, the Tour's impetus was to sell more editions of a motoring magazine, putting cycling to work in the pay of an intersection of the car and newspaper industries. With its resumption after the Civil War in 1941, Spain's *La Vuelta* covered the longest route in its history demarcating the victor's territory across the country and particularly the former Republican strongholds. For some years Franco restricted it to only Spanish participants. In modernity, these races all played their role in reinforcing the status of a unified territory, a people, a nation and its capital.

The Tours have also been the place that traditionally has allowed Europe to think of itself as the place where subjectivity could still 'do' rather than the place where subjectivity was simply relegated to 'being'. The Tours were centres of action in lands that might otherwise have been petrified into museums of the old world amongst the chaos of the new world and modernity.[23] But with the coming of

---

[20] Dauncey and Hare, 'The Tour de France' (n 19) 2.

[21] ibid, 3.

[22] ibid, 4. A part of the thesis we will develop here is that, rather than modern values, *the Tour* and sport now convey post-modern or neoliberal values.

[23] Was this the root of Europe's distaste for the American Armstrong?

the age of Empire, things changed. It was with the coming of those from outside Continental Europe that the practices of the peloton and, in particular, doping first become problematised.

It was with Tom Simpson's death in 1967 on Mont Ventoux – the Englishman whose success, prior to his death, had helped start the process of globalising the *Tours* – that doping first became a political matter. However, it remained an internal issue, something for the sport to deal with. The mid-1960s also coincided with the demise of national teams and the introduction of what are now known as the 'trade teams'. The late 1990s marked the point at which it became a matter for the sovereign – it was here with the *Festina* Tour, with national borders being crossed, that we saw doping becoming criminalised. It was here that we first saw cyclists being taken from their bikes to the jail cells. But it was in the age of Empire, an age that arrived with the American (and in the age of the second Bush Presidency a Texan no less), when things really start to escape their bounds.

An Aside on Bike Booms – Now and Then

We have already commented upon the manner in which the bicycle became affordable and thus widely available in the late nineteenth century and can add observations on the social history of the bicycle such as its use by the Imperial Japanese Army in Malaya or Chinese peasants and factory workers in Communist China. These situations can be readily contrasted with the bike boom of the early twenty-first century when bicycles became a status symbol of the middle class – the 'new golf' – and were certainly not affordable. A brief anecdote helps position the change. On the train to Melbourne one morning I overheard a middle-aged cyclist/lawyer talking to his colleague about his desire to sell one of his properties in order to buy a new racing bike. It seems that we have gone back to the time of the original velocipedes when the bicycle was an expensive plaything of the rich.

In this context it is also interesting to note that it was not until this same period that, for example, organised sport in Britain changed from being a way to keep idle young aristocrats busy, a form of 'formation' to deal with changing social conditions, to becoming the stuff of working men.[24] The interesting point vis-à-vis the globalisation of cycling and the bicycle is that, in modern times, it was the mass availability and affordability of the bicycle as a tool and mode of transport (for work, as work and the path out of work) that coincided with the massive growth of the sport within national boundaries. However, the contemporary, globalised bike boom has not coincided with such affordability. Here, the bike has become part

---

[24] See also, for a discussion of sport and leisure in the US as a nineteenth-century upper/middle class project, T Veblen, *The Theory of the Leisure Class* (Mentor Books, 1953). See also E Hobsbawm, 'Mass-Producing Traditions: Europe, 1870–1914' in E Hobsbawn and T Ranger (eds), *The Invention of Tradition* (Cambridge University Press, 1983) 263.

and parcel of the means by which global capital tends to reproduce itself, that is, through the creation of lifestyles and identities.

In this context, the boom in the bicycle has not been the result of a boom in sales of something accessible and cheap. With the globalisation of cycling in the late 1990s and beyond the price of the bicycle has soared. It is no longer a form of transport or a mere working tool; rather it has become the key to a 'healthy' neoliberal lifestyle.

Cycling, as the ad on TV tells us, is not a sport, it is a lifestyle. Unlike the modernist boom, with the post-modern boom, the price of the bike has skyrocketed. At one and the same time the production of the bike is no longer artisanal or a product of an industrial regime of production. No longer do French, Italian, or Basque makers handcraft bicycle frames. Just as the price increases, so does the number of top-level bicycle manufacturers in the new world. The post-modern bike is no longer composed of fire and steel but of carbon fibres and moulds. The post-modern bike is an out-sourced assemblage – the frames mass-produced anonymously in Taiwan, assembled by their European, American or Australian manufacturers at 'home'. The system of outsourced, networked manufacture, which typifies contemporary automobile production, has become the method of assembly of these post-modern carbon machines that has helped the cycling industry to create worlds and lifestyles. All this has been accompanied by a boom in clothing and accessories that enable the monitoring (heart rates, cadence, speed, power, routes) of each and every aspect of the cyclist's life.

1

Introduction

The Armstrong Era – Cycling in the Age of Empire

In terms of professional cycling, the underlying thesis here is that the changes which have occurred in pro-cycling and the problematisation of doping in pro-cycling cannot be properly understood without considering the broader processes at play within what is generally glossed as 'globalisation'.[1]

To flesh that claim out a bit, we can say that the Armstrong Era was in many ways the ultimate vehicle for the globalisation of cycling. That process had sown its seeds back in the 1980s with the beginning of an increasing Anglophone presence within the peloton.[2] Despite the ultimate revelations concerning the Texan's doping (see the Epilogue), there is no doubt that his presence played its part in the breaking down of the old European bases of the sport. In fact, following his fall from grace, the 'voice of cycling' Phil Liggett sought to excuse him on the basis that he was responsible for cycling's global growth.[3] His success was the success upon which the sport spread and 'grew' throughout the Anglophone world; from Johannesburg to Central Park the new cycling fans inevitably rode a Trek bike (his sponsor's brand) and more significantly, always dressed with an amulet of yellow.

The Armstrong Effect was this globalisation. From 1999 onwards the sport was marked by rapid economic growth in the new cycling world, particularly in the US, Australia, Britain and South Africa, along with a host of other new and emerging markets. Armstrong's success was central to this breaking down of cycling's European roots and it followed the years of individual Anglo-American riders undertaking the solitary task of breaking into the European peloton. Finally, the tables were starting to turn in respect of Anglo presence. Not only was the composition and the language of the professional peloton changing, now the sport's

---

[1] As will become apparent in the end this new way of the world is the world of neoliberalism and it will be that term that shall be settled upon within which to describe and characterise the changes brought about in sport and the law.

[2] For a coverage of this era see, eg, Samuel Abt, *Up the Road, Cycling's Modern Era from Lemond to Armstrong* (Velopress, 2005) or the more personal story of Alan Peiper in his autobiography, *A Peiper's Tale* (Mousehold Press, 2005).

[3] *Open letter from Michael Ashenden to Phil Liggett*, 30 August 2012, published on Velocity Nation, available at nyvelocity.com/content/features/2012/filthy-business-indeed.

patron was, for the first time, no longer a European. Along with that, for the first time, its fans began to loudly speak in (American) English.

We will return to Armstrong and his place in this story at the end of this work. Within this new world order of cycling, brought into existence by its redemption through the miracle of his victory over both cancer and the power of old Europe, certain nations began to be characterised as being more doping-prone or doping-friendly than others. The championing of Armstrong and the coincidence of various forces within the sport that rode on his back into these cycling greenfields was, at the same time, accompanied by a deepening suspicion and demonisation of the old cycling world. A decade before the European economic crisis, the same logic that was later deployed against the PIGS (Portugal Italy Greece and Spain), was deployed against the customs and traditions of the old cycling world; in particular Spain and Italy. Just as the European economic crisis pits lazy Latins against hard-working Anglos and Northern Europeans, this same logic played out during the Armstrong Era in respect of professional cycling and doping. At the same time, this distinction between good and bad Europe is an old theme, as Dumont notes over 'the course of centuries, the (social) Good was also relativized. ... "Truth this side of the Pyrenees, error beyond" noted Pascal ...'[4] Nevertheless, throughout the Armstrong Era (ie from 1999–2013) the popular myth sustained was that Anglo and Northern European riders were generally touted as being clean, good and culturally appropriate, whereas they were opposed and contrasted to the southern European and Latin riders, who were regarded as (naturally) prone to cheating, dirty and hence culturally inappropriate.

This new age saw the coming of a good Anglo rider, who had overcome the greatest of all battles (against cancer); his own personal rebirth was followed by the sport's rebirth and with it came the fulfilment of the sport's globalisation. Importantly for our task, in the process of globalising the sport itself, and because of its entanglement with the legacy of *Festina* and the emerging global anti-doping apparatus, cycling found itself bound up with a new form of law that came into being as a part of the wider process of globalisation. The law began to loom large over cycling, but the manner in which it operated, was deployed or applied, tended to suggest a new manner of it being done – a manner of doing law that signified a break with its modernist past. As we will see, it is this break that is so troubling to some anti-doping scholars.

Operación Puerto (see Chapter 2) provides us with the stepping off point for our focus and analysis. There was, however, during the Armstrong Era a fundamental contradiction at work in the manner in which anti-doping was carried out in professional cycling which *Puerto* helps illuminate. On the one hand, the Armstrong Conspiracy has described to us the networks of power and protection that operated to sustain the Armstrong Effect. On the other hand, others were

---

[4] L Dumont, *Essays on Individualism: Modern Ideology in Anthropological Perspective* (University of Chicago Press, 1986) 237.

sacrificed on the altar of anti-doping to ensure that the public pretence of the war on doping was being carried out with its full force. It appeared throughout this era that the deployment of the anti-doping apparatus did not treat all equally and fairly on a level playing field. Was it for the simple reason that some were more equal and more valuable to economic ends than others?

A Note on Terminology

Before proceeding, it is useful to provide some clarity to the development of this thesis by defining some key terms with which we will seek to analyse the problematisation of doping in cycling and its relationship to wider processes of globalisation. In this work, the term Government (with a capital G or the Government) is used to refer to the State institution of the Government recognised by classical liberal democratic theory as encompassing its three branches the Executive, Legislature and the Judiciary. Having said that, as will become apparent when we move to consider Law and administration (see Chapter 3) the State primarily carries out its activity of government through its first branch of the Executive. In this way the primary face of the Government can be seen as the exercise of Executive power through the activity of administration and policing. It is important to note, even at this stage, that the administrative and policing activities of the institution of Government are something quite different to the production of what we might call sovereign law. As will become apparent, administrative and police power focuses upon individual applications of power in the way that the law does not. To borrow from Agamben we can say that the bureaucrats – the angels and ministers of the sovereign and not the sovereign himself – carry out the administration.

The Legislative arm of Government in classical liberal democratic theory is responsible for the production of Law, or at least Legislation. Better put, the Legislative arm prepares the Law as in the end it is brought into being by sovereign will, for example by the sovereign, whether elected or not, giving their assent to the Law's being. Thus Law (with a capital L[5]) will be used to refer to the rules of general application and conduct, whether produced by the Legislature or the Common Law, and assented to by the sovereign, which establish a class of circumstances, things and people to which the rule or norm that it states applies. The hallmark of this form of Law is a rule of conduct or a declaration as to power, right or duty, in which some factual requirements are delineated that connect it to a given state of affairs and which are applied retrospectively.[6] Law does not look to the future

---

[5] In an attempt at consistency, for example, terms such as Legislation and Legality will be capitalised in the same way as Law when referring to Governmental bodies, instruments or actions, as will be the other branches of Government – the Executive and the Judiciary.

[6] *Plaintiff S157/2002 v Commonwealth* (2003) 211 CLR 476 – a decision of the High Court of Australia.

in what it judges, but to past events. Law does not seek to guide or conduct future conduct but only to decide past events.

The terms government, governance and governmentality (without a capital G) refer not to the institution of the State but, following Foucault, the idea of government as an activity rather than an institution.[7] My purpose here is not to engage in any post-Foucauldian debate concerning the demarcation and differences between, for example, the terms governance, governmentality, discipline, security, control or biopower (see, eg, in Chapter 4) but rather to point to the manner in which all of these terms describe activities, including regulatory, administrative and policing activities, that encompass institutions beyond the State institution of the Government. These activities of government are, in fact, carried out by a myriad or network of private and public institutions and actors, including the governed themselves. The activity of government is as such something greater and more wide ranging than the institution of the Government.

'Governmentality' in the first place was said by Foucault to involve

> the ensemble[8] formed by institutions, procedures, analyses and reflections, calculations, and tactics that allow the exercise of this very specific, albeit, very complex, power that has the population as its target, political economy as its major form of knowledge, and apparatuses of security as its essential technical instrument.[9]

Secondly, he understood governmentality as a tendency for the type of power he called government to take precedence over all over forms of power such as State sovereignty or the techniques of discipline. This tendency involves the development of specific governmental *apparatuses* and with them their specific knowledge. Finally, he understood it as the process of the legal State becoming the administrative State. Foucault's sovereignty typical of the State points us, of course, to specific and various *apparati* of administration beyond the State.[10] That is to an administrative hierarchy or State that exists and operates through and beyond the State.

Importantly for our work, Agamben has described the relationship between the etymology of the word economy and that of government. For Agamben governing involves looking after something and acquires the meaning of providing for the needs of life, nourishing.[11] The genesis of the term economy, *Oikonomia* refers to the administration of the house – something distinguished by Aristotle from

---

[7] P Dadot and C Laval, *The New Way of the World* (Verso Books, 2013) 4.

[8] An ensemble here is taken to be an apparatus. The position taken is that the use of the term ensemble here is a matter of translation and for our purposes does not signify anything different from the meaning Foucault gave to the term dispositif, which has been translated as apparatus. In relation to this, see the following definition of apparatus.

[9] M Foucault, *Security, Territory, Population: Lectures at the College of France 1977–1978* (Picador, 2007) 108.

[10] ibid, 108–09.

[11] G Agamben, *The Kingdom and the Glory: For a Theological Genealogy of Economy and Government* (Stanford University Press, 2011) 19.

politics – the polis and (democratic) politics is opposed to the economy of the house and despots. The house in this context is not that of the nuclear family, but 'a complex organism composed of heterogeneous relations, entwined with each other'.[12] Economic relations in this sense are linked by a paradigm that we could define as 'Administrative' ['gestionale'], and not epistemic: in other words, it is a matter of activity that is not bound to a system of rules ... but to a certain way of being ... This activity rather implies decisions and orders that cope with problems that are each time specific and concern the functional order (*taxis*) of the different parts of the *oikos*.[13]

Agamben cites Xenophon who compared the house with an army and a ship where the administrator '... knows each particular section so exactly, that he can tell even when away where everything is kept and how much there is of it'. Administration in this sense entails an ability to know the whereabouts of the things that are sought to be controlled so that they may be kept in an 'ordered arrangement'.[14]

Administration is a 'functional organization' that is a force that (following the Stoics interpretation) 'regulates and governs the whole from the inside'.[15] It is here with this idea of governing the whole from the inside that we begin to encounter what we might call the internalisation of government. As Dadot and Laval put it, to govern is not to govern against liberty, or despite it: it is to govern through liberty; that is, to actively exploit the freedom allowed to individuals so that they end up conforming to certain norms of their own accord.[16] Or, as I have written elsewhere, citing Thomas Pynchon: In this day and age law 'for the first time ... is put inside. [There is n]o more need to suffer passively under "outside forces" ...'.[17]

The various aspects of governmentality – for example, government, discipline, security, biopower or control; are not mutually exclusive from the form or forms of Law or Government. All these activities form part of a broader and overarching apparatus of government in a global society. The 'complex organism composed of heterogeneous relations, entwined with each other' of government exists and is itself intertwined with the Law. The problem, as we will soon encounter, is to discern the particular configuration as it stands at any particular time, what we may describe as a point in the Law-governance continuum, the particular point of place between these two poles.

Before moving on to deal with some of these issues we need to define one further term, that of the apparatus. Foucault's latter work did not focus upon the traditional approach to power based upon juridico-instrumental models

[12] ibid, 17.
[13] ibid, 17–18.
[14] ibid, 18.
[15] ibid, 19.
[16] Dadot and Laval, *The New Way of the World* (n 7) 5.
[17] M Hardie, 'Deleuze: Had I Not Done Philosophy I Would Have Done Law' (2007) 20 *International Journal for the Semiotics of Law* 81, 83.

but upon the concrete ways in which power penetrates bodies and forms of life. Rather than institutions, Foucault was concerned with the *dispositifs*, the apparatuses of power.

For Foucault the apparatus or *dispositif* is

> a thoroughly heterogeneous set consisting of discourses, institutions, architectural forms, regulatory decisions, laws, administrative measures, scientific statements, philosophical, moral and philanthropic propositions – in short the said as much as the unsaid ... the apparatus itself is the network that can be established between these elements.[18]

He continues by stating that it is 'a kind of formation, so to speak, that at a given historical moment has as its major function the response to an urgency'.[19]

Agamben draws out three elements in the Foucauldian definition:

a.   It is a heterogeneous set that virtually includes anything under the same heading: discourses, institutions, ... laws, police measures, philosophical proposition, and so on. The apparatus itself is the network that is established between these elements.

b.   The apparatus always has a concrete strategic function and is always located in a power relation.

c.   As such, it appears at the intersection of power relations and relations of knowledge.[20]

Agamben defines an apparatus as 'literally anything that has in some way the capacity to capture, orient, determine, intercept, model, control, or secure the gestures, behaviours, opinions, or discourses of living beings'.[21] For Agamben the apparatus as a pure activity of government is devoid of any foundation in being – it is a praxis, a practice, a strategy and always implies the process of producing its subjects.[22] The apparatus, the *dispositif* and *oikonomia* all refer 'to a set of practices, bodies of knowledge, measures and institutions that aim to manage, govern, control, and orient – in a way that purports to be useful – the behaviours, gestures, and thoughts of human beings'.[23] What is important here to note, other than the managerial or governing function of the apparatus is that, although it has no foundation in being, it performs its function in a way that purports to be useful. That use, as Foucault reminds us, is often a use in response to some sort of urgency (or for that matter emergency).

[18] M Foucault, 'The Confession of the Flesh' (1977) interview in M Foucault, *Power/Knowledge: Selected Interviews and Other Writings*, ed and trans C Gordon Vintage (1980) 194–228.

[19] ibid; and cited in G Agamben, *What is an Apparatus? and Other Essays*, Meridian (Stanford University Press, 2009), 2.

[20] Agamben, *What is an Apparatus?* (n 19) 2–3.

[21] ibid, 14.

[22] ibid, 5.

[23] ibid, 12.

In considering *What is an Apparatus?* Agamben undertakes a theological and philosophical genealogy of the term, a task he pursues further in *The Kingdom and the Glory*.[24] In the process of this task he proposes

> ... nothing less than a general and massive partitioning into two large groups or classes: on the one hand, living beings ... and on the other, apparatuses in which living beings are incessantly captured. On one side, then, to return to the theologians, lies the ontology of creatures, and on the other side, the *oikonomia* of apparatuses that seek to govern and guide them to good.[25]

In between these two classes he proposes the subjects, that is, 'that which results from the relation and, so to speak, from the relentless fight between living beings and apparatuses'.[26] With the 'boundless growth of apparatuses in our time' his argument is that 'there is not even a single instant in which the life of individuals is not modeled, contaminated, or controlled by some apparatus'.[27] Apparatuses are, in fact, 'rooted in the very process of "humanization" that made "humans" out of animals [a] division [which] separates the living being from itself and from its immediate relationship with its environment'.[28]

Oikonomia, according to Agamben, included 'the ordered organization of the human body',[29] and '*oikonomia* does not merely concern the management of the house, but the soul itself'.[30] Deleuze referred to the administration and management of life and extended Foucault's disciplinary paradigm to include that of a control society.[31] Hardt and Negri[32] and Lazzarato[33] refer to the manner in which worlds, lifestyles and forms of life are produced and governed in a global economy. Dicey referred to administrative law's concern with the care of social interests,[34] or Neocleous as the regulation of the internal life of the community, the regimenting of social life, or the management and direction of the population.[35] All these concepts point in one way or another to a world of governance and the contemporary application of power.

In undertaking our study of our particular subject matter we need to be guided by the analysis of these concepts, but, at the same time, recognise that the researcher, must abandon the texts that he has been analysing and proceed on his own.[36] In our case we must proceed to encounter our subject matter and, in so doing, we may produce new concepts and methods. Our task here is to do so in

---

[24] Agamben 2011.

[25] Agamben, *What is an Apparatus?* (n 19) 13–14.

[26] ibid.

[27] ibid, 15.

[28] ibid, 16.

[29] ibid, 29.

[30] ibid, 47.

[31] G Deleuze, 'Postscript on the Societies of Control' (1992) 59 *October* 3.

[32] M Hardt and A Negri, *Empire* (Harvard University Press, 1999); and M Hardt and A Negri, *Commonwealth* (Harvard University Press, 2009).

[33] M Lazzarato, 'From Capital-labour to Capital-life' (2004) 4(3) *Ephemera* 187.

[34] AV Dicey, *Introduction to the Study of the Law of the Constitution* (Macmillan and Co Limited, 1920) 328–29.

[35] M Neocleous, *Fabrication of Social Order: A Critical Theory of Police Power* (Pluto Press, 2000) 93.

[36] Agamben 2009 (n 19) 13.

the context of the growth of a global anti-doping apparatus. Within the context of our enquiry three immediate but overarching questions arise:

1. Within the context of *a global form of governance* what is it that is purported to be useful?
2. Similarly within the context of anti-doping policy what is it that is purported to be useful?
3. Is there any correlation between the two?

What is it that is useful for a global form of governance that causes it to operate through an apparatus of anti-doping, a network established between elements with a concrete strategic function that seems to be aimed at producing a certain type of subject: the clean athlete?

The New Way of the World

Our immediate subject matter – professional cycling and doping – leads and ultimately requires us to ask and consider the following: What is law in a global system, is it in fact 'Law'? How is it configured?

The global anti-doping apparatus established in the wake of *Festina* is a border-crossing assemblage[37] of legal and non-legal institutions and mechanisms. In essence, the World Anti-Doping Code (WADC) establishes a hybrid, global, transnational form of contractually based administrative law. It is hybrid in the sense that it is made, administered and enforced by a mix of private and public interests. It is global and transnational in that it encompasses and transcends the Law of any nation. The WADC, its subsidiary instruments of international standards such as the International Standard for Laboratories, the rules of sporting organisations at an international and national level, such as the International Cycling Union Anti-Doping Rules and relevant national laws or regulations, such as, in Australia, the Australian Sports Anti-Doping Authority (ASADA) Act and Regulations, comprise the relevant components of this system of Law. The institution known as the Court of Arbitration for Sport (CAS) gives the apparent consistency and rationality of this system and the appearance of Law. Importantly, CAS does not deal with Law in the sense that we have defined it, nor is it a Court. It is, at best, a private body that decides administrative matters by way of contractually based arbitration without any significant oversight by the institutions of Government.[38]

---

[37] P Zumbansen, 'Defining the Space of Transnational Law: Legal Theory, Global Governance and Legal Pluralism' in G Handl, J Zekoll and P Zumbansen (eds), *Beyond Territoriality: Transnational Legal Authority in an Age of Globalization* (Martinus Nijhoff, 2012) 83, citing S Sassen, *Territory – Authority – Rights: From Medieval to Global Assemblages* (Princeton University Press, 2006).

[38] In the Australian system there is a distinct separation between administrative tribunals that decide matters on the merits and the judicial organs, the Courts that decide matters based not on their merits but only principles of legality. Administrative bodies that have an adjudicative role in this system are known as Tribunals. Judicial bodies are known as Courts. Applying this distinction CAS is not a Court but a Tribunal. CAS is subject to an appeal to the Swiss Civil Courts. However, there is no evidence to suggest that this provides anything more than a procedural safeguard rather than subjecting its decisions to the Law.

The Code is intended to create a system that envisages and depends upon the interactions of private and State bodies, but nevertheless stands apart and autonomous from State bodies.[39] The anti-doping system, or apparatus, is a dispersed network without any centre being in complete control, but it is a hierarchy in the sense proposed by Dumont. For Dumont, hierarchy does not signify a ladder of command, nor is it to be strictly read as mere power or authority. Here a hierarchy exists or is introduced with the adoption of a value which allows the differentiated elements of the whole to be judged in relation to that whole.[40]

An outstanding question here is what value is it that allows for the differentiated elements of the whole to be judged? Or, to put it another way, following Hardt and Negri and their analysis of Empire, what is the single logic of rule[41] that brings the networked system together? An immediate answer may be given by referring to one of the questions we have posed above – the value or logic appears to consist in a concrete strategic function that seems to be aimed at producing a certain type of subject: the clean athlete. But this, as we shall see, in itself is insufficient. In the end this value or single logic is something even more fundamental to the processes we have reluctantly described as globalisation.

It is appropriate at this point to consider another term that will become important as we progress, a term that will replace globalisation, that is, neoliberalism. This will assist us in defining the key value and in guiding our enquiry into the Law-governance continuum. For, as we will argue, it is the value of neoliberalism that drives, not only the anti-doping apparatus, but also the changes in the Law and governance that we are living.

Dadot and Laval describe neoliberalism as a 'new global rationality'. Relevant to our identification of a value or single logic they go on to state that

> [b]y this we mean that such rationality is global in the two senses of the term: it is 'world-wide' in that it obtains on a world scale; and, far from being confined to the economic sphere, it tends to totalize – that is, create a world in its own image through its power to integrate all dimensions of human existence. A global rationality, it is at the same time a 'world-reason'.[42]

---

[39] See Arts 22.3, 22.4 and 24.3 WADC; D Paul, *A Guide to the World Anti-Doping Code: The Fight for the Spirit of Sport*, 2nd edn (Cambridge University Press, 2013) 6; S Cassese et al, *Global Administrative Law: Cases, Materials, Issues*, 2nd edn (Institute for International Justice and Law, 2008); Casini, Lorenzo, 'The Making of a *Lex Sportiva* – The Court of Arbitration for Sport "The Provider"', IILJ Working Paper 2010/5 Global Administrative Law Series (New York University School of Law, 2010). 439, 453–56 and 461.

[40] L Dumont, *Homo Hierarchicus, The Caste System and its Implications* (Paladin, 1972) 9, 104. A distinction within an identity; see the essay 'On Value, Modern and Nonmodern' 234, in L Dumont, *Essays on Individualism, Modern Ideology in Anthropological Perspective* (University of Chicago Press, 1986).

[41] Hardt and Negri, *Empire* (n 32) xii. 'Our basic hypothesis is that sovereignty has taken a new form, composed of a series of national and supranational organisms united under a single logic of rule. This new global form of sovereignty is what we call Empire.'

[42] P Dadot and C Laval, *The New Way of the World: On Neoliberal Society* (Verso, 2013) 3.

Neoliberalism is not adequately defined by privatisation or some sort of lessening of state power. Law and state power do not decrease with neoliberalism – the point is that their character and strategic function changes. We will develop this further when we consider the Rule of Law (Chapter 3) and its neoliberal mutation (Chapter 5).

Capitalism is an economico-juridical complex admitting of a multiplicity of unique forms including liberalism and neoliberalism.[43] Dumont has said that the economy as known under capitalism is an exceptional system, that is it constitutes an exception to the forms of organisation that have been dominant throughout human history.[44] That is, in capitalism, all other forms of rationality and organisation are subservient to the economy. Following this we could say, with a nod to Agamben, that in neoliberalism the exception is brought to the fore in a stark light. As Dadot and Laval put it, economics is at the base of a set of apparatuses for controlling the population and directing it. This experiences an unprecedented systematisation in neoliberalism where competition and the entrepreneurial model constitute a general mode of government, far exceeding the economic sphere in the habitual sense of the term. As they put it 'that is precisely what we see everywhere. The requirement of competitiveness has become a general political principle …'[45]

Significantly for our understanding of the changes brought about for the State, the Government and the Law neoliberalism is firstly and fundamentally a rationality, and as such tends to structure and organise the action of rulers, as well as the conduct of the ruled.[46] Neoliberal governance has assumed a political meaning and a normative significance in the context of the practices of government subject to the constraints of globalisation.[47] For Dadot and Laval the political category of governance, or, more precisely, good governance, plays a central role in diffusing the norm of generalised competition in such a way that it gradually supplants the outmoded, disvalued category of sovereignty. The neoliberal state is no longer judged on its capacity to ensure its sovereignty over a territory, in accordance with the classical western conception, but on its respect for the legal norms and economic good practice of governance.[48] The principal characteristic of neoliberal rationality is a generalisation of competition as a behavioural norm and the enterprise as a model of subjectivication.[49] This general principle of government through competitiveness precisely represents the extension of the neoliberal norm to all countries, all sectors of public activity, and all areas of social existence.[50]

[43] ibid, 11. See also G Arrighi, *The Long Twentieth Century: Money, Power and the Origins of Our Times* (Verso, 2010).
[44] L Dumont, *From Marx to Mandeville: The Genesis and Triumph of Economic Ideology* (University of Chicago Press, 1977).
[45] ibid (n 7), 11.
[46] ibid, 4.
[47] ibid, 218–19.
[48] ibid.
[49] ibid, 4.
[50] ibid, 13.

At the same time as neoliberalism transforms the character of the State, it also involves generating a relationship of the individual subject to him- or herself that is homologous to the relationship of capital to itself: very precisely, a relationship of the subject to him-or herself as human capital to be indefinitely increased – that is a value to be even further valorised.[51] Both the transformation of the State and the transformation of the relationship between the subject to him-herself are at play in our immediate subject matter: the anti-doping apparatus. Furthermore, as we will see this apparatus displays important aspects of the application of neoliberalism including the constitutionalisation of competition, a kind of an executive federalism that consecrates the primacy of the inter-governmental by public and private institutions and the increasing secondary station of social rights.[52]

Following Dadot and Laval we can come to define neoliberalism as a certain type of interventionism intended politically to fashion economic and social relations governed by competition.[53] This new discourse has generated a new governmental rationality that accepts the need for State intervention and rejects pure governmental passivity. The neoliberal is opposed to any action that might frustrate the operation of competition between private interests.

> State intervention here has a converse sense. It does not involve limiting the market through corrective or compensatory action but developing and purifying the competitive market through a carefully tailored legal framework. It is no longer a question of postulating a spontaneous agreement between individual interests but of creating the optimal conditions for the interplay of their rivalry to satisfy the collective interest. In this respect, neoliberalism combines a rehabilitation of public intervention with a conception of the market centred on competition, it extends the term that shift of the axis of liberalism by making competition the cardinal principle of social and individual existence ... It recognises that the market order is not a natural datum, but the artificial product of a political history and process of construction.[54]

Neoliberalism thus adopts 'a set of discourses, practices and power apparatuses aimed to establish new political conditions, to alter the rules of economic functioning, to transform social relations in such a way as to attain'[55] the objective of generalised competition as the principal norm of governance. Significantly for our understanding of the underlying single logic or value or, for that matter, the place of sport and anti-doping within this global apparatus we must contrast the homogeneity of neoliberalism with the heterogeneity of liberalism. Dadot and Laval make the point that

> for a long time, the so-called modern Western subject pertained to normative regimes and political registers that were heterogeneous and in conflict: the customary and religious sphere of old societies [pre-modern forms of particular law]; the sphere of

51 ibid, 15.
52 ibid.
53 ibid, 46.
54 ibid, 47.
55 ibid, 149.

political sovereignty; and the sphere of commodity exchange. This western subject thus lived in three different spaces: that of the services and beliefs of a still rural, Christian society; that of nation-states and the political community; and that of the monetary market in work and production. …

Liberal democracies have been worlds of multiple tensions and contrasting growths. … we can describe them as regimes which, within certain limits, enabled and respected a mixed functioning of the subject, in the sense that they guarantee both the separation and the articulation of the difference spheres of existence. This heterogeneity found expression in the relative independence of moral, religious, political, economic, aesthetic and intellectual institutions, rules and norms. This does not mean that the nature of the dynamic that inspired them is exhausted by this feature of equilibrium and 'tolerance'. Two major parallel growths occurred: political democracy and capitalism. Modern man was divided into: the Citizen endowed with inalienable rights and the economic man guided by self-interest; man as end and man as instrument. The history of 'modernity' has sanctioned an imbalance in favour of the second pole.[56]

Neoliberal life, therefore, comprises a multitude of human beings who are subject to a unitary order;[57] it provides the value that brings together the hierarchy, the single logic of its Empire. Liberal man was the calculating man of the market or the productive man of industrial organisations. Neoliberal man is competitive man, wholly immersed in global competition.[58]

The Law-governance Continuum

What we will attempt to illustrate throughout this work is that the anti-doping apparatus brings to the fore the myriad manners in which we are governed in a global system. It is no longer a simple question of simply doing sovereign or State Law and the Government, nor is it a matter of simply doing a new form of law. Hence, a part of our approach here will be to try and explain through this particular 'case', how law operates, or what it does, or tends to do and what it is not, in the present historical juncture. Rather than an essence of Law; which involves the eternal and possibly unanswerable question of what is law?[59] What we are concerned with is the operation or apparatus of governance, something that extends well beyond what we might have called, in modernity, Law (see Chapter 3) or even the Government.

Just as this is not a history, neither is it what we might call a Legal analysis. The point here is not to set out and ascertain the Legal meaning and status of anti-doping law but to consider the state, or shape of the law, in so far as it is Law,

---

[56] ibid, 256.
[57] ibid, 88–89.
[58] ibid 218–19.
[59] G-P Callies and M Renner, 'Between Law and Social Norms: The Evolution of Global Governance' (2009) 22(2) *Ratio Juris* 260, 262.

in the context and circumstances of cycling's globalisation. Rather than a history, or a legal analysis, what is at stake here is more of an archaeology, a genealogy, or possibly an anthropology of the anti-doping apparatus. In so far as we might be pushed to hang our hat on a 'discipline' Comaroff and Comaroff have suggested that the task of legal anthropology is being inexorably drawn towards interrogating the nature of sovereignty in the twenty-first century.[60]

In interrogating sovereignty (clearly we are interrogating something more than Sovereignty in the classical sense and following our definition of Law this may be our point of distinction from the Comaroffs) and in describing this apparatus as it is deployed in professional cycling, we are led towards the task set for us by both Agamben and Foucault concerning the tendency away from the primacy of Law and sovereignty, toward the primacy of governance. On his reading of Foucault, Agamben asks: what founds the juridical form when governance is primary to sovereignty?

> … up until the seventeenth century one limited oneself to deducing a paradigm of government from a theory of sovereignty, it then became an inverse process; given the growing primacy of the arts of government, it became a case of discovering the juridical form and theory of sovereignty that were able to sustain and found this primacy.[61]

As will become apparent this problem – of discovering the juridical form and theory of sovereignty that sustains the primacy of governance – goes to the core of the operation of the anti-doping apparatus. What founds the legal form, what form of legal institution, exists in the context of such an extensive legal, disciplinary and surveillance apparatus in a situation where (as we will see) governance is primary to Law and sovereignty? What founds a global spectacular and quasi-criminal policing apparatus that exists outside but with, at the same time, the blessing and support of the sovereign State? Or, as we have begun to already outline, what is the value that founds the hierarchy?

The problem posed by Agamben, towards the end of his work, *The Kingdom and the Glory*, arises from his reading of Lecture Seven of Foucault's College of France lectures on *Security, Territory, Population*.[62] In that lecture Foucault asks: 'What juridical form, what institutional form, what legal basis could be given to the sovereignty typical of the state?'[63] To anticipate our argument we could answer Foucault's construction of the problem by simply stating the *juridical form* is contract, the *institutional form* is private agreement, and the *legal basis* is consent. Alternatively, we might answer the question by reference to what we call the rubric of spectacle (*juridical form*), exception (*institutional form*) and functionality (*legal*

---

[60] JL Comaroff and J Comaroff, 'Reflections on the Anthropology of Law, Governance and Sovereignty' in F von Benda-Beckmann, K von Benda-Beckmann and J Eckert (eds), *Rules of Law and Laws of Ruling* (Ashgate Publishing, 2009) 31 at 40.
[61] Agamben, *The Kingdom and the Glory* (n 11) 272.
[62] Foucault, *Security, Territory, Population* (n 9) 108.
[63] ibid, 106.

basis). It may be that we need not be required to strictly and literally comply with the formula *juridical form – institutional form – legal basis*, but their worth as signposts for our enquiry should be kept in mind.

Foucault's construction has one element not immediately present in Agamben, what is founded by agreement is *a sovereignty typical of the State*; not of the State, but sovereign nevertheless. This is not to say that Agamben is not concerned with the question of sovereignty. It is clear his whole body of work is concerned with interrogating this topic and it is one that will continue to guide us, especially in respect of the concepts of the state of exception and that of *homo sacer*, but what Foucault's original gloss suggests is a form of sovereignty that exists beyond the State.

The apparatus established or coordinated by the WADC appears '*increasingly to evince a will to sovereignty*'[64] over what, following Agamben, I dub the bare life of the athlete as *homo sacer.* As Hardt and Negri's Empire shows us pointing to the holder of this sovereign power in any one instance may not be an easy task – it may be nowhere and everywhere simultaneously – the problem of the anti-doping apparatus requires us to begin to reconsider what sovereignty is, or what it does in this particular trans or supranational situation. Whether or not sovereignty is an adequate term in this context is arguable. It may be that what is required here in the end is a term other than sovereignty, or at least to distinguish clearly between the sovereignty of the State and this new form of emergent and global sovereignty. However, the Comaroffs may provide us with a useful and workable starting point when they define sovereignty as 'the exercise of control over the lives, deaths and conditions of existence of those who fall within its purview – and the extension over them of the jurisdiction of some kind of law'. However, their definition is useful only in so far as it highlights that these writers have not fully captured what is at stake in the Law-governance continuum.

What concerns the Comaroffs is, after Benjamin, the relationship between law making and power making. In order for power to transform itself into an assertion of sovereign authority there is need for an architecture of legalities, or their simulacra. Here this need arises in a situation where authority is outsourced to non-state institutions and has stretched deep into the management of bare life.[65] If the term sovereignty is of any use to us in the contemporary context it may be only in so far as it points us to interrogating the new conditions and the fact that what is founded by consent and private agreement is not a sovereignty of the State but *a sovereignty typical of the state* – that is a new form that exists beyond the State, but within which the State is an player. It is for this reason one of the principal aspects of this work seeks to interrogate the changing forms of law and their relationship to governance, discipline or control – what we describe in shorthand as the Law-governance continuum.

---

[64] Comaroff and Comaroff, 'Reflections on the Anthropology of Law, Governance and Sovereignty' (n 60) 38.

[65] ibid, 39, citing W Benjamin, Critique of Violence. In *Reflections: Essays, Aphorisms, Autobiographical Writings*, ed. Peter Demetz (Schocken Books, (1978), 277–300, 295.

Hardt and Negri provide us with a more nuanced and useful perspective on sovereignty in their analysis of Empire. What is at play in anti-doping law and policy is itself a symptom of the coming of what Hardt and Negri have described as Empire:

> The decline in sovereignty of nation states, however, does not mean that sovereignty as such has declined. Throughout the contemporary transformations, political controls, state functions, and regulatory mechanisms have continued to rule the realm of economic and social production and exchange. Our basic hypothesis is that sovereignty has taken a new form, composed of a series of national and supranational organisms united under a single logic of rule. This new global form of sovereignty is what we call Empire.
>
> The declining sovereignty of nation-states and their increasing inability to regulate economic and cultural exchanges is in fact one of the primary symptoms of the coming of Empire. The sovereignty of the nation-state was the cornerstone of the imperialisms that European powers constructed throughout the modern era. By 'Empire,' however, we understand something altogether different from 'imperialism.' ...

The passage to Empire emerges from the twilight of modern sovereignty. In contrast to imperialism, Empire establishes no territorial centre of power and does not rely on fixed boundaries or barriers. It is a decentred and deterritorialising apparatus of rule that progressively incorporates the entire global realm within its open, expanding frontiers. Empire manages hybrid identities, flexible hierarchies, and plural exchanges through modulating networks of command.[66]

What Hardt and Negri recognise is that a variety of contemporary processes are emerging to form a new global order which is a 'network power',[67] which brings 'together an oligarchy of diverse political bodies, including international institutions, the dominant nation-states, multinational corporations, continental and regional alliances, and so forth, which collaborate to create an open, constituent process'. This process is managed by practices and structures of global governance that provide an extraordinary plural and flexible process.[68]

As such Empire is a form of pluralistic regulation, established in the network and configured by a variable, multimodal, and/or polycentric geometry which includes

> an idea of the key constitutionalization and the governmentilization of 'dispositifs' of the production of law that takes command away from sovereignty, makes it adequate to the market, and distributes it among variety of actors.[69]

For Hardt and Negri, Empire is the paradigmatic form of governance and is a system, in the making, with a new logic and structure of rule. Sovereign power has

---

[66] Hardt and Negri, *Empire* (n 32) xii–xiii.
[67] ibid, xxii–xiv.
[68] Hardt and Negri, *Commonwealth* (n 32) 226.
[69] ibid, 226–27. *Dispotif* is translated to English as apparatus.

taken on a new form, and the consequence of its composition and its single logic is that State or national organs become mere local conduits of power, administration and management, of this global single logic. As Empire does not depend upon fixed boundaries or barriers it is a decentred and deterritorialising apparatus of rule that seeks to progressively incorporate the entire global realm and all forms of life within that realm within its open and expanding frontiers – it is a modulating network of command – and an administrative law of a cosmo-political society that completely over-determines domestic Law. We can see this configuration clearly in the world of anti-doping law and policy, with a multiplicity of organisations, hybrid, public, private, sporting, international, national that each exercise authority over the situation.

What is clear is that the activity of governance does not fully replace Law – for example, discipline and control are superimposed as technologies that focus upon the body and the mind; Law continues to play its part, although as we will see (Chapter 5) a new part within the apparatus, the question is one of articulation not of binary opposites. Given these new forms of law and new forms of governance tend to operate upon forms of life and life itself was Bataille pointing us along the right path when he located sovereignty within the body?[70] But, as we will see, these new forms of law operate to legitimise and 'regulate' governance through both more formal and informal mechanisms. Thus, the technologies of governance and Law, rather than being exclusive, are and must be articulated with each other. In such a situation all the various machines of law exist and operate at the same time, with varying degrees of weight and dominance.[71]

As we progress with our enquiry, we will see that there are further questions that arise for our consideration. These questions push us to consider either the role, or better, function of both law and governmentality within a global, transnational or supranational system. What is it that both Law and governance strive to achieve within what I will dub the society of competition? To repeat what we have already posed above, within the context of *a global form of governance* and within the context of a global anti-doping policy and apparatus, what is it that is purported to be useful? For that matter, what is it that is useful for a global form of governance that causes it to operate through an apparatus of anti-doping, that is a network, established between elements with a concrete strategic function, that seems to be aimed at producing a certain type of subject: the clean athlete? What does anti-doping tell us about how this *global form of governance* is configured and for that matter how law is configured? How does it differ from the sovereignty model of modernity? Is it that in the end we see laid bare before us the relationship between the athlete and the sovereign(s) in this *global form of governance*? Why is it that the sovereign comes to lick the feet of the wolf (see Chapter 6)? Despite what we might

---

[70] If biopower is taken as the defining feature of contemporary governmentality with its focus on the body Bataille here can be seen clearly as paving the way for the later work of Foucault and others.
[71] G Deleuze and F Guattari, *A Thousand Plateaus* (University of Minnesota Press, 1987).

call their privileged position can we really characterise the professional athlete as 'bare life'? Or does this in some way do an injustice to the 'traditional' conception of 'bare life' as being the poor and excluded of global society, whose archetypical figure is that of the refugee? It may be that we do not directly or adequately answer each and every one of these questions, but the purpose is at least to open them up for further consideration.

The End of Modernity?

In seeking to tackle these questions at times we take up as our academic proximate 'enemy' the work of the Danish anti-doping scholar, Verner Møller. Møller's work provides us with a counterpoint or launching off point in a number of chapters and allows us to situate our analysis and critique. In many ways it was in response to my reading of Møller's 'The Anti-Doping Campaign – Farewell to the Ideals of Modernity?'[72] that initially drove the trajectory of much of this enquiry. While the author shares, amongst other things, some sympathy with the issues raised by Møller, one of the tasks, taken on here in response, is to set out an analysis that highlights the way in which the liberal approach fails to take into account the fundamental changes that are at play in the world today. But one should not make too much of Møller's status as the enemy here; for in the end he is not. We share too many similar views and attitudes, but we do differ on parts of our analysis. By casting him as our proximate enemy, it helps illustrate the point that if we remain tied to old logics and tools, we cannot come to terms with the problematisation of doping in an adequate way. If there is indeed an enemy to be found here, it is that which I will dub neoliberalism and its 'society of competition'. It is within the 'society of competition' that we can begin to uncover the common or single logic or value that pervades both the global logic of governance, economy, sport and the anti-doping apparatus itself.

Before turning to Møller more fully, it is probably opportune to distinguish this work from others that have considered sport in the context of capitalism, globalisation or Neoliberalism. Brohm's classic Marxist text *Sport A Prison of Measured Time* is one that many liberal sports scholars reject because of what they perceive as its rejection of bourgeois individual autonomy and its focus upon the athlete as being exploited by the capitalism order. For some, the fact that the French Minister for Youth and Sport, Marie-George Buffet, responsible for the raid on the *Festina Tour*, was a Communist (and hence *ipso facto* a paternalist) and saw the riders as exploited workers, does not assist in the reception of 'left' or critical reflections on sport by the mainstream of liberal anti-doping or sport scholars.[73] Both Brohm

---

[72] V Møller, 'The Anti-Doping Campaign – Farewell to the Ideals of Modernity?' in J Hoberman and V Møller, *Doping and Public Policy* (University Press of Southern Denmark, 2004, 145).
[73] See, eg, ibid 150.

and, more recently, Collins[74] have considered the birth of modern sport and its links to the growth of industrial capitalism, the creation of sport by capital in its own image produces a playing field that is as much factory as it is a game.

Collins, as with other contemporary critics, importantly seeks to describe the linkages with the media – from print to satellite TV; and with global corporations and Empires. The use of corporate power and technology for marketing and sales purposes of both sport itself and its associated paraphernalia is also the subject of much work in this field. LaFeber's *Michael Jordan and the New Global Capitalism*[75] examines the dominion of companies such as Nike over a global marketplace brought about by an alliance of a triumphant capitalism and new technologies. The recent volume edited by Andrews and Silk, *Sport and Neoliberalism, Politics, Consumption and Culture*,[76] does begin to explore the relationship between sport and the neoliberal state and the manner in which sport becomes a vehicle for public governance. But we must distinguish ourselves even from this work in that in the end we will seek to posit sport as not just being another thing subject to neoliberal governance, but that it constitutes under Neoliberalism one of the highest forms of governance, thus leading us to ask whether, in fact, it is society that now mirrors sport rather than the opposite? Importantly, it appears that no one work has yet considered sport in the context of the particular shift from Law to governance in the manner that we have begun to outline above. It is here that we find our friend Møller as useful; not because he does, but because this particular Dane smells that something is rotten in the kingdom of sport.

Møller's characterisation of contemporary anti-doping law and policy as signalling the end of modernity is founded upon the view that the challenge manifested by the intrusion of the State and the WADA into sport's 'long tradition of self-governance' signals a 'growing lack of confidence in and an unease about the very project of modernity itself'. What Møller is bemoaning here is, of course, the loss of one of the heterogeneous spaces identified by Dadot and Laval that characterised liberal society, namely the autonomy of sport from the Government. What his analysis misses is the basis of this loss and the fundamental and homogenous nature of the new conditions. This unease, and the will to impose order that accompanies it, both exert pressure upon fundamental bourgeois legal principles and ideals of freedom and give rise to a call for their return.[77] One symptom Møller immediately identifies with this rupturous passage is the growing incidence and acceptance of trial by media. In this situation the end seems always to justify the means and anecdotal evidence seems to replace the sort of evidence that might previously have needed to withstand the modernist test of standing up in court.

[74] T Collins, *Rugby League in Twentieth Century Britain: A Social and Cultural History* (Routledge, 2006).
[75] W LaFeber, *Michael Jordan and the New Global Capitalism* (WW Norton & Co, 2002).
[76] M Andrews and D Silk (eds), *Sport and Neoliberalism, Politics, Consumption and Culture* (Temple University Press, 2012).
[77] Møller, 'The Anti-Doping Campaign – Farewell to the Ideals of Modernity?' (n 72) 145, 147.

Møller correctly identifies this tendency towards trial by media and anecdotal evidence as gaining acceptance and support in so far as it is 'in the service of the virtuous campaign against doping'.[78] Møller's position, or fear, is that what we are currently witnessing within sport 'may be a portent of a more general departure from the ideals on which the modern world is based'.[79] Such a view should not seem far-fetched and it, as has much of this thesis, has been reinforced, if not confirmed by events in Australia with the media coverage of the ASADA and the Australian Football League's case against the Essendon Football Club.[80] In the end, we suggest that this portent has further effects that extend beyond trial by media.

If the assumption that we have come to the end of modernity (as a period in history or as an organising concept) is correct, the question that we need to begin to consider is whereabouts are we now? *Operación Puerto* assists us in coming to terms with the situation as it introduces for us one example of how the media crisis and trial by media have taken over from the niceties of modernist practice of Law. As such, one way of understanding this, and of highlighting the points made by Møller, is by reference to the saga of *Operación Puerto*. Understanding the context and facts of *Operación Puerto* also assists us in setting the scene for the consideration of the various anti-doping strategies undertaken in its wake and the manner in which law and its forms appear to be in a process of transformation. But, as we will see, it also contains one of the essentials of our rubric of analysis – spectacle, exception and functionality.

In light of Møller's thesis and our consideration of *Operación Puerto* we move on to consider the question of Law in modernity and in light of a tendency towards a form of governance that itself appears as an exception to the Law. This sets the stage both for a later consideration of new or emerging forms of law and for an analysis of two specific anti-doping tools deployed as a part of the apparatus in the wake of *Puerto* – the Whereabouts system and the Biological Passport. Here, we not only bring to light these specific techniques of governance, but also begin to see disciplines become indistinct; are we talking about Law or not law? Is it Law, science or even the spectacle that decides and adjudicates? Here one of the symptoms of the passage that Møller has identified comes to light – all things, Law, politics, the economy, science and sport; tend to merge into a zone of indistinction.[81] The boundaries between the old disciplines are no longer clear and, in such a situation, it may even be unhelpful to try and isolate one from the other in a manner in which we may have in modernity.

It is from here that we begin to question the basis of Law in the contemporary age. References to the Rule of Law tend to be references to a static ideal, but what we try to describe is that the Rule of Law itself is not immutable and that our

---

[78] ibid, 148.

[79] ibid, 149.

[80] This is a matter that will have to be taken up elsewhere.

[81] G Agamben, *Homo Sacer, Sovereign Power and Bare Life* (Stanford University Press, 1999); and G Agamben, *The State of Exception* (University of Chicago Press, 2005).

whereabouts may be better ascertained by considering another form of the Rule of Law that has its roots in the shift away from Law to governance. Neoliberalism's form of law, or the society of competition, appears to be aimed as much at biopolitical production, or immaterial labour,[82] as at producing lifestyles. Production becomes more and more the production of affect (or governmentality) and here we are able to see a space where the 'economic' or 'Marxist' critique of the causes of doping can be mapped onto the more individualistic or affective understandings of the problem as put forward by Møller on other occasions;[83] sacrifice, the communication of intensities becomes what is produced, reproduced, bought and sold in a new economy. What is produced and sold today are, at their most basic, lifestyles, and here, at least, the sporting lifestyle, and, in this context, an analysis of the doping problem which seeks to continue to treat sport as some pure isolated (and autonomous) phenomena unconnected with the heady world of global business or politics is of little use to us.

Even if we just view professional sport with its emphasis on results, on *faster, higher, stronger*, Møller may be close to the mark when he remarks that 'there is no valid argument against doping that is not at the same time an argument against sport itself'.[84] However, as we will try to show (see Chapter 5), arguments against doping are not necessarily against sport or competition, but in their own way and within the particular logic of Neoliberalism, actually serve to bolster both sport and the society of competition.

Before continuing to develop this line of enquiry the point that needs to be raised is if we are experiencing fundamental changes in the way we 'do' law, we need also to think about the role and purpose of what might be called 'sport criticism'. Konig has criticised sports ethics as being a 'bad idealism with an antiquated knowledge'[85] and in some ways this is the point I seek to open up for further investigation. If what we are witnessing is, as Møller has highlighted, the end of modernity, and if we are going to deal with this juncture and all that it portends, we need to go beyond viewing anti-doping policy as just a matter for sport and concerning mere sporting rules. To take Konig seriously, we need to stop playing long enough; or really to play with it some more. We need to locate sport both historically and within the power relations affecting society now and not in some ideal of what is should be seen through the eyes of the nineteenth or twentieth century. Sport and its rules can only be understood against the background of the development and changes occurring within global capital and not by reference to

[82] See Hardt and Negri, *Commonwealth* (n 32); and, eg, M Lazzarato, 'From Biopower to Biopolitics' (2002) 13 *Pli: The Warwick Journal of Philosophy* 100, available at www.warwick.ac.uk/philosophy/pli_journal/vol_13.html.

[83] V Møller, *The Doping Devil* (International Network of Humanistic Doping Research, 2010).

[84] Møller, 'The Anti-Doping Campaign – Farewell to the Ideals of Modernity?' (n 72) 151. See also E Konig, 'Criticism of Doping: The Nihilistic Side of Technological Sport and the Antiquated View of Sport Ethics' (1995) 30(3)–(4) *International Review for the Sociology of Sport* 247.

[85] Konig, 'Criticism of Doping' (n 84) 257.

a set of values that arose in a different place and at a different time.[86] By recognising that what is at stake is not the purity of sport, but the control of the athlete, as labour and as commodity, and, fundamentally at the same time, the operation of the athlete within the spectacle as an expert, ambassador or minister of the society of competition, we might be able to start to tackle the problem. It might just then be possible to begin the task of constructing a useful critique of sport and doping policy that seriously takes into account the new conditions sensed by Møller.

Møller's assessment of anti-doping policy as the end of modernity immediately raises a number of issues which are at the heart of this work and which have ramifications that spread beyond the milieu of the world of sports, Law and doping. Importantly, what Møller puts on the table for discussion is the end of the modernist idea of the Rule of Law and the coming of the what has been termed the permanent state of exception;[87] it includes the idea of Law's rationality becoming law's functionality; and it includes the increasing playing out of these matters within a global society of the spectacle which adopts the tactics of a Just War where 'public pillorying (becomes) unmistakably punishment'.[88]

In one form or another it is these three factors – *spectacle, exception and functionality* – that come bundled together *under the rubric of a Just War* that serve as this work's rubric of analysis. The spectacle of trial and governance by media over-determining legal processes is apparent in many deployments of the anti-doping apparatus. *Operación Puerto* or, for that matter, the expulsion of Michael Rasmussen, so painstakingly documented by Møller (see Chapter 4) are emblematic of the spectacular examples herein. The Armstrong Era and its final playing out is also steeped in spectacular aspects. But, in the light of what has followed in other arenas (such as the case of the Australian Football club Essendon throughout 2013 and 2014) these examples, whilst telling and setting the future path, may be seen as shining only faint light on what was to come.

The law of anti-doping operates so as to move beyond and over-determines sovereign power and its boundaries. It is a policing power that appears more as an aspect of a global administrative or executive power than as a form of Law that has its source and place within modernity's separation of powers.

Spectacle and Exception are held together by Functionality. So long as the deployment of the apparatus is functional to the global system its extra-legal methods find their justification. Anti-doping sensed though the rubric of Spectacle – Exception–Functionality herald, as Møller has sensed, a change in the way we do law in a post-modern age. These factors are also consistent with many of the symptoms identified by Hardt and Negri as signalling the end of modernity and the coming of Empire (see Chapter 6).[89]

---

[86] L Bryson, 'Sport, Drugs and the Development of Modern Capitalism' (1990) 2 *Sporting Traditions* 135–36.

[87] Agamben, *Homo Sacer* (n 81); and Agamben, *The State of Exception* (n 81).

[88] Møller, 'The Anti-Doping Campaign – Farewell to the Ideals of Modernity?' (n 72) 149.

[89] Hardt and Negri, *Empire* (n 32); M Hardt and A Negri, *Multitude, War and Democracy in the Age of Empire* (Harvard University Press, 2004); and Hardt and Negri, *Commonwealth* (n 32).

The fascination of Møller and other liberal commentators with preserving the autonomy of sport and its 'long tradition of self-governance' is in many ways not a project of modernity or its form of legality. The fascination is one of the contradictions at the heart of the liberal analysis of sport and law. The liberal demands all to be equal before the Law of the sovereign whilst at the same time demanding that sport, at least in principle, remains autonomous from the Law of the sovereign. Preserving such autonomy can just easily be seen as a throwback to pre-modern times and, at the same time, a precursor of things to come. Sport's autonomy was itself an exception to the universalisation of the law characterised by modernity. One of the most basic tenets of the legality of modernity is the notion of all being equal before the same Law – something that this long tradition of self-governance challenges.

In the contemporary context, what the liberal analysis misses in its cherishing of the autonomy of sport is the changing nature of the Government and governance. It might be enough to point to the former East Germany and cry out that sport must be autonomous from the Government, but this clearly misses the point that the government of the population now extends beyond the formal structures of the Government.

There are at least two things at play here when we talk about equality before the Law. Firstly, there is the level playing field of a society where all are equal before the same Law – the modernist's vision of the Law. Secondly, there is the question of, what Møller likes to refer to as, the level playing field of anti-doping. This is the liberal idea that somehow the global anti-doping apparatus constructed upon the framework of the WADC seeks to treat all those that fall within its realm as equals and seeks to treat them equally. What should become apparent is that the exceptional nature of anti-doping law challenges both these ideas. Firstly, it is only the athlete and not the citizen that is subject to this particular form of law. Secondly, within the exceptional zone of the anti-doping apparatus not all are treated equally. Functionality and not Legal rationality determines treatment to a large extent. In light of this, I propose that, following Hardt and Negri, rather than equal application of the Law, what is at play within the realm of the anti-doping apparatus is the achievement of the flexible management of difference. Difference is managed within the framework of functionality aimed at the construction and maintenance a global market; in this case a global cycling market, and more generally, the society of competition itself. From this position it becomes apparent that not all are equal before their particular sovereign, nor that of global cycling, nor the market.

Chapter Summary

Throughout this work we will seek to describe the manner in which the law of the anti-doping apparatus is characterised by a move away from, a mutation of, the traditional concept of Law and the Rule of Law. We will introduce and deal with this latter concept, the Rule of Law in detail in Chapter 3 and develop it further in the neoliberal context in Chapter 5. The manner that law and governance is played out through:

- the movement of the place of adjudication beyond the state sphere and its sovereign boundaries to an exceptional, modulating and supranational Lex Doping and the spectacle (Chapter 2);
- the end of modernity and the transgression of the separation of powers characteristic of liberalism through forms of policing, administration and governance (Chapter 3);
- the intensification of Panoptic and Control mechanisms of governance and policing along with exceptional transformations of the place of the expert in the law (Chapter 4); and
- the instigation and subjection of all of society to the rules of competition (Chapter 5) are all examples of this.

In describing *Operación Puerto* and the *Valverde* cases, Chapter 2 seeks to highlight that the exception to the Law, that takes place within the anti-doping apparatus is, in fact, a permanent exception to the Law of the sovereign State that reigned throughout modernity's high water tide. The *Valverde* cases show us how a cyclist's consent, manifested by them joining a cycling club, or taking out a racing licence, sets in place a policing and disciplinary procedure in which sovereign boundaries are traversed and dissolved. Within the logic of the anti-doping apparatus State action in pursuit of the infrastructure and networks that contribute to doping on a systemic level are regarded as not being functional to the ends of the apparatus. Spanish law, with its procedures based upon the Rule of Law and which thus regards the preservation of the integrity of criminal procedures as taking precedence over disciplinary or even civil procedures, is treated as a hindrance and barrier to the Just War on doping. The same is said for principles of International or European Human Rights (things that proceed only from State agreement); where they are in conflict with the war on doping, that Just War takes precedence. Furthermore, *Operación Puerto* tells us how this primacy of the exception manifests itself increasingly by the spectacle's justification of both the ends of the war on doping and the inability of State Law and sovereignty to be able to adequately deal with the task.

As a reflection on aspects of the end of modernity, Chapter 3 seeks to highlight the fact that within modernity itself there was a tendency away from Law towards governance. Here, the works of Weber and Dicey, which in many respects are used as foundational stones for the liberal vision of the Rule of Law and the rational Law-bounded State, appear to have been written at a high-water mark of liberalism and modernity, such that from their lookout these two were capturing a glimpse of what was to come. Instead of describing what was set in stone, the vision of the

Rule of Law and the rational State takes on the character of an Owl of Minerva[90] moment where what is being described as the Now is, in fact, very much the Past. It is for this reason that we move in Chapter 3, from Weber and Dicey to Foucault, Hardt and Negri, Agamben and others such as Neocleous, in order to describe or pose some of the problems for an analysis that does not take into regard the shift along the Law-governance continuum and all its ramifications.

Chapter 4 describes two principal arts of government employed by the anti-doping apparatus – the Whereabouts and Biological Passport systems. Through mechanisms of discipline, control, biopower and security, the body and life of the professional cyclists has become the object of power in unprecedented ways, monitoring both the bodies' place and position but also its internal functioning and normality. Chapter 4 sets out for us aspects of how the cyclists' life is governed, piloted and fashioned. Furthermore, its shows us how its administrative and policing machinery actively searches out abnormality, rather than as was the case with the Law, waiting for and responding to the occurrence of a legal offence.

Chapter 5 sets out what appears to be, according to the logic of neoliberalism, and a theory of sovereignty that is different in form to that which preceded it. The transformation of the State into just another economic actor has given rise to a theory of sovereignty that we might call *Homo Econonimus* or the Society of Competition. No longer is it a question of the general will bringing forth the State and its system of sovereignty, but of individual will consenting to the injunction of having to be an entrepreneur of the self. Throughout the history of the State sovereignty has slowly but steadily moved from being vested in a transcendent God, to being vested in the figure of the monarch as God's representative, to being vested in the figure of the Law of the State, up until the contemporary context where, above all else, sovereignty appears vested in the economy. No longer do we move to the invisible hand of God, as within the new politico-theological structure of Empire we are now moved and governed by the invisible hand of the economy. It is at the most basic level that this theory of sovereignty performs the role of a single logic of rule or value that guides and governs the operations of everything else within its domain.

Chapter 5 concludes by positing the place of the athlete and the anti-doping apparatus within the society of competition. Both sport and neoliberalism seek to create the image of a level playing field. Both activities are shrouded in the great mist of the level playing field of pure competition. With the passing of the noble amateur, the conditions for competition in sport are maintained by way of the application of the anti-doping apparatus. In the context of sport, and of global governance, the anti-doping apparatus brings into play a hybrid mix of actors, sport, corporate and private associations, that seek to explicitly control the competitive environment by denominating and isolating good competition from

---

[90] GWF Hegel, *Philosophy of Right* (Oxford University Press, 2008), Preface: 'the owl of Minerva spreads its wings only with the falling of the dusk'.

bad competition. In doing so the anti-doping apparatus never seeks to address the root, systemic or structural, conditions of the bad forms of competitive behaviour.

In this world, it is the athlete that is posed as the (or at least a leading) expert of the society of competition. It is the athlete that embodies the injunction to become the entrepreneur of the self on the level playing field of life. The athlete is held up as an example of the possibility of living the dream and of making it on the global playing field of life. In this fantasy world of generalised competition, it is not greed, but factors such as hard work, dedication and integrity, and resilience, that have allowed them to not come up short. We may not all be able to achieve their privileged status, their success in the global sporting spectacle, but we can learn from their attitude and their ethic, the manner in which they have thrown themselves at the mercy of competition.

Chapter 6 serves as our conclusion to the main body of this work and seeks to bring together the entire edifice of neoliberalism's permanent state of exception, its new forms of law or quasi law carved out of spaces beyond State sovereignty, its administration and its policing operations and its spectacular and arbitral adjudications. We highlight that all these new forms of government are backed not by sovereign command and Law but by individual consent and contract. At its most basic, we can characterise our theory of sovereignty itself as one of the Permanent State of Exception. What grounds this element of the exception, along with all others is consent by contract. Contractual governance[91] or government by private agreement appears in our case study as the juridical form that supports and finds its basis in the theory of sovereignty we have identified. Consent by contract or otherwise gives rise not only to the border crossing or dissolving assemblage of private arbitration, but it also founds and justifies the panoply of governance tools we have encountered. Consent also appears by itself to not only justify the banishment of a violator but also their public pillory. Consent grounds the police – here the privatisation of the police is not the outsourcing of State policing functions to private corporations, but it is our consent to have our body and its location monitored and assessed and in the end banished upon grounds that do not easily sit with the Rule of Law or the rational state of modernity. If anything grounds the end of modernity here it is our consent to be governed by the economy.

If we identify the juridical form as contractual governance we can also identify the institutional form as that of the police and the administration, possibly better described in this case as contractual policing. Here we highlight that the Law and the police are different animals; the former clearly a mechanism of sovereignty, the latter appearing not only on the governance side of the continuum but also being a form of governance in which we ourselves actively participate.

In our Epilogue we return to the figure of Lance Armstrong and pose him as the paradigmatic figure of the neoliberal athlete. Lance 1.0, the young, driven precancer version who seized the opportunity provided by the society of competition

---

[91] P Zumbansen, 'Private Ordering in a Globalizing World: Still Searching for the Basis of Contract' (2007) 14(2) *Indiana Journal of Global Legal Studies* 181.

and played the game with verve and vigour. He was already a privileged expert and ambassador, already a minister or angel of the new order in construction. Being a player was the ticket to fortune and to a life free of the trailer park in which he was raised. Lance 2.0 was organised, disciplined and resilient, backed by a machine he overcame death to enforce a form of victory and dominance that gave him the status of the sport's patron, but also as an archetypical figure for us all – an inspiration. Lance 3.0 was the sovereign who returned to give us all hope. Even when he was pursued, Lance acted as a sovereign; as someone beyond the law, refusing right up until the end to recognise the law's power over him. But there is no post-confessional Lance 4.0. In the end, Lance as the outcast, as *homo sacer*, is simply the bare life, that is Lance after he stops having to be Lance.

2

Operación Puerto – It's not about the Blood

Operación Puerto

Operación Puerto (Operation Mountain Pass), is the name given to a criminal investigation conducted by the Spanish Guardia Civil. In many ways the events and commentary surrounding *Puerto* encapsulate and set the future trend for the manner in which the reality of the material processes occurring in anti-doping have become hidden and confused by both media crisis and an emerging form of law and governance. The portrayal of the Spanish investigation and trial by the media by many in positions of power within cycling and anti-doping brings into stark view Møller's concerns relating to the end of modernity, including that of trial by media. For administrators and policy makers, their aims – rational and good administration and the making of good policy – appeared at times to have taken second place to a perceived need to engage in the maintenance of an ill-informed and self-interested slanging match that sought to denigrate and override the niceties of the mechanisms of modernist justice. Rather than being a simple black-and-white question as it is generally portrayed, polarised around the binaries of 'clean' and dirty, or 'fair play' and 'cheating', what *Puerto* reveals is that the issue is one of critical complexity. Here the public stance and the media's portrayal of the situation belie the forces and movements at play as cycling's helmsmen sought to transform it into a global commodity. *Puerto* reveals a space of critical opalescence, where rumour, suspicion, media, law and politics all converge into a media-constructed zone of indistinction. *Puerto* reveals a space where the global system in construction pushes forth, utilising the tools of the spectacle, exception and functionality, brought together by the logic of Just War to over-determine modernist values and Law. It characterises as a hindrance, as tardy, as dysfunctional, as an outdated formality, the grand institution of modern Post-Franco Spanish justice.

In May 2006, the Spanish daily newspaper, *El Pais* published a series of stories concerning the *Guardia Civil* investigation of a network involved in the medical preparation of a number of professional cyclists and other athletes. At the centre of the storm was the Madrid-based gynaecologist, Dr Eufemiano Fuentes. It is cycling history now that the reporting of *El Pais* subsequently sent the cycling world into turmoil as the extent of Dr Fuentes' preparation programmes were revealed and the affair quickly took on a life of its own. At first, the focus was on the Spanish team, *Liberty Seguros*,[1] whose title sponsor quickly withdrew their financial support. The riders of the team, directed by Manolo Saiz, were forced to cover up their sponsor's name with tape as they competed in the 2006 *Giro d'Italia*.[2] Drama such as this had not been witnessed in a cycling race since the *Festina Tour*. Almost immediately other famous cycling names began to emerge, such as Jan Ullrich and Ivan Basso. This not only called into doubt their performances in that edition of the *Giro* but also cut the list of favourites of that year's *Tour de France* to shreds.[3]

Following the initial drama, the media's focus shifted to identifying all the cyclists involved and the matter of how they should be punished. This was also the main focus of the UCI and WADA; a constant calling for the riders to be disciplined in a manner that, deliberately or not, misunderstands what *Puerto*, as a criminal and judicial process, was all about. Hence this line of attack was not only reserved for the media; senior officials of both the UCI and WADA did nothing to shed light on the complexity of the situation.[4] But to begin to understand *Puerto* one needs to consider why the police had been engaged in the surveillance of Fuentes, Saiz and others in the first place.

By piecing together the police and court documents it appears that this surveillance emerged out of the intersection of two seemingly unrelated concerns in Spain. The first was the ongoing investigation by the Spanish *Guardia Civil* into the importation of prohibited medicines such as Insulin Growth Factor 1 (IGF-1) from Australia in *Operación Mamut* (Mammoth).[5] *Mamut* had uncovered a network of importation and distribution of IGF-1 from an Australian company, Gropep. That company, which is based in Adelaide, South Australia, was originally funded by an Australian governmental authority, the Commonwealth Scientific and Industrial Research Organisation (CSIRO), and the University of Adelaide. During the lead up to the Sydney Olympics in 2000 there had been stories circulating that Gropep was the source of substances used by Australian athletes in their preparation for the games.[6] At the time of the investigation Gropep had, in fact, planned to

---

[1] *Liberty Seguros* was the name of the team after it changed sponsors from ONCE at the end of the 2003 season.

[2] A Hood, 'Liberty pulls plug on sponsorship' *Velonews* (25 May 2006). velonews.com/article/9913; A Tan, 'Liberty Seguros terminate contract' Cyclingnews (2006) www.cyclingnews.com/news.php?id=news/2006/may06/may25news3.

[3] 'Ullrich and Basso deny involvement with Fuentes' Cyclingnews (2006) available at www.cyclingnews.com/news.php?id=news/2006/may06/may26news.

[4] 'Operacion Puerto: case closed' *Cyclingnews* (2009) available at www.cyclingnews.com/news/operacion-puerto-case-closed; A Hood, 'The scandal that just keeps on giving: Puerto investigation faces another delay' Velonews (16 October 2009) available at velonews.competitor.com/2009/10/news/the-scandal-that-just-keeps-on-giving-puerto-investigation-faces-another-delay_99302; S Stokes, 'Operacion Puerto delay scandalous, says McQuaid' Cycling News (16 October 2009) available at www.cyclingnews.com/news/operacion-puerto-delay-scandalous-says-mcquaid.

[5] Guardia Civil, Seccion de Consumo y Medio Ambiente de Guardiia Civil, Dilegencia de Exposicion de Hechos, March 2004.

[6] Cyclingnews 1998.

license the right to manufacture IGF-1 to the suspects in the *Mamut* investigation. Following the trail of Gropep's IGF-1 importation and distribution throughout Spain eventually led the *Guardia Civil* to the doors of Dr Fuentes and his cohorts. In the first instance it was this illegal importation and subsequent supply that the *Guardia Civil* were interested in cracking. Their interest was not in Fuentes, Saiz or their collaborators. Even more clearly it was not the cyclists involved. However, the fact of the matter was that it was the trail of IGF-1 from Adelaide that led the *Guardia Civil* to Fuentes and his collaborators. It was a trail that received no interest from either the Australian authorities or media.

During the course of the *Mamut* investigation the *Guardia Civil* became aware of the declarations of the ex-*Kelme* cyclist, Jesus Manzano, which had been published in the Spanish sports daily, *AS*.[7] Manzano set out in great detail his views on the system of rider preparation that existed within his former team, *Kelme – Communidad Valenciana*. This system, Manzano claims, was driven not by the individual cyclists but by those who managed and ran the team. Included amongst those were the team's various *Director Sportifs*, including the principal Director, Vicente Belda, who later stood charged alongside Fuentes and Saiz in the *Puerto* process.

In late 2005, the *Mamut* investigation intersected by chance with the disaster that arose for Spanish cycling after Roberto Heras's positive test for EPO in 2005 in the *Vuelta a España* (Spain's cycling *Tour*).[8] The repercussions for Unipublic, the race's organisers, sponsors, and the Spanish State were enormous. For a complex array of reasons, Spanish cycling was in crisis following Heras' positive test.

At the end of 2005 and in the dawn of what was then thought to be a post-Armstrong World, Heras was the only real Spanish possibility to conquer the Grand Tours (*Giro d'Italia*, *Vuelta España*, and the *Tour de France*). But he was in disgrace. The loss to Unipublic as a result of Heras' positive test drew into sharper focus the perceived problem of doping in Spain and the alleged attitude of impunity that existed there.[9] It may be possible to speculate that it was also this loss of credibility, both in the public eye and in terms of possible future sponsorship and television coverage, which drew the hunt of the *Guardia* closer to Fuentes. The *Guardia* files show that they certainly took note and started to take a closer look.

The evidence given by *Liberty Seguros' Director Sportif*, Manolo Saiz, both when he was detained by the *Guardia Civil* and later at the trial, provides some insight into both how the *Vuelta* disaster came to be and how the *Liberty* team became entangled in the ongoing investigation into illegal importation. Saiz had

---

[7] 'El lado oscuro del ciclismo: El escándalo destapado por Jesús Manzano y el Diario AS contado capítulo a capítulo' *AS* (2004).

[8] 'Roberto Heras, positivo por EPO' *El País* (2005) available at deportes.elpais.com/deportes/2005/11/08/actualidad/1131438112_850215.html; 'Heras: "Estoy completamente seguro de que soy inocente"' El Pais (2005) available at www.elpais.com/articulo/deportes/Heras/Estoy/completamente/seguro/soy/inocente/elpepudep/20051108elpepudep_7/Tes.

[9] 'Ullrich and Basso deny involvement with Fuentes' Cyclingnews (2006) available at www.cyclingnews.com/news.php?id=news/2006/may06/may26news.

been under video surveillance by the *Guardia Civil* and was arrested with a bag of cash to allegedly pay his team's outstanding account with Fuentes. The cash was in the mixed denominations of euros, Swiss francs and Australian dollars. The dollars were supposedly money left over from the team's *per diem* payments by the organisers of the Tour Down Under in Adelaide earlier that year. Saiz has had a long history in professional cycling, but unlike most other team directors, he had never been a professional cyclist. Nevertheless, his contacts extended far and wide throughout the cycling world and he had been, for many years, one of the most successful and complete *Director Sportifs*. Saiz was the mentor (or, at least, inspiration) for Lance Armstrong's *Director Sportif*, Johan Bruyneel, who rode and served his cycling apprenticeship with Saiz during the 1990s. Saiz also had close connections with ex-Australian professionals and cycling powerbrokers such as Neil Stephens and Stephen Hodge. In Spain his followers and contacts are known collectively as the '*Manolo-istas*' and they are anecdotally regarded as being closely linked to those who, at the time, brokered the power behind the UCI. It is of no surprise, then, that Saiz was also significantly a prime mover, along with former UCI President Hein Verbruggen and his protégé Alain Rumpf, in the creation of the Pro Tour (now World Tour) model adopted by the UCI. Saiz was also a key figure in mustering the numbers for the election of Pat McQuaid as Verbruggen's successor as UCI President in 2005.

When he was interviewed in detention, Saiz said that he had known Fuentes since his stint with the Spanish cycling team *ONCE* in the early 1990s, a time when his team was populated by a number of high-profile riders many of whom are still involved in the sport as administrators or *Directors Sportif*. Saiz said that, after Fuentes left the team, they had occasional personal contact but that it was in 2004, with his signing of Roberto Heras, that the relationship recommenced on a more-than-friendly level. Saiz said that, on his arrival at *Liberty* from the *US Postal Service* team (*USPS*), Heras had asked that if he could have Fuentes, as his personal doctor. According to Saiz, Heras wanted to deal directly with Fuentes. At first, Saiz said he had refused the request, as it did not seem to him to be the best way to manage the team. After much insistence on the part of Heras, Saiz gave in, but it seems that he decided to try and manage the relationship as best he could. Saiz was insistent in his evidence that it was Heras and other riders in his team, some of whom had also previously been in *Kelme*,who had pushed for the Fuentes connection. There, of course,was no love lost between Saiz and *Kelme's Director Sportif* Vicente Belda. During the previous years, Saiz had been instrumental for pushing through the Pro Tour and *Kelme's* exclusion from it. This exclusion had in part been brought about by this insistence of Saiz and others that *Kelme* was still engaged in cycling's old ways.[10]

---

[10] 'Saiz and Belda fall out over Valverde' *Bike Radar* (2004) available at www.bikeradar.com/news/article/saiz-and-belda-fall-out-over-valverde-9981; M Hardie, 'Liberty trifecta' *Cyclingnews* (2004) available at autobus.cyclingnews.com/road.php?id=road/2004/jun04/euskalbizikleta04/euskalbizikleta043.

The author interviewing Roberto Heras, Durango, 2004 (photo Iban Gorriti).

After Heras's positive test the *Guardia Civil* appear to have thought it worthwhile to see if there was any link between the substances being used by cyclists and their investigation of importation and distribution in *Operacion Mamut*. This, of course, was not the only event that had led them to the consulting rooms of Fuentes. The year before, the *Vuelta* had been hit by two positive doping tests for blood transfusions. The first to break was that of Tyler Hamilton, another ex *USPS* rider, who tested positive following his 11 September time-trial victory, over his soon-to-be teammate, Floyd Landis, in Valencia.[11] The second involved the post-race revelations concerning Hamilton's teammate Santi Perez.[12] On the road the *Phonak* team was managed by ex-*Kelme Director Sportif*, Alvaro Pino.[13] And, of course,

[11] M Hardie, 'Belda takes aim' Bike Zone (2004) available at www.bike-zone.com/news. php?id=news/2004/sep04/sep25news2; M Hardie, 'Tyler starts the fight club on September 11, *Cycling-news*, 2004. autobus.cyclingnews.com/road/2004/vuelta04/?id=results/vuelta048. Hardie 2004b; Jones 2004. On the day of the 11 September time trial as a part of his journalistic duties the author waited patiently outside of the *Phonak* team bus in an attempt to speak to Hamilton. Hamilton was unusually distant that day. A week or so later, driving from Granada to Caceres for the start of the next stage of the race the author rang through the news to Jones whose name ended up on the story which broke the news of the positive test. Another task the author had throughout that race was to ghost write the race diary of Floyd Landis. Six years later and not that long after his accusations of doping in the *USPS* team and by Lance Armstrong, Landis travelled to Australia to attend a conference organised by the author to discuss doping. That conference coincided with the 2010 World Road Cycling Championships in Geelong Australia. The conference was to be held at Deakin University's Alfred Deakin Institute but was moved off campus at the insistence of the Vice Chancellor as a result of commercial and political pressure arising because of the attendance of Landis.

[12] S Abt, 'Pérez of Phonak is accused' *International Herald Tribune* (1 November 2004) available at www.nytimes.com/2004/11/01/sports/01iht-phonak_ed3_.html.

[13] T Maloney, 'Six years, 11 doping scandals: The Phonak legacy' *Cyclingnews* (2006) available at www.cyclingnews.com/news.php?id=features/2006/phonak_legacy.

seemingly outside of the Fuentes affair, the next doping incident to really rock cycling was that of another ex-USPS rider, Floyd Landis.[14] These events involving Heras, Hamilton and Perez drew the *Guardia Civil* closer and closer to their stakeout of Fuentes.

Puertas Abiertas

In May 2006, the *Operación Puerto* story broke when *El Pais* published details from the leaked *Guardia Civil* files. Not only were Liberty *Seguros* embroiled but so, also, were Hamilton, Perez, a host of *Kelme* riders and two of the main challengers for that year's *Tour de France* – Jan Ullrich and Ivan Basso. All of this is old news. Most who follow cycling are now all too familiar with the stories of the blood bags, the nicknames[15] and the speculation that still continues to surround them. Bags of evidence have come to light regarding Fuentes and the methods he practiced. The riders both implicated and suspected and the subsequent disciplinary and criminal proceedings against many of them have all been in the news.[16]

Many seemed to believe that there was something else that Spanish justice needed to resolve, other than the prosecution of Fuentes and Co, which would assist cycling's 'renewal'. This was the continual line pushed by the media, the UCI and WADA. But the point that is often forgotten in the fog is that as far as the *Guardia Civil* investigation and the Spanish courts were concerned, the cyclists have never been suspects. Sure there were bags of evidence implicating various riders in the Fuentes' scheme, bringing to light for the first time the details of planning and administration that went on to help produce some 'great' rides,[17] but no

---

[14] 'Spanish soccer clubs linked to Fuentes?' *Cyclingnews* (2006) available at www.cyclingnews.com/editions/first-edition-cycling-news-for-december-8-2006; Canadian Broadcasting Corporation, 'Cycle of denial Implicated on the Internet' (2006) available at www.cbc.ca/sports/indepth/landis/instantmessage.html; Velocity Nation, Interview with Paul Kimmage, 'Fighting the Good Fight' (2009) available at velocitynation.com/content/interviews/2009/paul-kimmage; D Walsh, From Lance to Landis, Inside the American Doping Controversy at the Tour de France (Ballantine Books, 2007).

[15] Barthes is right in that he tells us that there is an onomastics of the Tour. But in the time since Barthes, in a manner the semiotician may not have envisaged, that onomastics has descended from the heights of myth and epic having the status of Greek gods. They have descended from being lofty signs of the valour of the ordeal, of beings signs of old European ways and ethnicity – Brankart le Franc, Bobet le Francien, Robic le Celte, Ruiz l'Ibere, Darrigade le Gascon; to being patronymics of the biopolitical, of *homo sacer* and the spectacle that sustains Empire. See R Barthes, 'The Tour de France as Myth and From Barthes to Foucault and beyond – Cycling in the Age of Empire', a paper delivered at *Foucault: 25 Years On*, Conference – University of South Australia, 25 June 2009, available at /esodoweb.net/pdf/agempire.pdf.

[16] 'Complete coverage of "Operación Puerto"' Cyclingnews (2009) available at autobus.cyclingnews.com/news.php?id=news/puerto_complete.

[17] For examples see M Hardie, 'Tyler starts the fight club on September 11', *Cyclingnews*, 2004. autobus.cyclingnews.com/road/2004/vuelta04/?id=results/vuelta048 M Hardie, 'Liberty trifecta' *Cyclingnews* (2004) available at autobus.cyclingnews.com/road.php?id=road/2004/jun04/euskalbizikleta04/euskalbizikleta043.

cyclist was ever charged, or was likely to be charged, with a criminal offence in Spain as a result of *Operación Puerto*.

In this context the consistent media reports of riders being cleared of any involvement by the Spanish judiciary are meaningless. The cyclists were always witnesses and, in some ways, possibly the victims of the network focused around Fuentes.

The approach of the Spanish courts is abundantly clear even from the reports in the cycling media. For example, one report even sets out in detail the questions that Investigating Judge Serrano intended to ask cyclists when giving evidence.[18] The questions point to the status of the cyclists as victims rather than perpetrators. The questions were:

1.   Is the witness still a professional cyclist?
2.   For which teams has he ridden since 2002?
3.   As a professional cyclist, does he know the doctors Eufemiano Fuentes, Yolanda Fuentes, or Alfredo Córdova? Has he received blood transfusions? If so, in what laboratory and with whose authority?
4.   During his career as professional cyclist, has he ever been sent by his doctor, manager, or other person to the laboratory of Dr. Merino Batres in Madrid?
5.   Has he ever ridden for a team for which Manolo Saiz was technical director or manager? Did he receive blood transfusions during that time?
6.   Assuming that he had suffered health disadvantages as consequence of the treatment by the doctors Fuentes and/or Córdova and/or the actions of Saiz, has he suffered any damage that he could claim in this process?

Their status, as such, is further illuminated by the comments made by one of the accused Merino Batres when he told the *Guardia*:

> Poor Mancebo, I believe that we swindled him a bit. He didn't need the transfusions for anything. He had such a high natural Haematocrit that we couldn't do half as much for him that we did for the others.[19]

Batres recounts how Fuentes and himself swindled Francisco Mancebo to the tune of €50,000 in 2005 alone. As a result of being caught up in *Puerto* (ie implicated but never charged with a criminal or doping offence) Mancebo's income fell from €1,000,000 in 2006 with the French team *Ag2r* to a low of €10,000 when he was riding in Portugal during 2008.[20]

[18] 'Spanish soccer clubs linked to Fuentes?' *Cyclingnews* (2006) available at autobus.cyclingnews. com/news.php?id=news/2006/dec06/dec08news.
[19] C Arribas, 'Queremos llegar al fondo de la trama' *El Pais* (12 February 2009) available at elpais. com/diario/2009/02/12/deportes/1234393206_850215.html. Author's translation.
[20] ibid.

In these circumstances, instead of pursuing the riders, what Spain sought to do was to deal with the public health issues arising from doping in sports and to deal with the supply of doping substances flowing into that country, from ironically what is regarded as a part of the new (and by implication 'clean') cycling world. The interest of the *Guardia Civil* was, and always remained, the importation of potential doping products and their distribution and administration throughout Spain. The *Guardia Civil* believed that Fuentes was probably in collaboration with other sports doctors implicated in doping practices and that these doctors and the groups that they formed constituted independent, but interrelated, criminal groups; acting independently but related through their shared objective of providing medical assistance to cyclists. These groups were interlinked with those seeking to import, manufacture and distribute the substances. Simply put, Spain had gone after the dealers and the pushers and not the end users or the victims. This, however, has never sat well with the media and WADA who wanted to catch cheats. Their focus was always individualistic not systemic.

Figure 1 Dr Fuentes' doping plan for Roberto Heras 2005

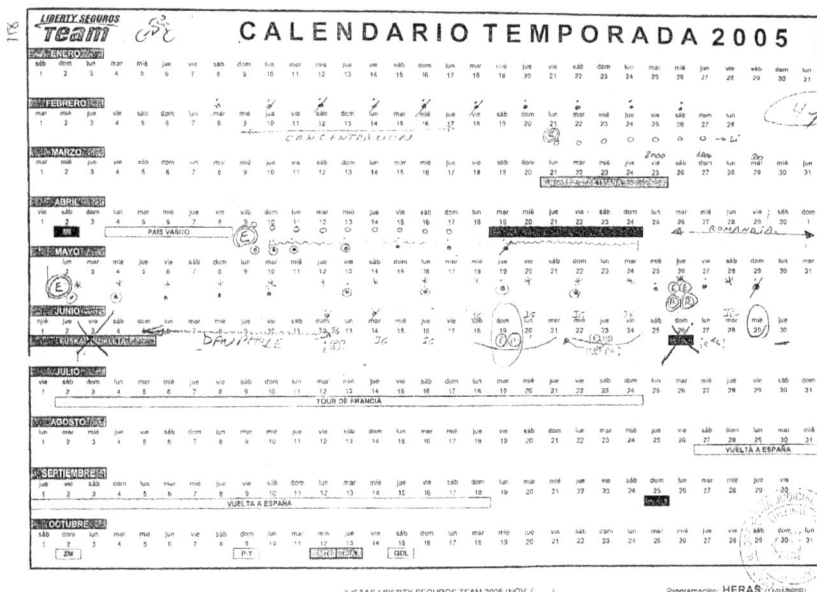

The conclusion reached by the *Guardia Civil* was that Fuentes and his gang developed and were involved in the practice of doping, which they described as the integral preparation of the riders based on illicit methods using medicines in a manner contrary to Spanish health laws. The illicit preparation methods of Fuentes used products which were imported into Spain without passing the normal controls applied to the importation of medicines, they were using the medicines for purposes other than those that they were designed, and many of the products used were beyond their use by date. The January 2009 appeal decision in *Puerto* has highlighted the grounds upon which the case against Fuentes and his cohort would proceed.[21] These include that the practice endangered public health in:

(a) that they did not extract blood and conduct transfusions in adequate premises;
(b) that they did not transport blood in adequate recipients;
(c) that the identity of the donors were not adequately recorded;
(d) that there did not exist a system to guarantee that the blood was stored at the correct temperatures or that the fridges and freezers had adequate back up electricity in the case of black out; and
(e) that the operation of extracting and transfusing blood was conducted in a clandestine manner.

Fuentes, Pantani and Chaba

The effect of Fuentes' practices on the health of the riders was one of the issues raised by the continuing post-appeal *Guardia Civil* investigation. It remained the focus of the matter when it finally came to trial in 2013. As the story of Pantani's relationship with Fuentes suggests, these practices of preparing cyclists clearly raise other important public health concerns. As does the death of Jose Maria Jimemez. These deaths were not the stated reasons for the *Guardia Civil* to continue to pursue the charge of endangering public health, but they serve to highlight the risks. Although there have been suggestions that the *Guardia Civil* may have investigated the links between Fuentes and Marco Pantani and Jose Maria Jimenez, the references to these two riders in the *Puerto* files have not been widely speculated about in the media. What the files do call into question is the assumption by Matt Rendell in his book, *The Death of Marco Pantani*, that in his final year *Il Pirata* (as Pantani is referred to) was not doping.[22]

Rendell documents Pantani's life during his last year in some detail: the plastic surgery, the outcome of the criminal and disciplinary trials and appeals, the visits to the psychiatrist and his doctors in Italy, the hospitalisations, the crack and

---

[21] Audienca Provincial de Madrid, Seccion no 5, Rollo 702/2008, Organo Procedencia: JDO Instruccion N 31 de Madrid, Proc Origen: Diligencias Previas Proc Abreviado no 4293/2006, Auto Numero 63/09, Ilmos Magistrados D Arturo Beltran Nunez, D Jesus Angel Guijarro Lopez, D Paz Redondo Gil, dated 11 January 2009.
[22] M Rendell, *The Death of Marco Pantani: A Biography* (Weidenfeld & Nicolson, 2006).

cocaine binges, on to his retirement and final death on 14 February 2004. During this time, it was thought that Pantani was, for racing purposes, clean, although he was using crack and cocaine after his retirement. Rendell recounts how doctors in Italy had warned him that racing itself might not be the best thing for his mental or physical health but that racing doped was far more dangerous.

Nevertheless, it was in this same period, painstakingly documented by Rendell, that the *Puerto* investigation tells us Pantani was also visiting Madrid and Dr Fuentes. During Pantani's last season on the bike, the one immediately before his death, commencing late January 2003, Fuentes equally painstakingly records an intense calendar of preparation including EPO (almost daily for over a month), IGF-1, T3 Levothroid (a hormone used in the treatment of menopause) and insulin. The programme lasted from late January until Pantani's retirement in June 2003.

The coincidence between this programme and Pantani's documented incidents of mental instability during his final year raises significant cause for concern as to the health implications of doping. These coincidences or mis-incidences of events in Pantani's last year of life have never fully come to light. Another Fuentes patient who also suffered from depression and instability, Jose Maria Jimenez, died a little over two months before Pantani.

Figure 2 Dr Fuentes' doping plan for Marco Pantani 2003

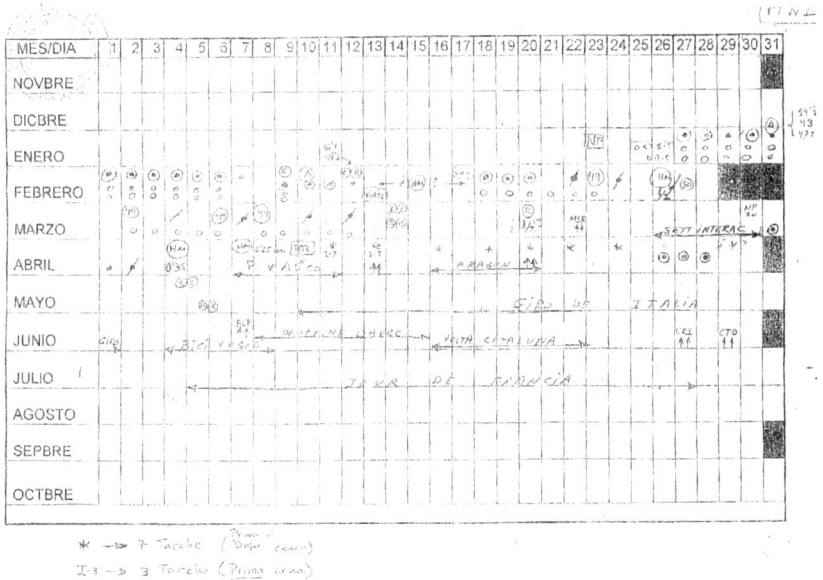

Figure 3 Annotations to Dr Fuentes' doping plan for Marco Pantani 2003

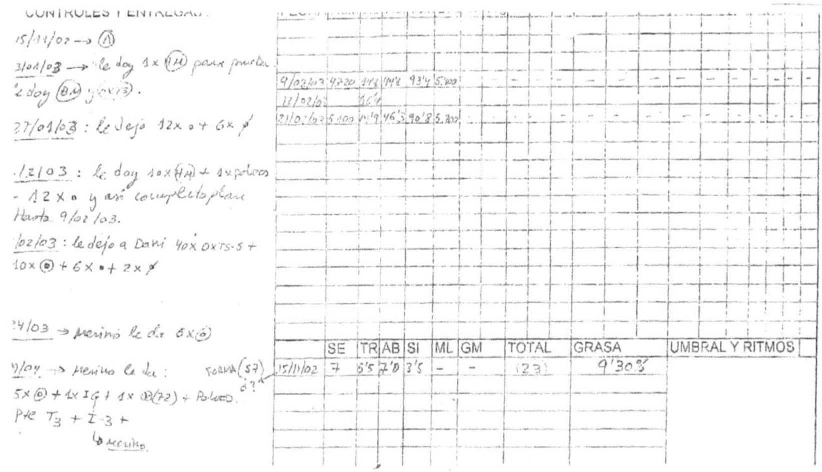

'We Don't Want to Know'

The Spanish judicial process, like any other judicial process, was not a linear affair. Interlocutory steps and appeals by various parties, including the UCI and WADA, all had their effect on the course of the proceedings. As did, from the outset, the interventions of ASO, the company which controls the *Tour de France* and the UCI, in demanding that a list of names be given to them prior to the 2005 *Tour* and before the investigation itself was complete. In 2007, Investigating Judge Serrano shelved the inquiry.[23] His finding was that he did not have enough evidence to obtain a prosecution against anyone involved, as doping was not, then, a crime in Spain. As well as that, in his view, the facts as presented did not fit within the concept of a charge of endangering public health. At that point it seemed that, to all intents and purposes, in Spain *Operación Puerto* was finished. Nevertheless, the damage rolled on as the riders who had been implicated, some of whom who had been 'cleared' by their national cycling federations or national anti-doping agencies, found it difficult to obtain a ride in a top-tier team.

Some were sanctioned, with Basso being the highest-profile rider involved. Others ended up either retiring, racing in lower-level teams or racing as refugees in places such as Portugal and the United States until things blew over. Out of the approximately 50 cyclists named or referred to in one way or another, probably as

---

[23] Juzgado de Instruccion Num 31, Madrid, DPA 4293706 H, Autosobreseimiento, dated 8 March 2007.

few as five have had meaningful careers post *Puerto*, despite the majority of them never being prosecuted or disciplined.

In the end, the sanction imposed on most of them has not been that meted out by the courts, nor their federations. It has, however, been dealt to them by the management and sponsors of the *Pro Tour* teams and the race organisers. This is evidenced by Mancebo's case referred to above, and as many of the other cases show, retribution for involvement in *Puerto* is not legal in the way we used to think about such things. Whatever the legal outcome might be, retribution manifests itself in one form as an inability to obtain a contract with a decent team. Both ASADA and the Royal Spanish Cycling Federation (RFEC) respectively, found that those involved had no case to answer. The comparison between Spain and Australia is telling, as in all the rhetoric one is painted as being 'out of step' and the home of the old ways of cycling, whilst the other is 'in step' and the home of the new ways of cycling, but both decisions were made on identical grounds. The comparison is also telling given the manner in which one Spaniard, Alejandro Valverde, was singled out for attention.

The issue is complex and defies the simple explanations concerning the old and new cycling worlds. On the one hand, there is the position that Judge Serrano had refused to formally release evidence to the relevant sporting bodies until at least the criminal process against Fuentes and his collaborators had been completed. This order of the Court has itself been highlighted in the media wars as further evidence of Spain not being in step with the new cycling culture. As we will see, it has also formed the basis of, or evidence for, the divergence between the law of anti-doping and that of the Spanish Constitution. There is no great conspiracy here. It is the simple application of ordinary principles of (modernist) justice in which disciplinary proceedings are suspended pending the outcome of criminal hearings. The Provincial Court of Madrid confirmed this approach in December 2009,[24] as did the Court in the final judgment in the case (see the *Puerto* Trial below). It is also consistent with fundamental principles of law and natural justice and to not be bound by them would place the integrity of the criminal trial at stake. However, the UCI received a bundle of 56 files encompassing the bulk of the *Operación Puerto* documents then in the possession of the *Guardia Civil*. The UCI retained a consultant to deal with the *Puerto* files and, in early 2006, subsequently passed these on to their respective national cycling federations. It was on this basis that, for example (the Italian Olympic Committee) CONI, disciplined Ivan Basso.

---

[24] Audienca Provincial de Madrid, Seccion no 5, Rollo 395/2009, Organo Procedencia: JDO Instruccion N 31 de Madrid, Proc. Origen: Diligencias Previas Proc Abreviado no 4293/2006, Auto Numero 3734/09, Ilmos Magistrados D Arturo Beltran Nunez, a Pascual Fabia Mir, D Paz Redondo Gil, dated 26 November 2009.

In the Australian case, of the 56 bundles of documents sent to the federations, it appears that only one page actually made it to the independent anti-doping body ASADA.[25] Without more than this one page consisting of a calendar accompanied by some handwritten and coded annotations, it is no surprise that ASADA found that there was no case to answer. The question that must be asked is where the chain of custody for these documents broke down. How did Cycling Australia, if that is indeed where the chain broke, fail to pass on all the relevant documents? Nevertheless, the UCI continued to hold out Australia as one of the representatives of the new cycling culture who have dealt with the *Puerto* problem is a comprehensive way, whilst Spain is characterised as an example of the old ways. Ways that must change.

In February 2008, the Provincial Court of Madrid reopened the case.[26] The three magistrates found on appeal that there was sufficient evidence for the charge of endangering public health to be pursued and they directed Judge Serrano to reopen his investigation into that charge. However, it may be that an equally important finding of the Provincial Court was that the cyclists had never engaged in fraud in respect of their employers or sponsors. This decision is important, not only for the riders, in so far as they continued to suffer at the hands of administrators and sponsors who feared the sullying of their good names, but also the continuing schizophrenic and paranoid manner in which *Puerto* and, more broadly, doping policy continued to be dealt with in cycling (or, for that matter sport in general). The Provincial Court finding suggests, in fact, that these very same sponsors and administrators have been all too well aware of the practices within their respective teams for too long – and thus are not in a position to have either their name sullied or to have been defrauded.

The 2008 Provincial Court decision rejected the argument of fraud as being openly artificial and stated that it was not realistic to try to fit acts such as those in question in *Puerto* within the Spanish law of fraud. Fraud in Spain, as with most jurisdictions, requires that either those contracting the cyclists (the teams) or those running publicity campaigns in concert with the cyclists (the sponsors), to be deceived, and to be deceived seriously, hence the concept and the offence of serious fraud. The court stated that

> when it is notorious that for many years there has been talk of irregular practices, when there have been cyclists who have died from the consumption of drugs, frequent

---

[25] ASADA's independence, or lack of it, has been an issue in relation to its cases against the players of the Rugby League Club Cronulla-Sutherland and the Australian Rules Club Essendon throughout 2013 and 2014. This is an issue to be tackled elsewhere.

[26] Audienca Provincial de Madrid, Seccion no 5, Rollo 566/2007, Organo Procedencia: JDO Instruccion N 31 de Madrid, Proc. Origen: Diligencias Previas Proc Abreviado no 4293/2006, Auto Numero 496/08, Ilmos Magistrados D Arturo Beltran Nunez, D Jesus Angel Guijarro Lopez, D Paz Redondo Gil, dated 11 February 2008.

disqualifications and sanctions, when cycling is the mirror into which other sports look with fear, when it is known that the caravans and logistic premises of cycling teams have been searched for stimulants, when random controls are necessary after each race or stage, and the cycling teams have their own specialist doctors, to affirm that the cyclists have defrauded those who have contracted them is to close one's eyes to reality … . there is at least an 'I don't want to know' attitude, and that is incompatible with the idea of serious fraud.[27]

The implication of this finding is clear. The Provincial Court felt that the sponsors, and the sport's administrators, had knowledge of the fact that there had been a number of doping cases in cycling in recent years and that doping existed within the sport. The further and more important implication is that both groups had been happy to turn a blind eye while it was in their interests. This finding undermines somewhat the simplistic rhetoric of (individual) cheating and fair play, often repeated by members of both these groups. This rhetoric pervades the discussion around doping in cycling in contemporary times and the arguably hypocritical situation whereby it is only the cyclists who are taking the blame for the problem (we will return to the individualisation of the problem later in this work). For all the talk of cultural change in cycling, there has still been little acknowledgment from the various levels of the sport's administration and sponsors that whilst many of them continue to build their own careers, they too were a part of cycling's old ways (eg see the Epilogue to this work). The Landis allegations and subsequent investigation by US Federal authorities and USADA reinforce this.

The *Puerto* files refer to various media reports, doping cases and allegations of such, that of Roux, Manzano, Heras, Hamilton and Perez in particular. All of this suggests that the widespread use of performance-enhancing substances in cycling was common knowledge. Drugs in cycling have a long history starting with the sport's birth in the nineteenth century.[28] As we know, it was Simpson's death[29] that brought the health and safety of the cyclists into focus as anti-doping controls developed during the 1960s.[30] It was also with Simpson's death in 1967 – the Englishman who helped start the process of globalising the Tours – that doping first becomes a political matter but it still remained an internal issue, something for the sport to deal with. As we have noted above it is the late 1990s that mark the point at which it becomes a matter for the State and it was with the *Festina Tour*, with borders being crossed, that we see doping first becoming criminalised. Even at the time of the *Festina* affair, the ethos behind anti-doping measures was health and safety. Only recently, as the pressures of a global market demanded, has that

---

[27] ibid.

[28] See JM Hoberman, *Mortal Engines: The Science of Performance and the Dehumanization of Sport* (The Free Press, 1992), where he chronicles the early links between cycling and medical research.

[29] W Fotheringham, *Put Me Back on My Bike: In search of Tom Simpson* (Yellow Jersey Press, 2003).

[30] B Houlihan, *Dying to Win: Doping in Sport and the Development of Anti-doping* (Council of Europe Publishing, 1999).

focus shifted to the risk management backed by the rhetoric of fair play and cheating to be monitored by a bio-political passport regime (see Chapter Five).

Puerto also reveals a new post-*Festina* 'post-modern' approach to the organisation of doping. *Festina* became criminalised because of the seizure of various illegal substances in Willy Voet's team car.[31] The riders, including Australian Neil Stephens, were held in police detention for days, with the almost 'blind' Swiss rider, Alex Zuelle even being deprived of his glasses. The *Festina* affair exposed the old team-based practices of preparation, where team doctors themselves were responsible for the team's doping programme. In the aftermath of *Festina*, that system began to break down and it seems that it was replaced by a more networked and outsourced preparation system. *Operación Puerto* exposes the outsourced network model that came into existence in cycling in great detail. It also suggests that *Liberty* returned to a more team-based approach as Saiz was aware of the dangers to his rider's health, not to say the team's reputation, if they were left alone and allowed to do their own thing. Journalist and ex-professional Paul Kimmage has argued that rather than dealing with its history and the problem of doping, in a post-*Festina* world these practices only became further perfected.[32]

Spectacle, Exception and Functionality

Spain and Australia, in the guise of Valverde and Davis, were the unfortunate focus of another *Operación Puerto* sideshow that was played out in advance of the 2007 World Cycling Championships in Stuttgart. Although at that point there was only speculation and rumour as to Valverde's involvement in *Puerto*, the Stuttgart Organising Committee decided that it did not want Valverde to compete in the 2007 World Championships to be held in that city. This involvement, they said, was sufficient to exclude Valverde; his presence was not consistent with the city's plans to give cycling a new start. The UCI quickly fell into line with their hosts and announced that, not only were they prohibiting Valverde from riding, but also that they would commence disciplinary proceedings against him. The problem for the UCI and Stuttgart was that they had opened a can of worms in that other riders who had been listed to start at the World Championships were in a similar or even worse position than Valverde in relation to their documented *Puerto* involvement. The problem here is clearly not one of proven guilt, but of suspicion of doping itself being sufficient for an athlete to be sanctioned. The Stuttgart organisers didn't want to be associated with the stench of disrepute that the media had whipped up. Rumour and notions of disrepute figure again in the later exclusion of Michael Rasmussen from the *Tour de France* (see Chapter Five) and away from cycling it

---

[31] W Voet, *Breaking the Chain, Drugs and Cycling – The True Story* (Yellow Jersey Press, 2001).
[32] Velocity Nation, Interview with Paul Kimmage, Fighting the Good Fight, 2009. velocitynation.com/content/interviews/2009/paul-kimmage.

was disrepute and the Kafkaesque claim that Essendon Football Club could not prove that they had not doped that drove the Australian Football League (AFL) through a crisis of its own making in Australia from 2013–2015.

On having the inconsistency of their position brought to their notice, the UCI quickly decided that the cases of Davis and Valverde were the same and that both, along with the Czech, Rene Andrle, would all be excluded from the race.[33] It did not matter that the Court in Spain had restricted the use of the *Puerto* evidence until that case was concluded, nor that the RFEC and ASADA had found that both Valverde and Davis had no case to answer. The law, or force of law, was now being simultaneously made, interpreted and applied by the UCI, the Stuttgart Race Organising Committee and sponsors of the World Championship. Even the agreement between the UCI and the RFEC to mediate the dispute in CAS rather than the RFEC seeking an injunction in a civil court did not bring about a result that the race organisers found to be satisfactory or binding. Davis also commenced proceedings in CAS and the matters seemed to be effectively resolved with the CAS Arbitrator considering

> … that a ban imposed on a cyclist, not yet recognised as guilty of doping, from participating in the World Championships constituted a form of advance sanction. … the UCI was prevented from implementing the type of procedure which would allow it to pronounce such a severe sanction whilst maintaining in an adequate manner the rights of the cyclist.[34]

In short, CAS found that the Organising Committee and the UCI had sought to deny the riders natural justice. Unimpressed by the outcome, the German Interior Minister froze the government's subsidy to the organisers of the race.[35] The crisis created in the spectacle was in the end not resolved by law, even sporting or anti-doping law, but by the application of the exception in order to achieve the functional outcome of cycling's perceived clean start.

Law, Beyond a Boundary

As we will come to see, when *Puerto* finally came to trial, the presiding judge, Justice Santamaría Matesan re-stated the earlier decisions by various Spanish judges and courts refusing to allow access to and the subsequent declaration of invalidity concerning the access gained by the CONI to one of the blood bags

---

[33] P McQuaid, Personal Communication, UCI President Pat McQuaid, 20 September 2007.

[34] Valverde cleared by CAS to ride World Championships available at www.cyclingnews.com/news/valverde-cleared-by-cas-to-ride-world-championships/.

[35] 'Valverde; Sinkewitz implicates Bettini; Minister freezes funds' Bike Radar (27 September 2007) available at www.bikeradar.com/news/article/valverde-sinkewitz-implicates-bettini-minister-freezes-funds-12592.

comprised in the evidence.[36] These orders were central the particular sideshow of the Spanish *Puerto* process that featured Alejandro Valverde and involved his prosecution by the Italian authorities for doping. It is, in fact, much more than a sideshow; being, in so far as the UCI and WADA were concerned, the main game.

Figure 4 Dr Fuentes' doping plan for Alan Davis 2005[37]

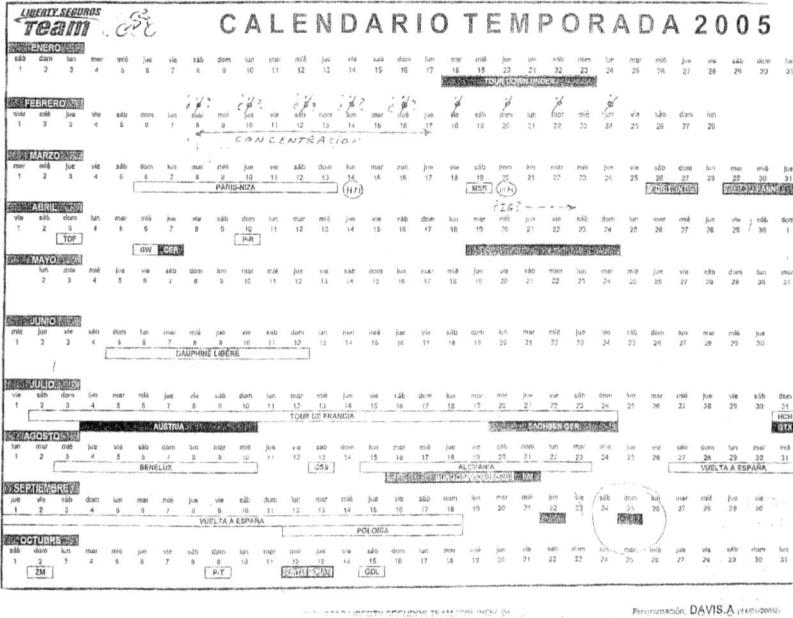

On 16 March 2010, three years before the finalisation of the Spanish criminal process in *Operación Puerto*, and two-and-a-half years after the Stuttgart events described above, the CAS delivered its award banning the Spanish cyclist Alejandro Valverde from competition for a period of two years, the result of what Martinez describes as 'a complex maze of administrative and arbitration processes'.[38] For our purposes, this maze raises issues central to the administration of anti-doping law and its interaction with the sovereign Law of the State. It is at this point that we will begin to more clearly distinguish the operation of Law in the sovereign and

---

[36] Juzgado De Lo Penal N° 21 De Madrid, Juicio Oral n° 52 de 2012., Doña Julia Patricia Santamaría Matesanz, Magistrada-Juez del Juzgado de lo Penal n° 21 de Madrid, SENTENCIA N° 144/13, procedimiento abreviado n° 4293/06: Eufemiano Claudio Fuentes Rodriguez, Jose Ignacio Labarta Barrera, Vicente Belda Vicedo,Manuel Saiz Balbas, Yolanda Fuentes Rodriguez (hereinafter Sentencia Final) 328–29.

[37] There are no similar documents of Dr Fuentes that relate to Alejandro Valverde.

[38] JL Martinez, 'El Caso Valverde: Un complejo entresijo de decisions y actuaciones legales' *Analisis del laudo TAS 2009/A/1879*, 42 RJDE30 A310: 413, 2010.

modernist sense from the transnational, or supranational, form, or force, of law called forth by the anti-doping apparatus.

The core question raised by Valverde's case, which itself provides the reason why it was so tenaciously pursued by WADA, is that it squarely raises (and decides) the question as to whether a sovereign state's domestic Law, its Constitutional rights and guarantees or even International or European standards of Human Rights, are overridden or over-determined by the transnational anti-doping apparatus. As we have seen, along with the complex Legal issues, this problem immediately gave rise to the charges that 'Spain is an open bar for doping' and that 'in Spain there are all kinds of obstacles placed in the way of punishing athletes for doping violations'.[39] To be clear the particular obstacle placed in the path of the Just War on doping that was being complained about was the Spanish system of Law based upon post-Franco notions of a Soveriegn *Estado de Derecho* (a State governed by Law, that is, in the Anglo sense, the Rule of Law).

The *Valverde* case, involved not one but three separate proceedings brought against him or appealed to CAS. The maze of decisions is further complicated by some of the proceedings being heard together. It must also be recalled that as far as the Spanish criminal proceedings were concerned, neither Valverde nor any other cyclist was ever treated as a suspect. In order of their date of decision the three CAS decisions are:

- *WADA & UCI v Alejandro Valverde & Royal Spanish Cycling Federation (RFEC)* (CAS 2007/A/1396 & CAS 2007/A/1402) decided 10 July 2008 (**Valverde 1**);

- *Alejandro Valverde Belmonte v Comitato Olimpico Nazionale Italiano (CONI)* (2009/A/1879 CAS) decided 16 March 2010 (**Valverde 2**); and

- *WADA & UCI v RFEC & Alejandro Valverde* (CAS 2007/A/1396 & CAS 2007/A/1402) decided 31 May 2010 (**Valverde 3**).

In summary, the first and last decisions concerned the refusal by the RFEC to initiate disciplinary proceedings against Valverde for alleged doping offences arising from the criminal investigation into *Operación Puerto*. The second decision concerns the proceedings brought against Valverde in relation to *Operación Puerto* by CONI and which sets the stage for the global ban imposed upon him by the final decision. It is the detail of the decisions of 16 March and 31 May 2010 that highlight for us some of the challenges brought about by the anti-doping apparatus and their effect on principles associated with notions of State sovereignty.

Since about 2004, Valverde had emerged as one of the most exciting professional cyclists on the scene – being competitive on all terrains except maybe the individual time trial; he had, he had, in his *Tour de France* debut in 2005, successfully challenged Lance Armstrong in the Alps on stage 10 from Grenoble to Courchevel. Many saw him as the emerging star of professional cycling.

---

[39] ibid, 413.

He brought style and passion to a cycling world that was dominated by the robotic Armstrong machine. One of the early occasions I saw him race brought that feeling of euphoria and goose bumps when one has witnessed something exciting, if not, indeed, marvellous. Valverde was also a product of Vicente Belda's *Kelme* team and not a protégé of the Saiz dynasty with its strong connections to both Armstrong's Director Bruyneel, and the UCI hierarchy, its President Pat McQuaid and cycling's godfather, Hein Verbruggen.

When in May 2006, the *Guardia Civil* seized blood bags and plasma and arrested, among others, Dr Eufemiano Fuentes, they found him to be carrying a business card from a hotel that had on the reverse side a notation: '*Valverde*'. Another business card found in the possession of Fuentes was that of the Head of the UCI Medical Commission, Dr Mario Zorzoli. Strangely, one of the few comments made by Fuentes to the *Guardia Civil* as they completed the search of his premises was 'did you find everything on Valverde?' Along with the business card, Report No 116 of the *Guardia Civil* in the *Operación Puerto* documents referred to a bag of plasma bearing the code '*18 VALV (PITI)*', – '*Bag No 18*'. It was this bag that, above all others, became the centre of attention in the *Puerto* media spectacle and it was this bag that would later be analysed by the Anti-Doping Laboratory in Barcelona, an analysis that detected high levels of erythropoietin recombinant (EPO). When and where the blood was extracted, when, where and in what circumstances the EPO was added was never explored by either the media or CAS.

As we have already seen, in October 2006, Investigating Judge Serrano had by two orders prohibited the use of evidence in the Spanish criminal proceedings in any disciplinary or administrative processes until such time as the criminal processes were concluded. We have already dealt with this and mentioned the final orders of the *Puerto* Court that again refused WADA access to the blood bags held as part of the evidence. But, as will become evident, it is the refusals and subsequent orders annulling access to *Blood Bag No 18* that the CAS decisions revolve around.

Valverde 1

The decision of CAS in *Valverde 1* begins by reciting the view that although the applicability of UCI's anti-doping rules ultimately derive their source from the membership of Valverde to the RFEC, that is by way of private agreement, nevertheless they 'may be more in the realm of a statute or a bylaw, or general conditions to a contract than a contract between the parties'.[40] This distinction was not determinative of the manner in which CAS dealt with the first of the two interlocutory issues before it, which related to the time in which an appeal should be commenced. But, for our purposes, what it points to is that on joining a sporting

---

[40] *WADA & UCI v Alejandro Valverde & Royal Spanish Cycling Federation (RFEC)* (CAS 2007/A/1396 & CAS 2007/A/1402) decided 10 July 2008 (*Valverde 1*).

federation, an athlete is said to accept implicitly or explicitly to be bound by the rules found in the WADA Code and reproduced in their own sport's rules. Furthermore, although that agreement is expressed by contract, and that the WADC is regarded as a being a species of contract and not an international treaty,[41] what is brought forth by the Code is an institution carrying with it, effectively for the lives of the athlete, constitutional powers. As we will continue to see, this single act of joining a sporting club brings with it a whole new universe of law and governance.

The second issue before CAS in *Valverde 1* is of direct interest to us in telling this particular part of the story. That issue concerned the request by the UCI and WADA to have Valverde subjected to the collection of a biological sample, such as hair or nail clippings, for the purpose of carrying out a DNA analysis. The point of WADA and the UCI requesting the DNA analysis was to enable them, if possible in the future, to carry out a comparison of Valverde's DNA with that of *Blood Bag No 18* held by the *Guardia Civil* as part of the evidence collected in *Operación Puerto*. CAS rejected the application for a biological sample, leaving the matter open to being revisited in the future. Their reasoning behind the rejection turned upon the fact that, at the time of this decision, the evidence gathered in *Operación Puerto*, particularly the blood bags, were not available for use in sporting disciplinary matters because of the orders of the Investigating Judge Serrano and his answer to a letter from CAS of 1 April 2008. Given the blood bag was not available as evidence until the Spanish criminal proceedings were determined, CAS decided that there was no point in taking a biological sample at that time as no comparison could, in fact, be made. Nevertheless, the question of access to Valverde's DNA and blood would not go away.

An Italian Passage

On the day *Valverde 1* was handed down, Valverde himself arrived second on the road in stage six of the *Tour de France* from Aigurande to Super-Besse Sancy. He had already won the opening stage of the *Tour* and was, along with Cadel Evans, one of the two main favourites for that *Tour*, which was eventually won by the veteran Spaniard, Carlos Sastre. The victory in stage six would later be awarded to Valverde after the Italian Ricardo Ricco tested positive for CERA (Continuous Erythropoiesis Receptor Activator) a week or so later.[42] I had been sitting in a

---

[41] *US Olympic Committee v International Olympic Committee*, CAS 2011/0/2422, states that the WADC is not an international treaty but a contractual instrument that binds its signatories in accordance with private international law: see paragraph 8.2.1. For a discussion of the Lausanne UNESCO Treaty and the origins of WADA see D Vidar Hanstad, A Smith and I Waddington, 'The Establishment of the World Anti-Doping Agency: A Study of the Management of Organizational Change and Unplanned Outcomes' (2008) 43 *International Review for the Sociology of Sport* 227.
[42] See at velonews.competitor.com/2008/07/news/road/riccardo-ricco-tests-positive-saunier-duval-team-withdraws-from-tour-de-france_80269.

bar in Barcelona airport, awaiting a connection to Bilbao; my Basque companion's comment on Ricco's *incredible* win was given in the form of him mimicking an injection into his arm. After the race in Bilbao, when I spoke to Ricco's team director, he told me that after seeing the win he grabbed the Italian and asked him '*what have you done?!?!*'.

Eleven days after the CAS decision in *Valverde 1* that had denied the application of WADA and the UCI for a bodily sample, stage 15 of the *Tour de France* travelled 125 of its 183 kilometres through Italian territory. Australian Simon Gerrans, who after advising his breakaway companions that he would not contest the finish, did exactly that and won the day; one of his breakaway companions Egoi Martinez later questioned his integrity. Valverde had finished that day in the main group of contenders for the overall classification about four minutes behind the Gerrans-Martinez group. It was on that Sunday, 20 July 2008, after the completion of the 83 kilometres from Embrun in France to Prato Nevoso, that an official from CONI performed an in-competition anti-doping control on Valverde. The control included a blood test. The test was the routine sort of in-competition test that cyclists are subjected to daily after they race. For all immediate intents and purposes these tests are to be used to determine if an athlete is doping in that particular competition. The test was negative and it gave rise to no evidence that suggested at the time Valverde was, in fact, doping. At the time Valverde might have thought nothing more of it. He may not have even recognised the name of the person, Dr Tiziana Sansolini, who carried out the test, but nevertheless, it was this test that set the scene for WADA, the UCI and CONI to outflank the Spanish and the decision of CAS in *Valverde 1*.

If we fast forward six months, to January 2009, Investigating Judge Serrano is on vacation from his chambers in Madrid, and in his place is Acting Judge Jimenez. On the basis of apparent *letters rogatory* received from Italy, Investigating Judge Jimenez authorised the Italian judicial police to proceed with an extraction of blood samples from the *Blood Bag Number 18* in the laboratory in Barcelona where the evidence was held. At the time there was some confusion as to whether the request in the *letters rogatory* were actually made by the CONI prosecutor or by the criminal prosecutor of Rome. *Letters rogatory* are a formal request to a foreign court for some type of judicial assistance, commonly in the case of service of documents. What will later become an issue is on whose behalf were the *letters rogatory* issued – was it CONI, an Italian governmental sporting body or the criminal prosecutor of Rome? In order to overcome any such legal barriers, the Italian police deputised, as acting Carbineri, the same Dr Tiziana Sansolini, the CONI official who had taken the sample of Valverde's blood in Prato Nevoso.[43]

---

[43] Adding to the confusion is the fact that previously Serrano had authorised two *letters rogatory* in the case of blood bags allegedly corresponding to the Italian rider, Ivan Basso and the German, Jan Ulrich. This authorisation had allowed the cyclist's respective federations to take disciplinary action against them. Probably, from Serrano's perspective, he treated these foreign nationals as being in a different position to a Spanish national subject to the RFEC's jurisdiction.

As a result of gaining access to the blood, in February 2009, CONI analysed the DNA from blood obtained in the *Tour de France* in 2008 and the DNA content of the plasma in *Blood Bag No 18* and concluded that there was a match. The scientific or evidentiary basis of the match does not seem to have been explored in CAS (see the discussion of the use of DNA evidence in respect of the Biological Passport Chapter 4 below). Thus began CONI's accusations against Valverde for doping, which were quickly picked up by the cycling media and took on a life of their own.

But this is not the end of the story. On his return from holiday, Judge Serrano issued an Order of Revocation[44] on the basis that CONI was not a judicial authority and that, under the Judicial Assistance Convention of 29 May 2000, such orders are only available in the case of public authorities. CONI's apparent status as a private sporting organisation meant that, in the eyes of the Spanish system, they were not entitled to seek such international judicial cooperation. The effect of this *Order of Revocation* under Spanish law was that the use by CONI as evidence of *Blood Bag Number 18* was not valid; and the cooperation procedure with CONI was declared to be null and void. It should be noted that this order came following the previous order prohibiting the use of the *Puerto* evidence in administrative or sporting disciplinary procedures until the criminal process against Dr Fuentes et al were concluded. CONI appealed the Revocation Order in the Spanish Courts. The *Audiencia Provincial de Madrid* dismissed their appeal on 18 January 2010.[45]

Notwithstanding this, on 11 May 2009, CONI's *Tribunale Nazionale Antidoping* (TNA) had already gone ahead and sanctioned Valverde giving him a two-year 'prohibitive' or 'precautionary' ban from competition in Italy. The TNA decided that the various orders of the Spanish Court had no effect in a proceeding taking place under the auspices of Italian sports law. Despite orders and later appeal decisions by the Spanish Courts, and the subsequent rejection of CONI's appeal, the TNA position was that the request for cooperation came from an international judicial authority (the police Prosecutor's Office of Rome) rather than CONI. The implication was that there was an existing criminal investigation into Valverde's activities by the Italian police. There was, however, never any criminal prosecution of Valverde in Italy, nor in any other place for that matter. In effect, a sporting tribunal, the TNA, decided that they could adjudge a Spanish citizen, for offences that allegedly occurred on Spanish territory, despite rulings of a superior Spanish Court prohibiting the use of the evidence, and on the basis of a matrix of circumstantial evidence not entirely related to the issue. All of these matters come to be agitated before CAS in *Valverde 2 & 3*.

[44] Dated 18 February 2009.
[45] Martinez, 'El Caso Valverde' (n 38) 439.

Valverde 2

In June 2009, Valverde appealed the TNA decision to ban him from competition within Italy to CAS. Consistent with CAS jurisprudence on the WADA Code, CAS found that given CONI had discovered the asserted violation, the matter would have to be decided according to the CONI rules and not those of WADA or the UCI.[46] The effect of this is that the appeal by Valverde was restricted to the preventive ban imposed under the CONI rules and not any possible further ban that might be sought to be imposed under the WADC or the UCI rules. Apart from this the question of what facts made out the violation, including when and where it had actually occurred is not one that has been ultimately decided with any clarity by the CAS decisions.[47]

It needs to be recalled that, at this point, Valverde's case had been considered and decided by the sporting authorities within Spain. The RFEC, as did ASADA in the Australian instance of Davis, decided that there was no evidence available upon which to proceed with any disciplinary action against the various cyclists. To Valverde, his case had been heard and decided in his favour and having to be prosecuted again by CONI amounted to a form of double jeopardy. Valverde maintained this argument throughout the various CAS proceedings. He also claimed that his prosecution was contrary to the guarantees of equal treatment under the Law provided by both the Spanish Constitution and the European Convention on Human Rights, and that there was no admissible evidence available to prove any case against him. Notwithstanding these arguments, and following hearing evidence from former Kelme rider, Jesus Manzano, who stated that Valverde had been involved in doping practices with Dr Fuentes at their former team, and from a Spanish journalist, Enrique Iglesias, who gave evidence that Valverde owned a dog named '*PITI*', on 16 March 2010, CAS confirmed the two-year preventative ban imposed by CONI in *Valverde 1* that prevented him from participating in competitions in Italy.

The reasoning of CAS highlights a problem that is central to our thesis: to what extent did this new form of law, this new global constitution that Valverde contracted to, take precedence over the Law of Spain and, for that matter, the human rights guarantees of the European Union. To what extent was the law of anti-doping autonomous from those systems and the principles that they were said to enshrine. Putting to one side the question as to whether the CONI prosecution constituted a form of double jeopardy – both cases, RFEC and CONI, involved the alleged use or attempted use of a prohibited substance or method, with the latter having the added element of the DNA 'match' – what is significant in terms of traditional conceptions of State sovereignty is whether, or on what basis, CONI

---

[46] *Alejandro Valverde Belmonte v Comitato Olimpico Nazionale Italiano (CONI)* (2009/A/1879 CAS) decided 16 March 2010 (*Valverde 2*) para 76.
[47] ibid, paras 78, 81, 82, 94.

could exercise jurisdiction in respect of a possible violation that was committed by a Spanish national wholly within Spanish territory. From a traditional perspective of sovereignty, what is raised here is the extent to which a sovereign is able to prosecute violations of the law by non-citizens that have occurred outside its own territory. The simple answer to this problem is given Valverde's consent to the contract to play sport gives rise to an exception to State sovereignty with the result that the WADC carves out a new juridical space within which power to sanction is distributed and modulated on principles very different to that of territorial sovereignty.

In relation to jurisdiction, CAS reasoned that the purpose of the CONI rules was to prevent individuals, including foreign athletes, who had committed violations, from participating in sporting activities in Italy. The problem, of course, was that at the point when CONI had prosecuted Valverde he had not been found to have committed a violation. CAS found the necessary connection between Valverde and the CONI rules to be the fact that he participated in races within Italian territory. But they said less about any necessary connection between the actual or alleged violation and Italy. The closest we get to a discussion of this is that it is sufficient for CONI to have discovered the violation. In the eyes of CAS, the violation is stated to be the attempted use of a prohibited substance or method that continued up and until the seizure of the blood bags by the Guardia Civil.[48] The violation is said to be constituted by its discovery and not by its occurrence and the identification of specified actions of Valverde, or even Fuentes, at any specified time and place. There is no specified guilty act, only a discovery of an asserted attempted violation. In a literal reading of the CONI Rules CAS found that they did not provide for any limitations regarding the place where the violation was committed.[49] That is, CONI's rules were not to be read against the backdrop and context of the rules of State sovereignty but on the basis of the functionality of a new constitutional apparatus. Given that Valverde had participated in the past and probably would participate in the future on Italian territory CAS regarded CONI's actions in asserting jurisdiction as being justified.

Furthermore, as we have seen, the RFEC had decided that given the prohibitions upon the use of evidence by the investigating judge there was no case for Valverde to answer. This latter element raised a related question of law regarding the use of both the documentary evidence and the blood bags held by the *Guardia Civil*.

In determining the questions relating to the admissibility of the evidence, including *Blood Bag No 18*, CAS directly considered questions relating to State territoriality and the limits of sovereignty. Rather than using these concepts as having a limiting effect, CAS turned them into tools to broaden, or at least justify their reading of the extent of, CONI's power. Noting that *Puerto's* Investigating

---

[48] ibid, 82.
[49] ibid, 94.

Judge Serrano had revoked the orders in relation to the supply of *Blood Bag No 18*, CAS considered that these orders had no effect beyond Spanish territory.[50] At its core CAS regarded the use of the evidence, in the face of the Spanish Order of Revocation, as not being inconsistent with principles akin to what we might call natural justice or due process and the Rule of Law.[51] Furthermore, CAS was adamant that its jurisprudence was clear in so far as it was not bound by the decisions of other (sovereign) courts or tribunals with jurisdiction, nor was it bound by the rules of evidence.[52]

But to get to the grist of the CAS reasoning we can put to one side the question of the legitimacy of the Italian criminal proceedings,[53] the manner in which the principle of territoriality is dealt with (the same principle appears at once to restrict Spanish power whilst expanding Italian power)[54] and the manner in which evidence was deemed admissible or reliable. The logical kernel of the CAS reasoning might well be identified in the statement towards the end of their decision where they find that 'the fight against doping is … preponderant over the Athlete's interest'. Whatever the merits of Valverde's reliance on Spanish or European law prohibiting the use of the evidence the preponderance of the 'fight against doping' took precedence. In a nutshell, what CAS was making explicit was that the Just (and transnational) War against doping justifies any breach of the norms traditionally associated with the Rule of Law, the principle of territoriality and human rights.

In the end, the only issue for CAS was that the DNA identification of the plasma in *Blood Bag No 18* was sufficient to prove the violation of use or attempted use of a prohibited method or substance.[55] It is the mere collection of the blood (at a time that is never identified) for non-therapeutic use that constituted the relevant violation.[56] It was on this basis that CAS confirmed the preventative sanction imposed by CONI preventing Valverde from participating in Italy for a period of two years commencing 11 May 2009.

Valverde 3

Valverde 3 concerned the appeal by WADA and the UCI from the decisions of the *Spanish Comite Nacional de Competicion Disciplina Deportiva* (CNCDD) and the RFEC, made on 7 September 2007, not to open disciplinary proceedings against Valverde. As noted above, similar decisions were made by other national

---

[50] ibid, 97–98, 102, 123, 124, 130, 131, 139.
[51] ibid, 102.
[52] ibid, 123.
[53] ibid, 130.
[54] ibid, 131.
[55] ibid, 165.
[56] ibid, 167.

cycling federations and anti-doping organisations in respect of other cyclists, such as Australia's Allan Davis. By the time of the hearing, the primary purpose of *Valverde 3* was for WADA and the UCI to seek to extend the CONI preventative sanction, confirmed in *Valverde 2*, into a worldwide ban under the WADC and UCI Rules. In doing so CAS found again that the relevant violation occurred on the discovery of *Blood Bag No 18* in Dr Fuentes' freezer on 6 May 2006.[57]

Valverde 3 recounts familiar ground as to that in *Valverde 2*, in respect of the admissibility of the documentary and blood bag evidence. CAS does not deviate from the position in *Valverde 2*. In dismissing the objections to the use of the evidence and submissions on the effect of the Spanish Court orders, CAS noted that this was a case where they felt it was 'appropriate to prevent a national federation [i.e. RFEC] from being too lenient'.[58] In recounting the findings in *Valverde 2*, CAS approved of the reasoning used to decide that the evidence could be used:

> … even if it was collected with violation of certain human rights, … there is an overriding interest at stake. In the case at hand, the internationally accepted fight against doping is a public interest, which would outweigh a possible violation of Mr. Valverde's personal rights.[59]

After considering the various strands of circumstantial evidence before it, the CAS Panel found that there was no violation of Valverde's rights and 'even if this was different, the overriding interest of the fight against doping would warrant this'.[60] Note that the 'public' interest to be served here is one derived from a private interest, that is, a sporting contract and that it overrides any rights that are themselves derived from Public Law. The public interest in maintaining fundamental legal, constitutional or human rights are overridden by a newly privately created 'public' interest. What exactly is meant by the international accepted fight against doping as a public interest is something that will be left for us to interrogate in the latter part of this work. But it is clear that this new public interest arises by way of private agreement and not sovereign command or Law.

As a result, on 31 May 2010, CAS decided in *Valverde 3* to extend the Italian sanction and suspend Valverde from all competition worldwide for two years based upon his involvement in *Operación Puerto*. The finding was primarily based upon the DNA 'match' alleged by CONI, which CAS found to be in breach of Article 15.2 of the UCI Anti-Doping Rules. Valverde was declared ineligible to compete until January 2012. He made his return to racing in the *Tour Down Under* in Australia that January and went on to win that year's *Vuelta España*.

As a member of a foreign (that is non-Italian) sporting federation (the RFEC), which in turn is affiliated with a foreign Olympic Committee, Valverde, in his

---

[57] *WADA & UCI v RFEC & Alejandro Valverde* (CAS 2007/A/1396 & CAS 2007/A/1402) decided 31 May 2010 (*Valverde 3*) paras 7 and 111.
[58] ibid, para 38.
[59] ibid, para 60.
[60] ibid, para 71.

defence, rejected the jurisdiction of CONI to prosecute him. How is it, asked Valverde, that a foreign sporting body, to which he was not affiliated, could adjudge a Spanish citizen, for offences that allegedly occurred on Spanish territory, despite rulings of a superior Spanish Court prohibiting the use of the evidence? This is what interests us – the CAS decisions squarely raise the supra-territorial nature or transnational character of the anti-doping apparatus. The CAS decisions highlight the issues relating to territoriality of national Laws and sovereignty and how these modernist Legal principles are at odds with the process of private arbitration that take place within this 'consensual' supranational jurisdiction. In this context it is the sporting spectacle's need for a speedy result that drives its own autonomous administrative and disciplinary procedures. Apart from questions of territorial sovereignty and questions relating to traditional Rule of Law principles as opposed to private administrative practices, the manner in which evidence is accepted and evaluated and the manner in which facts are found based upon that raise fundamental Rule of Law questions. We will turn again to the manner in which evidence is transformed in Chapter 4 below.

CONI is an Italian body which, in effect, administers the Italian sports law system. CONI's position is that, by virtue of private agreement, it is responsible for taking action which included making preventive and banning orders against both Italian and foreign athletes who are unaffiliated with Italian sports federations and who have breached regulations in force in Italy. These breaches are not required to have taken place in Italy but are discoverable by Italians. The purpose of CONI's anti-doping powers is said to be to ensure the protection of athlete's health and to ensure that athletes do not distort results to the detriment of just sporting competition. Other research we have conducted suggests that the relationship between health and doping is, at best, only a rhetorical one.[61]

Nevertheless, in the case of *Valverde 2*, no violation had occurred within Italian territory. Despite this fact (the doping control undertaken during the 2008 *Tour de France* did not return any positive result and only provided a DNA match to *Blood Bag No 18*) in both *Valverde 2 & 3* CAS rejected Valverde's arguments on jurisdiction. The reasoning of CAS proceeded on the basis that the version of the Italian rules in force in May 2006 provided for the imposition of an injunction against athletes not affiliated to the Italian federation. It appeared no territorial connection was necessary in order to enliven CONI's powers. It could, it seems, decide to prevent an athlete who had not been disciplined elsewhere from participating in Italy.

The reasoning of CAS appears to be informed by a reading of two specific provisions of the WADC. The first, Article 22.3, involves each government respecting 'arbitration as the preferred means of resolving doping-related disputes'. The second, Article 24.3, states that the WADA Code 'shall be interpreted as an independent and autonomous text and not by reference to the existing law or statutes

---

[61] M Hardie, D Shilbury, C Bozzi, and I Ware, *I Wish I was Twenty-One Now: Beyond Doping in the Australian Peloton* (Auskadi Samizdat, 2012).

of the Signatories or governments'. It may be that this second provision would raise constitutional problems in some States, however, judicial deference to sporting autonomy and the attitude of CAS seems to suggest that any such limitations would be rare in their application.

Based upon these provisions, the CAS Panel reasoned that the mere fact that Valverde had, in the past, participated in Italy, and would probably in the future compete in Italy, or in foreign races that passed through Italian territory, was sufficient for CAS to consider that CONI was justified in adopting restrictive measures. There is within this reasoning a kernel of a logic whereby Valverde is a potential threat to the integrity or reputation of competition, so he must be made an example of because of the state of Spanish cycling, doping and anti-doping, the leniency of the Spanish sporting authorities and the tardiness and errors of the Spanish judicial system.

In the context of neoliberalism it is important to point out that what the WADC provisions that give precedence to the rules of the body discovering the asserted violation achieve is to introduce the principles of competition to the investigation and prosecution of the anti-doping process itself. We will later consider the relationship between the society of competition and the anti-doping apparatus, but for present purposes, Dadot and Laval's observations about neoliberalism's form of law are apposite. Dadot and Laval note that, in the neoliberal world, the market itself becomes a principle of selection of the laws made by States and that, in such a system, the establishment of this competition between jurisdictions must itself be consecrated.[62] For them, there exists a principle that there must be competition between legal systems.[63] It is this principle which itself appears to be enshrined in the WADC and which gives rise to the condition whereby private sporting and State institutions, compete transnationally to be the first to discover a violation and thus assert jurisdiction. Those that do so are able to sustain their institutions as being purveyors of good governance, itself a principle that supplants the political category of governance, or Government, which was based upon a State's capacity to ensure its sovereignty over a territory. As Dadot and Laval put it:

> good governance, plays a central role in diffusing the norm of generalised competition
> …. It thus gradually supplants the outmoded, disvalued category of sovereignty. This
> state will no longer be judged on its capacity to ensure its sovereignty over a territory, in
> accordance with the classical Western conception, but on its respect for the legal norms
> and economic good practice of governance.[64]

The point is that to be considered functional or 'good' a State must apply the rules of private law to themselves. Harmonisation (something which the WADC explicitly seeks) is achieved through this type of transnational competition causing what Dadot and Laval characterise as an evacuation of liberal democracy 'by depriving

---

[62] P Dadot and C Laval, *The New Way of the World* (Verso Books, 2013) 212.
[63] ibid, 211.
[64] ibid, 218–19.

legislative powers of their main prerogatives'.[65] Harmonisation is achieved and derives not from above (ie sovereign command), but through the operation of markets and competition.

The *Puerto* Trial

Following the conviction of Valverde all eyes moved back towards Madrid for the final stages of the *Puerto* process. In a strange twist of fate, it is prior to the *Puerto* trial that the *Armstrong Era* finally unravels in late 2012. For our purposes, it is also useful to jump forward to the final resolution of *Operación Puerto* by the Spanish Courts in early 2013. In a Madrid courtroom, in mid-January 2013, the lengthy case against Fuentes and his co-accused is finally heard. At the same time, across the Atlantic in Hollywood, Armstrong is no longer in denial and heads to Oprah to confess and seek forgiveness from the people (see Epilogue).

On 29 April 2103, after a three-month hearing that had considered the 20,000 pages of evidence collected by the *Guardia Civil* and numerous witnesses, Judge Santamaría Matesan, in Madrid Criminal Court No 21, delivered her verdict concerning the crimes alleged to have been committed by Dr Fuentes and others against public health. In its judgment the Court found that the case against two – Fuentes and the former *Kelme* coach Labarta – of the five accused had been proven.[66] The Court imposed a one-year suspended sentence on Fuentes as a perpetrator of a crime against public health.[67] Fuentes was also disqualified from the practice of sports medicine for a period of four years. Labarta was found to be an accomplice to Fuentes and was also given a four-month suspended sentence. He was also disqualified from pursuing his work as a sporting coach or any professional activity related to cycling for a period of four months.[68] Yolanda Fuentes, Vicente Belda and Manuel Saiz were all found to not have any case against them proven.[69]

What is clear from this case is that the Spanish criminal justice system pursued and obtained jail sentences (albeit suspended) for the principal actors that had organised and operated a sophisticated network of doping within sport. The case was the first that saw a jail term given to a doctor (and his accomplice) for operating a doping network. The fact that the sentences were suspended is not a sign of any leniency on the part of the Judge, but recognition of the fact that Spanish law automatically suspends sentences of less than two years.

Puerto surpassed the acquittal of Richard Virenque and the suspended sentences of Voet and the team manager, Roussel, handed down in the *Festina* criminal trial

---

[65] ibid, 212.
[66] Sentencia Final (n 36) 12 ff and 357.
[67] Art 361 of the Spanish Criminal Code.
[68] Sentencia Final (n 36) 357.
[69] ibid, 15.

some 13 years earlier. Just as the *Festina* court had taken aim at the inactivity of the sport's governing bodies in dealing with doping, as we have seen, the Madrid Appeal Court also criticised the 'head in the sand' attitude of the sport's sponsors. In *Festina*, the UCI, the French Federation and the *Société du Tour de France* had sought symbolic compensation for the damage to their image caused by the affair. The damages claim had been rejected by the Court, which blamed the applicants for their slow and weak approach to the doping problem. The Court noted that this approach of the 'authorities' had influenced the light sentences given to the accused. Noting that EPO had been prevalent in the sport from as far back as 1993 with the knowledge of the sport's governing bodies, the *Festina* court stated:

> The court deplores that they remained for several years almost inactive before decid-ing on 1996 mainly to care about the excess of EPO. They never considered stopping competitions in a sport so plagued by doping and thus avoiding the harm to their image which they are complaining about.

Despite the anecdotal evidence that the French government had targeted the 1998 *Tour de France*, *Festina* had been a chance discovery by customs officials on a back-road border crossing. Prior to this, and during the first decade of the opera-tion of the WADA Code, the preferred method of discovering violations had been through testing urine, and later blood, samples. Importantly, *Puerto* prefigures the investigatory turn that anti-doping authorities would seek to pursue in the wake of the end of the Armstrong Conspiracy. The case against Armstrong also started as a criminal investigation headed by the Federal Investigator Novitsky, but as we will see later (Epilogue), that criminal case did not proceed to prosecution, in fact there were claims that the criminal case was derailed because of overt politi-cal interference. In the wake of this we should note that the US legal system was not subjected to the attacks visited upon the Spanish legal system throughout the whole *Puerto* process. Nevertheless, and notwithstanding the success of the *Puerto* investigation which dismantled an extensive global network of importation, distri-bution, supply and administration of doping products, a network that apparently extended beyond cycling, and the jail sentence handed out to its principal, the *Puerto* decision was immediately derided by the foreign and cycling press and by WADA. Once again, the criticism focused on what *Puerto* was not about. Despite the obvious importance of the case against Dr Fuentes, the fact that no cyclists (or other athletes) had been sanctioned meant to many that the decision was seen as inadequate. In the main, the criticism of and subsequent appeals centred on the decision of the court not to hand over the blood bags to WADA. *The Guardian* headline was consistent with the tone of the outrage:

> Doping doctor Eufemiano Fuentes' sentence shocks anti-drugs bodies – Anger at deci-sion not to hand blood bags to drug agencies.[70]

---

[70] *The Guardian* (30 April 2013) available at www.theguardian.com/sport/2013/apr/30/doping-doctor-eufemiano-fuentes-sentence-shock.

Of all the post-*Puerto* commentary, the piece that possibly best highlighted the 'us against them' logic was written by a self-appointed campaigner for a change in cycling in a post-Armstrong world. The intervention by Jamie Fuller, a Tasmanian businessman, who has made his fortune by selling Lycra tights to athletes and others who seek to live their particular dream, is significant as he purports to stand for change in cycling. His organisation or 'movement', *Change Cycling Now* proposed a future for the sport based upon 'transparency' and an adherence to rules. His complaint is a shining example of one that refuses to consider the context of the Spanish case and the positive aspects of its resolution. In the end, all Fuller could do was repeat the standard jingoistic Anglo attitude to Spain, by attempting to lampoon both the Judge and her decision. With the lead:

IS SPAIN TRULY CORRUPT? WE CAN'T BE BLAMED FOR THINKING SO ...[71]

Fuller compares the *Puerto* Court's decision unfavourably with those of the American TV personality Judge Judy. What could better provide us with a world-view that preferences law as spectacle over Law as a process or even justice? Fuller tells us that Judge Judy, a 'fully qualified lady' ... 'covers real-life cases' and that she 'uses basic common sense to hand down sensible, reasoned decisions'.

Of course, Judge Judy does not preside over a courtroom, but a reality TV show, in which the participants enter into contracts to abide by her 'arbitration'. Judge Judy's 'courtroom', unlike the one in Madrid, is scripted or at least partly so. Judge Judy does make 'decisions' in her reality TV arbitrations and the show's producers pay any awards she makes against any party.[72] As one commentator has noted:

> while the cases and people may be real, the courts could be held on the bridge of the Starship Enterprise and still have the same effect. It's all just part of the collective hallu-cination we call television.[73]

Nevertheless, for Fuller, Judge Judy's common-sense reasoned decisions provide us with some guide by which we can compare the dispensation of justice by, and the level of corruption within, the Spanish judiciary. For Fuller, Justice Santamaría Matesan:

> makes Judge Judy look like the real deal [as she on his version of reality] has courted her own publicity by effectively overseeing the biggest cover up in sports history.[74]

The 'biggest cover up in sports history' according to Fuller was constituted by the decision not to accede to the applications of WADA, the UCI and CONI, to have the blood bags handed over for further analysis. Unlike Judge Judy's reasoned deci-sions, Fuller claims that the decision to not hand the material over and to have it

[71] See watercooler.skins.net/2013/05/02/is-spain-truly-corrupt-we-cant-be-blamed-for-thinking-so/.
[72] See en.wikipedia.org/wiki/JudgeJudy.
[73] See consumerist.com/2007/12/17/judge-judys-tv-court-isnt-real/.
[74] See n 71.

destroyed was implicitly unreasoned and hence outrageous. For him the decision follows 'years of leg work and pushing shit uphill' by WADA and prevents 'them from receiving crucial information that could help make monumental advances in their work against the drug cheats'. For Fuller, the ultimate question is not whether serious inroads had been made into the practices of international doping networks stretching from Adelaide to Madrid, or even to Texas, but whether WADA can work efficiently with corrupt or inept judges, such as Santamaría Matesan who put unreasonable obstacles in their way. The upshot for him is a repetition of the past – a reaffirmation that Spain is soft on drugs in sport and that the country's criminal system (and Constitutional guarantees) undermine the message of unity of the anti-doping crusade. It is noteworthy that people such as Fuller use the word 'crusade' without flinching in this context. As we have seen in the *Valverde* cases, this crusade takes preeminence. For Fuller a suspended sentence and being struck off the medical register for four years was no deterrent. In the end the *Puerto* decision is a lost opportunity for Spain to show itself

> in a positive light in the fight against doping, but instead she's (Matesan) crucified their reputation with her final order". He concludes '... she was the judge for f#$k's sake' ...[75]

The simple and best answer to Fuller's rant is, of course, a perusal of the decision of Santamaría. Fuller could have satisfied himself more fully as to whether it stands up to the high standards displayed by Judge Judy and her reasoned collective hallucinations. But this is something we doubt he would have had the inclination or patience to do. But to start with the particular part of the judgment that deals with the applications to have the evidence handed over to WADA comprises 28 pages of the 361-page decision.[76] Throughout this part of the judgment there is a consideration of the relevant facts, the previous decisions in the case leading up to the trial, including those of the Madrid Appeal Court, along with the decisions and jurisprudence of Spanish and European Courts. In carrying out this task the Court makes it clear that when it comes to deciding questions of Law: just as in sport, not everything goes.

The Court is clear that it can only exercise power by respecting its jurisdictional limits

> limits that are constituted by scrupulously respecting the applicable limits of judicial power, and in particular our Magna Carta [the Spanish Constitution], and very especially the fundamental rights proclaimed in that Constitution.[77]

---

[75] ibid.

[76] Sentencia Final (n 36) 316–44.

[77] Indeed, Art 103 of the Spanish Constitution establishes that: 'Public Administration objectively serves the general interests and acts accordingly with the principles of efficiency, hierarchy, decentralisation, deconcentration and coordination, fully complying with the relevant legislation and the law', while Art 117 proclaims the independence and tenure of judges and magistrates, 'submitted only to the Rule of Law' and to whom corresponds the ability to 'exercise the power within jurisdiction in all kinds of action, judging and having judgments executed' according to rules that govern the powers and the procedures prescribed by Law.

While considering these limits, expounded in both Spanish and European decisions, the Court found that

> the application (by WADA and others) to have access to the biological samples (blood, plasma and concentrated red cells) cannot succeed.[78]

The *Puerto* Court made it clear that it had no doubt as to the legitimacy of WADA's application and that it was satisfied that the fight against doping in sport had a dual purpose: not only to pursue fraud in the outcome of the sporting competitions but also to protect the health of the athletes. The Court did not doubt the good faith of WADA in seeking to pursue disciplinary cases against athletes, but it was not convinced that the clearly stated purpose of the WADA request, that is: the future opening of disciplinary cases against athletes who may have engaged in practices prohibited doping was the issue that it had to decide. For the Court, the issue before it was the fate of the evidence, that is the biological samples (blood, plasma and concentrated red blood cells), and whether their being handed over to WADA or another body, could violate the fundamental rights of the defendants or others, such as cyclists or other athletes, who may be indentifiable following an analysis of the samples.[79] On its assessment of the Law, the Court could not be convinced that there would be no such violation. It is apparent to any reader that this position – one firmly based within the principles of Legal modernity and its conception of the Rule of Law; is in stark contrast, if not conflict with the findings of CAS in *Valverde 1,2 & 3.*

In its conclusions, the Court stated in relation to the requests for the evidence for the purpose of obtaining the blood bags to open disciplinary proceedings against athletes, whose identity had not been specified, and who have not been accused in the case, that it could not allow a prospective investigation (that is a 'fishing expedition'), or attempt to open a sporting law case that was incompatible with the constitutional principles and the Rule of Law.[80] Both the Spanish Constitutional and Supreme Courts were cited as authority for the proposition that the Rule of Law in a democratic society is incompatible with merely prospective activities, without there being a general requirement to satisfy the limitations on the interference with fundamental rights.[81] As we will increasingly see the anti-doping apparatus, unlike the law, tends to take on a prospective rather than retrospective aspect.

Nevertheless, in all the hubris surrounding the *Puerto* decision, one striking fact seems to have escaped those who point to Spanish corruption, or simply just

---

[78] Sentencia Final (n 36) 331. A number of grounds are given for the Court's refusal of the application. Some turn on the extent of Spain's obligations to cooperate with other European judicial authorities (which neither WADA, the UCI nor CONI are) and the generally recognised problems of interference in criminal processes by concurrent or subsequent disciplinary proceedings. Relevant also is the distinction between judicial and administrative powers that is, in many ways, vital to Continental jurisprudence.

[79] ibid, 321–22.

[80] WADA put forward no facts and allegations upon which they stated the evidence was relevant – their application was, in lawyers' parlance, merely a 'fishing expedition'.

[81] ibid, 340.

its bad decision making. The events that form the basis of the *Puerto* prosecution span from at least as early as 2002 until May 2006. The WADC carries with it an eight-year limitation period from the date the violation is asserted to have occurred, outside of which no action may be commenced against an athlete or other person for an anti-doping rule violation. Even if WADA had obtained the sought-after evidence in 2013 at best it would only be able to be utilised in pursuing athletes who may have doped, between May 2005 and May 2006, and not previously. This is not to say that there may not be potential suspects who fall within this period. But it is also the case that many that may fit this class have already either been disciplined or been found, by their respective anti-doping agencies, to have no case to answer. The relevance of the dates might might also have been a factor, for example, if CAS had thought it important to identify the date of Valverde's alleged violation, and the question as to whether any involvement he had had with Fuentes was prior to him leaving *Kelme* at the end of 2004 or whether the attempted use in question arose after that date. But in the end such legal argument is not our focus. For us, what is probably most important to highlight is the border-crossing nature of the anti-doping apparatus and the direct challenge it mounts to traditional or modernist visions of sovereignty and the Rule of Law.

It is in this manner that we can conceive of *Puerto* existing within the framework of the abandonment of old notions of Law and the construction of a new functional global system. It starkly brings into view the contrast between the principles of the Rule of Law (*Estado de Derecho*) and Constitutionalism and the needs and ends of the transnational apparatus and system of law in construction. As is apparent anti-doping, as it has been played out in relation to *Operación Puerto*, exemplifies Møller's fear – this is the end of modernity and law is, in fact, made in the media as much as it is made in the courts. In *Operación Puerto* we begin to see not only the contours of a new form of law and its clash with the old, but at the same time we find an example of the distance that exists between the rhetoric of the media crisis surrounding doping and the actual reality of the material processes that are occurring during cycling's process of global structural readjustment. In the case of *Puerto*, it is the media crisis that has driven sports policy and not the Rule of Law or Legal principles: it is this media crisis or a moral panic and the Just War on doping that it drives that has defined what *Puerto* is about.

At its most basic, those engaged in the rhetoric surrounding *Operación Puerto* have painted a picture of Spanish justice as being slow and out of step with the cultural change, which the purported 'new cycling world' is trying to embrace. Whether it was the then UCI President Pat McQuaid, or his self-anointed critic Fuller, the Spanish authorities (or just Spain) have been criticised for being simply 'too lenient in their approach to doping'.[82]

---

[82] D Renee, 'McQuaid: Spaniards Are "Too Lenient in Their Approach to Doping"' (2008) available at www.efluxmedia.com/news_McQuaid_Spaniards_Are_Too_Lenient_In_Their_Approach_To_Doping_21946.html.

The rhetoric is not only simplistic, it is also misleading, if not intellectually dishonest. It misses the point that Legal decisions, just like 'sporting' decisions are meant to be, are bounded by rules. But it also misses the point that it was not just the Spanish who can be accused of not dealing with the problem 'properly'. As noted above the same criticism could also be made of countries, such as Australia, that are said to represent the new cultural change within cycling. In light of all this, if there is one cyclist who has come to personify the assertions of corruption in Spain in relation to *Operación Puerto* it is, of course, Alejandro Valverde. But, more importantly, Valverde provides us with the figure of a person who, unlike others, could not escape the grasp of the expanding supranational apparatus.

3

Form(s) of Law

Forms of Law – Whereabouts are We?

In the previous chapter, which focused upon *Operación Puerto*, we tried to place Møller's End of Modernity thesis,[1] which, to restate it briefly, argues that the coming of global anti-doping law signals an end to 'Enlightenment principles', into some factual context. In order to make my point clearer, and to avoid any misunderstanding, it is appropriate to do so again. The immediate response by some to this problem appears to consist of an argument that, if this is the case, and if current anti-doping policy is *ipso facto* 'irrational' – that is, contrary to the logic of modernity – the problem can be resolved by a return and adherence to such 'Enlightenment principles' and, furthermore, the principle of the Rule of Law. This is not my position; I do not believe we can turn the clock backwards in such a way. In saying this, I do not disagree with Møller's insightful assessment that anti-doping law does signal a new way of doing law or governance. I do not disagree. I have tried to begin to outline, through the preceding discussion of *Operación Puerto*, that a moral panic does, in fact, exist in the form of a Just War that surrounds the question of doping in sports.

But this must be only the beginning of any enquiry. To state that there is a moral panic or crisis, and that anti-doping constitutes a new way of doing law is, in many ways, doing no more than merely stating the obvious. If an anti-doping critique is to mature beyond simply pointing out the obvious, we need to firstly come to grips with the present conjuncture and analyse how it is different from the past; only after that can we begin to think about other ways of doing law or anti-doping.

It is in this way that we can, at least, try to avoid the trap of a romantic longing for a return to the glory days of a bygone era of 'Enlightenment principles' or some pure and/or objective theory of the Rule of Law.

Is the answer to this irrational policy and this moral panic adequately countered by a call to return to 'Enlightenment' principles? To the logic and rationality of European modernity? My position, which I will attempt to further illustrate here, is plainly, no, this is not the case. Underlying my argument is that such a response itself is as emotional, irrational and as romantic as the panic it seeks to criticise. For present purposes, I do not wish to tackle headlong the received

---

[1] V Møller, 'The Anti-Doping Campaign – Farewell to the Ideals of Modernity?' in J Hoberman and V Møller, *Doping and Public Policy* (University Press of Southern Denmark, 2004).

wisdom that there is only one set of objective rational principles which we can derive from the Enlightenment, or that, as such, there is only one rationality and one logic that is applicable to thinking about the world. In the first place, I regard this approach as an overly Eurocentric view of the world, bordering, in fact, on a racist model. Browning for one reminds us that modernity is a highly generic term and that key components of modernity, such as the Enlightenment and reason, are interpreted in various ways.[2] More relevant is the description given to neoliberalism by Dadot and Laval[3] where they describe neoliberalism as a 'new global rationality'. It is from this rationality, not one from a past era, that we must judge and assess the anti-doping apparatus. Thus, my response to those who call for some return to modernist rationality is to argue that they fail to grasp the totality of the contemporary context in which 'globalisation', generally, and anti-doping policy, in particular, is taking place. In many ways the problem is that raised by Agamben when he suggested those who sought a return to the rational forms of the Law of the sovereign State have lost the keys to the scriptures of law, and appear as such themselves lost in our contemporary age.[4]

My position should be clear: yes, moral panic in the guise of Just War – backed by the state of exception and the police and played out in the global society of the spectacle – is one of the principal forms of contemporary governance. Nevertheless, before turning to the question of governance in more detail, it is first appropriate to describe how the tendency towards the pole of governance itself arises out of a transformation of the Rule of Law. Below, I will seek to introduce and outline two principle forms of law, which we might dub, for ease of reference, but for want of a better description, modern and post-modern, sovereign and administrative, or even State and Imperial. In doing so it may be suggested that it is not clear on which side of the fence I sit – which form of law I favour. However, it should be apparent, from what I have already stated above, that this response is itself misconceived. This is not an argument about one form of law being better, or more 'just' than another. Rather, the point is to attempt to highlight which form of law is presently and apparently tending towards becoming dominant and emerging as such on a global basis, or in other words, whereabouts we currently are able to locate ourselves in reference to the Law–governance continuum. If pushed, my position is that neither form of law is preferable, and the task is not to accept one or the other as a given: that is, to strive to return to the past or to accept the other as the way things are inevitably now done. The point is, simply, that with an understanding of both (or all) forms of law we might just then be able to begin to conceptualise a version of justice that is 'better' equipped to deal with a global and hybrid world. But this is not our present task; it is part of the circular search for justice and a problem that has been unresolved for 2,000 years.[5]

---

[2] G Browning, *Global Theory from Kant to Hardt and Negri* (Palgrave Macmillan, 2011) 5.
[3] P Dadot and C Laval, *The New Way of the World: On Neoliberal Society* (Verso, 2013) 3.
[4] G Agamben, *The State of Exception* (University of Chicago Press, 2005).
[5] J Gil, *Metamorphosis of the Body: Theory Out of Bounds*, vol 12 (Minnesota University Press, 1998).

Our present task is, therefore, to begin to contextualise the tensions we have already observed and in so doing begin to interrogate the Law-governance continuum more fully. This will set the stage for our consideration of the extension of the anti-doping apparatus beyond the realm of Law, and enable us to consider the place of particular forms of governance within anti-doping that concern the administration, the police and the deployment of an array of measures, an apparatus of discipline, control and biopower. This passage will assist us in answering the question we have set for ourselves as to what founds the juridical in an emerging supranational system.

Weber and Formal Law

Our ideas or conceptions about what law is, or how we define it, are influenced in many ways by a form of Law that found its high-water mark in the nineteenth century. It is this conception of law that informs Møller's vision. Two strands serve as examples. In the Anglo system, Dicey's conception of the Rule of Law is pervasive. On the continent, Weber conceived of a form of Law that was consistent with what he called Modern Rational Capitalism. Below, we will consider aspects of this form of Law, as understood by both Dicey and Weber and upon which our popular conceptions of law are based. However, as we will see, given their position at modernity's juridical high-water mark both were aware, in one manner or another, that this form of Law was itself in the process of deformalisation. Furthermore, Dicey's consideration of Continental Administrative Law assists us in understanding how the Rule of Law itself was construed differently in the Anglo system and on the Continent. This not only highlights the influence that the Continental system of Law has had on Law's continued deformalisation generally, but also points us directly to law's future.[6]

Along with the separation of powers of the Executive, Legislative and Judicial branches of Government, one of the principal and recognisable characteristics of both these conceptions of the form of Law include that such a system of Law emanates, and derives its force, from sovereign command. In particular, this form of Law emanates from a national sovereign who has exclusive power to rule and command over a definable territory and people. Already, it should be apparent that this particular criterion is not consistent with the situation we are attempting to deal with – the regime constituted by the WADC is not one that emanates from a single sovereign source, nor an agreement between sovereigns in the sense of public international law. Valverde's saga recounted above places this within our full view.

Law in such a situation also acts by way of a generality – it establishes a class of circumstances, things and people to which the norm that it states applies.

---

[6] M Weber, *Economy and Society*, vol 2 (University of California Press, 1978) 880ff.

The hallmark of this form of Law is a rule of conduct or a declaration as to power, right or duty, in which some factual requirements are delineated that connect it to a given state of affairs and which are applied retrospectively.[7] Law does not look to the future in what it judges, but to past events. Importantly, the Rule of Law applies equally to all those who find themselves within that definable people and territory. Subsequently, all those who are subject to this form of Law have recourse to the national system of courts existing within the given territory of the sovereign. These courts decide disputes after they arise – they decide past events according to Legal principle. This notion of Law being retrospectively applied resonates with the considerations of the *Puerto* trial court we have considered above. In the end it is the independence of the sovereign courts that provides the entire system of Law with its means of legitimisation.

The fact that Law applies equally to all within the territory of a single sovereign is one of the characteristics that Weber points to in order to distinguish it from the forms of law that preceded it. According to Weber, modernity's, or Modern Rational Capitalism's Law was preceded by particularist modes of closed, private and consensual forms of law. These forms tended to be either patrimonial or magico-religious, and they operated by way of the differential application of rules to different social groups, in different localities and which transcended, in certain circumstances, the boundaries of the nascent State: guilds, the church and local custom were prime examples.[8] *Lex Mercatoria* was another example that clearly transcended state boundaries.[9]

Weber believed that the creation of the rational (national) capitalist market economy (which we can later distinguish from later forms of capitalist organisation) required the demise of the particularist mode of creating law that had prevailed in the Middle Ages, or the granting of privileges of monopoly to certain closed organisations, for example printers' monopolies over books in early copyright law or the clergy and ecclesiastic law. Weber's rational capitalism abhorred different laws for different social groups or orders. The movement away from the particularist mode of creating law reduced the autonomy of organised status groups in two ways: by regulating non-state organisations, and by restricting the power of persons to create law by private ordering.[10]

Weber argued that what rational modernity required, and hence what it produced, was a calculable and uniform form of Law. Such a stable and uniform Legal environment was necessary to guarantee the needs of the growing markets. Calculable Law comprised abstract formal rules and regulations, non-arbitrary adjudication of Legal questions, especially relating to economic production,

---

[7] Plaintiff S157/2002 v Commonwealth (2003) 211 CLR 476 – a decision of the High Court of Australia.

[8] Weber, *Economy and Society* (n 6) 880ff.

[9] M Hardt and A Negri, *Multitude, War and Democracy in the Age of Empire* (Harvard University Press, 2004) 169ff.

[10] Weber, *Economy and Society* (n 6) 880ff.

enforceable contracts, and predictable economic rights. With this calculable Law the market economy could flourish. Calculable Law was accompanied by the rational bureaucratisation of the State, which itself reduced the autonomy of the forms of particularist law and limited the ability of those who had participated in them to create law by means of engaging in private agreement. Rather than law created by private agreement, henceforth rational Law would emanate from the single sovereign source of a Parliament. Thus, the transformation of these particularist, autonomous systems was driven politically by the growing strength of the State, and economically by the formally free competitive struggle of a market economy. The *privi-leges* (privatised law) attached to the old forms of autonomy were perceived as not being functional to either the Law or the market and, as such, the consolidation of Modern Rational Capitalism. Calculable and formal(istic) Law, calculable accounting and market relations, all of which applied equally to all: that is, citizens (of a sovereign nation) who themselves were formally equal before the general Law and the market. Such a form of Law emanated from a single sovereign source and underpinned the consolidation of Weber's Modern Rational Capitalism.

Here it is timely to recall the concern of Møller that anti-doping signals the end of modernity because it compromises the autonomy of sport and its 'long tradition of self-governance'. Was the autonomy of sport really both a project of modernity and at the same time an exception to that project? The autonomy of sport only appears to arise as an issue in the context of modernity's struggle to rationalise law. Sport as it arose and was organised in the nineteenth century was not a pre-modern institution, but its organisational autonomy does appear to hark back to the pre-modern forms that concerned Weber. The fascination with the autonomy of sports has its place at the heart of the liberal analysis of sport and law; however, from this perspective, the autonomy of sport was not a project of modernity or its form of Legality. It may also be that sport as an activity that occurs in a sphere outside what we might call 'normal' life gives rise to its special or exceptional status. Anderson uses the term 'qualified immunity' to describe the manner in which sport became or maintained its special status in regard to the application of aspects of the general Law.[11] The rise of sport in industrial society saw a change in the nature and function of games or sport. From customary or folk games, sometimes with a very different ethic to modern sport, developed a more rule-based, organised, form of sport aimed at developing a specific type of person, whether it be aimed at the idle aristocracy or workers with leisure time, and whether it be couched as either a civilising process[12] or a form of Muscular Christianity.[13] The proposition put forward by Anderson is that with the increasing organisation of sport (his example is the birth of Association Football in the UK) and with the

---

[11] J Anderson, *Modern Sports Law: A Textbook* (Hart Publishing, 2010) para [1.07].
[12] N Elias, *The Civilizing Process* (Blackwell, 1994).
[13] JJ MacAloon (ed), *Muscular Christianity in Colonial and Post-Colonial Worlds* (Routledge, 2008).

recognition by both the State and sporting bodies that sport had a role to play in civilising or educating the public at large there was, in effect, a *quid pro quo*

> the newly emerging sports governing bodies of the mid to late nineteenth century had received a reward for submitting to he civilizing process: the withdrawal of the threat of further legal intervention and the largely unrestricted liberty to self-regulate.[14]

What we can take from all of this is that, from its inception in industrial society, sport and sports administration has enjoyed some form of immunity and autonomy from the general Law. Furthermore, this immunity came about because of sport's role in the process of government. But whilst this immunity gives rise to something that Møller champions, it is equally this autonomy that gives rise to what he fears – that is, Law's deformalisation. Anderson continues to note that it is the increasing commercialisation or commodification of sport that has caused the Law surrounding sport to increase, and hence, in some ways, for its autonomy to be lessened. However, importantly, it appears that the intrusion into the space of sport's autonomy has not been brought about by an expansion of the modernist project of State building, but, in the end, by the proliferation of other forms of law and governance that both involve and exclude the State.

Dicey and the Law of Constitution

Patrimonial, magico-religious, local or particularist autonomy was perceived as involving discretion, which was equally perceived as being beyond measure and calculation and was hence characterised as abhorrent to the needs of Modern Rational Capitalism. Discretion itself was identified with absolute power, and in particular royal or monarchial prerogatives, exercised without the control of parliaments or the courts. Dicey viewed the exercise of discretion as something contrary to the Rule of Law, and it is not without coincidence that during this period, others, such as Bentham, argued against the Common Law – and its system of judge made (read arbitrary) Law – in favour of codification.

Like Weber, Dicey saw Law as being impersonal – that is, it applied to or by an authority based upon an office and not a person – a position summarised by the phrase, 'a government (or empire) of laws and not of men', which has its origin in Harrington's *The Commonwealth of Oceana*.[15] Law, as such, is embodied in abstract rules that are applied universally to all, and are not aimed at any particular individuals, groups or classes of people. As a result, and importantly, it is this abstract notion of transcendent Law that governs things and not the whim of mere fallible mortals or, for that matter, an administrative practice.

---

[14] Anderson, *Modern Sports Law* (n 11).
[15] J Harrington, *Commonwealth of Oceana* and *A System of Politics* (Cambridge Texts in the History of Political Thought) J Pocock, ed (Cambridge University Press 1992).

AV Dicey advocated a theory of the 'Rule of Law', which still holds, without question for the most part, a very strong currency today. In fact, the Rule of Law has been adopted (and transformed) by the 'international community' as one of its principle tools of intervention in States tying it to principles such as good governance and accountability.[16] Nevertheless, whether this rule of law is Dicey's Rule of Law is never brought to light. Similarly, it is also an idea of Law in which some on the 'left' have pronounced their faith as an 'unqualified human good', along it seems, with some anti-doping academics, who have fallen back upon it because it seems the only available bulwark against perceived authoritarian, discretionary or arbitrary rule.[17]

At the core of the Diceyan definition of the Rule of Law are three kindred concepts, each of which had a particular consequence. The first of these, already noted above, was the idea of the absolute supremacy of Rule of Law. The Rule of Law thus consists of a regular and consistent application of power and is opposed to arbitrary decision making, that is, any wide and discretion uncontrolled discretion. Secondly, the Rule of Law required that all persons were considered equal before the Law, and that this equality before the Law required that government, administrators and ordinary persons were all subject to the same Law. It is the corollary or analogue of Weber's opposition to the particularist modes of closed, private and consensual forms of law. Its particular consequence was that all persons are bound to follow the same Law. This is the basis of the criticism of the WADC for not providing a level playing field of the law. The third concept was that the particular constitution of any State is not the ultimate source of Law. This is probably the most overlooked and controversial aspect of Dicey's concept of the Rule of Law, as it implicitly challenges the received wisdom of the supremacy and sovereignty of parliament.[18] At its most basic, the consequence of this statement is that there is something more that stands behind positive Law itself. It opens up the debate around things such as natural law and equity that we might say have raged since the time of Antigone[19] and continues today in the work of Agamben. Any enquiry as to what might stand behind the law – some *just-i-fiable* good or just-ness – and how it is relevant to the current topic is an important task, but it is not the purpose of this particular work; it is something that must come as a consequence of knowing whereabouts we are now.

---

[16] See U Mattei and L Nader, *Plunder: When the Rule of Law is Illegal* (Blackwell Publishing, 2008).

[17] EP Thompson, *Whigs and Hunters: The Origin of the Black Act* (Allen Lane, 1975) 266; see, eg, the works of Scheuerman cited below.

[18] As we will see, in neoliberalism we might say consistently with Dicey that the society of competition and not a State's constitution is the ultimate source of the Law.

[19] Sophocles, *The Three Thebian Plays: Antigone, Oedipus the King, Oedipus at Colonus*, trans R Fagles (Penguin Classics, 1984) 82.

Dicey's Critique of Administrative Law

The words "administrative law," which are its most natural rendering, are unknown to English judges and counsel, and are in themselves hardly intelligible without further explanation.[20]

Dicey went to great lengths to distinguish the English conception of the Rule of Law from French Administrative Law (*droit administratif*), which he saw not only as being an arbitrary form but also as a form which breached the doctrine of the separation of powers.[21] Administrative Law, whether in the Continental model or in the way it has developed in the Anglo system since Dicey, is, by its very nature, concerned with Executive power. It is a form of Law that countenances and allows Executive discretion, whilst at the same time, seeking, at least procedurally, to regulate it. Forms of Administrative Law have also developed in such a way that they now apply to a variety of particular and specialised areas – for example, immigration, broadcasting, mining, workplaces, and of course, sport.[22] On their face, and especially in cases where supervision by the ordinary courts is lacking, these forms of Administrative Law appear inconsistent with the form of Law described by both Weber and Dicey.

The World Anti-Doping Code (WADC) system, which seeks to establish a transnational or supranational autonomous form of law, not subject to the supervisory powers of national courts, is a case in point. The law of the WADC neither emanates nor derives its force from the command of a single national sovereign, nor does it apply equally to all those who find themselves within that definable people and territory. The WADC establishes a particularist and autonomous global system of law, in which its text clearly states that it is not to be read in the light of, or bound by, the conditions that governed the Law of Modern Rational Capitalism.[23]

The anti-doping system established by the WADC is one of the preeminent examples of the new global form of Administrative Law that is being constructed in the process of globalisation. WADA has been described as being 'a body that is emblematic of the emergence of the new forms of hybrid private-public governance mechanism in the global sphere'.[24] The WADC is, of course, a particular form of law that applies only to athletes and their support staff, and prohibits for them only things that are not generally prohibited in the wider society. Moreover, it limits their recourse to a non-judicial body, controlled and established by the

---

[20] AV Dicey, *Introduction to the Study of the Law of the Constitution* (Macmillan and Co Limited, 1920) 326.

[21] For a contemporary survey of this system see B Latour, *The Making of Law: An Ethnography of the Conseil d'Etat* (Wiley, 2009).

[22] In Australia, the ASADA Act is a form of State Administrative Law.

[23] Recall Art 24.3 of the WADC: 'The Code shall be interpreted as an independent and autonomous text and not by reference to the existing law or statutes of the Signatories or governments.'

[24] L Casini, 'The Making of a *Lex Sportiva*: The Court of Arbitration for Sport "The Provider"', IILJ Working Paper 2010/5 (Global Administrative Law Series) (New York University School of Law, 2010).

global Executive of sport. It is not intended to be subject to the supervision of the courts of the national sovereign.

One demand resulting from the WADC's global reach is the requirement for some flexibility in its application by its various state and sporting princes. Flexibility and discretion are necessary, and allowed, in order to maintain the system's single logic (which I suggest may be something other than the integrity of the spirit of sport; whatever that might mean) and to achieve its local effectiveness. Thus, rather than by way of the general application of Law to all, the WADC operates and achieves local effectiveness by way of the flexible management of the differences it encounters. Harmonisation of laws should not be confused with all being equal before the same law. The opening paragraph of the WADC clearly supports this proposition, stating that it is

> specific enough to achieve complete harmonization on issues where uniformity is required, yet general enough in other areas to permit flexibility on how agreed-upon anti-doping principles are implemented.

For Weber, the increasing use of discretionary powers and the specialisation of law for different classes and sectors of society is, on this view, a sign of the deformalisation of Law. In his consideration of *droit administratif* Dicey observed the

> very contrast between administrative law as it exists in France ... and the notions of equality before the law which are firmly established in modern England.[25]

This contrast stemmed, in part, from the privileged position this form of Law possessed as a result of it being situated and administered within the Executive arm of Government and not being subject to the Anglo conception of the constraints inherent in the concept of the separation of powers. Dicey's concern, in part, was the manner in which the French system '*juridialised*' prerogatives of the Crown that had existed under the *ancien regime* and placed servants of the government outside of the purview of the ordinary courts of Law. As such, he argued that the French system was in stark contrast to the English system and was not in accord with

> the full meaning of that absolute supremacy of the ordinary law of the land ... which we have found to be a salient feature of English institutions.[26]

Searching for an adequate definition, he turned to the works of Alexis de Tocqueville and his contemporaries, French jurists such as Aucoc, who defined *droit administrative* as:

> (1) the constitution and the relations of those organs of society which are charged with *the care of those social interests* (interets collectifs) *which are the object of* public *administration*, by which term is meant the different representatives of society among which the State is the most important, and (2) the relation of the administrative authorities toward the citizens of the State.[27]

---

[25] Dicey, *Introduction* (n 20) 327–28.
[26] ibid, 325.
[27] ibid, 328–29 (emphasis added).

For us, the function of Administrative Law as being the constitution of organs of society charged with the care of social interests and public administration and the relation of these organs towards and with the citizenry is of particular significance. As an emerging form of a supranational, hybridised and globalised form of Administrative law, neither fully public nor fully private, which has been brought into being not solely by State actors but by an alliance or apparatus of non-State and State actors, the anti-doping apparatus has at its *raison d'être* the administration and care of what is defines as social interests. The supranational care of social interests is achieved by Law, law and what Agamben described as ~~law~~, that is, governance.[28] This transnational or supranational form of law is not International Law in the sense of Public International Law, which was a system that was based upon the notion of the inviolability of sovereign States and their free agreement. Furthermore, this emerging or new form of law, rather than a pure sovereign method of rule or right, is a form of trans-national governance, achieved both through means of Law, law and not law, which both Agamben and Dicey describe as having an 'exceptional character'.[29] Dicey had already foreshadowed in his own way the manner in which concepts such as governance, economy, the police, the exception and biopower, all aimed at the 'care' of social interests are embedded in the concept of administration.

The French system was, according to Dicey, based upon a fundamental misconception, which he attributes to Montesquieu, as to the meaning of the separation of powers. In the Anglo system, the separation of powers seeks to maintain the independence of each branch of Government by effectively placing the Parliament and the Executive under the supervision of the Judiciary, in so far as their actions must be consistent with both constitutional and Legal principles. On this view, the separation of powers is inextricably woven into the concept of the independence of the Judiciary – a condition that underpins the legitimacy of the whole sovereign system. But it

> means, in the mouth of a French statesman or lawyer, something different from what we mean in England by the 'independence of the judges,' or the like expressions. … it means … the government and its officials ought … to be independent of and to a great extent free from the jurisdiction of the ordinary Courts.[30]

Thus, for Dicey, within the realms of Administrative Law, firstly, not all were equal before the same Law, a special form of law or privilege attached to Legal persons because of their status, and, secondly, and as a corollary of that, unlike the Anglo position where the separation of powers placed the Law courts in a supervisory position, whereby they controlled and kept within their Legal powers both the Executive and the Parliament (as the case may be), on the Continent, the separation of powers was construed (or misconstrued) as meaning the courts had no

---

[28] G Agamben, *Homo Sacer, Sovereign Power and Bare Life* (Stanford University Press, 1999).
[29] Dicey, *Introduction* (n 20) 327.
[30] ibid, 332–34.

such power to interfere with the workings of the other branches of government. Unlike the Continental misconception, the independence of the Judiciary, rather than the independence, or the immunity, of the other branches of government from interference from the Judiciary, is fundamental to contemporary conceptions and rhetoric surrounding the Rule of Law.

The Continental system stemmed from the view that 'judges must never be allowed to hamper the action of the government'.[31] To allow courts to judge the Executive impinged upon that particular view of the separation of powers.[32] de Tocqueville's assessment of the situation carried with it as much (or even more) trepidation as Dicey's assessment, de Tocqueville wrote of judicial power being expelled from the sphere of government

> into which the ancient regime had most unhappily allowed its introduction, but at the very same time, as any one can see, the authority of the government has gradually been introducing itself into the natural sphere of the Courts, and there we have suffered it to remain as if the confusion of powers was not as dangerous if it came from the side of government as if it came from the side of the Courts, or even worse. For the intervention of the Courts of Justice into the sphere of government only impedes the management of business, whilst the intervention of government in the administration of justice depraves citizens and turns them at the same time into revolutionists and slaves.[33]

It is important for us to consider the ramifications of this position in the contemporary context. According to this conception of the separation of powers a global sovereign or executive power requires, and is justified in having, complete and unfettered discretion, a free reign in governance, a discretion which is not to be brought into question by existing national courts, or for that matter, international or transnational tribunals in construction, or at least other than those anointed by that sovereign or Executive. As in Imperial France, '[j]udicial functions must remain separate from administrative functions'[34] and thus judicial functions must not interfere with government or governance in the construction of Empire. We have already seen echoes of this logic in the reasoning of the CAS Panels in *Valverde 1, 2 & 3*.

Dicey was careful to note the changes in the nature of *droit administrative* throughout the nineteenth century[35] which was 'the outcome of more than a hundred years of revolutionary and constitutional conflict'.[36] He was of the view that it established

> a condition of things fundamentally inconsistent with what Englishmen regard as the due supremacy of the ordinary law of the land.[37]

---

[31] ibid, 335.
[32] ibid, 336–37.
[33] A deTocqueville, *Democracy in America* (1835) 174–75, cited in Dicey, *Introduction* (n 20) 353–54.
[34] Dicey, *Introduction* (n 20) 337.
[35] ibid, 327.
[36] ibid, 330.
[37] ibid, 328.

Droit administratif straddled the *ancien regime*, the revolution, the Thermidor and its successors.[38] These observations of Dicey's are relevant in considering the form of global law we face in the contemporary context. In constructing the new regime, the Imperial or Bonapartist model, sought to obtain the 'least interference by the Law Courts with the free action of the government'. Although Dicey later accepts that, over time, *droit administratif* took on a form which possessed some similarities to English Law, that it became more Law-like, more judicial and less a direct arm of Executive power.[39] The important point is that it is this very transformation that belies the observation of Hardt and Negri concerning the contemporary context:

> Eventually a new judicial function must be formed that is adequate to the constitution of Empire. Courts will have to be transformed gradually from an organ that simply decrees sentences against the vanquished to a judicial body or system of bodies that dictate and sanction the interrelation among the moral order, the exercise of police action, and the mechanism legitimating imperial sovereignty.[40]

Law's Deformalisation and the Need for Speed

As already noted, Weber recognised that his formalistic description of Law, as a rational and calculable system, was already giving way to a new form of law and to its deformalisation. The germs of this new form are what today is arguably becoming the norm; this is, in part, the lesson of Agamben. We have introduced one clear aspect of deformalisation which has been the increasing use of discretion and the growth of administrative and particularist forms of Law. Weber recognised that Modern Rational Capitalism's formal and calculable Law was undergoing a process of entropy – deformalisation of Law was *the thing* of the future. Weber's Continental vantage point, possibly, allowed him to perceive of this deformalisation before Dicey, who, of course, was bound by the self-acknowledged island of 'scrupulous legalism' and 'pedantic absurdity' of English lawyers.[41]

Weber recognised that the fact of the deformalisation of Law was related to transitions within the capitalist form. The late nineteenth century and early twentieth century saw the emergence of the crisis of liberalism, monopoly capitalism, and later, as one reaction to these things, the growth of the welfare and social democratic State. In this context, Law became increasingly made and addressed to particular social groups. As the State became increasingly complex and compartmentalised, so too did the Law and this growth itself also brought about a growth in forms of Administrative Law; quasi-Legislative Law such as Delegated Legislation,

---

[38] ibid, 330–32.
[39] ibid, 360ff.
[40] Hardt, Michael, and Negri, Antonio, *Empire*. Harvard University Press, 1999, 38.
[41] Dicey, *Introduction* (n 20) 358.

quasi-law such as policy and rule-making, and the increasing grant and use of discretionary powers. Each of these measures led to Law making being further removed from the daily life of Parliament and placed in the hands of the Executive and its bureaucracy. Parliament, it might be said, has been reduced to the creation of framework agreements under which the Executive and bureaucracy wielded real political and Legal power.

At the same time, the increasing complexity of society meant that Law started to merge with other disciplines such as science, technology and economics, and those disciplines themselves began to influence what had been previously purely Legal reasoning. Thus, towards the end of his career Weber came to qualify his Rationalisation of Law thesis. In *Economy and Society*,[42] and in the light of a number of developments he observed in the late nineteenth century such as the development of a division of labour and vocational interest groups with their own lawyers – labour law, corporations lawyers, etc, all contributing to an apparent regression back to the feudalisation of law. Different specific *privi-leges* applying to different status groups accompanied the development of a new privileged class of bureaucrats with the technical 'know-how' and who thus became indispensable to the administrative process.

William E Scheuerman has questioned the traditional belief in an elective affinity between economic liberalism and the Rule of Law. He argues that today it obscures the manner in which the process of economic globalisation threatens core features of the Rule of Law. For Scheuerman, because of its high-speed nature and its tendency towards deterritorialisation, contemporary capitalism is vastly different to its predecessors and, as such, the fundamental relationship between capitalism and the Rule of Law has itself been transformed. Because global capitalism consistently and constantly revolutionises the temporal horizons of economic action, its reliance on a robust model of the Rule of Law diminishes. Social acceleration and deterritorialisation have diminished the dependence upon traditional Rule of Law virtues and as such traditional modes of liberal Law decreasingly figure in the operations of the global economy. Soft law, international arbitration, private ordering and increasing Executive discretion have far more prevalent forms of governance than traditional forms of law.[43] We will turn to consider the changes brought about by neoliberalism to the Rule of Law (Chapter 5) but for now it is sufficient to note that, instead of the machine-like production of the formal and calculable law of Weber's modernity, which matched its machine-like production, what is increasingly required today, rather than calculability and equality before the Law, is flexibility.

Aristotle suggested in *Antiquity* that law in its normative form was inherently defective because of its need to state matters generally. Scheuerman notes that Locke proposed a similar thing in the instance of the body of the prince. Locke's

---

[42] Weber, *Economy and Society* (n 6).
[43] WE Scheuerman, *Liberal Democracy and the Social Acceleration of Time* (The John Hopkins University Press, 2004) 145.

argument was that the most sensible answer to the Legislative power's inherent tendency to commit mistakes in predicting the future is to place

> power in the hands of the prince to provide for the public good, in such cases, which depending on unforeseen and uncertain occurrences, certain and unalterable laws could not safely direct.[44]

This proposition is that Executive discretion is a real necessity in the Law, precisely for the reasons that Aristotle introduced equity as the fulfilment of justice. Scheuerman writes:

> Law is prospective because only rules announced beforehand can provide legal security, but also because legislation in its very nature is concerned with the task of predicting and coordinating future needs. The 'exigencies of the times' are 'impossible to fore-see' with perfection, however, and thus legislative power is inherently flawed.[45]

What is important about the contribution of Scheuerman is that he recognises that the condition of speed that characterises the contemporary global condition further accentuates the defective nature of Law. The necessity of Executive discretion to act beyond and even against the Law thus derives not merely from the necessity of acknowledging the limitations of inflexible and rigid Legislative statutes, but, from an even more fundamental need, to make sure that the present is free from an unduly slavish dependence on the dictates of the past. Here the rigidity of Law is merely a manifestation of the domination of the present by the past. Although future-orientated, Legislative activity inevitably generates rules that soon represent (past) predictions about the present and future, because 'things of this world are in so constant a flux, that nothing remains in the same state'.[46] Since the Legislature 'is usually too numerous, and too slow' only the Executive is likely to prove able effectively to break with the letter of the Law for the sake of rapidly adjusting Legislative authority to the dictates of a changing world.[47]

Scheuerman's point is that presuppositions about the space and time horizons of human activity shape many conventional assumptions about liberal-democratic decision making. Referring to Montesquieu and to Locke he observes that in liberal-democratic theory (unlike in Judge Judy's courtroom) it is the slow-moving nature of deliberation and decision making that contributes to its reasonableness and rationality.[48] He also noted how networked, checked and balanced forms of government, such as the American republic, were conceived as protecting

---

[44] ibid, 37.
[45] ibid.
[46] ibid.
[47] ibid, 37–38.
[48] Throughout so many sporting and particularly anti-doping cases we have seen that speed and the needs of the economy overdetermine Legality. Valverde's case and the example of the Stuttgart World Championships is one we have addressed here. The manner in which the AFL Commission dealt with Essendon's 'governance' issues is an even starker example.

democratic forms by decelerating the pace of political exchange. Referring to Hume he argues that along with both

> bicameralism and the separation of powers can be interpreted as tools for the sake of heightened cognitive merits.[49]

Ideas of majority rule also rest upon these same presuppositions of time and space, as do basic elements of the western system of Law, such as Constitutionalism and the Rule of Law.[50] The future orientation of law making and the stability it seeks to engender becomes

> problematic given the multiplication of settings in which legal rules inevitably encounter a greater variety of 'permutations and combinations of events ... which were never contemplated when the original rules were made' ... [N]ew instruments of production, new modes of travel and of dwelling, new credit and ownership devices, new concentrations of capital ... all of these factors of innovation make vain the hope that definitive legal rules can be drafted that will forever after solve all problems. As such when human relationships are transforming daily, legal relationships cannot be expressed in enduring legal form. The constant development of unprecedented problems requires a legal system capable of fluidity and pliancy.[51]

According to this view, the Legislature's capacity for generating clear and binding laws that are able to guide future action 'tends to decay' leaving the gaps to be filled through the exercise of judicial discretion. However, what Scheuerman does not address in this instance, given his desire to resurrect liberal democracy, is that the other holder of discretionary power, the Executive, through the myth of a representative Parliamentary democracy, seems to do all that it can to defeat the exercise of judicial discretion which it does not control itself. Nevertheless, he recognises the result that:

> However attractive from a normative standpoint, the classical dream of a relatively airtight legal code in which judicial discretion is rendered unnecessary tends to be systematically undermined by time and space compression and its resultant increases in 'the speed of movement of goods, people, information, messages, and the like'.[52]

The nineteenth-century hostility to discretion remains a dominant force within the Law, despite the global condition taking on an increasing form of speed and interconnectedness that presents an ever-increasing challenge to the traditional model of Executive–Legislative relations. Traditional Rule of Law rhetoric appears incapable of adequately addressing the problem of speed and time and space compression, with the resultant production of what Scheuerman fears as a *misfit*

---

[49] Scheuerman, *Liberal Democracy* (n 43) 43.
[50] Dadot and Laval argue that, in fact, liberalism and the Rule of Law are anti-democratic or anti majoritarian: Dadot and Laval, *The New Way of the World* (n 3).
[51] Scheuerman, *Liberal Democracy* (n 43) 56–57.
[52] ibid, 57.

between the time and space horizons of legislative activity and social and economic life.[53] Such a misfit is made all the greater as government has moved from a laissez-faire role through the welfare era, to one of a being a manager or regulator of the local conditions of a global market and society. In such a situation national Legislatures:

> are expected to do nothing less than react effectively to a multiplicity of rapid-fire changes in social and economic life while simultaneously maintaining fidelity to the traditional notion of its legitimacy as resting on wide-ranging forms of unhurried debate.[54]

In such a situation, contemporary Parliaments abandon their Law-making duties to both national and global executives which are envisioned as better equipped to grapple with the imperatives of speed. To the extent that the Legislature's ability to coordinate future activities is drastically curtailed by the process of time and space compression, the scope of discretionary executive authority grows accordingly. Indeed, this development has taken place, as the range of exceptional and even emergency executive authority has become sizable even in relatively stable liberal democracies. In our high-speed social world, the Legislature's inability 'to foresee, and so by laws to provide for, all accidents and necessities, that may concern the public' is probably a main source of the ubiquity of Executive discretion in modern-day liberal democracy.[55] In short, the slow-going character of deliberative Legislatures, or for that matter sovereign courts, increasingly leaves them poorly suited to the regulatory challenges of modern social and economic life. It is in this context that Carl Schmitt's diagnosis of the becoming of 'motorised legislator', operating in the context of an accelerated world where speed is at a premium, foreshadows both the more simplified and more complex apparatus that is tending to become commonplace.[56] The reduction of the classical liberal Legislature to a rapid-fire mechanical instrument for coordinating social and economic affairs was, for Schmitt, a consequence of 'liberalism's congenital misunderstandings about politics', but it also signals contemporary capitalism's indisputable need for rapid-fire regulatory activity.[57] Scheuerman's point is that the rise of the motorised legislature heralds the disintegration of the classical attributes of liberal Law making and, most importantly, its fidelity to the Rule of Law. Rather than a transcendent government of Laws and not of men, Law, or ~~law~~, functions as a technical device for overseeing high-speed economic affairs. For this reason, contemporary liberal Law making increasingly consists of vague and open-ended resolutions,

---

[53] ibid, 52.
[54] ibid, 48.
[55] ibid, 50.
[56] ibid, 104.
[57] ibid, 100.

exceptional and emergency norms, and poorly crafted statutes possessing a limited half-life.[58] In accordance with high-speed temporality of society:

> law making procedures become ever faster and more circumscribed, the path towards the achievement of legal regulation shorter, and the share of jurisprudence smaller.[59]

In our study what we have seen, to date, is that the requirement for speed manifests itself in an avoidance of the tardy processes of national Law courts, a preference for private arbitration, flexibility and the application of a modulating 'sovereign' power. Private agreement creates a particular, autonomous form of law, which forms the basis of the system's authority, not independent courts. Arbitration takes place in the context of disciplinary matters arising from contract and in a situation in which the accused has none of the substantive rights and liberties of a citizen under the Rule of Law, nor do they have the ability to defend, or even properly mitigate, an offence.

The strict liability regime of anti-doping requires that the only recourse available is of a formal procedural type. Furthermore, rather than the application of an autonomous and strict Legal principle and Legal supervision by independent, national courts, the WADC calls upon sovereign States to privilege private arbitration, such that decisions are made and arbitration is carried out by way of recourse to technical, economic and scientific standards, toggled onto the spectacle of a Just War against doping as the guiding principle of governance.

Private Governance and the Growth of Arbitrative Demand

The *privi-lege* of anti-doping law and of arbitration place our contemporary context well outside the Weberian and Diceyan conceptions of Law. Private arbitration has replaced the courts as a bastion of 'judicial' decision making, with consent giving rise to a system unrestrained by constitutional, rule of law or human rights restraints. Foucault foreshadowed the relationship between biopower, neoliberalism and the growth of arbitrative demand.[60] As we have seen, what is at stake for us in the first instance is the manner in which the consensual agreement to play sport includes the agreement to have disputes settled by an arbitration process that stands outside of the traditional Legal system.

According to Foucault, eighteenth- and nineteenth-century liberalism and its conception of the primacy of the Law required a reduction of the judicial function to the pure and simple application of the (transcendent) Law. Foucault sees this as

---

[58] ibid, 56.
[59] ibid, 104.
[60] M Foucault, *The Birth of Biopolitics: Lectures at the College de France, 1978–1979* (Palgrave Macmillan, 2008) 175.

being transformed with the coming of neoliberalism, such that now what stands as being the law is no more than a set of rules of the game, in which each remains master regarding himself and his part (we will consider this in more detail in Chapter 5). But this, according to Foucault, requires the juridical function, instead of being reduced to the simple function of applying the Law, to acquire a new autonomy and importance. The particular status of neoliberal man as the man of enterprise – itself being a way of behaving in the economic field in the form of competition – and a society that allows individuals the possibility of behaving as they wish in the form of free enterprise, gave rise to a growth in the multiple forms of the typical enterprise unit. Correspondingly, it gave rise to an increase in the number of surfaces available for friction and hence an opportunity for the occasions for litigation to multiply. Foucault's point is that the social regulation of these conflicts calls for a form of interventionism that tends to operate as arbitration, importantly, within the framework of the (particular) rules of the (particular) game; something other than the Law.

Neoliberalism's reduction of the number of functionaries (of the State) and its increased dynamic of enterprises produces the need for an ever-increasing number of 'judicial' instances, manifested increasingly as instances of arbitration. The problem identified by Foucault is whether this arbitration should be inserted within already existing judicial institutions, or whether it is necessary to create new institutions. For Foucault this is one of the fundamental problems faced by liberal societies where there is a multiplication of the 'judicial' and instances of and the need for arbitration.[61] What we have already seen in the case of sport and the anti-doping apparatus is that arbitration is increasingly a private affair removed from the sphere of influence and restriction of the State.

Globalisation indicates shifts in the kinds of controls over corporations, people and markets. Michael Hardt and Toni Negri identify three general categories that are in constant interplay in order for the globalisation process to be undertaken: private agreements, regulatory mechanisms, and general norms operating at an international or global level.[62] The first level of private agreement is characterised by emerging forms of private authority whereby business governs global economic activity outside the control of nation States or other Governmental structures. Hardt and Negri refer to this emerging form of private authority as the new global form of *Lex Mercatoria* which they credit with the ability of players involved to make contacts independently in areas outside State controls and based on shared customary Legal understandings. As the authors state, *Lex Mercatoria* originally referred to the Legal structures that governed trade among merchants in mediaeval Europe at centres outside the jurisdictions of all the sovereign powers. The new

---

[61] ibid, 176. The need for regulation also increases; the more 'liberalised' the market becomes the greater the need for regulation. See, eg, B Harcourt, *Illusions of Free Markets: Punishment and the Myth of Natural Order* (Harvard University Press, 2011).

[62] M Hardt and A Negri, *Multitude, War and Democracy in the Age of Empire* (The Penguin Press, 2004) 169.

Lex Mercatoria provides a legal framework within which one is not dependent upon any national Legal system or systems. Its purpose is to function outside of, and to be a supplement to, national structures in the realm of global business. For Hardt and Negri this *Lex Mercatoria* is not validated by nation States but simply constructed by the law firms that serve the multi- and transnational corporations.[63]

There is no doubt that contemporary *Lex Mercatoria* is much more extensive than in the past, not only in its territorial reach and its speed of operation, but also in its subject matter, whereby even the social reproduction of the population becomes a subject of this new form of law. We can clearly see this in the domain of sport and in particular its anti-doping rules, where the reproduction of a certain type of population is at stake and where private agreement has become the 'constitutional' norm. Importantly, this new form of law provides the minimum conditions under which the business of sport is capable of taking place. It is a regime internal to the sporting body itself which, at the same time, purports to be an arm's-length consensual agreement between all those who wish to partake in the game.[64]

The second point made by Hardt and Negri is that private authority emerges only with the backing of the political authorities. In one way or another, *Lex Mercatoria* depends upon Public Law to guarantee its existence, obligations and sanctions.[65] In the case of the particular aspect of *Lex Sportiva* or *Lex Doping*, established by the WADC and with CAS at its peak, it is Swiss Federal Law that guarantees its force of law. In Australia the Commonwealth's ASADA Act inserts itself into the supranational regime but in a manner that seeks not to act as any guarantee of Legality. But this, in itself, tells us nothing about who or what exercises sovereign power. Nevertheless, the WADC arrangement still required the agreement of the interested governments in the form of the Lausanne UNESCO Treaty[66] and most importantly the various international and national sporting federations, along with the International Olympic Committee (IOC), for it to come into being. Thus, at this second level identified by Hardt and Negri, we find bilateral and multilateral agreements that tend to and, in fact do, create truly global forms of authority, which are, in turn, given deference by and backed by both public and private institutions. Not only do we have an interregnum that is halfway between the national and the transnational, but it is also one that is halfway between the public and the private, which acts to create a new global form of governance supported by a vast array of legal authorities, normative systems and procedures. For this reason, it appears as both supranational and transnational and in a manner that privileges the private, 'consenual' basis of its constitution. It is also this array of authority

---

[63] ibid.

[64] ibid, 169–70.

[65] ibid, 171.

[66] Lausanne Declaration on Doping in Sport, Adopted by the World Conference on Doping in Sport, 4 February 1999, Lausanne, Switzerland, available at www.sportunterricht.de/lksport/Declaration_e.html.

systems and procedures that comes together to form the anti-doping apparatus. In Chapter 4 we will consider specific deployments of this apparatus.

The third level of arrangement, discussed by Hardt and Negri, are the supranational or transnational institutions that emerge as a result of multilateral agreements.[67] The focus of the authors in their work is on institutions such as the World Bank and the International Monetary Fund. For our purposes, the two primary institutions that we have encountered and have authority within the new global transnational system are the WADA and the Court of Arbitration for Sport (CAS). But again, even in this situation, the bearer of sovereign power modulates. The competition between anti-doping and sporting agencies exemplified by Valverde's case is a testament to this modulation of power.

In contrast to what we might term Rule of Law romanticists, Goldman has analysed the place of globalisation in the Western Legal tradition by examining what he calls recurring patterns of law and authority. Of particular interest to Goldman is the manner in which pre-modern forms of law, contrary to the principles of modernity, were themselves of a particularist or local nature. We have already described Weber's view on these forms of law. In examining the emergence of private agreement in the age of globalisation of interest to Goldman is 'the nature of the contractual mechanism for triggering arbitration and the institutionalisation of authorities in adjudication outside the state'.[68] Within these realms of private agreement or governance, Goldman identifies a tendency towards a 'useful universalism' within the particular universe established by the contract in question.[69] It is this 'useful universalism' within the particular world in question that we would call the functionality required by what Hardt and Negri describe as the system's 'single logic' or, in the language of Dumont, the system's value that gives rise to the hierarchy formed of the dispersed elements of the whole. For Goldman, contractual arbitration mechanisms conjure a problem of logic: a paradox of self-reference, which, without more, affects its enforceability.[70] Hardt and Negri identified the need for State or public backing in order to ensure enforceability. Goldman also notes that voluntary compliance based upon peer pressure contributes to an acceptance of a particular process in order to preserve one's livelihood.[71]

In effect, the societal context of the international commercial contract can become a substitute authority by creation of the parties, tending to exclude domestic law, as the parties 'autonomise' their Legal relationships. Such privately created law may be enforceable by government although not necessarily requiring that level of coercion.[72]

---

[67] Hardt and Negri, *Multitude, War and Democracy* (n 62) 172.
[68] DB Goldman, *Globalisation and the Western Legal Tradition: Recurring Patterns of Law and Authority* (Cambridge University Press, 2007) 287.
[69] ibid, 288.
[70] ibid, 288–89.
[71] ibid, 289.
[72] ibid.

For Goldman:

> the transactional community creates allegiance from the shared history and prospective reward of future deals. … The externalisation of the resolution and enforcement process in an independent arbitration institution … adds perceived political objectivity to the process. These factors combine to ground the contract in the interior, moral consciousness of individuals, by virtue of the personal, contracted creation of the process. Contracting itself can then become for this community a source of law with validity at a global level.[73]

This source of law, or power, operates at a paralegal or extra-State level.[74] It also raises in our minds some of the arguments of neoliberal legal scholars such as Posner, around the utility of social norms as a more efficient means of governance.[75] It is for this reason that Goldman recognises that globalisation 'represented by the accelerated interconnections amongst things that happen in the world' is stimulating a new facet of jurisprudence reflected in the semantic shift from the word Government to governance.[76] Along with it we find a world constructed in relative freedom from State coercion and which appears autonomous enough to avoid the need for the redress of redistributive effects, or the guarantees for that matter, of State Law. In this context, the Diceyan idea of the universality of Law becomes confined to the needs of a particular universe of a particular community and importantly unconstrained by ideas of territory and traditional conceptions of the Rule of Law.[77] It is no longer a transcendent form of Law that governs but an immanent contractual arrangement that is interiorised.

It should be apparent from this reflection on Weber and Dicey that we no longer live in the world of Modern Rational Capitalism and its Law. We tend more and more to move in a system in which the sovereigns of modernity continue to reign but no longer govern. The fundamentals of both Weber and Dicey's systems have clearly changed; Law is no longer solely the product of a single sovereign source that governs a definable people and territory under their control. The sovereign's courts, in a growing instance of situations, are no longer the courts of final recourse. Governance is increasingly carried out at the behest of networks of international organisations and corporations, on the basis of technical, economic and scientific standards, leaving the remnants of the State to perform an implementation and management role in respect of global policy, and of primarily ensuring, through its presence as an institutional backer, its local effectiveness.

That there is a fundamental change in the nature of global organisation and the deformalisation of sovereignty and its form of Law should not be in doubt. Despite the misgivings of many, it will continue to have profound ramifications for

---

[73] ibid, 290.
[74] ibid.
[75] EA Posner, *Law and Social Norms* (Harvard University Press, 2009).
[76] Goldman, *Globalisation and the Western Legal Tradition* (n 68) 290.
[77] ibid, 292.

what, until now, we have called Law and Legal principle. What we are witnessing with the construction of the global system could be described on one level, and by way of analogy, as an increasing return to pre-modern systems of particularist, specialist and compartmentalised law, along with a subsequent and increasing use of arbitration, rather than judicial processes. It is a return to dispute resolution by way of private agreement, rather than recourse to the sovereign's courts. But added to this mix is the increasing reliance on technical, economic and scientific standards, as the guiding principle of governance, rather than Legal method, which involves the retrospective application of autonomous and strict Legal principle in order to resolve disputes.

The lesson of Foucault, and more recently Agamben, is that more diffuse mechanisms and apparatuses now perform these functions. Governance tends to become a question of biopower (the administration and management of bodies) within a global society of the spectacle, rather than a question of mere sovereign command. In this system of global governance, rather than an international form of Law agreed upon by equal sovereigns, things and mechanisms that are not themselves Law (law) appear to have the force of Law. The question may well become not, is it Law? or does it operate according to Legal principle, or for that matter the Rule of Law? – but – following, Deleuze and Guattari, what does it do? How does it work? Even, does it work like Law? That is, does it affect in the way in which we have previously conceived of the role and function of Law?

The Police

> [T]he Rule of Law continues to play a central role in the context of the contemporary passage: right remains effective and (precisely by means of the state of exception and police techniques) becomes procedure.[78]

Consent to private arbitration looms large as the central aspect of the construction of a global system or systems of law and governance that we are encountering. The other aspect that we have begun to touch upon is the manner in which consent does not appear to construct a system that mirrors the rights and guarantees of modernity, but rather seems to carve out a space for the exceptional care of social interests. The administration and discretion bleeds into policing and it is the activity of global policy that demonstrates the real effectiveness of the new Imperial order described by Hardt and Negri. The two initial coordinates of the authority of Empire are the juridical power to rule over the exception and the supranational capacity to police. In this context whilst right remains effective, by way of the operation of the exception and the police, there is a continuing role for the Rule of Law, not as a substantive guarantor of rights, but as merely a guarantor of formal

---

[78] Hardt and Negri *Empire* (n 40) 26–27.

procedure. Consistently with this, the only rights given to athletes in the WADC are of a procedural nature – a right to doping-free sport and a level playing field and the right to certain formal procedural guarantees in the testing system. We will return to the former in more detail below. In respect of the latter, most departures from these procedures are not, of themselves, sufficient to invalidate any process.

These elements of imperial rule – police, exception and right conceived of as procedure – provide us with better-equipped tools for the task of understanding the anti-doping apparatus. Police power better illustrates the function of discretion and procedure than does Legality and the Rule of Law. It also provides a focused lens through which we can begin to understand the concept of exception or, in other words, the tendency towards the governance pole of the Law-governance continuum. Here, the work of Neocleous on the police is instructive, for it allows us to conceive of a genealogy of the practice and procedure of the global administrative apparatus. With such an understanding we are also better able to contextualise particular instances of its deployment.

Neocleous points to the roots of the word *'police'* in French-Burgundian and how it spread and was adopted throughout Europe in the fifteenth century. The meaning, or function, he gives to the police has interesting parallels for us with Foucauldian concepts of biopower and discipline and with Dicey's definition of *droit administratif* referred to above. The meaning of police has remained constant

> denoting the legislative and administrative regulation of the internal life of a commu-
> nity to promote general welfare and the conditions of good order ... the regimenting of
> social life ... the management and the direction of the population by the state.[79]

Although the meaning is constant (save that we would say that the police, or the concept of policing, now extends beyond that of being a State institution) the reach of the police has been, over time, capable of encompassing all of society, and as such there is no human problem that cannot become the proper business of the police.[80] The institution of the police is the Diceyan care of social interests by an administrative power. In the end, the police function is that of the administration and management of life.[81]

Neocleous goes on to question what he refers to as the parallel myth between Law and order in that 'policing is considered to be related to order via law: the police maintain order by enforcing the law'.[82] Contrary to this position, Neocleous argues cogently

> the way in which the police institution is consistently collapsed into 'law' is fundamen-
> tally misleading. If we are to think of *policing as a form of political [rather than legal]*
> *administration* ... We need to consider at greater length the administrative nature of
> police power ... as historically policing was an exercise of administrative power as much

---

[79] M Neocleous, *Fabrication of Social Order: A Critical Theory of Police Power* (Pluto Press, 2000) 1 (emphasis added).
[80] ibid, 93–94.
[81] G Deleuze, *Foucault* (University of Minnesota Press, 2000) 92;
[82] Neocleous, *Fabrication of Social Order* (n 79) 94.

as anything else ... the police function should be seen through the lens of administration as much as the law ... the lens in question should be the *law-and-administration continuum*. This is because it is through the continuum of law and administration that the state *administers civil society politically as part of the fabrication of social order*.[83]

Neocleous is concerned with the concept of the police within the context of the State, but his argument, despite his reluctance to align himself with Hardt and Negri, is apposite to a consideration of the role of the police in the global context of Empire. Furthermore, his consideration of a 'law-and-administration continuum' rather than a simple binary of law and not law is capable of being read consistently with the thought of Foucault, Agamben, and Deleuze and Guattari, where law and governance form two poles between which practice fluctuates. An interrogation of the 'law-and-administration continuum' is what is at stake if we are to take up the task of Legal anthropology and interrogate sovereignty. It is what is at stake if we are to interrogate the juridical form and theory of sovereignty that is able to sustain and found the primacy of governance over Law.

Neocleous distinguishes the Rule of Law model, from that of policing, and notes that in the

crime control model in which crime prevention is the most important police function and to which other issues, such as individual rights, can be regarded of secondary importance.[84]

Through an analysis of the power of arrest in England and its relationship to a subsequent prosecution, Neocleous shows how the administrative function of the police gradually colonised the practice of prosecution process without any Legal authority. Arrest which was originally a mechanism to bring a person before a magistrate in order to determine whether a prosecution could proceed – a practice that supported the idea that the police act purely according to Law – gradually became a practice whereby the police themselves took control of the prosecution process, such that by the mid-nineteenth century the police not only apprehended an offender, but also prepared the case against him.[85] The practice, and importantly, the tension between the police and Legal authority was not a nineteenth-century curiosity, and when the practice was found to be illegal in the first half of the twentieth century, the tension was resolved on the side of the police by their assumption of powers that the Law denied them, merely because they felt them necessary and that there was a 'moral justification for getting around the rules'.[86]

In pointing out that the Law is very much a product of the police, Neocleous refers to Laws (eg Vagrancy Acts as early as 1824) which introduced stop and search powers, reversed the traditional presumption of innocence and introduced concepts such as strict liability, in which the suspect might only be able to mitigate

---

[83] ibid, 94–95 (emphasis added).
[84] ibid, 95.
[85] ibid, 96.
[86] ibid, 96–98.

a penalty, rather than be able to prove their own innocence.[87] All of these now have familiar descendants in the global anti-doping apparatus and are, of course, readily criticised by anti-doping critics and academics as being contrary to the Rule of Law. But what is important is that the content of Legal rules, and the conception of fundamental Legal principles, which formed a part of the Rule of Law, changed because of the necessities of police practice, and not some higher abstract ideal of the Rule of Law. These practice-based changes are generally accompanied by calls to some overriding moral justification. They point back to our rubric of spectacle, exception, and functionality in the context of the Just War on doping.

Discretion is the key feature of the practice of police power – Lord Scarman, cited by Neocleous, stated that: 'the exercise of discretion lies at the heart of the policing function'.[88] Discretion is such a central concept to policing

> that one cannot understand the police function without understanding the place of discretion in the police role. First, because the discretion of law enforcement agencies is near absolute. Second, because … individual police officers have the legal right and duty to enforce the law as they see fit, including whether to arrest, interrogate and prosecute … And third because identifying some of the issues surrounding discretion reveals some of the key features of police power.[89]

Absolute discretion is, of course, perceived to be at odds with the Rule of Law's notion of equal treatment before the Law, of a level, Legal playing field. Discretion as a form of selective Law enforcement and order maintenance is inherently discriminatory, its application is group specific, and it is intended to be so. Discretion shares

> a common root referring to the act of separating, distinguishing and judging. By definition the exercise of police discretion defines who is a deviant in any social context and how that deviant is controlled. Some laws may be enforced more strictly against some groups than others, while at other times certain techniques of maintaining order will be utilized for different groups.[90]

Furthermore, the act of taking control of the body of a suspect, and its violation in order to demand bodily samples, in whatever form, is the quintessential act of police discretion. It is not by reference to medical ethics or concepts such as consent to treatment that we should try to understand anti-doping instruments, such as the Biological Passport (see Chapter 4), but by reference to the nature of police power and its role in the biopolitical governance of populations.

> The citizen who is deemed to be suspect stands stripped of his canopy of rights, and the police can lawfully take control over and work on his body and mind … The fact that discretion is so integral to the exercise of police powers tells us something important about the police and its relation to state power, for discretion is a key feature of

[87] ibid, 105.
[88] ibid, 99.
[89] ibid, 99.
[90] ibid, 99–100.

state power generally. … While liberal jurisprudence tends to treat discretion entirely in terms of its place in judicial decisions, police *discretion can in fact be understood only by considering policing less as a form of juridical power and more as a form of political administration.*[91]

The exercise of discretion, as a type of administrative or Executive power, is entirely consistent with the growth of new administrative forms that have developed since Weber first grasped the signs of law's deformalisation and its production of quasi-judicial forms. It also allows us to begin to understand the importance of the Schmittian phrase '*Sovereign* is he who *decides* on the *exception*' – discretion as an Executive, rather than Judicial function, points squarely to the power of the sovereign to decide the Law, or more precisely, the exception to the Law. Agamben's discussions of Schmitt begin, in fact, with a discussion of the development of new forms of Administrative Law in the early twentieth century, the same passage foreseen and described in outline by Weber and Dicey.[92] Furthermore, Agamben's concept of the state of exception refers to more than an exercise of an administrative power; it also encompasses a situation in which the old boundaries of disciplines, institutions or powers tend to blur into a zone of indistinction or critical opalescence. This place that straddles borders, is also where Neocleous locates the police. The difficulty of where to place the police in the traditional Rule of Law institutional structure arises because rather than

> sitting uncomfortably in both judicial and executive spheres, the police … straddles the boundary between these spheres naturally, operating most comfortably in *the 'open border'* between the spheres of state power and giving the police an independence which no other institution of the state appears to have.[93] (Emphasis added).

The concept of the police operating in a global zone of indistinction is a much more adequate manner in which to conceive of the practice of anti-doping law than by way of reference to Legality and the Rule of Law. Policing appears as a border crossing assemblage in a way that the Law and Rule of Law does not.

Discretion allows the exercise of power with law standing at arm's length, deferring to the power of administration but using its own symbolic and political significance to confirm the same power.[94]

In the case of anti-doping law, we are no longer in the midst of an exercise of State power but the constitution of a form of global hybrid State/non-state administrative power. To continue to critique it as not conforming with the Rule of Law, is to sadly miss the point; in anti-doping we are dealing with the global administration and management of a form of life, with its policing.

---

[91] ibid, 101 (emphasis added).
[92] Agamben, *State of Exception* (n4) 7, 11ff.
[93] Neocleous, *Fabrication of Social Order* (n 79) 106.
[94] ibid, 103.

4

A Global Apparatus of Control

Anti-Doping Law and Global Governance

As we have already noted and as we have tried to contextualise by our foray into and beyond Weber and Dicey, one of the more forceful criticisms levelled by liberal commentators of anti-doping law and policy is that the manner in which the system established by the World Anti-Doping Agency (WADC) operates is not consistent with traditional notions of the Rule of Law and the separation of powers. It is the premise which, to a large part, underlies Møller's analysis of the scapegoating of Michael Rasmussen, and is made explicit in the quotation from the United States journalist Michael Hiltzik:

> What has evolved to protect competitive purity since then [the establishment of WADA] is a closed, quasi-judicial system without American-style checks and balances. Anti-doping authorities act as prosecutors, judge and jury, enforcing rules that they have written, punishing violations based on sometimes questionable scientific tests that they develop and certify themselves, while barring virtually all outside appeals and challenges.[1]

Møller's book on Rasmussen is important as it sets out in detail the manner in which the Union Cycliste Internationale (UCI), the directors of the *Tour de France*, the media and Rasmussen's team, *Rabobank*, handled, or mishandled, the adminis-tration of the Whereabouts System that operates in that sport. Møller painstakingly documents the manner in which the 2007 *Tour de France* leader, and at that point, probable winner of the race, was 'retired' by his team for no better reason than to quell a media storm played out in Debord's *Spectacle*.[2] Møller's documentation shows us that Rasmussen was not in breach of any rules that justified his exclusion from the race. He had not received the three Whereabouts warnings necessary to constitute an Anti-Doping Rule Violation (ADRV) and a two-year ban from competition. Furthermore, contrary to the Whereabouts rules, details of his file were leaked to the media by the Danish anti-doping authorities. In *I Wish I was Twenty One Now – Beyond Doping in the Australian Peloton* there appeared one

---

[1] V Møller, *The Scapegoat: About the Expulsion of Michael Rasmussen from the 2007 Tour de France and Beyond* (Akaprint, 2011) 281.
[2] G Debord, *The Society of the Spectacle* (Zone Books, 1995) 147.

quote in respect of the Rasmussen case.[3] The questions and the responses of the professional cyclist interviewed put into context the gravity of the events that took place in Pau in July 2007:

> Q: Are you ever amazed that Rasmussen is still alive? I actually think sometimes; I really seriously am amazed that he hasn't committed suicide.
>
> A: Yeah, that was I think an oversight on Rabobank's point of view, I don't know. I was there and I'm part of that team and I don't know enough about that. But I think it was an oversight on them when they kicked him out of the Tour, to leave him alone that night. They put him in a hotel room 100km up the road or something, with that, driven there by a PR lady or something. Really, somebody should have been on suicide watch.
>
> Q: Well, I'm still amazed about it.
>
> A: Taking the Holy Grail away from somebody.

This chapter is not about the Rasmussen case, but nevertheless this does help us situate the operation and effect of the Whereabouts System and how Møller's theoretical perspective fails to consider the mutations and the different logics or rationalities of the Rule of Law. Furthermore, his analysis does not take into account the manner in which the emphasis of government has moved from one of Law in the formal sense, towards a question of governance. It is the zone of indiscernibility between Law and governance within the anti-doping apparatus that we will now focus upon.

It is probably by now apparent that one aspect of this general movement from Law to governance that interests me is the manner in which, within a global world of generalised competition, sport itself acts as a form of general global governance. We will turn to this as we move on; however, what I wish to develop here is a more particular or localised example of governance drawn from cycling and deployed in its full intensity in the wake of the *Operación Puerto* revelations in 2006. Rather than the deployment of mechanisms of the arbitration of disputes, what concerns us here is the manner in which the daily lives, activities and bodies of professional cyclists are themselves increasingly governed by way of two principal instruments or tools: the Whereabouts System and the Biological Passport. What is it that these tools tell us about the changing relationship between Law and governance?

In order to understand these instruments of the global anti-doping apparatus we need to descend into the hidden abode of the athlete's world and, in particular, the manner in which this apparatus deals with, supervises, and governs their daily lives and activities. What follows in this part is an overview of the manner in which the individual cyclist, by their membership of the global population of cyclists, is made the object of an intense regime of testing and surveillance. By doing this, we can begin to uncover the manner in which the operation of these two anti-doping instruments contribute to making the private lives and bodies of professional

---

[3] M Hardie, D Shilbury, C Bozzi, and I Ware, *I Wish I was Twenty One Now: Beyond Doping in the Australian Peloton* (Auskadi Samizdat, 2012) 110.

cyclists visible to those who function as administrators of this apparatus. In doing so, the hidden act of doping is itself sought to be made visible, not by way of strictly legal mechanism but by administrative measures which, in turn, challenge and transform legal principle. In considering these two tools we will again use as our counterpoint for analysis the work of Møller and his critique of anti-doping scholarship which sought to justify the Whereabouts System by reference to Foucault's work on the Panopticon. This approach helps us understand what is at stake and highlights the political nature of these tools. It points to the limitations of the different strands of liberal analysis and suggests that a closer reading of Foucault's paradigm of the Panopticon is, in fact, applicable to the Whereabouts System and to the anti-doping apparatus more generally. My point is that the paradigm of the Panopticon, and its extension through concepts such as biopower and the society of control, do, in fact, assist us with a better understanding of what is actually at play. They help us grasp how the apparatus makes the invisible act of doping visible and in its process how the Law is again transformed. They also point us back to the concept that seems to underpin this policing – consent.

Before undertaking that task it is worth making the point that this apparatus forms a part of what Marazzi has described as a wider 'experiment in post-Fordist governance'.[4] Like myself, Marazzi is concerned with 'the gradual transformation of politics into administration' and the place of the 'emblematic problems of post-Fordist societies' in this transformation, among which he includes drugs.[5] These issues go to the heart of the problem raised by the Law–governance continuum and the interrogation of sovereignty that we have set as our task. For Marazzi, the manner in which these problems are dealt with become technical (rather than legal or democratic) problems in which the

> drug addict strays from the consensual and 'discursive' democracy, ... to consider him as a citizen would be contradictory in terms of representative democracy. The drug addict is incapable of representing the whole of civil society: he is in fact, a marginal, he is not included in a representative democracy whose rules he does not abide by, he is an 'impossible subject', irreducible to the norms of common living. As such, he can only be considered an 'administrative subject', outside of the democratic debate on the deeper causes of his existence ... the question of democracy ... (has been) liquidated through a purely technical approach to the issue of drug addiction.[6]

Marazzi's point is that public measures against drug addiction reflect larger issues relating to the post-Fordist construction of a

> democracy "without rights" ... the drug addict, the refugee, the unemployed are the "human material" on which to experiment with the new technologies of social control ...[7]

---

[4] C Marazzi, *Capital and Affects: The Politics of the Language Economy* (Semiotext(e), 2011) 136.
[5] ibid, 135.
[6] ibid, 138–39.
[7] ibid, 141.

To the conception of 'democracy without rights' we can add that of 'law without rights' which itself operates as a technical or administrative measure, as a form of governance. My point is that this system of law without rights not only includes what we might call parts of the population of the global poor, but also those who seemingly inhabit a space reserved for the global elite or aristocracy. In this manner it is not just, for example, the drug addict, the refugee, or the unemployed – who may at the same time be seen as potentially impossible subjects – or, for that matter, figures of Agamben's *homo sacer*.[8] In the case of the anti-doping apparatus the experiment is also being carried out on those who, simultaneously, perform a role in the governance and propagation of the generalised system of global competition. The broader context and ramifications of the anti-doping apparatus are brought home to us by comments such as those by the former Australian Minister for Sport, Kate Ellis at the 2010 Australian New Zealand Sports Law Conference, where she stated that the Whereabouts System was, in fact, a model which could be deployed throughout society. Furthermore, the Western Australian branch of the Liberal (conservative) party called for random drug testing to be carried out on welfare recipients, with the proposal that any positive test should result in the withdrawal of benefits.[9]

It is important to note that the anti-doping regime does not differentiate between the amateur and the professional; by taking out membership with a cycling club and receiving a 'cycling licence', all those who join consent to become objects of this regime. The only difference being the professional is subject to the extreme intensification of the anti-doping apparatus. It is primarily the Whereabouts System and the Biological Passport that constitute this intensification and they are at the forefront of this experimentation. The two instruments also constitute the primary manner in which the space of surveillance is constructed. This space of surveillance not only locates and makes visible the physical location of each individual cyclist, it also, in turn, makes visible their internal bodily functions, in this case the composition and the fluctuations of the composition of their blood. The combination of the Whereabouts System and the Biological Passport thus makes the cyclist visible. These systems cannot, by themselves, cause the actual act of doping to be identified with any certainty; rather what they do, by casting the place of the body and the constitution of its blood in terms of abnormalities, is to suggest a probability that doping may have, in fact, occurred. Increasingly, this probability determines guilt.

Anti-Doping Offences

Within the academic literature on anti-doping there exists a high preponderance of psychological analysis that addresses the problem of doping as one of

---

[8] See, eg, L Kreft, 'The Elite Athlete: In a State of Exception?' (2009) 3(1) *Sport, Ethics and Philosophy* 3.
[9] PerthNow.2011 available at www.perthnow.com.au/news/nsw/dole-drug-tests-homeswest-reform-proposed-at-wa-liberal-conference-ng-5b1a8ff40c3570f1bf264654d8a961d6. These kinds of proposals continue to gain much wider acceptance.

moral reasoning.[10] According to the logic of moral reasoning, anti-doping targets misplaced motives framed as unacceptable morals and thus these authors assume that a doping offence is due to lack of knowledge, ignorance or unfairness on the part of the offender. Consistent with the individualisation of the problem, the anti-doping apparatus constructs the im/moral individual as the sole focus of attention and regulation. This is done despite the fact that in some cases the question of whether doping is not a moral but a technical question. For example, in the 2009 *Tour de France*, the US team *Garmin Slipstream* (widely regarded as a clean and ethical team) made extensive use of the drug pseudoephedrine (known internally as pseudo-bombs) which, at that time, was not banned in sport.[11] The following year, 2010, pseudoephedrine was again placed on the list of prohibited substances. Similarly, blood doping in its various forms is banned, while processes such as altitude training or methods that reproduce the same effect are not.[12] The question of its use was simply whether it was on a list of banned substances. This was a technical question, not an issue of morality.

As the global constitutive or framework document for the anti-doping apparatus, the WADC establishes two primary norms that may be transgressed by an athlete – the presence of a prohibited substance in their body and the use of a prohibited substance or method. The individualisation of the problem is clear from the text of the WADC and its embodiment of the principle of strict liability. Article 2.1 of the 2009 WADC establishes the offence (or ADRV) of the presence of a prohibited substance in a bodily sample taken from an athlete. The relevant parts of the article state that 'each athlete has duty to ensure no prohibited substance enters their body'. In order to make out the offence: '… it is not necessary to show intent, fault, negligence or knowing use on the part of the athlete, such that the (mere) presence of a prohibited substance is of itself sufficient proof'.

Furthermore, in most circumstances (other than certain specified substances), the presence of any quantity of the substance constitutes a violation. The strict liability principle has been criticised by some as being contrary to accepted principles of Law and human rights.[13] This was an issue in the Alberto Contador case which led the then President José Luis Rodríguez Zapatero to comment on the government's Twitter page, 'there's no legal reason to justify sanctioning Contador', a position supported by his opponent and successor, current President Mariano Rajoy, and by Angel Juanes, the President of *Audiencia Nacional* (the Spanish High Court)

---

[10] See, eg, T Long et al (2006). 'A Qualitative Study of Moral Reasoning of Young Elite Athletes' (2006) 20 *The Sport Psychologist* 330; and ID Boardley and M Kavussanu, 'The Moral Disengagement in Sport Scale-short' (2008) 26(14) *Journal of Sports Sciences* 1507–17.

[11] Hardie, Shilbury, Bozzi, Ware, unpublished research data.

[12] For example, hyperbaric chambers have been used by Australian Football Clubs, including the Essendon Football Club, in recent years as a legal form of blood doping.

[13] See RH McLaren, 'CAS Doping Jurisprudence: What can we Learn?' (2006) 1 *International Sports Law Review* 4; JE Coleman and JM Levine, 'The Burden of Proof in Endogenous Substance Cases: A Masking Agent for Junkscience' in McNamee and Møller (eds), *Doping and Anti-doping Policy in Sport: Ethical and Legal Perspectives* (Routledge, 2011).

who questioned the constitutionality of the strict liability principle, in so far as it removed the presumption of innocence.[14] Soek notes that although the burden of proof is on the prosecuting authority (the anti-doping or sporting organisation) to prove the offence, the practical effect of the strict liability principle is that the athlete appears prima facie guilty whenever a prohibited substance has been shown to be or has been present in their body.[15] The one exception to the strict liability principle, which in reality is not really an exception, as it does not excuse the offence but only mitigates any penalty, involves the situation where an athlete can show how a substance entered their body, that it was not intended to enhance performance, and that there was no fault or negligence on their part.[16] If an athlete is able to adduce corroborating evidence of these elements, to the standard of conformable satisfaction, any penalty can be reduced from the standard two years of ineligibility (ban) from competition.

Article 2.2 of the WADC establishes the ADRV of use or attempted use of prohibited substance or method. Accordingly, it is each athlete's personal duty to ensure that they do not use a prohibited substance or method. Once again, intent is neither a necessary element of the offence nor is whether an attempted use was carried through or was, in fact, successful. The provisions of Article 2.2 in effect create a wider 'catch-all' situation, allowing for cases to be proven where no substance has been detected in an athlete's bodily sample, or where there is evidence of an attempt to dope which itself has not been fully acted upon. Although Article 2.1 adopts the principle of strict liability, which it is argued is necessary in order to properly carry out the fight against doping, Article 2.2 requires evidence other than a positive test result, such as actual evidence of use, or, for example, other circumstantial evidence based upon the Biological Passport. This, as we will see, raises another set of difficulties in respect of proof. Already in the *Valverde* decisions, we have seen that such use, or attempted use, can be made out on highly contested, circumstantial or even tenuous pieces of evidence.

In respect of both provisions, the standard of proof to be met by the prosecuting authority is said to be that of comfortable satisfaction, something greater than the balance of probabilities used in civil cases, but generally not quite as high as the criminal standard of beyond reasonable doubt. The standard was adopted by the Court of Arbitration for Sport (CAS) from the jurisprudence of the Australian High Court and its decision in *Briginshaw v Briginshaw*.[17] We saw in *Valverde* how this standard may not be given its full effect and, importantly here, we will see how the manner in which scientific evidence is used in Biological Passport cases effectively lowers this apparently high standard of proof.

---

[14] 'Cronologia del "caso Alberto Contador"' *El Mundo* (2011) available at www.elmundo.es/elmundodeporte/2011/02/15/ciclismo/1297794357.html.
[15] J Soek, *The Strict Liability Principle and the Human Rights of Athletes in Doping Cases* (Asser Press, 2006) 41.
[16] Art 10 WADC. This is what gave rise to Contador's contaminated steak defence.
[17] *Briginshaw v Briginshaw* (1938) 60 CLR 336. A decision of the High Court of Australia.

However, the crucial point to be made here is that the WADC ultimately brings its disciplinary weight to bear upon the individual and their behaviour. As competition individualises everything, in the end it makes the individual ultimately responsible for their own actions and their own body. Dadot and Laval[18] highlight the individualisation of choice and fate in a neoliberal world when they speak of the manner in which the management of the self and management of the enterprise and all such practical exercises in self-transformation tend to transfer the whole burden of complexity and competition exclusively onto the individual. In neoliberalism, they argue, techniques of the self and techniques of choice merge completely. Once a subject is fully conscious and in control of his choices, he is also fully responsible for what happens to him, giving rise to an infinite responsibility of the individual for his own fate.[19] 'To be a personal enterprise assumes living entirely in risk'[20] whereby external causes and problems of the system are transformed into personal failure.[21] The WADC assumes that the individual is in a position to access the information required to make the correct choice and that, by establishing what it calls the Prohibited List[22] of substances and methods, what is facilitated is a transfer of risk to the person who chooses such that any decision correct or otherwise belongs entirely to the individual.[23] In the world of the war on the doper there is no such thing as society.[24] This is the logic that also informs the rejection of the Spanish *Puerto* case, and its focus on the dealers and distribution networks, in favour of a global hunting down of the cheats.

The WADC also operates in conjunction with five international technical standards issued by WADA. The stated aim of these standards is aimed at bringing harmonisation among anti-doping organisations in various technical areas, namely, the prohibited list, testing, laboratories, therapeutic use exemptions, and protection of privacy and personal information. WADA states that the standards have been the subject of lengthy consultation among WADA's stakeholders and are mandatory for all signatories of the Code. Given their mandatory status, the norms articulated in the standards seep into the decisions of both sporting and State anti-doping documents and decision making.[25] Any departure from the norm must be proven by an athlete on the balance of probabilities, but even when this is possible, certain provisions of the WADC, UCI Rules and, for example, the ASADA National Anti-Doping (NAD) Scheme, contain 'no invalidity' clauses that seek to ensure that departure from the norm does not invalidate any positive doping test

---

[18] P Dadot and C Laval, *The New Way of the World* (Verso Books, 2013) 272.

[19] ibid, 274.

[20] ibid, 275.

[21] ibid, 277.

[22] The Prohibited List and its 'catch all' provisions are notoriously difficult to interpret.

[23] Dadot and Laval, *The New Way of the World* (n 18) 278.

[24] R Butt, 'Margaret Thatcher: Interview for the Sunday Times – The First Two Years' *Sunday* Times (3 May 1981) available at www.margaretthatcher.org/document/104475.

[25] P Berman, 'From International Law to Law and Globalization' (2005) 43 *Columbia Journal of Transnational Law* 485, 510.

results.[26] Straubel argues that the WADA system is 'nearly incapable of addressing the inherent imbalance of power between athletes and their accusers'[27] and that under the current WADC an athlete must prove both a departure from the ISL and that the departure was likely to have caused the positive result constituting 'an exhibition of unchecked power'.[28]

Whereabouts Surveillance

Paul Dimeo[29] sets out in great detail the history of anti-doping and the development of the drug-testing regime in sport. For our purposes, what interests us is the transition that occurred in the late 1980s from purely in-competition anti-doping testing, that is testing that took place only at sports events, to unannounced out-of-competition testing, that is testing that could take place at any time and place outside of events.[30] The Whereabouts System was introduced ostensibly as a mechanism to improve the administration of out-of-competition doping tests. In cycling, the system is linked in its operation and purpose to the Biological Passport such that it is regarded as a necessary and complementary tool without which the Biological Passport would not be complete. Whereabouts is said to target out-of-competition testing by requiring individual athletes to state their physical location within set timeframes and, thus, make themselves available for the collection of both blood and urine samples. These tests, in turn, provide information for the Biological Passport, which itself contributes to the refinement and better targeting of such testing. It is because of this that the UCI regards the information gathered through the Whereabouts System as being imperative, in that it is said to enable anti-doping tests to be conducted anywhere in the world, at any time.[31] From 2008, the requirement to complete Whereabouts information was extended to include a large section of the professional cycling peloton. As such, all members of UCI professional teams and those in the Registered Testing Pools of their National Anti-Doping Agency (NADO) must provide online to the UCI or their NADO a schedule of their whereabouts. In doing so, riders are required to complete their Whereabouts information in advance and in quarterly blocks.

---

[26] See, eg, XZTT and Anti-Doping Rule Violation Panel (2012), AATA 728, available at www.austlii. edu.au/au/cases/cth/AATA/2012/728.html; and *Anti-Doping Rule Violation Panel v XZTT* [2013] FCAFC 95, available at www.austlii.edu.au/cgi-bin/sinodisp/au/cases/cth/FCAFC/2013/95.html?stem =0&synonyms=0&query=xztt.

[27] MS Straubel, 'Lessons from USADA v Jenkins: You Can't Win when you Beat a Monopoly' (2009) 10(1) *Pepperdine Dispute Resolution Law Journal* 119.

[28] ibid, 138.

[29] P Dimeo, *A History of Drug Use in Sport, 1876–1976: Beyond Good and Evil* (Routledge, 2007).

[30] B Houlihan, *Dying to Win: Doping in Sport and the Development of Anti-doping* (Council of Europe Publishing, 1999) 151.

[31] UCI, Whereabouts & location forms, 2008. Available at www.uci.ch/templates/UCI/UCI2/layout.asp?
MenuId=MTI1Njk.

The information provided by the athlete is intended to be strictly confidential and must only be used for the 'relevant purposes' and, once the three-month period has elapsed, the information must be destroyed. As the relevant purpose is the planning, coordinating and conducting of out-of-competition testing, the strict application of the rule would mean, for example, that after 30 March the information provided for the three months preceding is required to be destroyed as it is no longer relevant. Given the privacy concerns, one might expect these rules to be strictly interpreted – in a similar way that punitive or criminal provisions are always strictly interpreted so as not to impinge upon fundamental rights. However, Møller's work on Rasmussen shows that this rule has not always been followed. His analysis of Rasmussen's case illustrates that the requirement of confidentiality may be overridden by the arbitrary requirements of the Spectacle.[32] Despite Møller's objections, Rasmussen's expulsion would no doubt be justified by claiming that the fight against doping warrants such a breach even if confidentiality was expressly set out in the rules.

The provisions of the rules[33] relating to Whereabouts information require riders to provide the UCI, at a minimum, with a one-hour time slot each day where the cyclist guarantees to be available for an anti-doping test, their residential address for each day – that is, the place where they will be sleeping, their training schedule, their competition schedule and their travel schedule. The information must be provided for each day of the year and before the commencement of each quarterly period and it must be updated whenever the cyclist becomes aware of a change to their schedule. The required information is entered online by the cyclist into the Anti-Doping Administration and Management System (ADAMS). Interestingly and in a seemingly Orwellian manner, the US Anti Doping Agency considers the staff they employ to enforce the requirement to complete this information as one of the 'athlete services' they provide.

As set out above, Article 2 of the WADC details the provisions that deal with ADRVs. Pursuant to Article 2.4, a failure to provide proper Whereabouts information may constitute an ADRV. Under the provisions, any combination of three missed tests and/or filing failures within an 18-month period, as determined by anti-doping organisations with jurisdiction over the athlete, shall constitute an ADRV. The explanatory notes to the WADC go on to state that a failure to provide proper Whereabouts information may also constitute a breach of Articles 2.3 and 2.5 which deal with refusals and failures to submit to a test and tampering with an anti-doping control, respectively. Violations of, for example, Article 2.4 carry with them, pursuant to Article 10.3.3, a minimum of a one-year and a maximum of a two-year period of ineligibility (ban).

[32] Møller, *The Scapegoat* (n 1); V Møller, 'One Step Too Far – About WADA's Whereabouts Rule' (2011) 3(2) *International Journal of Sport, Policy and Politics* 177.
[33] UCI Regulations, Ch V of Pt 14, rules 81–119.

Mr. ADAMS by Pedro Horrillo

Mr. Adams entered my life at the same moment as we started the New Year, on January 1st, 2008. To tell the truth, I never approved of him, but he didn't seem to care: he had come to stay and was aware that I knew it. Also, he certainly knew that I could never reject him. Ours has been since then a relationship full of ups and downs – something predictable in any forced relationship- but keeping no secrets at all. I have always told him everything I have done, whom with, where, when, whenever I come and go … Of course it is not the case, but if by any chance it occurred to me, let alone lying to him – that would be really serious – but hiding something from him or telling him just a half-truth – it is the same for me – God help me if he ever finds out! Then I would be risking the whole family and their bread and butter. Mr. Adam's shadow is very long, extremely long.

So you'd better not take it to heart, as living with Adams is not easy at all. That's why we cyclists usually make jokes about the matter and mean to send a message to brother Adams when we think of going to the pictures, for instance. Of course you are free to go out without telling him, although in that case you'd rather pay attention to your mobile phone, select the silence mode and be ready to leave the cinema, may he happen to visit your house. To go to the pictures, for a walk with some friends, play with the kids in the park, have dinner in a restaurant, … in any situation you like you have to act the same way.

And now a year since our first encounter, in another turn of the screw, Mr. Adams makes me give him daily notice of the exact place and the time that I will be available for him.

If he turns up and I am not there, I will have a big problem, even if my absence is justified.

So that's how things stand. To begin with, I am of the opinion that random drug testing is one of the most effective ways to fight against fraud. Even though most of them are mere red blood cell extractions for the biological passport program and not doping tests, strictly speaking. But Adams' demands wear me out; they overwhelm and saturate me to the extent that sometimes, out of rebelliousness, I just provide him with the minimum necessary information.

What a rebellion! You might think. Still I can't nor should complain about it, as we, the cyclists have accepted taking part in that program and its consequences. And on the other hand, being a sportsperson, I have undertaken the same commitment with my team under contract.

The irony of fate! I started riding the bike because nothing else had ever given me such sense of freedom before. I carried on cycling, free as a bird, and eventually managed to make a living (of it). It is everybody's dream to be able to work in something you love. And all thanks to the bike. However, I have never felt so inhibited like now when it comes to make decisions. I am not free to improvise in my own life, to hesitate, to make hasty and last-minute plans. That is over, freedom is no longer there. Well … not exactly, some people say, you always have the option to get a computer, search for a connection and voilé! Adams is changed. Or even better, to send an SMS. For some people it is basically the same thing, but not for me. If you'll pardon the expression, I call this the being given the third degree.

So that is how it is and far from complaining, I chose to accept it. Given the choice between adapt or die, I prefer the first one, because I want to be a cyclist as long as possible, therefore, I won't pay heed to your attempts to put off my desire to continue, Mr. Adams.[34]

Panopticism? and the Internalisation of Control

Predictably, part of the liberal reaction to the Whereabouts System has been a critique of its impact on personal privacy and debates regarding whether it can be defended as a 'morally' valid system of surveillance. However, work with Australian professional cyclists has observed a tacit acceptance of the system as a necessary evil.[35] In that study it was observed that the Whereabouts System was widely considered as an imperfect, but still largely useful and moderately successful, deterrent and detection system for otherwise virtually undetectable doping methods. The following excerpt from the interviews conducted in that project suggest that the 'paperwork' involved in complying with the Whereabouts System is regarded by some to be of the same nature as other forms of regulation that one might need to comply with as a small businessperson or entrepreneur, that is, they are just facts of doing business:

> I have to do Whereabouts and I have to do this, things can always be better sure but it doesn't seem like it's that big a deal. I think any vocation you're going to have this paperwork to deal with and all this bullshit or licensing and stuff like that.[36]

Legal or ethical issues generally took second place to a pragmatic acceptance that Whereabouts was essential to a working anti-doping apparatus. One former cyclist commented that:

> It addresses a key method that people have used to avoid control, so I would have thought it is an eminently reasonable expectation if you have an anti-doping program because that is the way people have got around controls: not being there.[37]

---

[34] Adams: Antidoping Administration & Managing System. Translated by Martin Hardie, Original published in *El Pais* in Spanish. www.elpais.com/articulo/sociedad/senor/Adams/elpepisoc/20090210 elpepisoc_2/Tes.

[35] Hardie et al, I Wish I was Twenty One Now (n 3).

[36] Hardie, Shilbury, Bozzi and Ware 2010, unpublished interview.

[37] Hardie et al, I Wish I was Twenty One Now (n 3) 93.

What is clear from these interviews was that, even at their most negative, there wasn't any clear objection on what we might term ethical or moral grounds to the Whereabouts System itself. Even at its worst, the system was regarded as a necessary evil, and was generally rationalised by the interest in notions of rider health, fair play and, most importantly, the economic necessity of presenting a 'clean' sport. Most complaints arose initially at a technical level that may be understandable given that managing data on the daily movements of any given individual is a mammoth task.

Discussion of whether the system is 'morally justifiable' becomes more pressing when it is considered that three failures to comply result in an ADRV – that is a two-year ban from competition or, worse, it can mean the end of a contract, reputation and, in the end, a career. It is from this perspective that academic analysis has concentrated – the question as to how the regime is to be justified vis-à-vis an athlete's human rights or civil liberties. Below I consider two articles, both by leading anti-doping scholars, which have both discussed Foucault's concept of Panopticism in the context of the Whereabouts System. Hanstad and Loland were the first to consider this issue.[38] They used as their starting point Foucault's concepts of a surveillance regime. Later Moeller responded to their analysis.[39]

To start with, Hanstad and Loland accepted that the reactions of athletes to the system as a form of unacceptable surveillance seemed more cogent than criticisms based upon perceptions of justice.[40] How the two concerns – unacceptable surveillance and injustice – are so neatly separated was not made clear, but the authors concluded:

> We began by asking whether WADA's compulsory reporting system can be defended on moral grounds. Our answer is conditionally affirmative. The arguments against the WADA-system do not seem powerful enough to reject it. Everyday surveillance of individuals is far more extensive, it is concealed and also more problematic. The WADA requires active participation from the person being watched. Hence, the system does not seem to involve undue violation either on the principles of justice or on athletes' autonomy and right to self-determination.[41]

Hanstad and Loland's conclusions regarding the Whereabouts System seem to rest upon two propositions: that 'Everyday surveillance of individuals is far more extensive, it is concealed' and that the 'WADA requires active participation from the person being watched'. In their analysis of the system, the authors referred to the claims of some Norwegian athletes that Whereabouts constituted a 'Big Brother system', a perception they believed was 'strengthened by the system not only affecting the individual's life as an athlete, but also their whole lives'.[42]

---

[38] DV Hanstad and S Loland, 'Elite Athletes' Duty to Provide Information on Their Whereabouts: Justifiable Anti-doping Work or an Indefensible Surveillance Regime?' (2009) 9(1) *European Journal of Sport Science* 3.
[39] Møller, *The Scapegoat* (n 1); Møller, 'One Step Too Far' (n 32) 177.
[40] Hanstad and Loland, 'Elite Athletes' Duty' (n 38) 7.
[41] ibid, 9.
[42] ibid, 7.

Hanstad and Loland accepted that surveillance regimes have increased in scope and complexity and that the 'need to regulate can go too far'. In considering this aspect and in pursuit of striking a balance they turned to Foucault's work for a 'critical approach'.[43]

Their analysis commences with an acceptance of the proposition that Foucault's work on the Panopticon 'appears as a model for the development of Western society'.[44] They note Bentham's 'good intentions' in drawing up his plans for the model prison, and that Foucault points to opposite consequences: 'far more subtle, disciplining and "normalizing" processes that more effectively reduce the individuals opportunity for autonomy and right to self-determination'.[45] Interestingly, and possibly without fully grasping Foucault's point, they argue that, in light of the Norwegian population's reported lack of concern about the misuse of personal information, the claim of opposite consequences is a paradox.[46] Rather than being a paradox, the apparent acceptance of surveillance and the mis/use of personal information may, in fact, be one of the consequences of such regimes that Foucault himself suggested. That is, the docility of the population brought about by techniques of discipline results in them not being concerned, in their tacit acceptance of the fact that they are being observed and that the fruits of this observation may be used not only for their benefit but also contrary to it.

In the context of the prospective nature of the surveillance, Hanstad and Loland then note that unlike convicted criminals or others, who are controlled following their release from prison

> athletes have committed no crime or rule violation ... [having] to meet the demands of compulsory whereabouts reporting just because they might violate the rules ... is without doubt unusual.[47]

It is correct that the only other members of society subject to similar location surveillance and reporting appear to us to be persons serving jail sentences, such as home detention and convicted but released paedophiles. In the interviews done by Hardie, Shilbury, Bozzi and Ware, one participant commented on the situation as follows:

> Q: Do you think other people in society should be subjected to surveillance like athletes are?
>
> A: No.
>
> Q: No? So nobody should be subjected to that sort of surveillance?
>
> A: No. But I think we are, though.

---

[43] ibid, 8.
[44] ibid.
[45] ibid.
[46] ibid.
[47] ibid.

Q: We don't have to report. You know we might be with cameras and all that, but I don't need to report in. I don't even have to tell my boss where I am any more. But who are the other people who are subject to such a reporting scheme?

A: Criminals.

Q: Not even criminals. Just paedophiles who have been released.

A: Probationary people.

Q: Yeah. They've obviously got this one going.

A: It's like saying everyone's guilty before they've even done the thing.[48]

Another participant in that study commented:

Q: Who else in society do you think is subject to such a … ?

A: No one.

Q: Paedophiles?

A: Yeah, exactly, that's probably it, sex offenders … but I don't think theirs is as strictly watched as ours.

Q: No. It says something about your role in society, I think, yeah?

A: I guess so.[49]

Subjecting athletes to such measures of surveillance and location reporting, despite the fact that they have not actually violated any norm, is no doubt an exceptional measure within the bounds of what is perceived as a liberal democratic society.[50] If one turns to the original text of Foucault it is apparent that he considered this type of surveillance to be an aspect of the Panopticon that, in fact, perfects power, by allowing it:

to intervene at any moment and because the constant pressure acts even before the offences, mistakes or crimes have been committed … [in these conditions, its strength is that it never intervenes, it is exercised spontaneously and without noise, it constitutes a mechanism whose effects follow from one another].[51]

However, in their analysis, Hanstad and Loland either ignore or do not pick up on this normalising aspect of the Panopticon and its 'pre-crime'[52] operation. The authors then go on to point out what they consider two significant differences that distinguish Whereabouts from other forms of surveillance and which, in fact, tend

---

[48] Hardie et al, *I Wish I was Twenty One Now* (n 3) 102–03.

[49] ibid, 103.

[50] I Waddington, 'Surveillance and Control in Sport: A Sociologist Looks at the WADA Whereabouts System' (2010) 2(3) *International Journal of Sport Policy and Politics* 255.

[51] M Foucault, *Discipline and Punishment: The Birth of the Prison* (Vintage Books, 1991) 206.

[52] Pre-crime was the term used in the 2002 film Minority Report set in a future where a special police unit can arrest murderers before they commit their crimes.

to legitimise it. It is necessary to cite in full their proposition, as it deserves close analysis and comparison with the original text of Foucault:

> First, athletes themselves have to submit all the information about where they are, and second, violation of the regulations is followed by clearly defined consequences. This can hardly be described as a Big Brother-system where the athletes are being watched covertly. The whereabouts system is clearly detectable and open, and all athletes know the consequences of violation. There is a difference here between the criminal being electronically monitored as well, since athletes can withdraw from the surveillance. The point argued by, among others, Rune Andersen of the WADA, of sport as a voluntary practice in this fundamental *sense is a relevant one.*[53]

In essence, the differences between criminal surveillance and Whereabouts (which, it is argued, tend to legitimise the latter) rest upon four propositions. Firstly, sport and thus submission to the regime is voluntary or contractually based. Secondly, that the *surveillee* actively participates in the process (that is, by providing the necessary information and as a consequence of the first proposition voluntarily). Thirdly, surveillance is not covert but known (and because of the first and second propositions, accepted). Finally, the consequences of any violation are known and open. On this basis, the implicit position of Hanstad and Loland is that the Whereabouts System is not an example of the Panopticon and thus can be justified as 'morally' legitimate. Alternatively, at best, if it is an example of the Panopticon, the good intentions and beneficial nature of the system mitigate against its possible opposite consequences. The fight against doping of course warrants the internalisation of control. But the problem with this 'critical' analysis is, at its most basic, that their interpretation of Foucault's Panopticonic paradigm does not do justice to the original text.

We have accepted the proposition that sport is a voluntary activity and that submission to anti-doping rules is a matter of contract.[54] We have also sought to outline how private agreement tends to form an increasing part of the body of global law and that it increasingly underpins the general organisation of neoliberal society. Furthermore, even Foucault noted that although the disciplinary paradigm of the Panopticon was 'not under the immediate dependence or a great extension' of the juridico-political structures of a society, 'it is nonetheless not absolutely independent'.[55] The rhetoric of contract has, in fact, formed the 'ideal foundation of law and political power; Panopticism constituted the technique … of coercion'.[56] In these passages Foucault described the disciplines

---

[53] Hanstad and Loland, 'Elite Athletes' Duty' (n 38) 8.
[54] Reference was also made to this point in our work with Australian professional cyclists (Hardie et al, *I Wish I was Twenty One Now* (n 3) 61).
[55] Foucault, *Discipline and Punishment* (n 51) 221–22.
[56] ibid, 222. Note also on the coercive nature of contract, P Zumbansen, 'The Law of Society: Governance through Contract' (2007) 14 *Indiana Journal of Global Legal Studies* 191.

as both an 'infra-law' and 'counter-law' mechanisms that constituted the law but on a different scale creating

> between individuals a 'private' link, which is a relation of constraints entirely different from contractual obligation; the acceptance of a discipline may be underwritten by contract; the way in which it is imposed, the mechanisms it brings into play, the non-reversible subordination of one group of people by another, the surplus of power that is always fixed on the same side, the inequality of position of the different 'partners' in relation to the common regulation, all these distinguish the disciplinary link from the contractual link, and make it possible to distort the contractual link systematically from the moment it has the content of discipline. We know, for example how many real procedures undermine the legal fiction of the work contract: workshop discipline is not the least important.[57]

What better description is there of the manner in which the contract to voluntarily participate in sport is transformed into a disciplinary (or control) mechanism by the incorporation of the Whereabouts System? From a reading of the text we can see that it is, in fact, the voluntary nature of the acceptance of surveillance by contract, rather than distinguishing the Whereabouts System from the Panopticon paradigm, which supports the application of Foucault's model of power to it.

If it is accepted that what is at stake in anti-doping is fundamentally an administrative or policing activity, what we can begin to contemplate here is the instrumental manner in which discipline or control is, in fact, internalised by way of an agreement: that is, an agreed submission to be policed. In this respect, the privatisation of the police constitutes a form of the *publicisation of private life* in a manner that finds its analogue in the *privatisation of public life*. Thus, in this context, the privatisation of the police can be understood, not only as being constituted by the out-sourcing of, for example, policing activities to private security firms, but also as this process by which we consent, by way of a voluntary private agreement, to being surveilled by a transnational policing apparatus. In this situation it is our own individual consent that constitutes the privatisation of the police.

This brings us to the second factor by which Hanstad and Loland's distinguish Whereabouts from the Panopticon. Their argument was based on the fact that the *surveillee* actively participates in the process of their own surveillance by providing the necessary information that allows them to be observed. It is the corollary of the first, contractually based, voluntary proposition dealt with immediately above. To argue that a system is not disciplinary because individuals actively participate in a subtle process of surveillance and normalisation appears to miss the point of the Panopticon paradigm as a whole. Rather than being the paradox referred to by Hanstad and Loland above, the effect of the Panopticon is 'a far more subtle, disciplining and "normalizing" process' – a 'body is docile that may be subjected, used, transformed and improved'.[58] The docility and normalising process can only

---

[57] Foucault, *Discipline and Punishment* (n 51) 222–23.
[58] ibid, 136.

be magnified when discipline and control is internalised and when it becomes a part of a project undertaken by the athletes themselves. Within the Panopticon of Whereabouts, the athletes are 'caught up in a power situation of which they themselves are the bearers'.[59]

Without the athlete participating in the system the body is not normalised, which is the point of the whole operation – knowing that one is under surveillance is a key to its operation and one participates actively in this normalisation. The 'pain in the arse'[60] of continually providing and updating information to the computerised ADAMS system is one of the mechanisms by which the desired disciplinary effect is achieved. This, combined with the inability to know when the anti-doping controllers may arrive at one's door to undertake either a blood or urine test, manifestly reinforces the disciplinary effect. The athlete must always be on guard, to ensure that their whereabouts are reported fully and without any fault or mistake, always ready, at any time, for the tap on the shoulder or the knock on the door:

> He who is subjected to a field of visibility, and who knows it, assumes responsibility for the constraints of power; he makes them play spontaneously upon himself; he inscribes in himself the power relation in which he simultaneously plays both roles: he becomes the principle of his own subjection. By this very fact ... the more constant, profound and permanent are the effects ...[61]

Hanstad and Loland's third proposition, again a consequence of the first two, is that Whereabouts is not the Panopticon because the athlete knows that they are being watched. As can already be seen, the fact that surveillance is not covert severely misreads Foucault's paradigm. The point is not that surveillance is covert; it is the relationship between visibility and invisibility that is crucial. The observed in the Panopticon is fully aware that they are being observed; there is no covertness at play. The architecture of the paradigm is such that the observed is always actually or potentially visible to the observer. This visibility is the very trap of the Panopticon: 'the mechanism arranged spatial unities that make it possible to see constantly and to recognize immediately'.[62]

What, then, is the immediate purpose that is served by the Whereabouts System other than the ability to constantly see and recognise where an athlete is at a given time in order to undertake an anti-doping control. The athlete's daily activities, breakfast, stretching, the gym, shopping, training on open roads, visiting friends, going to a restaurant or the movies, sleeping, all become visible through their reporting of their whereabouts. The athlete does not see the controller until and when the controller wishes to be seen. But at the same time the athlete is always on the alert for the ever-present possibility of this occurrence. Hence, the cyclists complain that they provide a time when they are available to be seen, but the controller always seems to arrive at another time: 'He is seen, but he does not see;

---

[59] ibid, 201.
[60] Hardie et al, I Wish I was Twenty One Now (n 3) 94.
[61] Foucault, *Discipline and Punishment* (n 51) 202–03.
[62] ibid, 200.

he is the object of information, never a subject in communication.'[63] The athlete in the system knows this, and they know that failure on their part to be visible brings with it severe consequences. The invisibility of the anti-doping controller is the guarantee of order.[64] The fact that the system is not covert is, in fact, its very point. The major effect of the Panopticon is to induce 'a state of conscious and permanent visibility that assures the automatic functioning of power ... surveillance is permanent in its effects, even if it is discontinuous in its action'. It may well be that an athlete subject to Whereabouts is hardly ever, or perhaps never, tested as a result of their reporting their location, but it is this perfection of power that actually achieves and renders testing unnecessary in many cases. This perfection is brought about not by the system being covert, but by it being visible, by the athlete's active participation and by the time and place of the arrival of the controller being unverifiable ... never knowing when, but always knowing it is possible.[65]

It should be now apparent that a reading of Foucault's original text cannot support the propositions put forward by Hanstad and Loland. Equally, their fourth proposition, that the consequences of any violation are known and open, is similarly unsupportable on this basis. The inmates of the prison, the pupils of the school, the workers in the factory, all were more than aware of the punishment that might follow from their disobedience to the necessities of power. If openness is a criterion with which to distinguish the Whereabouts System from the Panopticon, the authors have forgotten that one great feature of the disciplinary mechanism is its 'democratic' nature, its openness constantly accessible 'to the great tribunal committee of the world'.[66] As should be remembered, it was this great tribunal of the Spectacle and not the application of the Law that convicted Michael Rasmussen.

The Panopticon as Paradigm

Verner Møller has sought to rebut the Hanstad and Loland analysis in support of Whereabouts himself by reference to the Panopticon. Møller's principal objection to the application of the Panopticon paradigm to the Whereabouts System is framed initially as a response to Hanstad and Loland's article discussed above. In an attempt to distance himself from them he deals with what he calls the 'Foucault *cul de sac*'[67] and, in turn, offers Orwell as a better theorist of the problem. Both these arguments are problematic. Firstly, his reading of Foucault, albeit for different reasons from Hanstad and Loland, appears to be equally flawed. While the Norwegians appeared to have set out to bolster the Whereabouts System, Møller clearly wants to demolish it. In doing so he takes issue

---

[63] ibid.
[64] ibid.
[65] ibid, 201.
[66] ibid, 207.
[67] Møller, 'One step too far' (n 32) 183.

with their reading of Foucault, but, on the way, he unfortunately also seems to miss the point. If he had approached Foucault with a more sympathetic or open mind, Møller could have demolished the Norwegian analysis with much greater rigour. Secondly, his favouring of Orwell, while interesting in that he foregoes his desired scientific reason to privilege literature, raises the question of resistance to power, only to champion a vague and ill-defined concept of human nature.[68] It is not Møller's use of Orwell but his misuse of Foucault that is relevant here.

Møller does not fall into the error of arguing that the mere fact of participating in and having knowledge of surveillance distinguishes Whereabouts from the Panopticon. Møller accepts Foucault's proposition that inmates in the jail are objects of information and that they feel as if they are under constant surveillance, without having the least idea whether, in reality, they are or not and it is this that causes the system to become a system of self-surveillance.[69] Thus, the criticisms I have made of the second and third of Hanstad and Loland's propositions do not apply to Møller. Nevertheless, he goes on to state that Foucault's idea is thought provoking but that his 'analysis does not match up to the impact it has had'.[70] The error in the use of Foucault, according to Møller, stems from the misapplication of Foucault's paradigm outside the realm of the prison:

> Many people today make use of Foucault without considering the range of his analysis. It might, therefore, be appropriate to remind ourselves that Foucault was focusing on inmates. He is primarily concerned with those who are locked up in prisons. It is true that he also mentions the sick, the mentally ill, workers and school children, but here, too, his point of departure is internment ...[71]

Hence, our first point of contention with Møller must be his narrowing of the Panopticon to merely apply to inmates in prisons or cases of internment. It is by virtue of this claim that Møller can go on to dismiss the relevance of Foucault. But in doing so, Møller commits the error he seeks to lay at the door of others – he doesn't consider the range of Foucault's analysis. It may be correct to point out that Foucault's point of departure was the prison, but this, of course, was neither the end of his journey, nor the range of his analysis. This is more than clear from a reading of the Panopticon text itself; of course, it would be even further illuminated if we were to proceed to consider the whole of Foucault's trajectory. From this claim, Møller then goes on to argue that the Panopticon does not have the normalising effects that Foucault suggested; it will be seen that this second claim stems from the error contained in the first.

Møller's error stems from the fact that he is unable to distinguish between the Panopticon as a jail and the Panopticon as an apparatus of rationality.[72] What is apparent from any fair reading of Foucault and from the plain text of

---

[68] ibid, 178–79.
[69] ibid, 183.
[70] ibid.
[71] ibid.
[72] Dadot and Laval, *The New Way of the World* (n 18) 316.

his chapter in *Discipline and Punishment* entitled 'Panopticism' is that what he is proposing is a model of power, a paradigm of power, 'a generalizable model of functioning'[73] which 'was destined to spread throughout the social body'.[74] Immediately before the paragraph that Møller cites – as proof that Foucault was only concerned with prisons – the Panopticon is described as a 'marvelous machine' which may be put to 'whatever use one may wish to put it to':[75]

... the Panopticon must not be understood as a dream building: it is a diagram of a mechanism of power reduced to its ideal form; its functioning, abstracted from any obstacle, resistance or friction, must be represented a pure architectural and optical system: it is in fact a figure of political technology that may and must be be detached from any specific use ... It is polyvalent in its applications ...[76]

Agamben has directly addressed the idea that what Foucault proposes is not one concrete example confined to the range of the prison, but a paradigm of power able to be applied in a variety of circumstances. This is plainly clear from the text of Foucault cited above. According to Agamben, the Panopticon functions as a paradigm in the strict sense

it is a singular object that, standing equally for all others of the same class defines the intelligibility of the group of which it is a part and which, at the same time, it constitutes. Anyone who has read Discipline and Punishment knows not only how the Panopticon, situated as it is at the end of the section on discipline, performs a decisive strategic function for the understanding of the disciplinary modality of power, but also becomes something like the epistemological figure that, in defining the disciplinary universe of modernity, also marks the threshold over which it passes into the societies of control.[77]

What concerns us, and what is ultimately at stake with the Whereabouts System, is both the disciplinary modality and the manner in which it marks, in combination with the Biological Passport, the threshold or passage from discipline to societies of control. The Panopticon is thus both a concrete, singular, historical phenomenon, and at the same time '*Panopticism*': a model of functioning which can be generalised, which allows the definition and establishment of new sets in the relationship between power and the everyday life of man:

To understand how a paradigm works, we first have to neutralize traditional philosophical oppositions such as universal and particular, general and individual, and even also form and content. The paradigm analogy is bipolar and not dichotomic, it is tensional and not oppositional. It produces a field of polar tensions which tend to form a zone of undecidability which neutralizes every rigid opposition. We don't have here a dichotomy, meaning two zones or elements clearly separated and distinguished by a caesura, we have a field where two opposite tensions run.[78]

---

[73] Foucault, *Discipline and Punishment* (n 51) 205.
[74] ibid, 207.
[75] ibid, 202.
[76] ibid, 205.
[77] G Agamben, *The Signature of All Things: On Method* (Zone Books,2009) 17.
[78] G Agamben, 'What is a Paradigm?', Lecture at European Graduate School (August 2002) available at www.egs.edu/faculty/giorgio-agamben/articles/what-is-a-paradigm/.

Contrary to what Agamben refers to as the tensional nature of this analysis – something inherent in the tensional concept of a Law-governance continuum – Møller criticises Foucault and the success of his ideas such as that of discipline normalising and creating docile bodies on the basis that they rest 'to a large extent on his tendency to take matters to extremes'.[79] It is an interesting criticism to be kept in mind when we turn to the manner in which Møller analyses the problem. Møller adopts a position at the other end of the binary spectrum to Foucault (and for that matter Hanstad and Loland). If Foucault says that discipline has a normalising effect, Møller 'disproves' it by showing that the opposite exists, and if the opposite exists, Foucault's claim is baseless. Taking things to the extreme, to the opposite binary position, avoids entering into the complexities of thought, and allows one to take refuge in the safety and comfort of their own personal or academic Chestnut Tree Café.[80] Just because people in jail might behave in a certain way as a result of surveillance, it does not mean people outside of jail will – for Møller this is proven by the fact that we still scratch our nose or crotch when under the gaze of close circuit cameras or even rob banks so equipped

> ... it will be natural for someone to test the power of the tower at some time. There might first be minor infringements of the existing order. If nothing happens, their audacity will increase just as when hungry birds test out a scarecrow.

For that same reason he [Foucault] needs to be read critically. If mankind were as capable of being moulded by a system as he describes, revolt and attempts to escape would be unthinkable once the architecture of the 'house of certainty' had been implemented.[81]

Later, referring to Orwell, Møller accepts that the description of Big Brother

> comes close to Foucault's view that the experience of permanent surveillance makes those subjected to surveillance internalize it. But surveillance as extensive as that which Smith is subjected to ought, according to Foucault, to result in resignation and subjection. Orwell's novel shows, however, that human beings respond in a different way. While it is true that they develop the ability to conform to given conditions in order to avoid punishment, the discomfort felt at the inhuman system stimulates resistance.[82]

Lest I mention the Chestnut Tree Café again? But Møller knows too well the story of one who has tested the power of Whereabouts System. His work on Michael Rasmussen's expulsion from the *Tour de France* for alleged violations of the system, rather than supporting the 'if nothing happens' option shows

---

[79] Møller, 'One Step Too Far' (n 32) 183.
[80] G Orwell, *Nineteen Eighty-Four* (Secker & Warburg, 1949): 'Under the spreading chestnut tree, I sold you and you sold me.' See also K Bowrey, *Law and Internet Cultures* (Cambridge University Press, 2005) 81: 'In Orwell's 1984, the Chestnut Tree Café is the haunt of free spirits – artists and musicians, members of the underground, outcasts, enemies, untouchables. It is a space for human contact and some sense of community, even though it co-exists within the strictures of the repressive state.'
[81] Møller, 'One Step Too Far' (n 32) 183.
[82] ibid.

precisely how attempts to test (to resist) the system are met.[83] They have not increased the audacity to challenge the system but, instead, brought Rasmussen to the very edge of his existence, as both an athlete and a living being. The justice of the manner in which Rasmussen was dealt with is the very point – his sacrifice reinforced the system, its operation, its acceptance by others and thus the deployment of power.

Making a scapegoat of the one who tested the system reinforces, rather than undermines, the system.

On another level, this statement by Møller also ignores the whole trajectory of Foucault's work on power and, in particular, his later work on forms of resistance to power and the importance to Foucault of the power/knowledge relationship. It is not possible here to deal with this aspect in detail; nevertheless, a reading of the original text can refute all the arguments of Møller, Hanstad and Loland. But, again, Møller takes the extreme binary position: because resistance may occur or be possible (despite the obvious consequences to Rasmussen and the effect on others of those consequences), the Panoptic model is of no value for our analysis. This claim – it is not an argument – is bolstered apparently by the proposition that surveillance itself does not do away with power!

> It is not, however, the surveillance itself that exerts the discipline, but the power that lies behind it. The panopticon does not, in other words, make power redundant.[84]

As is apparent from the above discussion, Foucault never argued that Panpoticism makes power redundant. Rather his position was that it is a mechanism, a technology for deploying and exercising power.[85] That is, the Panopticon does not operate to do away with power but rather to deploy it in more economical ways. For Møller, it is not the deployment of power that modifies and normalises but our own enlightened rationality:

> It is true that the cameras have a preventive effect. For obvious reasons, criminals will gravitate to areas where the risks of being discovered are smallest. If one bank has an effective surveillance system and another has not, then the bank robber will, other things being equal, plan to rob the latter. This is rational behaviour that has nothing to do with the disciplinary mechanism of anonymous surveillance.[86]

If this is 'rational behaviour' it is disingenuous to argue that the disciplinary system plays no part in it. This so-called 'rational behaviour' is, in fact, the very normalising effect of which Foucault speaks. In any event, the purpose of the disciplinary machine was never to be the universal panacea for crime. To argue that Panopticism does not end crime and is thus inapplicable to the situation again misreads the text. In their early forms, disciplinary institutions were

---

[83] Møller, *The Scapegoat* (n 1).
[84] Møller, 'One Step Too Far' (n 32) 183.
[85] Foucault, *Discipline and Punishment* (n 51) 206.
[86] Møller, 'One Step Too Far' (n 32) 184.

expected to end such dangers to society: 'to neutralize dangers, to fix useless or disturbed populations, to avoid the inconveniences of over-large assemblies …'.[87] Their focus and their deployment tended to play not a negative role, but a positive one – to increase the possible utility of individuals, to fortify, to develop the body: 'the disciplines function increasingly as techniques for making useful individuals. … Hence also their rooting in the most important, most central and most productive sectors of society'.[88] For every dissenting Rasmussen, one hundred normalised others are created.

The prevalence of mechanisms of surveillance, discipline and/or control within the anti-doping apparatus of sport is focused upon making the athletic body useful within the global Society of the Spectacle. To say this is to say that this productivity extends beyond the actual and singular body and its 'fitness' per se. It extends beyond the conditioning and disciplining of the physical body. In the society of competition, where governance extends beyond the producing the docile, it has an economic and governance function. In so doing, the effect of the disciplinary measure transcends the immediate effect upon one individual. At the point where disciplinary society and biopower converge, both the individual and the population, generally – and here specifically the sporting population – are the subjects of these technologies. Rasmussen's sacrifice may show that resistance or dissent exists[89] – that not everybody buys fully, with their heart and soul, into the system – but what these instances also show is that, overall, there is an increasing acceptance and 'improvement' of the individual and the population. The docile athlete, like the docile soldier, is a useful athlete – in fact what is being produced is a kind of docile activity, a certain kind of activity. Nevertheless, it is in this way that the Panopticon of Whereabouts plays a role of amplification – it arranges power, it makes power more economic and effective (to the point that in some cases their application is rarely or never needed). In so doing it strengthens the social forces involved in sport – increasing the production of the myth of fair competition on a level playing field, developing the virtue of the pure athlete, the economy and education. Neither power nor crime is made redundant; its aim is to 'raise the level of public morality; to increase and multiply'.[90]

On any fair reading of Foucault's text, it is clear that the Whereabouts System fulfils the triple objective of the Panopticon. Firstly, the cost–benefit objective – to obtain the exercise of power at the lowest possible cost; secondly, that of intensification and expansion – allowing the effects of power to obtain their maximum intensity and extension; and finally, the productive objective – of linking the techniques to economic growth.[91] But, most importantly, it organises and

---

[87] Foucault, *Discipline and Punishment* (n 51) 210.
[88] ibid, 210–11.
[89] Or, for that matter, the interviews in Hardie et al, *I Wish I was Twenty One Now* (n 3).
[90] Foucault, *Discipline and Punishment* (n 51) 207–08.
[91] ibid, 218.

fixes a population in the place that is necessary for it to be controlled – it is a centre of observation disseminated throughout the society in question,[92] it is an anti-nomadic technique[93] deployed against the nomadic athlete. The docility it contemplates is the consent of the useful; those who do not consent are no longer regarded as such and are thus expendable.

It is hoped that this examination of Foucault's text goes some way to showing that the paradigm of the Panopticon is a useful tool for the critical analysis of the Whereabouts System. It also is hoped that we are beginning to see the contours of the governance pole of the Law–governance continuum with a little more clarity. However, in order to properly locate the mechanism of Whereabouts within apparatus of global governance, it is necessary both to consider it along with the Biological Passport and to consider the manner in which Foucault and others have built upon and extended the Panopticon paradigm. For if Møller is correct about one thing, the Panopticon is not the be-all and end-all of the story; in the end, it is but one aspect of the apparatus.

Beyond Panopticism

Whatever the limitations of Møller's analysis of Whereabouts, what it does reveal is that a mechanical application of Foucault's primary text on the Panopticon does not give us the complete picture of the paradigm as it currently stands. Deleuze referred to the administration and management of life and extended Foucault's paradigm to include that of a control society.[94] According to Agamben, *oikonomia* included 'the ordered organization of the human body',[95] and '*oikonomia* does not merely concern the management of the house, but the soul itself'.[96] Hardt and Negri[97] and Lazzarato[98] refer to the manner in which worlds, lifestyles, and forms of life, are produced and governed in a global economy. Dicey referred to administrative law's concern with the care of social interests[99] or Neocleous as the regulation of the internal life of the community, the regimenting of social life, or the management and direction of the population.[100] All these concepts point in one way or another to the Panopticon paradigm's extension and crossing of the

---

[92] ibid, 212.

[93] ibid, 218.

[94] G Deleuze, 'Postscript on the Societies of Control' (1992) 59 *October* 3.

[95] G Agamben, *The Kingdom and the Glory, For a Theological Genealogy of Economy and Government* (Stanford University Press, 2011) 29.

[96] ibid, 47.

[97] M Hardt and A Negri, *Empire* (Harvard University Press, 1999); M Hardt and A Negri, *Commonwealth* (Harvard University Press, 2009).

[98] M Lazzarato, 'From Capital-labour to Capital-life' (2004) 4(3) *Ephemera* 187.

[99] AV Dicey, *Introduction to the Study of the Law of the Constitution* (Macmillan and Co Limited, 1920) 328–29.

[100] M Neocleous, *Fabrication of Social Order: A Critical Theory of Police Power* (Pluto Press, 2000) 93.

threshold to a world of governance. They are all, in one way or another, relevant to any contemporary application of the Panopticon paradigm. I don't want to dwell on the detail of these concepts, nor an in-depth analysis of what they have in common or what differentiates them, but a cursory examination points to their relationship to the Panopticon and their relevance to the Whereabouts System.

Michel Foucault dubbed the involvement of State power into the health and wellbeing of the population, 'biopower'. Biopower is one of the concepts by which Foucault extended the range of his Panopticon paradigm. His aim, in part, was by relating it to other forms of governance to show the manner in which these different forms coexisted with each other in different mixtures and concentrations at any given juncture. He did not try to place a wall between Law and discipline, or any of these other concepts in order to essentialise them, just as one cannot attempt to place a wall between his development of the concept of biopower, for example, and his work on the disciplines. Nevertheless, in considering what they term an anthropology of neoliberal man and the apparatus of government, Dadot and Laval point out that the very concept of government – acting on the actions of individuals who are supposedly free to choose – makes it possible to redefine discipline as a technique of government peculiar to market societies.

> The term discipline may be a cause for surprise here. It implies, seemingly at any rate, a certain real orientation vis-à-vis the meaning given to given it by Foucault … For Foucault, the model of discipline was Bentham's panopticon. However, far from contrasting discipline, normalisation and control, … Foucault's reflections more and more clearly reveal the matrix of this new form of conduct of conducts, which can vary, depending on the case under construction, from imprisoning prisoners to monitoring the quality of products sold on the market. If to govern is to structure the potential field of action of others, discipline can be redefined more widely as a set of techniques structuring the field of action, which differ depending on the situation in which individuals find themselves.[101]

Biopower, for Foucault, was the situation where life becomes the object of power and in which what is at stake in power is the production and reproduction of life itself.[102] Having conceived of biopower as having come into prominence during the nineteenth century (a position which Agamben has sought to refine with his work on, for example, *Homo Sacer* and *oikonomia*) Foucault identified two interrelated strands; the development of specific technologies of the body and the politicising of the body as a reproductive force.[103] The shift to biopower signalled a transition in the nature of sovereignty from its classical form – where one of the basic

---

[101] Dadot and Laval, *The New Way of the World* (n 18) 168–70.

[102] It is useful also to note here Arrighi's notion that the 'highest form of capitalism' or at least the one currently in formation (which he points to China as an example) seeks to internalise all the costs and processes of the reproduction of human beings: see G Arrighi, *The Long Twentieth Century: Money, Power and the Origins of our Times* (Verso, 2010).

[103] D Andrews, 'Desperately seeking Michel: Foucault's Genealogy, the Body, and Critical Sport Sociology'(1993) 10(2) *Sociology of Sport Journal* 148, 157–58.

attributes of the sovereign was the power over the life and death of his subjects (the right of the sword) – towards a new form in the nineteenth century whereby power became the right to let live and to let die. This shift saw the emergence of techniques of power that were essentially centred on the body. These emerging techniques included those to take control of the body or bodies, and to increase their productive force. Jason Read expands Foucault's observation that biopower was an indispensable element in the development of capitalism in the manner that it required the controlled insertion of bodies into the machinery of production and the population's adjustment to the processes of the economy:

> What is essential for Foucault is the manner in which the investment of the State into the life and death of the population, the environmental conditions of the cities, and the health and longevity of the working class in each case is a properly political relation forming a biopolitics. In each instance the goals of the intervention are political: Biopolitics functions to increase productivity while at the same time reducing the conditions and causes for revolt. Thus, it is more accurate to say that biopolitics works for both economic and political goals, or better, it is constituted at the point at which political power becomes inseparable from economic power.[104]

Read's observations will assume a greater relevance as we turn to consider in more detail the society of competition; nonetheless, in its emergent forms in the eighteenth and nineteenth centuries the techniques of biopower involve emergent fields and concepts such as the work of early demographers, the concept of public health, the medicalisation of society, insurance, risk management and the control of the human milieu and environment brought together in an economically rational way. This is the whole project of the taming of chance.[105] Biopower initially determines its field of intervention in this period in terms of birth rates, morbidity, various biological disabilities and the effects of the environment. What is important or different from what came before is that intervention is at the population level.

Biopower focuses upon the population as a 'political problem ... that is at once scientific and political, as a biological problem and as power's problem'. The control of life is a task and a technique of the administration and management of 'collective phenomena with economic and political effects that have become pertinent at a mass level'.[106] The techniques of forecasting, of statistical estimates and overall measures differ from the technique of discipline as they seek to intervene at the level of generality. They appear as regulatory mechanisms that seek to maintain a balance and compensate for variations within the population. They also, as part of this tendency to intervention, require security mechanisms designed to maximise and extract forces from the population. In a manner different to discipline, they no longer train the individual at the level of the individual body but take control

---

[104] J Read, *The Micro-Politics of Capital: Marx and the Prehistory of the Present* (State University of New York Press, 2003) 141.

[105] I Hacking, *The Taming of Chance* (Cambridge University Press, 1990).

[106] M Foucault, *The Birth of Biopolitics, Lectures at the College of France, 1978–1979* (Palgrave MacMillan, 2008) 245–47.

of life and the biological processes of man-as-species and of ensuring that they are not necessarily disciplined but regularised.[107]

In the case of the Whereabouts System we can say that it operates at the level of the individual body but, at the same time, it operates at the level of the entire population of athletes. This is what Møller fails to recognise in his critique of Foucault's so called *cul de sac* – the manner in which the System produces a regularisation or normalisation of the professional cycling population, even though at the same time it might produce instances of resistance or dissent. No matter that some may try to beat the system, the overall effect, at a population level, is one of compliance, docility and as such an increase in their productive force.

Biopower's regulatory controls encompass a vast array of collective measures undertaken to regulate the population. The disciplines constitute their own concrete form of domination and means of integration to the social order. Disciplines are, in effect, techniques of power that provide procedures for training and for coercing bodies. In this way we can consider the emerging nineteenth-century science of physical education as both a disciplinary and as a biopolitical technique. Physical education provides a set of teaching methods, principles, and conditions through which a desired set of (individual) bodily practices are inculcated. At the same time, the overall effect of physical education and its promotion acts at a population level. Thus, it operates at the interstices between individual (disciplinary) and collective (biopolitical or administrative) controls of the body and serves both sets of interest. Therefore, it should be of no surprise that Foucault regarded 'medical science as the crucial link at the level of knowledge between the discipline of the individual bodies by professional groups and the regulation of populations by panopticism'.[108] In the case of sport and physical activity, the profession of physical education, human movement and later sports science and marketing themselves accomplish the function of knowledge generation.

Thus, discipline and regularisation are not mutually exclusive, the latter does not replace the former, but the two are superimposed upon each other with one technology focusing upon the body, the other upon life itself. The two can be and are articulated with each other; as Deleuze might say there are no pure machines … all machines exists and coexist at any given time. In his work Foucault gives the examples of housing estates for workers and the question of sexuality to illustrate this articulation. It is the example of sexuality that gives us something close to what is at issue in sport – or at least that which provides us with a starting point to consider the manner in which sport becomes an object of power, of science, medicine and the State. Foucault asks: why did sexuality become a field of such vital strategic importance in the nineteenth century? We could similarly ask why has the sporting body and the problematisation of doping become of such strategic importance in the twenty-first century? Foucault's answer to his own question

---

[107] ibid.
[108] BS Turner, *The Body and Society* (Basil Blackwell, 1984) 33–35.

includes a whole host of reasons, and it is here that we can see, or at least begin to develop, the parallels between the sexual body and the sporting body. In the nineteenth century we are told that sexuality, as an 'eminently corporeal mode of behaviour, is a matter for individualizing disciplinary controls that take the form of permanent surveillance'. Sexuality also, quite obviously, has procreative effects – it is 'inscribed, takes effect, in broad biological processes that concern not the bodies of individuals but the element, the multiple unity of the population. Sexuality exists at the point where body and population meet. And so it is a matter for discipline, but also a matter for regularization'.[109] Dadot and Laval expand upon this when they discuss both sport and sexuality in the context of neoliberalism's methods of accounting and performance, noting that in the instance of sexuality and the 'vast psychological discourse that analyses them, encourages them and surrounds them with every advice of every kind today, sexual practices become exercises in which everyone is encouraged to compare themselves with the socially requisite norm of performance'.[110]

It is within this context that biopower's links with scientific knowledge begin to contribute to the tendency towards the medicalisation of society. Stepping back from Foucault for a moment we see a similar situation emerging in the nineteenth century in relation to sport and its medicalisation. Hoberman's accounts of the history of doping – of the systematic production of 'mortal engines';[111] can be read as a part of the chronicle of biopower taking the sporting body and in turn the entire population as its object. Whether the object of the production of mortal engines was for sporting, or for other wider purposes, what is clear is that the new sciences of modernity – physiology, anatomy, economy etc.; all used the sporting body to one degree or another as a testing laboratory for knowledge pertinent to the broader population. More recently, the French sociologist Christophe Brissoneau[112] has considered the confluence of the American system of management and doping developed in the late twentieth century with the Soviet Bloc's methods of sports training and preparation (including doping) which form the basis of contemporary sports science and management.[113] He has highlighted the manner in which the coming together of these two models was adopted by sports physicians in the West as the basis of a new method of managing and preparing the athlete. Importantly, in Brissoneau's analysis, these techniques did not stand alone in the world of sport but were inextricably linked to questions of productivity and endurance in other sectors of production – including, for example, the economy, industry, the military and space exploration. Hence, it should be of no real surprise

---

[109] Foucault, *The Birth of Biopolitics* (n 106) 249–52.
[110] Dadot and Laval, *The New Way of the World* (n 18) 281.
[111] J Hoberman, *Mortal Engines: The Science of Performance and the Dehumanization of Sport* (The Free Press, 1992).
[112] C Brissoneau, 'Doping in France (1960–2000): American And Eastern Bloc Influences' (2010) 27(2) *Journal of Physical Education and Sport* 33.
[113] Brissoneau's example is that of the entry into cycling of the French entrepreneur Bernard Tapie.

when we discover that the origins of what we now call blood doping, the very techniques that the Biological Passport was designed to tackle, have their roots in the experimentation by the US Military on dogs in the 1970s.[114] Similarly, as Agamben recalls in *Remnants of Auschwitz*, the experimentation by SS doctors on the Muselmann, which in itself suggests the link between the military and experimentation with endurance as having equally sinister roots:

> It was December, 1940 ... After a few minutes, we were all shivering from the cold; they made us run around the room to heat ourselves up, until we were all covered in sweat. Then they said, "Sit Down", and we did as they said. Once our bodies had cooled down, and we were once again cold, it was time for more running – and so it lasted for the whole day.[115]

Biopower is one manner in which Foucault asked himself the question concerning the trajectory of disciplinary societies and the development of complementary mechanisms or apparatus. In his *Postscript on Societies of Control*, Deleuze identified himself as continuing Foucault's brilliant analysis of the use of enclosures to compose productive forces. Deleuze highlighted Foucault's recognition of 'the transience of this model' and that 'in their turn the disciplines underwent a crisis to the benefit of new forces'. Deleuze adopted 'Control', the name proposed by Burroughs 'as a term for the new monster, one that Foucault recognizes as our immediate future'. Citing Virilio, Deleuze noted that ultrarapid forms of free-floating control had replaced the old disciplines.[116]

In another work Deleuze wrote:

> A control is not a discipline. In making highways, for example, you don't enclose people but instead multiply the means of control. I am not saying that this is the highway's exclusive purpose, but that people can drive infinitely and "freely" without being confined yet while still being perfectly controlled. This is our future.[117]

This is our future, to be able to move freely while still being perfectly controlled. 'Controlled' in one sense denotes having to pass through gates or follow certain paths. Referring to an imagined city of Felix Guattari, Deleuze stated that in control societies 'what counts is not the barrier but the computer that tracks each person's position – licit or illicit – and effects a universal modulation'.[118] A control tends to pilot behaviour. A control is both a method of individual discipline but a normalising and regulatory instrument. A control is also the word used to describe the

---

[114] DH Horstman et al, 'Effects of Hemoglobin Reduction on VO2 Max and Related Hemodynamics in Exercising Dogs' (1974) 37(1) *Journal of Applied Physiology* 97; and DH Horstman, M Gleser and J Delehunt, 1976. 'Effects of Altering O2 Delivery on VO2 Ofisolated, Working Muscle' (1976) 230(2) *American Journal of Physiology* 327.
[115] G Agamben, *Remnants of Auschwitz: The Witness and the Archive* (Zone Books, 2002) 170.
[116] Deleuze, 'Postscript on the Societies of Control' (n 94) 3–4.
[117] G Deleuze, Gilles, 'Having an Idea in Cinema', trans E Kaufman, G Deleuze in E Kaufman and KJ Heller (eds), *New Mappings in Politics, Philosophy and Culture* (University of Minnesota Press, 1998) 18.
[118] Deleuze, 'Postscript on the Societies of Control' (n 94) 7.

process by which athletes are tested within the anti-doping apparatus – athletes must pass anti-doping controls. Anti-doping controls form the basis of the Biological Passport. At the same time, being subjected to the Whereabouts System controls the fluid and nomadic population of the professional cycling peloton. The peloton and its members are essentially free to move about, to train and race and to live their lives subject to the piloting and control of the anti-doping apparatus. In the case of the anti-doping apparatus power and subjective freedom are no longer counter posed, the art of governing consists not in transforming a subject into a mere passive object but in leading the cyclist to do what he agrees to want to do[119]

> ... to govern is not to govern against liberty, or despite it; it is to govern through liberty: that is, to actively exploit the freedom allowed individuals so that they end up conforming to certain norms of their own accord.[120]

Biopolitical Passports

The Whereabouts System does not stand alone but is integrated into another instrument – the Biological Passport – which extends the scope and purpose of anti-doping controls. The Biological Passport is, by its very nature, technical and scientific and its method of surveillance and monitoring is probably more far reaching than the Whereabouts System. Rather than just monitoring where a particular body is at a given time, the Passport seeks to actually enter the body and measure processes occurring within them. Importantly, by its very nature, it also challenges traditional concepts of legal proof. Just as the disciplines depended upon and modified the operation of sovereignty and the law, the Biological Passport adapts and modifies both the nature of Panopticism and the law. By going back to Deleuze we can begin to grasp the manner in which the Biological Passport manifests the crisis of law itself:

> The apparent acquittal of the disciplinary societies (between two incarcerations); and the limitless postponements of the societies of control (in continuous variation) are two very different modes of juridicial life, and if our law is hesitant, itself in crisis, it's because we are leaving one in order to enter the other. The disciplinary societies have two poles: the signature that designates the individual, and the number or administrative numeration that indicates his or her position within a mass. This is because the disciplines never saw any incompatibility between these two, and because at the same time power individualizes and masses together, that is, constitutes those over whom it exercises power into a body and molds the individuality of each member of that body ... In the societies of control, on the other hand, what is important is no longer either a

---

[119] Dadot and Laval, *The New Way of the World* (n 18) 282.
[120] ibid, 5.

signature or a number, but a code: the code is a password, while on the other hand disciplinary societies are regulated by watchwords (as much from the point of view of integration as from that of resistance). The numerical language of control is made of codes that mark access to information or reject it.[121]

As we have noted above, the rationale for such an extensive surveillance regime as the Whereabouts System is to plan and conduct out-of-competition testing. The results obtained from out-of-competition testing have, in turn, provided the basis for what is known formally as the Athlete's Biological Passport. The Passport has been heralded by the UCI as a major breakthrough and the avant-garde of anti-doping policy.[122] The Panoptic nature of the Whereabouts System should not be considered in isolation, as the full picture cannot be drawn without reference to the Biological Passport. According to the UCI, the Biological Passport is a new tool that will allow better detection of the cheats.[123] Although the two instruments are different, they stand or fall together. The UCI has stated that the provision of accurate and timely Whereabouts information is critical to the success of the Biological Passport.[124] It is used to plan out-of-competition testing which serves to collect data for the Biological Passport. One function of the Biological Passport is to allow those planning the testing to better target those they suspect of doping. As one interviewee with experience in developing the Passport has stated

> … the other thing is, if they see abnormal blood results and it's not abnormal enough that they think they can sanction or even take further steps, at least they can really be on top of them. They can test the hell out of them, they can scare them – they can scare them into awareness or into action or be, you know, make their teams aware and they will be caught, that's the thing. Sooner or later, if that conscience is not there and they're not aware of what they're doing, they won't get away with it forever. We've seen riders like that in the last couple of *years*.[125]

It is of vital importance to emphasise that the Biological Passport is not used to detect the presence or absence of a Prohibited Substance or a Prohibited Method. Rather, it is used to detect the effects associated with the Prohibited Substance or Method on the human body. The logic of the approach is that if effects associated with a Prohibited Method are observable in a tested person, then perhaps that person might have been using the Prohibited Method. Equally, it must be stressed that the Biological Passport only points to a probability that a person might have been using the method. It is only a tool for the indirect detection of a Prohibited Method, as no banned substance is revealed nor is any direct evidence of the use of a Prohibited Method revealed. All the science seeks and is able to compare are

---

[121] Deleuze, 'Postscript on the Societies of Control' (n 94) 5.
[122] UCI, Information on the Biological Passport (2007) available at www.uci.ch/Modules/ENews/ ENewsDetails.asp?MenuId=&id=NTQzOA&LangId=1.
[123] ibid.
[124] ibid.
[125] Hardie et al, *I Wish I was Twenty One Now* (n 3) 115.

the parameters of a test sample, with previous samples, to identify any 'abnormal' fluctuations in an athlete's blood values. These 'abnormalities' may, in turn, indicate a probability that a person may have been using the Method. The science and the Passport cannot say with any absolute certainty what caused the 'abnormality'. The matter of these abnormalities is not a question of strict liability as with a positive doping test result, but the use and the privileging of one piece of indirect circumstantial evidence consisting of an interpretive opinion which challenges traditional notions of legal proof.

The Biological Passport is an individual, electronic record maintained for each athlete, in which the results of all doping tests over a period of time are collated in the ADAMS system. The results are analysed using the Athlete's Biological Passport Software (ABP Software), developed by the Swiss Laboratory for Doping Analyses. The ABP Software produces a quantitative stream of data that is, in turn, used by the UCI Biological Passport Expert Panel to determine the likelihood of doping. The Biological Passport contains results of individual urine tests, results of individual blood tests, a haematological profile consisting of the combined results of haematological parameters analysed in a series of blood samples, and a steroid profile consisting of the combined results of steroid levels in a series of urine samples. The Biological Passport allows a series of tests from each rider to be organised into a profile which enables individual limits for each rider to be established. Rather than a comparison with a population limit, it allows each test sample to be compared with the rider's own individual 'normal' haematological levels.

The UCI states that any significant variations can then be assessed for possible blood manipulation and argues that a haematological profile created by the Biological Passport 'opens new doors in the detection of riders who choose to manipulate their blood'. Importantly, the UCI regards the Biological Passport as applying 'similar principles to those used in forensic medical science to determine the likelihood of guilt'.[126] The veracity of this claim has been questioned[127] and is important as it points to the manner in which the law is transformed by the use of the Passport. Nevertheless, the procedure adopted is that once:

> sufficient evidence is gathered which determines guilt at an agreed level of certainty, scientific experts will recommend that the UCI open disciplinary proceedings for an anti-doping rule violation. It is expected that a profile of six tests will enable the detection of blood manipulation. In some cases, a fewer number of tests may be needed to detect doping.[128]

The penalty prescribed for such a violation is a ban from competition for two years. The accuracy of an inference that a person has used a prohibited substance and the role of the scientific experts in giving evidence before any disciplinary

---

[126] UCI, Information on the Biological Passport (n 122).
[127] Hardie et al, *I Wish I was Twenty One Now* (n 3) 120ff.
[128] ibid, 116.

committee become crucial steps in the process of proof. Again, it must be stressed that the Biological Passport is only an isolated piece of material evidence, namely a piece of processed instrumental data and that, ultimately, an allegation of doping or manipulation is based only on this indirect and circumstantial evidence (measured blood parameters) as opposed to direct expert evidence (detection of a prohibited substance in a blood or urine sample; which is at Law only itself a form of circumstantial evidence). Any opinion in interpreting the instrumental data is, by necessity, heavily reliant on statistics.[129]

Trust the Science

The result is that prior to any hearing, the science and expert commentary is determinative at two points – when the ABP Software analysis is undertaken and when the Expert Panel conducts its review of the Biological Passport data. At the point at which the UCI may have a discretion to open a case (following the receipt of the Panel's opinion) the science would also seem to effectively determine the issue. In its promotion of the Passport, the UCI made public statements to the effect that the national cycling federations have to trust the science provided by the Expert Panel. Traditionally, the Law requires scientific evidence to be of a certain standard and that it should be presented in a certain manner in order to safeguard the fairness of any hearing process. Thus, in judicial processes, scientific evidence should be communicated in such a manner as to allow the ultimate decision maker to be able to weigh it against all the other evidence, including other scientific evidence that goes to its reliability. However, the UCI has insisted on the need for national cycling federations to trust the science that lay behind the Biological Passport. The role of the expert in interpreting data produced by the ABP Software and the Biological Passport itself can be readily contrasted with that insisted upon by judicial processes:

> Our rules advise them [the federations] to follow a number of steps. Obviously, these will be new and difficult cases for them and we've offered them any assistance they want. They also have access to our scientific experts and data. What we're expecting them to understand is that we have the best experts in the world and that they've reviewed the data properly. The federations have to trust the review that has been conducted by our experts. Normally, we give them a piece of paper from the lab that says, we've found EPO or Nandralone, but instead we're giving them a statement signed by three experts with data and rider profiles. We expect them to trust us.[130]

---

[129] N Faber and B Vandeginste, 'Flawed Science "Legalized" in the Fight against Doping: The Example of the Biological Passport' (2010) 15(6) *Accreditation and Quality Assurance* 373. PE Sottas, N Robinson and M Saugy, 'The Athlete's Biological Passport and Indirect Markers of Blood Doping, Doping in Sports: Biochemical Principles, Effects and Analysis' (2010) 195 *Handbook of Experimental Pharmacology* 305. Again, these issues were canvassed by Hardie et al, *I Wish I was Twenty One Now* (n 3) 138ff.

[130] D Benson, 'Exclusive: Anne Gripper breaks silence on blood passport'. *Cyclingnews* (2009) available at www.cyclingnews.com/features/exclusive-anne-gripper-breaks-silence-on-bloodpassport.

The Biological Passport does not involve a positive test for a banned substance. The national federations (or NADOs or ultimately the CAS), who in the end must make a decision in respect of any finding of the UCI, are asked to trust the science as proof of doping.

> ... you can't expect the National Federation to be able to unravel what led to that deci-
> sion. It's not as simple as – well, that value's that, that's there and this here, therefore
> that's doping. You can't easily reverse engineer how you got to that decision. So, in that
> sense you've got to trust that we've been through this process, that was our decision,
> but if you've got another argument, you get an opportunity to challenge our opinion.[131]

Thus, given the nature of the data, the science and the expert commentary, the decision to make visible the alleged act of doping is an expert's opinion incapable of being communicated in a way that can be unravelled by reverse engineering. Notwithstanding the way it is expressed, the decision of the Expert Panel is no more than an opinion, and an opinion as to likelihood of doping, but nevertheless, at this point in the process, it takes on a decisive character.

The Expert Panel's recommendation is couched in terms of the likelihood that the cyclist in question has doped – that is, as a determination 'as to the likelihood of guilt'. The opinion of the Expert Panel states that there is no reasonable explanation of the blood profile other than the use of a Prohibited Method. It may be given, based on the preliminary nature of the opinion at this stage, that there is not a problem with statements 'as to the likelihood of guilt' by the Expert Panel. Statements phrased in terms of the 'likelihood of guilt' are not consistent with the principles of those 'used in forensic medical science to determine the likelihood of guilt'.[132] Forensic medical science in traditional Legal processes does not determine 'the likelihood of guilt'. Evidence based upon forensic science in Judicial proceedings must be set out in a particular way so as to guard against the expert's opinion usurping the role of the decision maker. It must comply with the rules of evidence. The Biological Passport cases decided by the CAS have sought to rely upon Article 3.2 of the WADC (Methods of Establishing Facts and Presumptions) that states '[f]acts related to anti-doping rule violations may be established by any reliable means'. The explanatory note to that Article states that, for example, a NADO may establish an anti-doping rule violation based on 'conclusions drawn from the profile of a series of the Athlete's blood or urine Samples'. Similarly, the comments to Article 2.2 state that:

> [i]t has always been the case that Use or Attempted Use of a Prohibited Substance or
> Prohibited Method may be established by any reliable means" and continue that these
> include conclusions drawn from longitudinal profiling, or other analytical informa-
> tion which does not otherwise satisfy all the requirements to establish "Presence" of a
> Prohibited Substance under Article 2.1.

---

[131] Hardie et al, *I Wish I was Twenty One Now* (n 3) 120.
[132] UCI, Information on the Biological Passport (n 122).

The WADC appears to studiously not refer to or use the word 'evidence' in its provisions on the proof of doping. However, both the claims of the UCI and Dr Sottas point to a comparison with the traditional methods of proving facts by the use of forensic or scientific evidence. The problem with the reasoning of the CAS in these cases is that the reference to 'any reliable means' appears to widen the scope of the method of proof beyond that which would be required for that means to constitute evidence in the Legal or Judicial sense.[133] If one trusts the science and ignores traditional methods of proving facts by forensic science the phrase 'any reliable means' appears to be able to roam at large.

The point here is that the reception of scientific evidence and, in particular, evidence which interprets data based upon types of statistical evidence, such as that which underpins the Biological Passport, has been strictly controlled by the courts in order to ensure that any Legal process is conducted fairly and without prejudice to the accused. The courts are also vigilant to ensure that the 'experts' do not usurp their position as the decision maker. From an examination of the Law, it is apparent that if the opinion of the expert in a Biological Passport case is phrased in terms of the 'likelihood of guilt' then it is *not* used in accordance with the principles applied to the reception of forensic medical science by courts. In fact, the manner in which evidence of the Passport is presented is in contradiction to those principles. If this is the case, the expert's opinion would be inadmissible as reliable evidence. Its basis as a reliable means of proof in the context of a court must, therefore, be questioned. Redmayne clearly states the distinction between the permissible and impermissible manner of giving expert opinion:

> The expert's error lay in confusing two different questions, namely: (1) What is the probability of finding the evidence, given that the defendant is innocent? (2) What is the probability that the defendant is innocent, given the evidence? The difference between the two questions may not be immediately obvious, but it should become clear when two different questions which have the same logical structure are considered: (1) What is the probability that an animal has four legs, given that it is a cow? (2) What is the probability that an animal is a cow, given that it has four legs?'[134]

The difference between the two ways of framing the evidence of the expert's opinion can be seen if we frame the statements in terms relevant to the Biological Passport:

1.   What is the probability of the abnormal blood value given the athlete has been at altitude?

---

[133] The point is not simply to refute this analysis by saying it is permissible because the WADC allows it, as Despina Mavromati has sought to do, but to highlight the changes in the nature of law that such a situation brings about. See D Mavromati, 'Indirect Detection Methods for Doping from a Legal Perspective: The Case of the Athlete Biological Passport' (2014) 6(2) *International Journal of Sport Policy and Politics* 241.

[134] M Redmayne, 'Presenting Probabilities in Court: The DNA Experience, 1996–1997' (1996) 1 *The International Journal of Evidence and Proof* 187.

2. What is the probability that the athlete is innocent (of an ADRV) given the abnormal blood values?
3. What is the probability of the abnormal blood value given the athlete has blood doped?
4. What is the probability that the athlete has blood doped (and is guilty of an ADRV) given the abnormal blood values?

Statements (1) and (3) would be permissible as evidence, whereas statements (2) and (4) would not. The WADA Guidelines state the Expert Panel's opinion in terms of their being a high probability that the athlete blood doped given the blood values – that is, in the impermissible form similar to (2) and (4). The impermissible form is known as the Prosecutor's Fallacy. In the Biological Passport process, the Prosecutor's Fallacy is institutionalised at the point of the Expert Panel giving their 'opinion'. The problem for the anti-doping apparatus is that it requires a method to make visible something that the Law has been incapable of visualising. The functional purpose of the Biological Passport is exactly to overcome this problem. The result is that rather than a Legal question decided according to Legal standards of evidence, the proof of the determination of doping becomes an administrative and technical decision based upon scientific and statistical standards. The Biological Passport seeks to penetrate a space that the Law cannot. It seeks to see what the Law cannot see or, as Agamben has written in the world of biopower, 'the physician and the scientist move into a no-man's land which at one point only the law and sovereignty could penetrate …'.[135] The proof of doping is no longer a Legal question but a scientific one in which the law can only blindly trust.

The Great Observer

Returning to the question of the Panopticon paradigm, Foucault was well alive to the coming of control societies. In noting that 'The 'Enlightenment', which discovered the liberties, also invented the disciplines',[136] Foucault asked:

> What Great Observer will produce the methodology of examination or the human sciences? … The ideal point of penalty today would be an indefinite discipline: an interrogation without end, an investigation that would be extended without limit to a meticulous and ever more analytical observation, a judgment that would avoid at the same time be the constitution of a file that was never closed, the calculated leniency of a penalty that would be interlaced with the ruthless curiosity of an examination, a procedure that would be at the same time the permanent measure of a gap in relation to an inaccessible norm and the asymptotic movement that strives to meet in infinity. The public execution was the logical culmination of a procedure that was governed

---

[135] G Agamben, *Homo Sacer, Sovereign Power and Bare Life* (Stanford University Press, 1999) 159.
[136] Foucault, *Discipline and Punishment* (n 51) 222.

> by the Inquisition. The practice of placing individuals under 'observation' is a natural extension of a justice imbued with disciplinary methods and examination procedures. Is it surprising that the cellular prison, with its regular chronologies, forced labour, its authorities of surveillance and registration, its experts in normality, who continue and multiply the functions of the judge, should have become the modern instrument of penalty?[137]

In constructing this new alliance between doping and the law and in opening up a new manner in which the invisible can be visualised, many of these features of this Foucauldian (or Kafkaesque) Great Observer to come are present. The Whereabouts System and Biological Passports operate as indefinite disciplines and as interrogations without end. They operate and extend without limit a meticulous and ever-more analytical observation of the daily aspects of life and the internal functioning of vital aspects of the body. They constitute, through the ruthless curiosity of an examination, a file that is never closed and which seeks to close a gap between the improvable and invisible (at law) act of doping; they operate between the invisible act and the inaccessible norm. They are the natural extension of the disciplines manifested by the practice of placing individuals under permanent observation by experts in normality, who assume and multiply the functions of the judge.

In such a procedure and, increasingly, in a society of biopolitical control based upon an accounting of the body and bodies – the administration of bodies using techniques such as continual monitoring and surveillance, the internalisation of control and an instrumental or functional rationality – the old law's techniques of deciding disputes after the event of their occurrence are replaced. Moving away from Foucault, Bauman's analysis of the Holocaust's rational administrative machinery exposes the connection between the bureaucracy, the task of administration and that of biopolitical control:

> Bureaucracy started from what bureaucracies start with: the formulation of a precise definition of the object, the registering those who fitted the definition and opening a file for each. It proceeded to segregate those in the files from the rest of the population, to which the received brief did not apply. Finally, it moved to evicting the segregated category from the land of the Aryans which was to be cleansed …[138]

Bauman's description of bureaucracy can be readily mapped onto the outline of the anti-doping apparatus set out above. The elements of this apparatus are consistent with the elements described by Bauman. But in this case, they are distributed throughout a network on a global scale.

Consistently with Bauman we have present:

- *a precise definition of the object of the ideology*: to cleanse sport of the doper who is a threat to the ethical order of the level competitive playing field of sport;

---

[137] ibid, 227–28.
[138] Z Bauman, *Modernity and the Holocaust* (Cornell University Press, 1989) 105.

- *the identification and location of the object*: by way of the regime of in and out of competition urine and blood testing, including the Whereabouts and Biological Passport systems;

- *the opening of a file for each object*: ADAMS and the Athlete's Biological Passport;

- *the segregating of those in the files*: the sorting of results by the ABP Software and then by the Biological Passport Expert Panels; and

- *the evicting of the segregated categories*: by way of anti-doping rule violation cases decided by disciplinary arbitration, bans imposed or by the spectacle of moral/media/institutional/public condemnation.

In successfully carrying out these five steps, the three manifestations (and perpetrators) of Bauman's description of instrumental rationality are also present and all work in tandem:

- *the machine* (the Whereabouts System, ADAMS, blood and urine sampling and analysis, ABP Software, and the Biological Passport itself);

- *the professional* (sports officials, accountants, the information technologists, statisticians, blood and physiological scientists, psychologists, academics, anti-doping lawyers); and

- *the bureaucracy* (the National Governments, NADOs, the IOC, national and international sporting organisations, corporate and state sponsors, WADA and the CAS).

The anti-doping apparatus and, more generally, neoliberal bureaucracy constitutes a transformation and not a withdrawal[139] – what Dadot and Laval term neomanagement – 'is not anti-bureaucratic. It corresponds to a new, more sophisticated, more individualised, more competitive phase of bureaucratic rationalisation …'.[140]

Our Whereabouts System is a long way from the traditional conception of the Rule of Law. What we are faced with is a very different machine to that of the boundary retained, backward-looking and dispute-resolving system of the old Law of the State system. In this world of biopolitical governance, as described above by Foucault, and just like in Kafka or Lewis Carroll, everyone is potentially guilty. The system demands, that, rather than waiting for an offence to occur and become visible, the anti-doping apparatus must actively search out abnormal bodies. The administrative machinery extends globally to all places and all times. The system demands that in situations where the processes of the law cannot see, the expert and their commentary visualise the invisible. Thus, process constitutes the invisible as visible and in turn decides which of these bodies are not worthy of remaining within the system, and therefore must be segregated.

---

[139] Dadot and Laval, *The New Way of the World* (n 18) 182.
[140] ibid, 262.

This space of surveillance not only locates and makes visible the physical location of each individual cyclist, it also, in turn, makes visible their internal bodily functions, in this case the fluctuations of their blood. The combination of the Whereabouts System and the Biological Passport in making the cyclist visible does not allow the cause of doping, or the event of doping to be known or observed, but rather it casts the body in terms of abnormalities whose cause cannot be identified with any certainty, but which suggest that doping may have occurred.

The ultimate effects are twofold. Firstly, an internalisation and continual monitoring of one's self at a personal and at a population level, coupled with the monitoring by the authorities. Secondly, a radical change in the nature and the definition of the offence of doping. No longer is it positive evidence of doping that is punishable, but what becomes punishable is an abnormality, in the cyclist's location, or their body, which suggests a probability that the invisible act of doping may have occurred. In the course of this process, accepted manners of proving an offence through evidence are transformed.

The Whereabouts System and the Biological Passport open up a new manner in which the invisible can be visualised. Through its discourse and the attendant commentary of the expert, a new alliance between doping and the law is constructed. It is a redistribution of the way in which the law treats the symptoms and the signified act of doping.

Faced with the coming of this apparatus of control, one must ask: 'Is this our future as well?'

5

The Society of Competition

Another Rule of Law (Is Possible)?

We have moved from a consideration of the *Operación Puerto* case and questions around the law of anti-doping to consider problems raised for us by Law's deformalisation in post-modernity. After raising the spectre of Law's deformalisation we turned to consider particular instances of the anti-doping apparatus in the context of governance and the policing and administration of bodies. In doing so we have started to consider the way in which productive bodies are produced by these governmental mechanisms of discipline and control. What we now turn to do is to put some meat on the bones of what I have already dubbed 'the society of competition and its particular relationship to the Law–governance continuum'. We will seek to show that governance here extends beyond the 'mere' control of the cyclist's body, or even their mind, to extend its grip throughout society at virtually every level.

The traditional conceptions and accounts of the Rule of Law – Weber, Dicey, even Scheuerman – have tended to treat the concept as a fixed and eternal standard against which one can measure societies and their law. In recent times it has become a 'democratic standard' – the gold standard – of democracy and global progress against which nations are measured. In the task of international nation building, catchphrases such as the 'Rule of Law' and 'good governance guide administration' – become, along with principles of economy, the measure of all justness, good and virtue: the system's single logic or value. What we need to do now is to return to the question of the Rule of Law to consider its more recent mutations and its place in the genealogy of the global project.

Foucault's lectures on *The Birth of Biopolitics* at first glance seem not to consider this topic in very much detail at all. Instead, the focus of direct attention is the birth of neoliberalism. Despite this first impression it is clear that the achievement of the conditions of neoliberalism, in their infancy at the time of Foucault's lessons, are the terrain upon which a biopolitical society is built. What is important for us in a discussion of forms of law, and the genealogy of the Rule of Law is Foucault's description of the manner in which neoliberalism transformed the concept of the Rule of Law. At the same time, this transformation points to substantial movements along the Law–governance continuum. Without neoliberalism's redefinition of the concept, the stage is still not set for the complete expansion of the biopolitical, administrative or governmental apparatus. For the pendulum to swing further towards governance the role of Law, and what is understood as the Rule of Law, had to necessarily change.

The Marxist geographer David Harvey has described neoliberalism as

> in the first instance a theory of political economic practices that proposes that human well-being can best be advanced by liberating individual entrepreneurial freedoms and skills within an institutional framework characterized by strong private property rights, free markets, and free trade. The role of the state is to create and preserve an institutional framework appropriate to such practices. The state has to guarantee, for example, the quality and integrity of money. It must also set up those military, defence, police, and legal structures and functions required to secure private property rights and to guarantee, by force if need be, the proper functioning of markets. Furthermore, if markets do not exist (in areas such as land, water, education, health care, social security, or environmental pollution) then they must be created, by state action if necessary. But beyond these tasks the state should not venture. State interventions in markets (once created) must be kept to a bare minimum because, according to the theory, the state cannot possibly possess enough information to second-guess market signals (prices) and because powerful interest groups will inevitably distort and bias state interventions (particularly in democracies) for their own benefit.[1]

Harvey's description does not really tell us how the Rule of Law in neoliberalism differs from that of liberalism. But what it does do is highlight certain aspects that drive its logic, including that the role of the State is that of creating and maintaining market conditions. Dadot and Laval's definition of neoliberalism as a new global rationality goes beyond Harvey's description in several important respects as they provide an opportunity to enlarge the focus beyond that of the role of the institution of the State and government. They point out that neoliberalism is not merely destructive of rules, institutions and rights derived from the State, but that it operates to produce 'certain kinds of social relations, certain ways of living, certain subjectivities'. At stake for them in neoliberalism is 'the form of our existence – the way in which we are led to conduct ourselves, to relate to others and to ourselves'. In this way the authors highlight, in much starker terms, the governmental and biopolitical nature of neoliberalism, something that Harvey does not, particularly the new existential norm that 'enjoins everyone to live in a world of generalised competition'.[2] Unlike Harvey, and following Foucault, Dadot and Laval highlight not only that the ruler (the State) is structured and organised in new ways, but also the conduct of the ruled.[3]

Of immediate relevance to us here is how the theorists of neoliberalism revised the concept of the Rule of Law. It was in his lectures on *The Birth of Biopolitics* that Foucault directly tackled this revision. It is here that we encounter a description of the transformations of the Rule of Law that enable us to begin to see more clearly that the traditional idea of one static and eternal conception of the Rule of Law is far from accurate. The deeper one digs into Foucault's analysis the more one sees

---

[1] D Harvey, *A Brief History of Neoliberalism* (Oxford University Press, 2005) 2.
[2] P Dadot and C Laval, *The New Way of the World* (Verso Books, 2013) 3.
[3] ibid, 4.

that even the liberal or modernist conception was not a static concept. Already, we have seen the apparent differences between, for example, Montesquieu, Weber and Dicey, which highlighted the differences between the Continental and Anglo conceptions of the Rule of Law, the separation of powers, the role and nature of administrative law and the increasing focus on managing and administering social interests. These may only be surface differences that tend to obscure the way in which the various approaches sought to manage the same problems.

In the modern, liberal conception of the Rule of Law it is probably fair to say that the negative conception is dominant. At the core of the concept is the idea that the Rule of Law entails some bulwark, some safeguard, to ensure that the State does not interfere with the private lives and affairs of individuals any more than is necessary necessary (eg, in terms of some notion of the social contract). The usefulness of Foucault's approach to the Rule of Law is that rather than just describing its formal or institutional aspects (eg, characteristics such as an independent judiciary, or how the problem of administrative law was dealt with) he pries open its function and how these functions might be achieved, exercised or, in fact, transformed again in the future?

What are the principal characteristics and functions of the Rule of Law as a concept? What does it fundamentally seek to achieve? How does its content vary? How does it legitimise the exercise of power in each of its reformations? These questions are all on the table if one moves to explore and understand the various permutations and mutations of the concept.

The first definition of the Rule of Law given by Foucault in his 1978 course on 'The Birth of Biopolitics' has its origins in the eighteenth and nineteenth centuries and is mirrored in continental terms such as *l'Etat de droit, de Rechsstaat,* and *El Estado de derecho*.[4] This form of the Rule of Law is, in essence, defined in opposition to two things: despotism and the police state. Despotism is that which identifies the obligatory character and form of the injunctions of the public authority with the sovereign's will such that in despotism the sovereign's will is the source of public power. Despotism refers any injunction made by public authorities back to the sovereign's will and to it alone, or, rather, it makes it originate in this will.

The police state, which is different from despotism, is a system in which there

> is no difference in kind, origin, validity and consequently of effect, between, on the one hand, the general and permanent prescriptions of the public authorities – … roughly … the law – and, on the other hand, the conjunctural, temporary, local and individual decisions of these same public authorities – … at the level of rules and regulations.[5]

The police state establishes an administrative continuum which, from the general Law to the particular measure, makes the public authorities and the injunctions they give one and the same type of principle, according it one and the same type of value. In the police state there is a special kind of affinity between executive and

[4] M Foucault, *The Birth of Biopolitics, Lectures at the College of France, 1978–1979* (Palgrave Macmillan, 2008) 168–69.
[5] ibid.

administrative power and the discretion and the concept of the police. The police state establishes a continuum between every possible form of injunction made by the public authorities, whatever the origin of their coercive character.

In one manner the police state may be democratic in a way that the sovereign's will is not – power may flow from some other body other than the sovereign (ie, in the form of a monarch), for example, Cromwell or the Jacobins, or even in some ways, the bureaucratic administrative model of the State. Thus, the police state may also rely upon measures other than the sovereign's Law to achieve its particular ends (eg, discipline, control and other biopolitical forms of governance).

We are easily able to overlay this description given by Foucault with the one of Neocleous above. What the latter suggests is that the police state is alive and well in liberal democracy. Nevertheless, in order to respond to these two threats – the despotic sovereign and the police state – the first liberal definition of the Rule of Law requires that the actions of public authorities will have no value if they are not framed in Laws that limit them in advance. The function of the Rule of Law is to ensure that the public authorities can only act within the framework of the Law. Thus, the Law replaces the sovereign as the principle and origin of the coercive character of public authorities. The source of power is removed or devolved from the transcendent figure of the sovereign's body to the transcendent and autonomous figure of the Law.

This first liberal conception of the Rule of Law arose as a response to forms of power and public Law at the end of the eighteenth century. It presupposed a difference of kind, effect, and origin between Laws, which are universally valid general measures, and in themselves acts of sovereignty and particular (administrative/ policial) decisions of public authorities. In such a conception, the Rule of Law is a State in which legal dispositions, the expression of sovereignty and administrative measures, are distinguished in their principal effects and validity.[6] From what we know of Dicey's view of administrative law, this conception appears closer to his understanding of the Rule of Law and his treatment of the French administrative system. According to Foucault there are, therefore, two aspects of this definition of the Rule of Law: one opposed to despotism and sovereign power, the other opposed to the administrative–policial State.

Towards the second half of the nineteenth century a new conception of the Rule of Law emerged.[7] In this period the Rule of Law tends towards a formulation in which every citizen has the concrete, institutionalised, and effective possibility of recourse against public authorities. From one perspective, it raises the question of the democratisation of the legal process and, with it, the problems of elections and of judicial or administrative review of governmental action. The core of the concept of Anglo judicial review (which appears to have lain dormant from the time of Lord Coke's battles with the Stuarts until Chief Justice Marshal in the early nineteenth century US Supreme Court) is not something that had been widely

---

[6] ibid, 169.
[7] ibid, 170.

acknowledged in the English system where the concept of the sovereignty and supremacy of Parliament took over from the sovereignty and supremacy of the monarch – which, in effect, replaced one unquestionable (unreviewable) power with another. The beginning of the acceptance of judicial review and of early forms of administrative law signals a subtle shift in the nature of the Rule of Law. This tends towards a situation that requires more than just a State that acts in accordance with the Law, and within its framework. The Rule of Law becomes a State in which there is a system of Law, that is to say, Laws, but it also means that judicial power is capable of intervening and deciding disputes between individuals and the government. Foucault discusses this by way of reference to the problem of administrative courts and the question as to whether the Rule of Law requires that recourse against public authorities takes place (only) in specialised administrative courts established to arbitrate for this purpose (the continental position) or whether recourse by citizens against public authorities occurs (only) in the ordinary courts (Anglo position). This is exactly the Dicey versus France conception of the Rule of Law debate we have outlined above.

These first two conceptions of the Rule of Law are what we can describe as 'liberal' conceptions. They are the starting point for the neoliberal attempt to redefine capitalism which changed in the post-Second World War period and especially after 1968 and the economic crisis of the early 1970s. It was in this period that neoliberalism's re-configuration of society and the Law began to take hold. What then emerged was a third conception of the Rule of Law which marked a fundamental shift in the rules of the game.[8]

The Third Way!

In respect of the birth of neoliberalism Foucault traces two paths: one being the ordoliberal school in Germany and the other the US neoliberal school. The distinctions are not immediately important for our purposes, but it is probably correct to say that, in many respects, the two have merged and that neoliberalism today is the child of both. In Germany, the idea of asserting the principles of the Rule of Law in the economy was a response to the Hitlerite 'state' in which the State had ceased to be a legal subject. In the Nazi 'state' popular acclamation had replaced the State and its institutions. However, the search for a redefined Rule of Law was directed at forms of legal intervention in the economic order (eg, in the US, the New Deal, elsewhere the social democratic welfare state). By 1968 and its aftermath capital needed to reconfigure itself to gain ground on the growing demands of the new politics, decolonisation, the peace movement and the strength of the worker's movement. Out of both the ordoliberal and neoliberal projects (especially the Chicago School) grew the principle of the Rule of Law in the Economic Order

---

[8] ibid, 171.

whereby the State is justified in making legal interventions in the economic order only if these take the form solely of what is described as the introduction of formal principles. In the neoliberal conception of the Rule of Law there can only be formal economic legislation. This new conception was also aimed against the State; it was about about curbing State power but, in this case, it was against the manner in which the democratic State was able to adopt policies that were inconsistent with the 'economy' (eg, the policies of redistribution embodied in the New Deal and the Welfare State). The only legitimate policy from this point on would increasingly become a formal economic principle.

As with its predecessors, the neoliberal redefinition of the Rule of Law is aimed against State power, at banishing State power from the private realm, but in a manner that is more far reaching than simply requiring the State to act and be accountable within the bounds of the Law. The requirement of only formal economic legislation carries with it 'radical' consequences for the role of the State and the Law. What does it mean that legal interventions have to be formal? Foucault answers this question by reference to Hayek.[9] For him, the Rule of Law is the opposite of a Plan.

To the neoliberal, it appears that the word 'plan' conjures up images of social-ism or communism; both pose a threat to the 'free market' economy. The answer, it seems, is to banish the plan from both the economy and government in order to protect liberal values. The Plan was defined as an aim, or the adoption of precise and definite economic ends which allow for (planned) intervention in the form of corrections, rectifications, suspension of measures and alternative measures. In the context of the Plan, the public authorities have a decision-making role and they replace individuals as the source of decisions. Under the auspices of the Plan, public authorities rather than private individuals become economic deci-sion makers themselves (public works). For the neoliberal, the Plan presupposes that public authorities can actually master all economic processes; for the fact is a plan requires a universal subject of knowledge who is able to see and oversee the order of the economy. Nothing is further from the truth for the neoliberal and, as such, the State, as the public sphere, must be banished from the economy. The crux of the neoliberal objection to the Plan is that public authorities make policy decisions rather than leaving things to individuals. It is from this basic tension between public policy and individual choice that the neoliberal idea of the Rule of Law has developed.

The Rule of Law for Hayek includes five principles. Firstly, that Law has the possibility of formulating certain measures of a general kind but that these meas-ures must be completely formal in the sense that they must never pursue an end. The Law only tells people what they must and must not do. There is an interest-ing result here whereby jurists such as Cotterell[10] talk about the Law becoming

---

[9] ibid, 171–73.

[10] R Cotterell, 'Law's Community: Legal Theory and the Image of Legality' (1992) 19(4) *Journal of Law and Society* 405.

increasingly policy based in recent times. It may be that there is some affinity between Cotterell's idea of policy and Hardt and Negri's idea of a single logic of Empire (ie, policy is essentially the core logic of neoliberalism). So, the qualification might be that policy in Law is acceptable if it achieves the ends of the neoliberal project. To put this another way, we could say, following Dumont, that the core logic or policy is a value that underpins the entire system. That value or logic requires that the Law's purpose is always to act in a necessary and normally exceptional manner in order to pursue the ends of competition. Even if neoliberalism abhors, the 'plan' it is itself the subject of a plan, in so far as it plans to construct the conditions for competition. As Agamben[11] and others such as the transnational jurist, Zumbansen[12] recognise, the functionality of the Law comes to the fore.

Secondly, the Law must be conceived of, a priori, in the form of fixed rules; importantly, these must not be rectifiable by reference to the effects produced. In this way, any collateral damage caused by the implication of the known fixed rules is not a relevant consideration for the Rule of Law. Thus, the Law is known and fixed and those who transgress it, knowingly or otherwise are aware (or are taken to be aware) of the consequences, no matter how unjust. In this case, the structural adjustment necessary to achieve the ends of the neoliberal project pain is a necessary byproduct that cannot be avoided. Thirdly, and following from the second principle, the Law must define the framework within which economic agents can freely make their decisions such that every agent (all agents are now economic) knows that the legal framework is fixed in its action and will not change. This underscores the principle of certainty that is required by the market. One could read from this that discretion is thus banished. However, things are not that simple as it appears that the discretion that is functional actually increases in scope but, as the fusion debate in equity and its clamouring for certainty over the length of the Chancellor's foot exemplifies,[13] any discretion that allows people to avoid the rules of the game, or contracts on the basis of some justness or unforeseen consequences is clearly abhorrent to the Neoliberal conception of the Rule of Law. Fourthly, the Law binds the State as much as it binds others. This ensures that economic agents have knowledge of the certainty of the actions of public authorities. But, and this is crucial, it also reduces the State (and even removes it from its transcendent position) to becoming just another individual economic actor – this is the world of the contracting State,[14] not the sovereign State. Fifthly, and finally, there is no

---

[11] G Agamben, *Opus Dei, Archaeology of Duty* (Stanford University Press, 2013).
[12] P Zumbansen, 'Law after the Welfare State: Formalism, Functionalism, and the Ironic Turn of Reflexive Law' (2008) 56(3) *American Journal of Comparative Law* 769; P Zumbansen, 'Defining the Space of Transnational Law: Legal Theory, Global Governance and Legal Pluralism' in G Handl, J Zekoll and P Zumbansen (eds) *Beyond Territoriality: Transnational Legal Authority in An Age of Globalization* (Martinus Nijhoff Publishers, 2012).
[13] See, eg, S Chesterman, 'Beyond Fusion Fallacy: The Transformation of Equity and Derrida's "The Force of Law"' (1997) 24(3) *Journal of Law and Society* 350.
[14] I Harden, *The Contracting State* (Open University Press, 1992).

universal subject of economic knowledge who can oversee all economic processes. The invisible hand – an intimately biblical concept[15] – guides everything.

In the three models of the Rule of Law outlined by Foucault we can observe a movement and transformation of the concept which can be traced from a State in which there was an unquestionable and unconfined sovereign (pre-Rule of Law) to a desire to confine the State and its actions by Law (the first liberal definition), to a desire to ensure that individuals are able to seek redress against the State (the second liberal definition) and finally to a desire to make the State and the individual equal legal or economic actors and to remove the ability of the State to impose public policy (the Neoliberal definition). The question that follows as a result of this genealogy is what happens to the concept of Law having a sovereign source if the State is no longer the universal subject of the law? If the liberal definition of the Rule of Law moved sovereignty from the body of the sovereign to the body of the law, where has it moved to in the Neoliberal definition? If no one can be in control, from where does law emanate? Who or what is sovereign? And what, in fact, is law in this context? Is it really useful to refer back to the Rule of Law and its traditional or popular liberal conceptions at a time when the Neoliberal model seems to have well and truly taken root?

Furthermore, what has all this got to do with sport, cycling and anti-doping? What is the connection between what we might term the total subsumption of society under the economy, mechanisms of governance and the sport in a global economy? The beginnings of one answer might be in the difference that Foucault draws out between liberalism and neoliberalism; a difference embodied in the logic of the game.[16]

The Rules of the Game

According to the neoliberal, the economy and the law are, and must henceforth be, a game. Accordingly, the neoliberal conception of its Rule of Law sets out the most 'rational' framework within which individuals are able to engage in their activities in line with their personal plans. Hence the main (or only) function of a system of jurisprudence is to govern the spontaneous order of economic life. The system of law must develop and reinforce rules according to which the competitive mechanism operates. Hence, a system of laws is equivalent to the rules of the game and it draws its inspiration not from the Law but from the game itself. Without doubt, this is a matter immediately relevant in respect of its ramifications not only for our understanding of the Rule of Law, but also in respect of the role that sport

---

[15] G Agamben, *The Kingdom and the Glory: For a Theological Genealogy of Economy and Government* (Stanford University Press, 2011).
[16] Foucault, *The Birth of Biopolitics* (n 4) 173–74.

and anti-doping play in its instrumental function as governance mechanisms of a global society.

Inherent in the logic of the neoliberal notion of the game-setting mechanism of law is that what is sought to be accomplished by way of this idea of law is the development and reinforcement of rules according to which the competitive mechanism takes place. The role of law in the neoliberal rational highlights the need to continually create and maintain the conditions of competition. We will begin to see that, despite the logic, competition itself is not a natural given but something that must be created. Competition itself is not human nature, it does not come prior to anything and hence it must be constructed. Karl Polanyi's *The Great Transformation*, published in the same years as Hayek's *Road to Serfdom*, is instrumental in this regard as it shows us that competition and the dominance of the market within society is a very recent construction.[17]

In relation to the instrumental role of sport is this regard it is more than interesting to note that mediaeval folk or peasant games were driven not by a logic of competition or of an individual trying to win, but by the logic of ensuring that not one of the players was left behind; that no one became a victim or a scapegoat.[18] Cooperation appears here prior to competition (in a manner related to debt being prior to exchange?[19]) What the game requires before competition may occur is, in the first place, cooperation. Everyone must agree and cooperate in establishing the game and its rules before competition can take place. As Dadot and Laval put it, the

> rules of the game and that apparatus for impartial supervision of those rules which are just as necessary for the competition as for a sporting contest if it is not to degenerate into a mere riot. A general competitive system which is at the same time just, fair and which functioned properly cannot exist without permanent supervision of the conditions under which competition must fulfill itself as a really effective system.[20]

The point is that the competitive, rational mechanism, logic or value of neoliberalism and the logic of competition is something quite different from that which drove both the liberal idea of the Rule of Law and economy, namely the idea of exchange. Rather than exchange, which started from the formation of an equilibrium defined by formal conditions, neoliberalism commenced from the competitive struggle between agents.[21] Furthermore, to a certain extent, market exchange required

---

[17] K Polanyi, *The Great Transformation: The Political and Economic Origins of Our Time* Paperback (Beacon Press, 2001). See also, of course, L Dumont, *From Marx to Mandeville: The Genesis and Triumph of Economic Ideology* (University of Chicago Press, 1977).

[18] See, eg, H Eichberg, 'Three Dimensions of Playing the Game: About Mouth Pull, Tug-of-War and Sportization' in V Møller and J Nauright (eds), *The Essence of Sport* (University Press of Southern Denmark, 2003); R Bastin, 'Ritual Games for the Goddess Pattini' (2001) 45(2) *Social Analysis*, 120.

[19] G Deleuze and F Guattari, *Anti Oedipus, Capitalism and Schizophrenia* (University of Minnesota Press, 1977).

[20] Dadot and Laval, *The New Way of the World* (n 2) 86–87.

[21] ibid, 103.

some form of equality and rights. Along with this, liberalism also envisaged some sort of levelling out to achieve equality – some measure of redistribution in order to ensure the security of the market system. However, neoliberalism apparently privileges growth as the pure possibility of making it. Rather than carrying with it some measure of equality, competition is inherently unequal; its purpose is to show us who is better, that is, to highlight who is more outstanding or unequal than the rest. In the logic of competition, as opposed to exchange, it is not the players that are equal, but it is simply that the rules are set in advance to create what is touted as a level playing field. Here neoliberalism's order 'consist[s] mainly in inequality'.[22] In reality, the level playing field does not create equality. Instead, it tends to act as merely a set of rules that brings certainty to the game. The essence of neoliberalism 'consists not in exchange (more equality), but in competition, itself defined as a relationship of inequality between different units of production or enterprises … The idea of the equality is replaced by the level playing field upon which unequal players compete'.[23] In this neoliberal reality, everything and every-one, from the State down to the level of each individual actor, becomes no more than an enterprise engaged in competition with everyone else. The People and the State are deprived of their public character and become corporations, or better entrepreneurs. In this way the State is much more than just the 'the 'vigilant guard-ian of this framework, but is itself subject to the normal competition in its own action'. If it was otherwise, the State could not perform its function as 'there are no grounds for the state forming an exception to the rules of law for whose application it is responsible. Quite the reverse, any form of self exemption or self subtraction on its part can only disqualify it in its role as an inflexible guardian of such rules …'. The governmental function of competition thus prevails over sovereignty with the consequence that there is 'a gradual hollowing out of all the categories of public law, which tends not towards a formal abrogation, but to diffusing their opera-tional validity'.[24] According to the logic of neoliberalism the State is not removed from the picture, it does not necessarily become more democratic, nor does it yet wither away; what occurs is that its role and function change. The political order that is devised and constructed is one where the State is under the supervision of the market, rather than the inverse situation of the Rule of Law's prehistory where the market was supervised by the State.[25] Henceforth, the only one true and funda-mental social policy of the political order is economic growth.[26] The result is the emergence of 'a radically economic state' completely different from the problem of classic liberalism, whereby the existence of the State is based upon a non-State

---

[22] L Dumont, *Essays on Individualism: Modern Ideology in Anthropological Perspective* (University of Chicago Press, 1986) 266.

[23] Dadot and Laval, *The New Way of the World* (n 2) 310.

[24] ibid, 302.

[25] Foucault, *The Birth of Biopolitics* (n 4) 116.

[26] ibid, 144.

space of economic freedom.[27] No longer was it a matter of cutting out or contriving a free space of the market within a political society, but rather

> how the overall exercise of political power can be modeled on the principles of a market economy. So, it is not a question of freeing an empty space, but of taking the formal principles of a market economy and referring and relating them to, of projecting them on to a general art of government.[28]

In neoliberalism, competition itself becomes the formal structure and the guiding policy. Intervention is carried out by the State (only) in the name of creating and maintaining the competitive framework. Competition within the rules of the game is opposed to the Plan, which shows how the resources of society must be consciously directed in order to achieve a particular end (ie, competition). That is there is no particular end, merely the possibility of a result within the rules, means that the end or aim of both law and sport here coincide.

This is the great transformation wrought by neoliberalism on the concept of the Rule of Law and, in these new circumstances, an analysis which merely cites the Rule of Law as a static, timeless, or eternal concept tends to miss the point – when the Rule of Law is spoken of, the question must become: which rule of law? As economic processes are decoupled from social mechanisms by the idea that the economy is a game which permeates the whole of society, the essential role of the State is, therefore, to define the economic rules of the game and to make sure that they are, in fact, applied.

What are these rules? What is their purpose? What do they achieve? Firstly, the rules must make the game as active as possible and to the advantage of the greatest possible number of people. They must simply operate on the surface of contact without real penetration of the economic and the social, thus they are merely supplementary and unconditional. The rules must ensure that it must be impossible for one of the partners in the game to lose everything and be unable to continue playing, a limiting rule that changes nothing in the game, but prevents one from completely dropping out of it. In this context, no one originally insists on being part of the game, but at the same time and consequently, the rules seek to ensure that no one is excluded without ever having explicitly wished to take part. All are virtual players of the game in which the only point of contact between the economic and the social is the rule safeguarding players from being excluded. What appears is, in effect, an inverted 'social contract' whereby all those who will the social contract, that is those that virtually or actually subscribe to it, form part of this gaming society. That is – and this is the crux of the matter for our purposes where the anti-doping apparatus enters the picture in the case of sport – until such a time as they cut themselves off from it by repudiating the rules inherent in this virtual 'social contract'. This is the logic of playing the game and thus being able to

---

[27] ibid, 86–86.
[28] ibid, 131.

'Live Your Dream' and 'Just Do It'. Other than Foucault's rule of non-exclusion – that is, the potential of all who are suitable to play to actually play – the game itself must follow its own course. Being capable of being culturally fit to play becomes the touchstone of this potentiality.

Thus, in liberalism, the function of the Rule of Law was for the State to leave people alone to live their lives without undue interference. However, in neoliberalism, the function of the Rule of Law is transformed to allow for the management of people on the purely economic grounds of pure competition.[29] Liberalism's *Homo Juridicius* is a very different creature to neoliberalism's *Homo Oeconomicus*. The interest of *Homo Juridicius*, or Liberal Man converged with that of others by way of a social contract – by the giving up of rights in return for protection from the State. *Homo Oeconomicus*, or neoliberal man, is someone who pursues his own interest and whose interest is such that it spontaneously converges with the interest of others. The Law of the State governs *liberal man* whereas *neoliberal man* (and the neoliberal State) become governable by the subtleties of the market and self-interest and not the will of the sovereign or the people constituted as a polity. Self-interest and the Law are not necessarily reconcilable as is exemplified by these neoliberal and liberal figures having a very different relationship with the State and hence the Law. If they can be reconciled, it is through a reconfiguration of the Law and their relationship to governance. Unlike the situation whereby the liberal State is the ultimate source of the Law, the neoliberal State is the local agent of the economy in a situation where the State, and hence the Law, cannot know or control it.

What happens when the State is marginalised, or rather, transformed, in this way? When and what new judicial mechanisms are established outside of the State structure to manage the rules of the game when all is based around the enterprise, competition, and being master of one's own games within the framework of the rules? As we have asked ourselves, what juridical form is able to form and sustain this system? In the context of eighteenth- and nineteenth-century liberalism, and its primacy of the Law, the judicial was reduced to the pure and simple application of an autonomous and transcendent Law. However, in circumstances where the law is no more than the rules of the game and in which each remains master regarding himself and his part, then the judicial, instead of being reduced to the simple function of applying the law, acquires a new form of autonomy and importance. This new autonomy of the law is at the same time immanent with the economic as *Neo Liberal Man* is the man of enterprise and not that of exchange.

Here enterprise is not just an institution, but a way of behaving in the economic field in the form of competition and in a situation where everything is

---

[29] ibid, 270.

encompassed or subsumed within the economic field. Enterprise society allows individuals the possibility of behaving as they wish in the form of free enterprise, with the result that with the multiplication of the forms of the typical enterprise unit, there is an increase in the number of surfaces available on which friction occurs. The occasions for litigation multiply and the regulation of these conflicts and any irregularities of behaviour (ie, rule breaking as opposed to the spontaneous economic regulation by competition) calls at times for judicial and other forms of interventionism that have to operate as arbitration or moments of finality within the framework of the rules of the game. The Law constitutes the playing field and law becomes the game's referee. The ever-increasing reduction in the size of the State and the number of its functionaries driven by the logic of economics and competition and the increased dynamic of enterprises has produced the need for an ever-increasing number of decisions to be adjudicated. For Foucault, one of the fundamental problems produced by this dynamic within neoliberalism was whether this arbitration should be inserted within existing judicial institutions of the State, or whether it is necessary to create new ones.[30]

What seems to be apparent with the process of globalisation is that the logic of neoliberalism has increased and the adjudicative or better arbitrative function has, in many cases, tended to move away from the judicial institutions of the State and towards instances of private arbitration.

The logic of competition and the requirement for rule enforcement within the game of the economy places enormous strain on the judicial structures of the State such that, on the basis of this same economic rationality, there occurs a simultaneous drive to the privatisation and spectacularisation of the 'judicial' or arbitrative function – of its contracting out and transformation where necessary and possible. Posner's championing of social norms and shaming as a more efficient mechanism for contractual governance over adjudication must be read within this context.[31] If Foucault is correct in saying that, in its various forms, the Rule of Law always challenges the State, neoliberalism has reduced the State to an instrument of the economy, another albeit very special, player in that game. It might be possible to characterise the situation as an inversion of the Law–governance continuum, whereby rather than the liberal model of governance being under or subject to the Law, what the neoliberal transformation achieves is a situation where the sovereign and the Law is under, or subject to, governance, the administration and, in the end, the police. That is, the economy governs, although it may appear that the sovereign continues to enjoy a restful reign. Along with this we could say that neoliberalism has also provided us with a theory of sovereignty based upon economic man.

---

[30] ibid, 175–76.
[31] EA Posner, *Law and Social Norms* (Harvard University Press, 2009).

Competition as Government

From Foucault's analysis of the neoliberal turn of the Rule of Law a number of points arise that are pertinent to our consideration of the anti-doping apparatus:

- the law's role in game setting;
- the privileging of competition as a form of governance; and
- the increasing need for other non-state forms of resolution and finality including a preference for private arbitration over that of sovereign judicial systems.

What, then, is the place of the anti-doping apparatus in the wide system of global governance? In trying to unpack this it is useful to consider the idea of competition as governance before turning to the question of how it is reflected or relates to the anti-doping apparatus. As we are beginning to see, in the context of a study of sport and law, at first glance one of the striking things about the analysis of the Rule of Law as game setting and its privileging of competition is that these two other fields of play are, in themselves, based upon similar logics. If we add to that mix the idea of competition as governance, we quickly have before us four models of power (sport, law, economy, governance) which all privilege, in their own (and in the same way), principles of competition. All are brought together by the same value.

Here, the rules are not themselves concerned with just outcomes but with establishing a procedure by which the players must abide in order to produce competition. The rules of sport, of the economy, of law and of governance are thus no more than ('cooperative') procedures to be followed to produce the outcome: a competitive winner. Justice here 'is nothing other than the just recompense of merit and skill in the struggle. Those who fail owe it solely to their weakness and advice'.[32] The outcome (ie, who wins) is formally irrelevant so long as the procedure is known and thus perceived to be itself just or fair.

In comparing competition in the economy to sport, examinations and experimentation in science, Hayek stressed the nature of competition as procedure, 'first and foremost a discovery procedure'.

There is no pre-determined range of known or 'given' facts which will be taken into account. All we can hope to secure is a procedure that is, on the whole, likely to bring about a situation where more of the potentially useful objective facts will be taken into account than would be done in any other procedure which we know we can judge the value of results only by the conditions under which it was conducted, not by the results.[33] Neoliberalism 'regards competition in the market as a process of discovery of relevant information, as a certain mode of conduct on the part of the subject, who seeks to outstrip and proceed others in discovering new

---

[32] Dadot and Laval *The New Way of the World* (n 2) 36.
[33] F Hayek, *Law, Legislation and Liberty: A New Statement of the Liberal Principles of Justice and Political Economy, Vol III* (Routledge & Kegan Paul, 1976) 67–68.

opportunities for profit.[34] The procedure of competition thus takes into account the most useful or functional facts, not necessarily the most just. The Rule of Law as a discursive machine continues to be present as game setting and with this mutation right becomes, at the non-discursive level, no more than procedure.[35] The law (or politics) ideological idealising of itself as justice manifests itself with an insistence at the most on formal procedural concerns law is not synonymous with justice, but with the finality of a result within the rules of the game. Agamben describes law's aim of finality clearly:

> As jurists well know, law is not directed toward the establishment of justice. Nor is it directed toward the verification of truth. Law is solely directed toward judgment, independent of truth and justice. This is shown beyond doubt by the force of judgment that even an unjust sentence carries with it. The ultimate aim of law is the production of a res judicata, in which the sentence becomes a substitute for the true and just, being held as true despite its falsity and injustice. Law finds peace in this hybrid creature, of which it is impossible to say if it is the fact or rule; once law has produced its res judicata, it cannot go any further.[36]

If, from here, we start to try and theorise about both sport and law there is a striking, possibly more than simply illustrative, resemblance between the actual and unconscious structure of each. Møller is well aware of this resemblance: 'Cleansed of all its decorations, the essence of sport becomes visible. The result is what it is all about.'[37] If we delve a little deeper, firstly, taking the pure idea of justice as a starting point, we find in the end not an actual incarnation of pure justice, but an actual incarnation of law embodied in the result. Justice is not the great determinant of the law. Law is exhaustively determined in the result – in the idea of *res judicata* – a bringing to an end, finality in the contest between the disputing parties. This law is a function: this is law's function. Justice itself is indeterminate, only determinable by reference to the unequal and differential relations that exist between the parties to the contest. Law is not determined objectively by reference to some higher (transcendental) notion or requirement of justice, but it is determined by reference to its objects of experience, its time and space, and the relationship of the contestants to this time and space and to each other.

In the end law is completely determined with respect to this singular point at which the contest occurs and is decided. It is completely determined for here and for now without reference to an identity of justice or some inherent legality. It is the exception and not the generality, the identity or the norm, that is the hallmark, the determinant and the motor of the law. The mighty summit of the law that we catch a glimpse of, what we perceive and what emerges out of the mist, its actual incarnation, is not justice but the resolution of the contest of competition. What we mistake for justice, what we think of as a solution, is the result of law's functionality.

---

[34] Dadot and Laval, *The New Way of the World* (n 2) 103.
[35] M Hardt and A Negri, *Empire* (Harvard University Press, 1999) 26–27.
[36] G Agamben, *Remnants of Auschwitz: The Witness and the Archive* (Zone Books, 2002) 18.
[37] V Møller, *The Doping Devil, vol 1* (International Network of Humanistic Doping Research, 2008) 99.

Sport is also meant to be fair (as we are told, again and again, by its scholars and administrators[38]). A level playing field cannot exist between individual players, but sport seeks to create the image of one. It shrouds this fact in the great mist of the level playing field of pure competition. The great contradiction at the heart of sport, that of *Citius, Altius, Fortius* and fairness, is embodied in the governing law of sport.[39] Competition is sport's guiding principle: some might say its essence or true spirit. Writing before the neoliberal turn, and in order to aggrandise sport and cycling as an epic in the manner of the Greek gods, Barthes called sport 'the world of total competition.[40] Despite what the neoliberals say about the unnaturalness of competition, athletes tend to accept, or we might say, have been governed to accept, that this 'the world of total competition' is, in fact, a natural state. Interview participants in the Australia study often referred to this, for example:

> Sport is a very important part of life. Sport is everything really. Sport is the battle of man against man battling it out, fighting it out to see who is the better athlete. So sport is the instinct we have, the competitiveness we have. The competitiveness of mankind, which is genetically imprinted in our brain and which enables us to excel in sport, but not only sport, it could be education. Basically mankind would be doomed if we didn't have this competitive spirit. … Athletes are competitive in a different way because the battle is visual to everyone because it is a one on one battle or team on team battle. It is a primal instinct. Sport is a primal instinct we all have.[41]'

'They are Learning'

In considering Foucault's analysis of neoliberalism I have stated that competition itself is inherently unequal and not based upon equality in the manner that liberalism conceived of it. In this regard Lazzarato has written that:

> For Neoliberalism, the market is not the spontaneous or anthropological expression of the tendency of human beings to exchange, as Adam Smith believed. Instead of exchange, they underline competition as the organizing principle of the market,

[38] See, eg, RL Simon, *Fair Play, Sports, Values and Society* (Westview Press, 1991); S Loland, *Fair Play in Sport: A Moral Norm System* (Routledge, 2002); and G McFee, *Sport, Rules and Values: Philosophical investigations into the Nature of Sport* (Routledge, 2004). 'WADA is a unique partnership between the sport movement and governments, with its main aim being to protect the clean athlete and provide a level playing field for all. This unique partnership helps foster the combination and complementing of sports' and governments' respective resources and assets, and results in a coordinated and cohesive approach to anti-doping. Furthermore, it underlines the fact that if we, the anti-doping community, are to succeed in levelling the playing field, it will require the will of everyone who wants, and believes in, pure and fair sport.' WADA President's Welcome Message, www.wada-ama.org/en/who-we-are/presidents-welcome-message.

[39] Citius, Altius, Fortius ('Faster, Higher, Stronger'), the Olympic motto proposed by Pierre de Coubertin on the creation of the International Olympic Committee in 1894.

[40] R Barthes, 'The Tour de France as Myth' in R Barthes, *Mythologies* (Editions du Seuil, 1957).

[41] M Hardie, D Shilbury, C Bozzi and I Ware, *I Wish I was Twenty One Now: Beyond Doping in the Australian Peloton* (Auskadi Samizdat, 2012).

specifically, competition between enterprises and between workers. Whilst exchange relates to equality, competition relates to inequality. The new mode of government substitutes the couple inequality/enterprise in place of the couple exchange/equality. For the neoliberals the market can operate as a regulatory principle only if competition is made the regulatory principle of society. For Neoliberalism, competition, like the market, is not the result of the 'natural play' of appetites, instincts or behaviours. It is rather a 'formal play' of inequalities that must be instituted and constantly nourished and maintained. Thus, appetites and instincts are not given: only inequality has the capacity to sharpen appetites, instincts and minds, driving individuals to rivalries.[42]

Lazzarato is, of course, pointing out what the neoliberals themselves say. Hayek states that

> ... rational behavior is not a premise of economic theory, though it is often presented as such. The basic contention of theory is rather that competition will make it necessary for people to act rationally in order to maintain themselves.[43]

He continues that competition

> is as much a method of breeding certain types of mind as anything else ... Competition is, after all, always a process in which a small number makes it necessary for larger numbers to do what they do not like, be it work harder, to change habits, or to devote a degree of attention, continuous application, or regularity to their work which without competition would not be needed.[44]

In discussing the manner in which neoliberalism has extended market mechanisms to what he terms the 'lifeworld', Hilgers highlights its governmental aspect 'Neoliberalism must change people' he writes

> this is why, from Lippmann to Thatcher's famous formulation, 'Economics are the method, but the object is to change the soul', Neoliberalism is a political project. The necessity of making people adapt to a world of generalized competition supposes a radical reform that transforms the way in which they perceive their destiny.[45]

The new government of subjects brought about by neoliberalism presupposes an instrument and space of competition, in which the subject

> must constantly strive to be as efficient as possible, to appear to be totally involved in his work, to perfect himself by lifelong learning, and to accept the greater flexibility required by the incessant changes dictated by markets. His own expert, his own employer, his own inventor, his own entrepreneur: neoliberal rationality encourages the ego to act to strengthen itself so as to survive competition. All its activities must be compared with a form of production, and investment, and a cost calculation. The economy becomes a personal discipline.[46]

---

[42] M Lazzarotto, 'From Biopower to Biopolitics, Pli' (2009) 13 *The Warwick Journal of Philosophy* 100, 116–17, available at www.warwick.ac.uk/philosophy/pli_journal/vol_13.html.
[43] Hayek, *Law, Legislation and Liberty* (n 33) 75.
[44] ibid, 76–77.
[45] M Hilgers, 'The Historicity of the Neoliberal State' (2012) 20(1) *Social Anthropology* 80, 82.
[46] Dadot and Laval *The New Way of the World* (n 2) 263.

Thatcher herself said:

> People have forgotten about the personal society. And they say: do I count, do I matter? To which the short answer is, yes. And therefore, it isn't that I set out on economic policies; it's that I set out really to change the approach, and changing the economics is the means of changing that approach. If you change the approach you really are after the heart and soul of the nation. Economics are the method; the object is to change the heart and soul.[47]

Competition is thus aimed at changing, directing, piloting people's behaviour. It is a manner of governing them. As the Iron Lady said: 'They are learning.'[48]

Sport as Governance and the Problematisation of the Individual Doper

> And I say to them, "don't blame your unemployment on to me. It is your fault." People are realising that we live in a competitive world and we shall always be up against that reality. It is a manner of governing them.[49]

As discussed in Chapter 4, the anti-doping establishment and the vast majority of academic literature on anti-doping privileges a form of psychological analysis which addresses the problem of doping as one of individual moral reasoning.[50] Competition individualises everything, it makes individuals responsible for their own actions and their own bodies. This is the basis of the strict liability principle in anti-doping and it helps explain why the CONI and UCI prosecutions of Valverde were functional (as they focused on the immoral individual athlete) to the anti-doping apparatus in a way that *Operación Puerto* (with its systemic focus) was not.

Although most people would consider sport to be in some way pure and highly instrumental in enhancing morality, enabling people to follow rules and respect each other, thus creating good citizens in everyday life, Long et al[51] argue that some studies in sports psychology suggest that the game reasoning of sport does not necessarily lead to character development but to a moral transformation in which an egocentric or self-interest perspective is considered a legitimate means of pursuing the goal of competition. We would say that this egocentric or self-interested perspective is what is called forth by the game of neoliberalism such

---

[47] R Butt, 'Margaret Thatcher: Interview for the Sunday Times – The First Two Years' *Sunday Times* (3 May 1981) available at www.margaretthatcher.org/document/104475.

[48] ibid.

[49] ibid.

[50] See, eg, T Long et al, 'A Qualitative Study of Moral Reasoning of Young Elite Athletes' (2006) 20 *The Sport Psychologist* 330; F Lucidi et al, 'The Social-cognitive Mechanisms Regulating Adolescents' Use of Doping Substances' (2008) 26(5) *Journal of Sports Sciences* 447; and ID Boardley and M Kavussanu, 'The Moral Disengagement in Sport Scale-short' (2008) 26(14) *Journal of Sports Sciences* 1507.

[51] Long et al, 'A Qualitative Study' (n 50).

that, contrary to the position of Long et al, we would say that the 'bracketed morality' of the sporting context is not distinguishable from everyday life. The moral atmosphere of sport – its higher self-centered ego orientation and aggressive tendencies that lower 'moral reasoning' – is the moral atmosphere of the society of competition. Contrary to the idea that sport constitutes some sort of bracketed morality, Dadot and Laval are much closer to the mark when they propose that the

> new subject is a man of competition and performance. The self entrepreneur is being made to succeed, to win. Much more so than the idealised figures of heads of enterprises, competitive sport is a great social theatre that displays of modern gods, demi-gods and heroes. While the cult of sport dates from the early twentieth century, and proved perfectly compatible with fascism and Soviet communism, as well as Fordisms, it experienced a major turning point when it permeated the most diverse practices from within, not only by lending them a vocabulary, but, more decisively, through a logic of performance that trend transforms its subjective meaning.[52]

Rather than being contrary to wider societal values, the character developed and brought about by the generalisation of game reasoning in neoliberalism's society of competition in fact seeks to achieve a moral transformation in which an egocentric or self-interest perspective is not only considered legitimate, but also the only way of being. Neoliberal man is competitive man, wholly immersed in global competition.[53]

The Complementary Nature of Free Competition and Anti-Doping Regulation

Franco Berardi[54] has written that competition 'implies a risky narcissistic stimulation' whereby 'many are called but only a few are chosen'. In such a situation the society of competition and its 'fairness' must, itself, be justified. At one and the same time self-interest is promoted while its excesses that may lead to perceptions of 'market failure' must be constrained. Excess, ecstatic excess, excessive enjoyment and any form of immeasurability beyond the rules of the game (and the logic of neoliberalism) require policing and demonisation in order to justify failure within this situation and without 'questioning its own ideological fundaments, and even its economic efficiency'.[55] If we accept the characterisation of the role of law put forward by the neoliberals, that the main function of a system of law is to govern the spontaneous order of economic life, we come up against what, prima facie, may appear to be a contradiction in the context of the war on doping and the creation of the conditions for pure competition. Savulescu, for example, has

---

[52] Dadot and Laval, *The New Way of the World* (n 2) 281.
[53] ibid, 255.
[54] F Berardi, *The Soul at Work: From Alienation to Autonomy* (Semiotxet(e), 2009) 99.
[55] ibid, 100.

argued that allowing everyone to dope would level the playing field, removing the effects of genetic inequality, so rather than being unfair, allowing doping promotes equality.[56] The reasoning behind this kind of laissez-faire-ism is that anti-doping is essentially anti-competitive. If, as I have suggested, the spectacle of sport plays an important functional role in the creation and maintenance of the conditions for such competition, rather than being a contradiction, the argument we are developing here is that the anti-doping apparatus in fact complements and contributes to these same instrumental functions and mechanisms of this gaming society. That is, the anti-doping apparatus is an instrument that contributes to the creation of the conditions of competition, not simply because it purportedly creates a level playing field, but because it seeks, at its most basic, to justify the image of that level playing field. If this is the situation, this raises questions such as how is it that transgression of such a seemingly anti-competitive measure, or better, restraint on the nature of competition, constitutes repudiation of the rules inherent in the virtual social contract of neoliberalism? Leaving aside why some who transgress are not excluded from the game, why and for what purpose is it that those that transgress become culturally unfit to play? As already noted above, in the context of a study of sport and law, at first glance, one of the striking things about the analysis of the Rule of Law as game setting and its privileging of competition is that these two other fields of play are in themselves based upon similar logics. Sport, like the economy, is meant to be a place where anyone who buys into the game can compete as an entrepreneur of the self. The conditions for competition in both cases are (meant to be) fair. We are told again and again that both sport and the economy seek to create the image of a level playing field. Both activities are shrouded in the great mist of the level playing field of pure competition. The great contradiction at the heart of sport between that of *Citius, Altius, Fortius*[57] and that of fairness is embodied in both the governing law of sport and the anti-doping apparatus.

As a biopolitical project, competition as governance has as its object all of life and all of its intensity – its focus is the totality of the population, as well as each and every body (ie, each and every aspect of life and each and every regime or field in which life is played out). Ehrenberg has been keen to point out how the increased attention being paid to the values of economic competition and sports rivalries has propelled the 'trajectory-individual' to a conquest of their personal identity and an increase in their own social status. In both the economy and

---

[56] J Savulescu, B Foddy and M Clayton, 'Why We Should Allow Performance Enhancing Drugs in Sport' (2004) 38 *British Journal of Sports Medicine* 666.

[57] The Olympic motto proposed by Pierre de Coubertin on the creation of the International Olympic Committee in 1894, is not only relevant to sport but also the intensification of work brought about in neoliberalism: see M Gollac and S Volkoff, 'Citius, altius, fortius [L'intensification du travail]' (1996) 114 *Actes de la recherche en sciences sociales* 54. Les nouvelles formes de domination dans le travail (1), cited in Dadot and Laval *The New Way of the World* (n 2) 289.

sport, individuals, according to Ehrenberg, are commanded to surpass themselves in the great entrepreneurial adventure of life.[58] As Franco Berardi has put it, capitalism 'expects enthusiastic participation in a universal competition where it is impossible to win without fully and convincingly deploying all of our energies'.[59]

The injunction to compete is, in the end, not an invitation but it is manifestly something that must be undertaken with passion. It is a duty; something that we 'have to be', 'having to be' a competitor in the great entrepreneurial adventure of life that forms the basis of existence.[60] It is in this duty of 'having to be' a functional member of the society of competition that we begin to encounter the reason why Agamben says that the camp is the paradigm of contemporary politics; of the way we live post-Auschwitz. If read literally, this claim might be very easy to dismiss as an exaggeration. But is its kernel contained in the dream of Primo Levi, referred to by Agamben: '"Wake Up!" shouted each morning in a foreign voice? In that situation whereby each and every day we do things, in effect, that we do not want to do?'

Both competition and doping arise in the context of this constant and perpetual injunction that requires us to construct ourselves as 'having to be' something within the society of competition. Doping becomes problematised as a matter of (free) choice made by those who are too morally weak to compete fairly on the level playing field of life. It is moral weakness that has led them to repudiate the rules of the game such that they are now unfit to particpate in that game. Neoliberalism does not merely grant the individual the freedom to compete and act according to their self-interest, it does so at the same moment that it considers them 'incorrigible rogues, potential criminals'. As we have seen in Chapter 4, the society of competition inaugurates 'the panoptical moment directed to the glory of the monitoring of each by all and all by each'.[61] This panoptical moment is necessary in order to reinforce the discursive and governmental spectacle of pure and natural competition, which glorifies the conduct of pure and natural bodies, all aimed at reinforcing the myth of competition as a natural and pure state carried out on a level playing field. Only upon this mythical field can we all (have to) be, can we all make it, as entrepeneurs of the self.

Boltanski and Chiapello's description of the 'spirit of capitalism', in their meticulous study of changes in the language and techniques of French management, goes some way towards helping us to understand the interplay of competition and anti-doping. The 'spirit of capitalism' they describe is an ideology that justifies people's commitment to capitalism, and which renders this commitment attractive.

---

[58] A Ehrenberg, *The Weariness of the Self: Diagnosing the History of Depression in the Contemporary Age* (McGill-Queen's University Press, 2010) xxii.
[59] Berardi, *The Soul at Work* (n 54) 91.
[60] Agamben, *Opus Dei, Archaeology of Duty* (n 11).
[61] Dadot and Laval *The New Way of the World* (n 2) 258.

They argue that, in its different mutations, three dimensions play a particularly important role in providing a concrete expression for the spirit of capitalism:

(a)   The first dimension indicates what is 'exciting' about an involvement with capitalism – in other words, how this system can help people to blossom, and how it can generate enthusiasm. This "excitement" dimension is usually related to the different forms of "liberation" that capitalism offers.

(b)   A second set of arguments emphasises the forms of security that is offered to those who are involved, both for themselves and for their children.

(c)   Finally, a third set of arguments (and one that is especially important for our demonstration) invokes the notion of fairness, explaining how capitalism is coherent with a sense of justice, and how it contributes to the common good.[62]

Although there are clearly elements of excitement and liberation offered by both sport and neoliberalism, something that Dadot and Laval refer to as the pleasure/ performance apparatus and which we will return to shortly, for present purposes Boltanski and Chiapello specifically identify this third dimension with the spirit of neoliberal capitalism. It is in the context of this third set of arguments surrounding the notion of capitalism as invoking a notion of fairness coherent with a sense of justice that we begin to appreciate the role that the anti-doping apparatus plays in respect of the generalisation of competition as a mode of governance. Although Hayek was clear that the logic of competition (at the non-discursive level) is not concerned with justice or fairness, the discursive function of anti-doping invokes and promotes the rhetoric of its fairness – of competition as liberty and justice. Hayek relies upon Locke, and even Rawls, in support of his proposition that in neoliberalism, what needs to be just are the rule of the game, the rules of the competition itself, but the outcome, the result, is not just but, as we have said, inherently unequal: it is only the way in which competition is carried on, not its results, that can be just or unjust.[63] Here the role of the law is to ensure the correct procedure.

The Law itself provides another way in which we might comprehend the relationship between competition and anti-doping and the manner in which the latter reinforces rather than contradicts the former. As is in the case of anti-trust law, or competition law's anti-monopoly provisions,[64] which seek to ensure that monopolies do not develop, anti-doping offers both a spectacular claim to the law's role in providing justice and fairness and at the same time an individualised band-aid fix

---

[62] L Boltanski and E Chiapello, *The New Spirit of Capitalism* (Verso, 2005); and L Boltanski and E Chiapello, 'The New Spirit of Capitalism' (2005) 18 *International Journal of Politics, Culture and Society* 161, 164 (emphasis added).

[63] F Hayek, *Law, Legislation and Liberty: A New Statement of the Liberal Principles of Justice and Political Economy, vol 2* (Routledge & Kegan Paul, 1976) 73–74, 179, fn 16.

[64] There is something very telling about the fact that in the USA the protection of the playing field of competition is referred to as anti-trust law!

to the excesses of pure competition. As Desautels-Stein has written the of the US legal context the

> paradigmatic example of the manner in which government would come to constrain competition was the establishment of a federal antitrust law in 1890. With this law and the body of jurisprudence it would spawn, the state would explicitly work to control the competitive marketplace, isolating "good" competition from the "bad".[65]

In the context of sport, and of global governance, the anti-doping apparatus brings into play a hybrid mix of actors including sport, corporate and private associations, who seek to explicitly control the competitive environment by denominating and isolating good competition from bad competition. This mix of actors, which revolves around WADA and the various anti-doping organisations, possesses an exceptional power, albeit in perfect conformity with neoliberal logic, by conferring power to establish the rules of the game on a technical body situated above governments.[66] These institutions that exist within the global anti-doping apparatus never seek to address the root systemic or structural conditions of the bad forms of competitive behaviour. The anti-doping apparatus is always one step behind the bad in its detection tools, just as in the case of 'competition' law; all that it can propose to do is to deal with the consequences of competition and not its roots:

> This point may at first seem too subtle, but there is a striking difference between the two kinds of approaches. The first approach, which I label "modern liberal," refrains until the end from any critical analysis of those legal rules which are constitutive of the classic liberal style and focuses entirely on the consequences of that style. Thus, the modern liberal style confronts symptoms with no worry about causes. The second approach, which might be labeled "progressive," is actually concerned with the deeper and more fundamental causes of social inequality. This might mean an attack on the classic liberal conception of contract and property rights themselves. The modern liberal style does not do this, nor does antitrust law. Antitrust law, even at its most ambitious, simply responds. It never attempts to re-create.[67]

On Desautels-Stein's analysis, the band-aid nature of anti-doping law is neither progressive nor modern liberal, as it never seeks to deal with the deeper and more fundamental causes of what it has sought to problematise. Nor is it classical liberal as it operates at the other extreme of the Law-governance continuum.

The Smear of Jouissance

Why is it then that the fairness the anti-doping apparatus seems to seek is so often promoted and accepted as a 'just cause' or 'war'? Is it here that an analysis of the

---

[65] J Desautels-Stein, 'The Market as a Legal Concept' (2012) 60 *Buffalo Law Review* 387, 427–28.
[66] Dadot and Laval, *The New Way of the World* (n 2) 209.
[67] Desautels-Stein, 'The Market as a Legal Concept' (n 65) 428.

production of subjectivity under neoliberalism may be of real assistance? One of the important questions posed by Madra and Özselçuk is 'what are the subjective conditions that cultivate a passionate attachment to the bourgeois axiom, "to each according to their contribution"?[68] Relevant to our work, what they are exploring is an analysis of the subjective investments that produce the passionate attachments which, in turn, provide the conditions for the justification and maintenance of neoliberal capitalism.[69]

In Chapter 4 we discussed Møller's criticism of the use of the paradigm of Panopticism in the context of the Whereabouts System. It was noted at that point that while everybody may not buy fully with their heart and soul into the system, there is, overall, an increasing acceptance and 'improvement' of the individual and the population brought about by Whereabouts. Madra and Özselçuk theorise that there is an 'implicit behaviourism' in much of the government literature which stems from a 'too quick ontologization of the behaviorist propositions of Chicago neoclassicism'. Their point is that:

> even though economic rationality may not hold at the level of the individual and even though concrete individuals behave in random ways, competitive dynamics, functioning like a selection mechanism, will make sure that economic rationality gets realized at the level of markets.[70]

It is at this point that the biopolitical nature of the apparatus of governance overcomes the distinctions between control and discipline operating at the level of the individual and biopower operating at the level of society. *Homo Economicus* is the

> working assumption of neoliberal governmentality ... it is the grid of intelligibility ... the surface of contact between the individual and the power exercised on him ... an interface between the individual and the government ... What Foucault offers is an analysis of 'governmental reason,' of those types of rationality that are implemented in the methods by which human conduct is directed through a state administration.[71]

For Madra and Özselçuk, Foucault's analysis is not a 'behavioral assumption from which neoliberal reason sees and attempts to engineer the world ... seamlessly realized in actuality ...'.[72] Hence, they approach subjectivity in terms of social fantasies that ... enable the constitution of a social link (in Althusserian terms, a "society effect" or, in psychoanalytic terms, "social transference") in the face of its central and constitutive derailment by the smear of jouissance.[73] The key to grasping the analysis of Madra and Özselçuk is what they term the 'entrepreneurial injunction'[74] and its relationship to this concept of *jouissance*.

---

[68] YM Madra and C Özselçuk, 'Jouissance and Antagonism in the Forms of the Commune: A Critique of Biopolitical Subjectivity' (2010) 22(3) *Rethinking Marxism* 481, 481.
[69] ibid, 484.
[70] ibid.
[71] ibid, 484–85.
[72] ibid.
[73] ibid, 487.
[74] ibid, 491–92.

This concept is something that encompasses more than its common English translation of 'enjoyment'. As Žižek puts it, to enjoy, the imperative of *jouissance*, Enjoy! is 'something we do as a kind of weird and twisted ethical duty'.[75] Dean has explained this ethical duty to Enjoy! as an excessive, intense please-pain, as that "something extra" for the sake of which we do what otherwise seems irrational, counterproductive, or even wrong … a special kind of agony, one that makes us feel more fully alive than anything else.[76] I want to revisit this 'special kind of agony' shortly, when viewing the cyclist's sense of drive and passion through Agamben's lens, that is, the sense of 'waiting for Christmas every day and it never comes', as an aspect of the condition as described by the British-Finnish rider, Charlie Wegelius. Nevertheless, before moving to consider this directly within the context of sport and anti-doping it must be made explicit that the imperative to Enjoy! entails more than this pleasure–pain seeking but also includes 'the extra element of pleasure attached to the painful experience of repeatedly missing one's goal'.[77]

For Žižek in the construction and maintenance of neoliberalism the imperative to Enjoy! performs a specific ideological function. If we follow Žižek and take ideology as something more than a discursive formation that covers over a fundamental incompleteness or impossibility, ideology also includes an 'extra, irrational nugget of enjoyment that attaches the subject to a formation'.[78] Here, in the construction and maintenance of the Real[79] of neoliberalism, ideology takes hold of the subject by promising to provide the subject with enjoyment. In the society of competition this enjoyment, or the hope of it, is manifested by the figure of the entrepreneur of the self, one who is able to compete in the great entrepreneurial adventure on the ideological fantasy of life's level playing field. The attachment to being a player in this game becomes the attachment to the fantasy, an all-consuming twisted and weird ethical duty of competition on the supposed level playing field of life.

In the construction of this ethical duty of competition, the law and the *apparatus* of governance perform the role of delimiting the good from the bad. For the lawyer, or the moralist, we are back in the realms of isolating the 'good' from the 'bad'. It is here we begin to move back into the realm of, for example, 'competition law' or for that matter and, more specifically for our enquiry, the law and apparatus of anti-doping. Lacan theorises *jouissance* in relation to law,[80] 'the taming of perverse *jouissance*'.[81] Law and governance institute the regulation of 'an infinite movement of desire within a delimited frame'.[82] The essence of the law here is

---

[75] S Žižek, *How to Read Lacan* (Granta Books, 2006) 79.
[76] J Dean, 'Enjoying Neoliberalism' (2008) 4(1) *Cultural Politics* 47, 51.
[77] ibid.
[78] ibid, 51–52.
[79] ibid, 52, citing Žižek.
[80] ibid, 490.
[81] J Lacan, *The Seminar, Book VII: The Ethics of Psychoanalysis*, trans D Porter (WW Norton, 1992) 4.
[82] Madra and Özselçuk, 'Jouissance and Antagonism' (n 68) 491.

to 'divide up, distribute, or reattribute everything that counts as jouissance'.[83] The morality of the law 'affirms itself in opposition to pleasure'[84] such that:

> in the subject's unstable relation to a law that demands the subject *to enjoy, but not to do so excessively* ... this transgressive superegoic injunction to enjoy, which underlies the prohibitive and regulative role of public law, is what really makes the subject "stick" to the law.[85]

In the construction and maintenance of the society of competition both the law and apparatus of governance perform a dual role. To the liberal or libertarian, at first glance, these appear to be contradictory, but they are actually complementary roles in the sense that the injunction to compete must also be complemented by an ideological explanation of certain excesses of competition as transgressive immoral moments.

At one point in his work, *The Doping* Devil,[86] Møller seems to be suggesting that the essence of sport is the result and its existential significance is the performance thus making a spectacle the process of active creations, not something that is just created. Active creations and performance on one level points us towards Foucault's aesthetics, but we are also led to this condition of ecstatic excess. Møller's consideration of Bataille puts on the table the place of the anti-doping apparatus in taming the excess that is inherent in Bataille's notion of sovereignty. Even in the festival or sport, where excess is a factor and permitted, excessive moments are constrained if they might threaten (economically) productive activity.[87] From this perspective we might say that the apparatus seeks to capture the performance and its excess but only its utility, which are its measurable or functional forms. Here the 'mission impossible' of both competition and anti-doping – the actual construction of a fair and level playing field beyond that of an ideological fantasy of the Real – reveals itself. The law and the *apparatus* of governance seek 'to administer and domesticate jouissance, [but] these efforts inevitably fail since it is impossible to balance out, apportion, or stitch together jouissance' which itself is 'ambiguous, excessive, and unstable'. It is thus important 'not to fall into a form of reproductionism where jouissance glues all the cultural, political, and economic processes snugly together in an everlasting "institutional equilibrium"'.[88] Are we here on the cusp of understanding what the anti-doping apparatus seeks to achieve: the impossible balancing out of the imperative to Enjoy![89] – Is it this and not immoral greed that is the reason that the testers and the apparatus is always one step behind the dopers?

The injunction to become the entrepreneur of the self, on the level playing field of life, is itself sustained by the false promise that all can, in fact, achieve full

---

[83] ibid, 490.
[84] Lacan, *The Seminar, Book VII* (n 81) 20.
[85] Madra and Özselçuk, 'Jouissance and Antagonism' (n 68) 490 (emphasis added).
[86] Møller, *The Doping Devil* (n 37) 103–10.
[87] ibid, 103–05.
[88] Madra and Özselçuk, 'Jouissance and Antagonism' (n 68) 490.
[89] ibid, 489.

enjoyment 'the mythical figure of the Entrepreneur fills in the empty place' of this false promise, such that 'the Entrepreneur is a fiction with material effects'. In the act of measuring oneself against the fantasy of the Entrepreneur, of 'continuously striving toward attaining it' one always comes up short.[90]

The figure of the athlete (let's call him Lance) can thus be conceived as one who can 'enjoy (and deserve this enjoyment) on our behalf'. In this manner the athlete on one level at least relieves 'us of our duty to measure up to the idealized figure of the Entrepreneur'. For Madra and Özselçuk[91] this relief (or interpassivity?) assists us in making sense 'of the resilience with which social subjects remain committed to capitalism'.[92]

Applying their approach to our problem, and to paraphrase a remark towards the end of their article, perhaps a realistic and sober explanation for the attraction and investment people place in the anti-doping apparatus is that of the backlash against the 'greed' of the doper, it is 'an attempt to isolate it as the symptom that blocks the fulfillment of the fantasy of a truly fair, efficient, and scientific capitalism'. Approached this way, the shift to near universal support for the Just War on doping, its necessity and its truth, is based upon a deference to 'the privileged expert subjects' of that apparatus 'who are supposed to know how to remedy and regulate the failures and excesses of competitive markets'.[93]

The Pleasure/Performance Apparatus

Before moving to consider the athlete as an expert of the society of competition and in order to develop the idea of the injunction to Enjoy! it is useful to consider the manner in which the new panoptic moment combines surveillance, especially in the forms of management and accounting, with striving for pleasure and enjoyment. In describing neoliberalism as a new subjective norm, Dadot and Laval note that what they term the neo-subject in the process of being formed, 'is a correlate of an apparatus of performance and pleasure'.[94] Here techniques of the self and techniques of choice merge. The correlate of the irresponsibility of a world that has become ungovernable by dint of its global character is the infinite responsibility of the individual for his own fate, for his capacity to succeed and be happy.[95]

> Not being weighed down by the past, cultivating positive expectations, having effective relations with others: the neoliberal management of oneself consists in manufacturing a high performance ego, which always demands more of the self, and his self-esteem paradoxically grows with its dissatisfaction at past performance.[96]

[90] ibid, 491–92.
[91] ibid, 493.
[92] ibid.
[93] ibid.
[94] Dadot and Laval, *The New Way of the World* (n 2) 255.
[95] ibid, 274.
[96] ibid.

Dadot and Laval's argument is that we cannot understand the scale of the deployment of neoliberal rationality if it is regarded in the way that Møller attempted to distinguish the Panopticon by characterising it as (or only as) the imposition of a mechanical force on society and individuals who are its external points of application. The neoliberal subject is undoubtedly one of competition and performance being made to succeed and to win. All of life becomes an exercise in which all are encouraged to compare themselves with the socially requisite norm of performance.[97] Performance is measured at every turn, whether in calculating our progress and improvement or, as we have seen, our deviation or deviance. Sport

> has become a ubiquitous principle of action and competition model of social relations. Coaching is simultaneously an index and a means of the constant analogy between sport, sex and work. More so, perhaps then economic discourse on competitiveness, this model has made it possible to naturalise a duty of performance, which is diffused to the masses, normal activity centred on generalised competition. In this apparatus, the enterprise readily identifies with winners …[98]

Sport is the terrain, or better, the method or model of governance in which all are 'requested to produce evermore and enjoy evermore'. Sport is, in this way, 'directly connected to the surplus enjoyment that has become systematic. Life itself, in all its aspects, becomes the object of apparatuses of performance and pleasure … Managerial discourse makes performance a duty and advertising discourse makes pleasure and imperative … subjects are enjoined to surpass themselves, to push back the limits …'.[99] The striving to Enjoy! constitutes from this perspective an 'extraction of surplus – pleasure from oneself' or 'an excess of self over self, or boundless self-transcendence' and it is this factor that makes the individual and the enterprise in the society of competition function.[100]

There is no end, no final, 'stable condition of self-possession, but a beyond the self that is always receding, which is constitutionally aligned in its very regime of the logic of enterprise and, over and above that, with the cosmos of the world market'.[101] The lack of any stable condition within neoliberalism is neatly crystallised in the '*Journey to Better*' marketing campaign for the Srixon golf ball[102] where the Northern Irish professional golfer, Graeme McDowell recounts that '[t]here's never really a "good enough" in golf. There's always better … We're always on the journey to better … That's the thing about better. You can't own it. You can

---

[97] ibid, 281.

[98] ibid.

[99] ibid, 284. They continue 283: 'We are the champions – such is the hymn of the new entrepreneurial subject. From the song's lyrics, which in their way heralded the new subjective course, the following warning in particular must be retained: no time for losers. What is new is precisely that the loser is the ordinary man, the one who, in essence, loses.'

[100] ibid.

[101] ibid.

[102] 'The Journey to Better' available at srixon.com/thejourney/.

only pursue it. Stalk it. But once you've tasted it, better is never truly beyond your reach.[103]

The body in the society of competition is now the product of choice, style, self-fashioning.[104] All of us must work towards a situation where we are always able to (try to) surpass our capacity, our performance and pleasure. This 'same discourse equalises everyone in the face of these new obligations: no handicap of birth or environment represents an insurmountable obstacle to personal involvement in the general apparatus'.[105] Hence, we have sport for all, and institutions such as the Paralympics but, crucially, we have the athlete as the expert of the society of competition, the athlete as the one who can teach us how to perform and to Enjoy!. Fair play becomes an iron discourse in a velvet vocabulary.[106]

The Athlete – An Expert of the Society of Competition

We have already seen the role that the privileged expert subjects, for example in the Biological Passport, play in the justification and fulfilment of the ideological fantasy of the society of competition and the effect that such expert knowledge has in mutating traditional concepts of Law and Legal evidence. Furthermore, the athletes themselves are employed both in the service of generalised ambassadors of competition and as ambassadors of its inherent purity, naturalness and good-ness. The athlete performs (with pleasure and privilege) in a 'great social theatre' lending the rest of us a vocabulary. It is within this realm that we both are relieved of the failures of our inability to achieve the fantasy – to live the dream – but, at the same time, we are continually driven to strive to achieve it. The athlete as societal 'role model' encompasses this inherent contradiction of the society of competition.

On one level, the athlete embodies the fantasy of the entrepreneur of the self. At the same time, they are, given the relief they provide us through their exper-tise, privileged subjects and, in so being, they are measured against an idealised norm imposed by the law and the anti-doping apparatus, which itself is informed by the fantasy and promise offered by neoliberalism. The privileged expert who lives the athletic dream is one of 'pure performance' and is an entrepreneur of the self, '100% me!'.[107] The clean athlete is heralded as being honourable, ethical, sincere, having pledged 'to do their best using only natural talent and hard effort, never using performance enhancing drugs or knowingly bringing the sport into disrepute'.[108] It is not only the level playing field, but also the scientist or the athlete

---

[103] 'The Journey to Better – Graeme McDowell' (Extended Version) Srixon TVUSA, available at www.youtube.com/watch?v=6CoVE-UN9G4.
[104] Dadot and Laval, *The New Way of the World* (n 2) 295.
[105] ibid.
[106] ibid.
[107] 'Pure performance' is the mission statement of ASADA, while '100% me' is that of UK Anti-Doping.
[108] Bike Pure Rider Honour Code, available at bikepure.org/resources/.

(ie, the privileged expert) in whom we place our trust in order to found and sustain our commitment to, and hope in, the society of competition.

The Australian Sports Anti-Doping Authority (ASADA) is a government statutory authority whose stated purpose is to protect sporting integrity through the elimination of doping and whose vision is to be Australia's driving force for pure performance in sport. When launching ASADA's web-based educational programme, former Australian Minister for Sport, Mark Arbib, stated that: 'Pure Performance is a world-leading anti-doping program that will give our athletes the confidence to proudly compete drug-free on the world stage.'[109] ASADA's website proudly states the Pure Performance programme is a solution for developing 'a level playing field in sport'.

Bike Pure is the name of 'an independent not for profit organization' which promotes honest ethical cycle sport. Bike Pure is 'strongly opposed to doping and stands together in a united position to begin a new era for cycle sport'. It is an 'independent voice for honest, ethical cycling on a global scale, sending a powerful message that you don't have to resort to taking illegal performance enhancing drugs to compete in cycle sport'. It was conceived 'out of the doping scandals that tarnished the 2008 Tour de France' and with the 'profound message of promoting honesty and integrity in sport'. Their website sets out their 'philosophy' at length:

> The continuous aim of Bike Pure is to help develop and sustain a future generation of sincere role models who young athletes can aspire to. Our aim is also to help to educate young athletes that they can compete and be successful in sport without having to resort to cheating against their opponents .... Bike Pure feel that correct guidance given to the next generation of riders will have a foundational effect on the decisions athletes make if they are ever faced with a decision to dope .... We encourage athletes and teams to adhere to our 'Honour Code', declaring that they are opposed to doping in sport. Bike Pure are lobbying for stiffer penalties for doping offenders – 4-year ban minimum and life bans for repeat offenders. It is through the actions and support of our members that we can apply pressure on authorities for these measures to be implicated.
>
> We are not naive to think this is a complete solution, but it is an important first element in getting the riders who are opposed to doping to join forces with the supporters and lay a foundation to protect the mental and physical health of future champions and the integrity of our wonderful sport.
>
> Bike Pure's Athlete Honour Code:
>
> - I pledge to respect and adhere to the rules of my sport.
> - I pledge to compete to the best of my own natural ability.
> - I pledge to commit to compete without using banned substances.
> - I pledge to respect my fellow competitors.
> - I pledge that as an ethical Bike Pure role model I will adhere to clean, honest, ethical sport and not knowingly bring my sport into disrepute.[110]

---

[109] Senator The Hon Mark Arbib, Assistant Treasurer, Minister for Small Business, Minister for Sport, Media Release, 16 February 2012, 'Most Comprehensive Anti-Doping Program for Australian Olympic and Paralympic Athletes'.

[110] Bike Pure Rider Honour Code, available at bikepure.org/resources/.

The UK Anti-Doping Agency is 'a Non-Departmental Public Body which is accountable to Parliament through the [UK] Department for Culture, Media and Sport' and acts as 'the principal advisor to government on drug-free sport, UK Anti-Doping is responsible for protecting sport from the threat of doping in the UK'.[111] Its website states that:

> Substances and methods are banned for a reason. Doping, the use of artificial enhancements to gain an advantage over others in competition, is cheating and is fundamentally contrary to the spirit of sport. Further, doping robs true athletes who play by the rules of their right to competition that is safe and fair.
>
> Doping affects not just top athletes, but also future generations who may be influenced by what top athletes do. Only by taking a concerted and comprehensive approach to the fight against doping in sport is it possible to protect the integrity of sport, the health of athletes, and young aspiring sports people worldwide.[112]

UK Anti-Doping's principal education programme, which promotes a number of ambassadors is entitled '100% me':

100% me: Pure Sport, True Talent

100% me is about being a true athlete. It's about being able to say my performance is 100% me. There is no secret to my success – just hard work, determination and talent.

From plimsolls to podium

100% me is here to help you throughout your sporting journey. 100% me supports, informs and educates athletes throughout their careers by providing anti-doping advice and guidance. It is your guide to ensure you can 'be clean and stay clean'.

100% me ambassdors

Many of the UK's top athletes support 100% me and champion doping-free sport ....

Values of 100% me

As an athlete you will no doubt also embrace the values of 100% me. The 100% me campaign is about being successful, confident and retaining the values of clean, fair competition. 100% me embodies and celebrates five key values:

- Hard work
- Determination
- Passion
- Respect
- Integrity

… 100% me is here to help you throughout your sporting journey. 100% me supports, informs and educates athletes throughout their careers by providing anti-doping advice and guidance. It is your guide to ensure you can "be clean and stay clean".[113]

The logic and the values expounded by these organisations are inherently biopolitical in nature – they are concerned with the administration and management of

---

[111] UK Anti-Doping What We Do, www.ukad.org.uk/what-we-do/.
[112] ibid.
[113] What is 100% Me?, available at www.ukad.org.uk/athletes/100percentme.

life itself. It is a form of politics that has taken life as its object. Furthermore, the values and characteristics it seeks to promote are those of the 'good': a valuable and productive member of the society of competition, hard work, dedication, purity, passion and resilience. Neocleous has commented on the rise of resilience during neo-liberalism's development as a significant political category that has

> expanded to straddle the private as well as the public, the personal as well as the political, the subjective as well as the objective, and so organisational resilience is connected to personal resilience in such a way that contemporary citizenship now has to be thought through 'the power of resilience'. ... The anxious citizen is acknowledged as the resilient citizen and championed. ... the relationship between the economic development of neoliberal subjectivity and the political development of resilient citizenship.[114]

With reference to the observations of Marx and capitalism's objective roots in uncertainty, instability, restlessness, agitation and change, he notes that

> ... capital thrives on anxiety. The neoliberal intensification of this process ... has been compounded by this articulation of resilience as something personal as well as systemic. Resilience is thus presented as a key way of subjectively working through the uncertainty and instability of contemporary capital. The neoliberal subject can 'achieve balance' ... can 'overcome life's hurdles' ... and just 'bounce back from whatever life throws at us' ... The policing of the resilient citizen coincides with the socio-economic fabrication of resilient yet flexible labour. *Neoliberal citizenship is nothing if not a training in resilience.* ... anxiety and resilience are now core to the jargon of neoliberal authenticity ... the jargon of neoliberal authenticity is the jargon of neoliberal authoritarianism. *This is police power at its most profound, shaping subjectivity and fabricating order ... coaching us in our resilience.* And it is a police power par excellence in closing down alternate possibilities: we can be anxious about what might happen, but our response must be resilience training, not political struggle. We can be collectively anxious and structurally resilient, but not mobilised politically.[115]

That the athletic expert is a counsellor of resilience is evident from the laudatory euphoria throughout the media in the wake of Cadel Evans' 2010 *Tour de France* victory. This can be illustrated by reference to a couple of blog pieces written at that time, one on 'better parenting' and another on 'personal bests'. The first speaks of a 'story that's come along at precisely the right time'.[116] Evans is contrasted with our politicians who do not inspire us, who are not good role models and who are not trusted by the public

> along came Cadel Evans, and his winning ride. Finally, there is someone worthy of emulation by our kids. He showed all the qualities of grit, determination and mental toughness that most parents I meet would love their kids to develop.

---

[114] M Neocleous, 'Anxious Resilience' *Mute* (18 August 2011).
[115] ibid (emphasis added).
[116] M Grose, 'Parenting Ideas' (2010), available at www.parentingideas.com.au/Blog/July-2011/Cadel-Evans-is-one-tough-hombre,-and-one-great-rol.

Evans is someone who has

> worked long and hard to master his craft. … He didn't let disappointment deter him. … he didn't let setbacks and bad luck derail him. Learning from these past experiences, and taking lessons in preparation from past winners, he came back stronger and more determined than ever to make this race his own. … Evans' feat was a shining story of resilience. His ability to hang in both physically and mentally when times were tough was astounding.[117]

Along with his resilience, Evans is an example to us all that we are all winners. We are all winners because we can always strive to achieve our own personal bests (this is why triathlon is the neoliberal sport par excellence):

> PB – a term most often associated with sport – describes an achievement that surpasses anything an individual has ever achieved before. When athletes achieve a PB they are elated. A PB taps into one of our most basic human needs – the need for accomplishment. A PB is a measure of our performance and also represents the realisation of our fundamental human need to improve. … Sport teaches us that being your best is not only about skill and talent, but also requires tapping into the vast pool of psychological resources available to us. … By way of example, look no further back than those three sleep-deprived weeks in July, when Australia witnessed one of our greatest-ever sporting moments – Cadel Evans winning the Tour de France. The Tour, 3,000km of relentless physical and mental endurance, is the most gruelling sporting event in the world today. … What does it take to win the Tour? Well, apart from the obvious physical capabilities, including skill, fitness and stamina, there's grit, determination, courage, persistence, focus, desire, resilience … the list goes on, and Cadel has them all. … But here's the thing – we may not all be elite bike riders (or musicians or scholars or leaders), but every single one of us, no matter what our level of skill, talent or circumstances, can be better. We all have the capacity to develop these psychological traits that give us the edge and help us realise our full potential.[118]

At its core, unlike the liberalism of modernity, living in neoliberalism is not about specialisation, but inspirational and passionate performance, improvement, adaptability, multi-tasking, versatility and resilience. The object is for man to change himself in an 'economy in constant motion' where 'adaption … [is] always a current task'.[119] The intensification of work on the self, brought about by *Citius Altius Fortius*, depends upon a system of incentives and sanctions that give rise to controlled autonomy and flexible constraint. The subject, like the athletic expert, is one of self-control, always aiming to internalise constraints and the new norms of productive efficiency and individual performance brought about by generalised competition. The position of the athlete shows us that there has not been a reduction of hierarchical controls, but only 'their gradual alteration in the context of a new management that has been able to rely on modes of organisation, new

---

[117] ibid.
[118] ibid.
[119] Dadot and Laval, *The New Way of the World* (n 2) 64–65.

accounting, recording and communication technologies, and so on'.[120] The athlete as expert 'is reactive, more flexible, more innovative, technically more effective, more specialist, less subject to statutory rules' and at the same time subject to an intensification of a global governmental apparatus based upon their consent to take part in the performance–pleasure apparatus.[121] This consent is brought about not so much by sovereign command but by a multiplication of contractual relations that stand beyond the State. The athlete is both technical and tactical and like 'enterprise man are economic agents who only respond to the logic of their own self-interest'.[122] The logic of individual calculation is reflected throughout the anti-doping apparatus as it is throughout the society of competition of which the athlete is the expert and ambassador. The athlete is the archetype of hypermodern, uncertain, flexible, precarious, fluid and weightless man today.[123] Through his compulsory involvement brought about by 'choice' and 'consent' in the anti-doping apparatus and his internalised flexible constraint, he is able to seize the opportunity to freely fashion his life while at the same time eroding everything that is stable in his personality. No longer does work provide a stable framework, a predictable career, and a set of robust personal relations. What the athlete as expert normalises is the need to consider nothing but immediately utilisable competences. This explains both the need to constantly change and the need to discard as obsolete the past ('[y]ou've always got to prove yourself; it is necessary to start all over again') as much as it does the rapid obsolescence and eviction of those unhealthy, unsuitable or culturally unfit (dopers) for the society of competition.[124]

In a world where competition is the main lever for enhancing responsibility, the athlete as expert provides everyone with the model against which they must constantly measure and prove themselves in order to merit the conditions of their own existence. 'Life is perpetual risk management, requiring strict abstention from dangerous practices, constant self-control, and a regulation of one's own behaviour that blends asceticism and flexibility.'[125] The athlete is the perfect embodiment of the value of the society of competition as they

> have no hesitation in selling themselves to the highest bidder without any considerations of loyalty and fidelity. Furthermore, maintenance of one's body, self-improvement, the search a powerful sensations, fascination with extremes, the taste for active leisure, and the idealised overcoming of limits indicate that sporting model is not reducible to the entertaining spectacle of the powerful devouring one another.[126]

The athlete is held up as an example of the possibility of living the dream and of making it on the global playing field of life. In this fantasy world of generalised

---

[120] ibid, 177–78.
[121] ibid, 230–31.
[122] ibid.
[123] ibid, 255.
[124] ibid, 289.
[125] ibid, 166–67.
[126] ibid, 282.

competition, it is not greed, but factors such as self-control, hard work, dedication and integrity and resilience, that have allowed them to not come up short. We may not all be able to achieve their privileged status, their success in the global sporting spectatcle, but we can learn from their attitude and their ethic, the manner in which they have thrown themselves at the mercy of competition. In the society of competition, we can all be winners and achieve our PB. We mere mortals are told to learn from the athletic expert and to 'Just Do It'.

Excursus: Competition, *Jouissance* and the Non-language of Sport

Cycling, Benjo Maso has suggested, can only be written,[1] it can never be seen in its completeness and, possibly, it cannot ever be said. Even in the times of complete television coverage there is an impossibility of bearing witness to the whole event (is this why there is always a loathing of the television commentator for their misstatements and mistakes?). In Maso's statement, and his rationale for the invention of heroic sports journalism,[2] there might be another suggestion of what is at play in sport, in anti-doping and its relation to the state of exception and Agamben's figure of *homo sacer* – the unspeakable, unsayable zone of indistinction between the animal and the human and between the exception and the norm.

In discussing the need for sovereignty to politicise bare life, Agamben briefly turns to a passage from Aristotle's *Politics*, which situates the proper place of the *polis* in the transition from voice to language. In doing so, Agamben equates this to the link between bare life and politics.[3] Throughout his trilogy, which examines the state of exception, which comes to fruition but not an end, the inability to speak plays an important part in capturing what is at play within this zone of indistinction. The inability of bare life to speak and the ability of political life to speak are the two poles between which the idea of humanity oscillates. In our reading of these texts, this is also the first point at which we can start to draw some analogy or an approximation between Agamben's subject of *homo sacer* and the subject of sport and the position of the athlete. Is it that sport is prior to language or is itself unable to be directly spoken through language?

The Greek word ἄφατος (afasia) carried with it the meaning of something not uttered, nameless, untold, unutterable, ineffable. It was something extraordinary – in the sense of there not been a way to say how something is done.[4] Denis Hauw has commented on the athlete's condition of alexithymia (from the Ancient Greek words λέξις (lexis, 'diction', 'word') and θυμός (thumos, 'soul, as the seat of emotion, feeling, and thought') – literally 'without words for emotions' – a term coined by psychotherapist Peter Sifneos in 1973 to describe a state of deficiency in understanding, processing, or describing emotions.[5] Hauw et al have considered

---

[1] B Maso, *The Sweat of the Gods* (Mousehold Press, 2005) 14, 20.
[2] ibid.
[3] G Agamben, *Homo Sacer, Sovereign Power and Bare Life* (Stanford University Press, 1999) 7.
[4] HG Liddell and R Scott, 'An Intermediate Greek-English Lexicon' (1889), available at perseus.uchicago.edu/Reference/MiddleLiddell.html.
[5] Alexithymia Wikipedia en.wikipedia.org/wiki/Alexithymia.

this condition in the context of a review of anti-doping research conducted during the first decade of the twenty-first century.[6] One research priority pursued by some in this area has been based around ideas of addiction and sensation seeking, that is, the addiction or dependence arising in some athletes and their subsequent post-athletic feelings of emptiness. It is in a context related to this that Hauw has raised the condition of alexithymia.

These two terms, afasia and alexithymia, are both related to an inability to say or express emotions through speech. It might be trite to say that in sport it is the body which communicates, but, more than that, what it communicates is an intensity, an emotion, and thus, something prior to language. How many times do we hear that such and such a sportsperson is in fact 'an animal' or is animal-like? The Swiss cyclist, Fabian Cancellara rides like 'an animal', Barthes has his heroes of Greek myth, and Carlos Arribas has said that the performance of the climber is a matter for the Gods.[7] It is here that this fundamental categorical pair of politics of Agamben's – that of bare life and political existence; come into play in the realm of sport. There is politics – that is something other than an animal; because man separates himself from the animal, opposes himself to his own bare life through language. Is that what is at play here, both in sport and within the apparatus of anti-doping, in this oscillation between animal and human?

How many times are we unable to express in words the feeling or emotion we encounter doing or even observing sport? Firstly, what is it that cannot be expressed? Does Agamben, again, give us a clue in *Remnants of Auschwitz,*[8] in his discussion of the idea of *festus* (the festival or celebration). In discussing the writing of Kimura Bin, he identifies three stages of the idea of the festival applied to a psychology of the subject. These are *post festum, ante festum* and *intra festum.*

The concept of *post festum* – the 'I was' – represents an irreparable past, a melancholic state which comes with the arrival of things already done. This melancholic state might be equated with an athlete's feeling post-event. It could also be equated with the living death that the athlete encounters post-career, whether that career has ended 'normally' by way of retirement or has been enforced by way of a ban.

Ante festum involves a state where this direction of the melancholic's orientation to the past is inverted. The 'I' here is never a certain possession but it is always something to be attained, a potentiality or possibility of being oneself in the act of the performance of the event; 'the essential problem here is the problem of one's own possibility of being oneself, the problem of the certainty of becoming oneself, and, therefore, the risk of being alienated from oneself'.[9] Here, rather than

---

[6] J Bilard, G Ninot and D Hauw, 'Motives for Illicit Use of Doping Substances among Athletes Calling a National Antidoping Phone-help Service: An Exploratory Study' (2011) 46(4) *Substance Use Misuse* 359.

[7] C Arribas, 'The Giro and the Dolomites', available at newcyclingpathways.blogspot.com.au/2009/05/giro-and-dolomites-more-on-myth-and.html.

[8] G Agamben, *Remnants of Auschwitz: The Witness and the Archive* (Zone Books, 1999) 125–28.

[9] ibid, 126.

a melancholic past, one gives primacy to the future in the form of projection and anticipation. But this future always risks itself and risks not being present at the point of its own celebration. Is it like the state of unattainable enjoyment bound up with the concept of *joiussance,* the waiting for a Christmas every day that never comes for Wegelius.[10]

Agamben states that *intra festum* one might expect is the point where human beings finally gain access to self-presence, but that this is not so, and in explaining this he refers to two examples given by Bin that are not celebratory. The first is obsessive neurosis, a condition whereby one attempts to document their own presence at a celebration that constantly eludes them. This condition suggests the obsessive athlete who never quite achieves it despite the (overly) meticulous calculation, management and administration of both their *ante* and *intra festum* states. Despite their obsession with achieving their 'true' selves, despite this meticulous planning, they never quite make it – the condition of Cadel Evans until he made it to the top of the podium in the 2011 *Tour De France,* and where he found himself again after that victory.

The second example proposed by Bin is that of epilepsy, which is a particular form of self-loss achieved through a kind of ecstatic excess over presence. Agamben asks: why does the epileptic lose consciousness? and answers: because that is the point in which the 'I' is about to adhere itself in the supreme moment of celebration. The epileptic crisis confirms consciousness' incapacity to tolerate presence, to participate in its own celebration.

Is that what communicates to us in sport this ecstatic excess of the celebration? Is this unspeakable, unsayable zone of sport and athletic celebration somehow related to this supreme moment of celebration where the 'I' is able to elude the demand to 'Wake Up!'? and for a moment achieves the imperative of 'Enjoy'! In Agamben's consideration of Bin and the *festum,* there is a reference to Dostoevsky:

> There are instants that last no longer than five or six seconds, in which all of a sudden you hear the presence of eternal harmony, in which you have reached it. It is not earthly. But I do not want to say that it is heavenly either; only that an earthly man is incapable of tolerating it. He must either be physically transformed or die.[11]

One professional cyclist interviewed described the sensations they enjoyed in their work as follows:

> A: It's like I enjoy doing my job, that's why I do it, I enjoy the day to day things of it, I enjoy riding the bike in the fresh air, and I enjoy periodising, and a big sensation is putting your body … like when you've just gone out, and just got it dialed, and you just get it tweaked, that fine tuning. That's what I get a lot of satisfaction out of. That's like mastering your trade you know. Or I get back on my mountain bike and I haven't touched it for six or eight months and it's perfect, it's just how I know it. I grew up

---

[10] Charlie Wegelius in T Kolln, *The Peloton: Portrait of a Generation* (Rouleur Limited, 2010).
[11] Agamben, *Remnants of Auschwitz* (n 8) 127.

riding, I feel I have complete competence at how to control my bike, get down a hill or doing a skill you know, that's what I really like.

Q: I don't want to get all, you're probably as much a hippie as I am …, I don't want to get all mystical on you, but is it sort of like that feeling when it's all dialed, it's all happening, and you put your body on the line, and you're away in a break, or something's going to happen, whatever it is, is it sort of like an out of body experience?

A: Oh absolutely it is. When your form is that good, and probably the best seasons I've had, and this is why this season has been so frustrating for me, I've sucked basically all year. Maybe, in every other year I've had a point, I've had a day or two days, or 10 or 12 of them, where it's like perfect you know, you don't feel anything, there's no pain, you're in complete control, you are out of body pretty much. I've even, for example, now you guys are going to think I'm crazy, but I go and see a yoga instructor. … I mean I don't do any stretching or anything like that, it's the breathing stuff, and a lot of visualisation stuff, and they basically teach you, and this is how those yogis and people like that, when they meditate, it's that 'out of body' experience pretty much and that's when you're most content, you're just happy with the moment, you know, and when you're doing that and you've perfected your skill, your trade, because you've practiced at it, and you've worked over and over, and just to get it there, and it all lines up, but you use those principals of just being in that moment as they call it.

Q: Well what you're presenting is again a really positive image of what cycling is or could be.

A: If I can make a living doing that, I'm a happy bloke. If I can live a good lifestyle and have that experience, I'm content you know. Does that make sense? Is that off track to what you …?

Q: No look, when you were saying that, I remember once chasing down a break in the Top End Tour, when I used to race, and I remember that feeling of no pain, you just sort of, it's just like pure joy and I thought fuck, I'm in 54/13 here, and I'm just churning up the Stuart Highway, chasing these guys down and was just going you know, I wasn't doing anything, I was turning those pedals and I was thinking fuck.

A: The experience, I mean I don't want to sound like I've got an ego or something but the one I refer it to, I was junior world champion … For an hour 20 I was just in bliss, I spent 12 months preparing for the event. Two hours after I was vomiting and shitting and couldn't eat for six hours, and I was in, you know while I'm in the doping control, but for an hour 20 I ran at 190 heart rate average and maxed at over 200 and did not feel a thing. I was world champion at it. That's the ultimate you know? That's mastered, I had it dialed for an hour 20 in 12 months and that's all that mattered.

Q: You said to me in the email, is this all about your thesis or something else? This is sort of heading towards the stuff I want to do in my thesis but there's something …[12]

To be in this zone, to be dialed in and to achieve this ecstatic excess of celebration, the pleasure and pain of *joiussance* is the ultimate athletic experience. The athlete is the world champion of pleasure and pain, the champion of the performance/pleasure apparatus.

---

[12] Hardie, Shilbury, Bozzi and Ware 2010, unpublished interview.

Is there something at play in the depths of the apparatus of anti-doping which seeks to humanise this figure of bare life? To create a human out of an animal, or at least to capture and control this animal element in the wider process of governmentality? This thing, this condition that alludes the call to 'Wake Up!', the momentary achievement of the imperative to 'Enjoy!' is it also a part of the system of administration and management of life for the ends of a global economy, is it this that is at stake in the sovereign conception of anti-doping? And if so, is there, another way for us to rationalise anti-doping apart from this? Is the husk, the shell of competition, which the liberal analysis tells us is the true spirit, the true essence of sport, simply a blanket with which this is covered over and captured? And is this shell or blanket the same one, or at least analogous to the shell that clothes Law as justice? Or, for that matter, the ideological fantasy of the entrepreneur in neoliberalism?

6

Conclusion

Functionality – Exception – Spectacle

One of the principal things that we have tried to show throughout this work is that the law of the anti-doping apparatus represents something different from simply doing something that we once knew as the Law. The anti-doping apparatus is a part of a general tendency away from, a mutation of, the traditional concept of Law and the Rule of Law. This apparatus operates in a profoundly different manner from the Law of modernity and carries with it a movement of the place of adjudication beyond the State sphere and its sovereign boundaries. Adjudication takes place throughout an exceptional, modulating, and supranational framework, consisting of an emergent *Lex Doping* and mechanisms of governance, including that of the spectacle. This was first introduced in Chapter 2 with our discussion of the end of modernity and *Operación Puerto*. In Chapter 3 we sought to provide a sketch of the modernist conception of the Rule of Law and the Law, while highlighting that, within modernity, the seeds of their transgression were already present through forms of policing, administration and governance. Chapter 4 considered the intensification of these forms of policing, administration and governance through panoptic and control mechanisms that are accompanied by exceptional transformations of the place of the expert in the law. Chapter 5 brought us face to face with our contemporary form of law and its rule of law with the instigation and subjection of all of society to the rules of competition.

However, this brief overview does not, by itself, answer the question posed at the beginning of this study. That is, what juridical form and theory of sovereignty is able to sustain and found the primacy of governance over Law and sovereignty? What does our case tell us about the configuration of the Law–governance continuum? What answers does it offer to the questions we have posed? We can set out in a table below a schematic answer in order to bring together the various threads woven into our story.

Early in this work we proposed the rubric of Spectacle-Functionality-Exception in order to point, in shorthand, to significant changes in the way that law is done and to express something inherent, or embodied, within Moeller's fear concerning the end of modernity. We now develop this rubric further before continuing to answer our question. I have used the term functionality to describe the way in which the Law or law plays an instrumental role. The functionality of the Law is inscribed in neoliberal rationality; it is an instrumental rationality that always seeks to adapt means to ends. In doing so it excludes the kind of rationality that

Møller regards as the cornerstone of modernity and enlightenment principles, that is a rationality that makes reflecting on action a condition of acting properly.[1] The end of the Law in neoliberalism is that of creating the conditions, or we might say constitution, for the construction of competition as the value or single logic that underpins the totality of the world. The goal of generalised competition is the rationale. This is Law's function in a neoliberal world.

A.   *Given the growing primacy of the arts of government (over the law and sovereignty)*
        [Permanent State of Exception]

B.   *It is a case of discovering:*

     I.   *The Juridical Form and*
            [Contractual Governance]

         i.   *juridical form*
                [contractual governance]

         ii. *institutional form*
                [the administration & police]

         iii. *legal basis*
                [arbitration, functionality, spectacle]

     II.   *The Theory of Sovereignty*
            [Homo Econonimus and Society of Competition]

C.   *that were able to Found and Sustain A*
        [Glory [B.II] + Effect [B I.iii] -> [Permanent State of Exception [A.]]

                      – sovereignty typical of the State [of exception]

The originality of this new way of the world is that it replaces the binary opposition of intervention/non-intervention by the State with a new question surrounding the nature of State intervention.[2] It is this change that has had a profound effect on the Law of modernity and forms of law that have followed it. Tangled up in this is that there has also been a profound change or affect upon the meaning of what is known as the 'public interest'. As we have seen in Valverde's case, the Court of Arbitration for Sport (CAS) took the view that the public interest in the fight against doping took precedence over the cyclist's legal, constitutional and human rights. But as we pointed out, this so-called public interest did not emerge from any political or social contract; its source was not public law in the sense that we have come to know it. Instead, for the CAS, the public interest arose because of Valverde's personal consent or choice to participate in sport. Therefore, in this instance, the public interest arises because of private (not public) agreement – an individual (not a social) contract.[3] At play in determining this public interest, and in determining

---

[1] P Dadot and C Laval, *The New Way of the World* (Verso Books, 2013) 114.
[2] ibid, 121.
[3] ibid.

or differentiating between legitimate and illegitimate intervention,[4] is what we mean by society. As Dadot and Laval put it, 'at stake is the meaning of a little word: social' such that in the world of neoliberalism the 'only social objective is the market and competition'.[5] In this new way of the world, the only value underpinning 'society' and the Law/law is the end of generalising, or totalising, competition.

A brief detour into legal theory helps to position this shift. Hayek rejected the entire lineage of the legal positivism of modernity commencing with Hobbes and passing through Bentham, Austin and Kelsen that posited Law as emanating from sovereign will. This is the form of Law we described in Chapter 3. For instance, and in a similar way to our description, Hobbes defined the Law 'as the command of him that hath the legislative power'.[6] Bentham's view was that the Law is only made by the legislator, and this explains his antagonistic position on judicial discretion and the common law. 'In Hayek's view, John Austin and Hans Kelsen merely extended this intellectual tradition, which reduces Law to the will of the Legislator, in contrast with the liberal tradition, which asserts the precedence of law over Legislation'.[7] The law, then, for Hayek was not the Law. Dadot and Laval argue that what is partly at stake here is the distinction between the Greek terms *nomos* and *thesis*:

> It will be recalled that the Greeks carefully distinguish between nomos and thesis: private law alone is nomos, whereas public law is thesis – which means a public law is 'enacted' or "constructed", and in this sense constitutes a "manufactured" or "artificial" order, whereas civil law is essentially a "spontaneous" order. Rules of conduct, which alone make possible the formation of a spontaneous market order, are there for themselves derived not from the arbitrary will of a few men, but from a spontaneous process of selection operating over the longue durée.[8]

From this perspective, then, private law is not the Law emanating from sovereign will, but law, which, as with the market, is a product of a process of discovery through competition. The function of private law is nothing other than the ordering of the affairs of those within neoliberal society. Not being enacted, constructed, or manufactured, and simply being a mechanism to ensure the operation of the competitive market, private law appears as having no end in itself. In this way we can say that neoliberalism's law, as with its market, has no end that stands outside of itself; neoliberalism, the market, competition, law, have no (governing) value other than themselves. Furthermore, as we have seen, in this system the only value of the Law and the Rule of Law is to create and maintain the conditions for competition to take place. Dumont might have said that in this respect what we have constituted as a whole is a moribund hierarchy.[9] We will return to this shortly.

---

[4] ibid, 121.
[5] ibid, 122.
[6] See, eg, ibid, 128–29.
[7] ibid.
[8] ibid, 127–28.
[9] L Dumont, *Homo Hierarchicus, The Caste System and its Implications* (Paladin, 1972) 306.

Again, Dadot and Laval assist us in illustrating this when they point to Hayek's distinction between the market – which is independent of any goal – and the economy. Their description of the economy is one which echoes Agamben's discussion of *oikonomia*; the market, they say, must not be confused with the economy, the latter is 'an intentional organization or arrangement ... for a purpose ... which pertains to taxes'.[10] Private law thus pertains to the realm of the market; public law is, on this view, a mechanism or institution of Government. In this situation, the role of the Law (as with the Rule of Law) is only to create the conditions for competition, to ensure the cohesion of the market order through the making and application of formal rules that apply by virtue of their generality. The Law's only proper role is to construct the competitive playing field and to prohibit certain kinds of activity; public law should go no further than this.[11] It is only through prohibition that public law guides and pilots conduct, in a similar way to the World Anti-Doping Agency's (WADC) Prohibited List, which never spells out what one should do, never what is permitted (what Hayek terms 'a command'[12]), only what is prohibited. Public law is not the conduction of conduct. Public law is the mechanism that establishes and defines the market or space of competition; it is in this way that the neoliberal market is established and defined by Law. But this is a new kind of Law aimed at constituting a new kind of society.

Thus, the teleology of public law only has one value, simply that of creating the conditions for the market, which, of course, has no value other than itself. Within the space of market relations, the only bond is that of economic relations – 'the market order is not an economy, but it is composed of economic relations'.[13] Economic relations based upon competition are the only social bond; this is a society that is constituted by 'pure performance' where all are simply '100% Me'. The economic relation of competition becomes the preeminent tool of governance and, within this realm, the only real (neoliberal) law is private law, which itself is based upon or derived from the order of economic relations.

We take Dumont's concept of a moribund hierarchy to mean a hierarchy that forms a whole and is governed by a totalising value, or a single logic, but which has no governing end in or other than itself. Our hierarchy is one totally governed and informed by the economic relation of competition. For Dumont the term:

> ... value designates something different from being, and something which, while the scientifically true is universal, is eminently variable with the social environment, and even within a given society, according not only to social classes but to diverse departments of activity and experience ...[14]

---

[10] Dadot and Laval, *The New Way of the World* (n 1) 124.

[11] ibid, 124–25.

[12] ibid, 125.

[13] ibid.

[14] L Dumont, *Essays on Individualism: Modern Ideology in Anthropological Perspective* (University of Chicago Press, 1986) 239.

In the new way of the world of neoliberalism's Empire there is no variation of value within the social environment; crucially, this value posits itself on a global basis as the only way of being. Without being provocative, and if taken as a set of principles associated with the base word 'total', we can quite confidently say that the value of competition the value of competition today is totalitarian. There can be no doubt that the ideology of competition seeks to exert total authority over society while seeking to control all aspects of public and private life. The kind of value represented by competition is not really a value at all – 'the end cannot be its own means'.[15] Rather than being a value, the single logic of Empire performs the function of

> … annihilating values entirely … ends are reduced to means: having construed a cate-gory of "instrumental values," they proceed to deny the distinct existence of "intrinsic values," that is, of values proper … a dead end of individualism.[16]

A hierarchy constituted by a single value of the market economy of competition is a hierarchy that has no external value – in neoliberalism, law has no end in itself – the law and the market only have a function.

In describing *Operación Puerto* and the *Valverde* cases, Chapter 2 sought to highlight that the exception to the Law that takes place within the anti-doping apparatus is, in fact, a permanent exception to the Law of the sovereign State that reigned throughout modernity's high-water tide. The *Valverde* cases show us how a cyclist's consent, manifested by joining a cycling club, or taking out a racing licence, sets in place a policing and disciplinary procedure in which sovereign boundaries are traversed and dissolved. Within the logic of the anti-doping appa-ratus, State action in pursuit of the infrastructure and networks that contribute to doping on a systemic level are regarded as not being functional to the ends of the apparatus. Spanish law's procedures were based upon the Rule of Law, which, as a result, regarded the preservation of the integrity of criminal procedures as taking precedence over disciplinary or even civil procedures; as a result, these were treated as a hindrance and barrier to the Just War on doping. The same can be said for principles of international or European human rights (things that proceed only from State agreement) – where they are in conflict with the war on doping, the Just War takes precedence. Furthermore, *Operación Puerto* showed us how this primacy of the exception manifests itself increasingly by the spectacle's justi-fication of both the end of the war on doping and the inability of State Law and sovereignty to adequately deal with the task.

---

[15] 'Whatever the peculiarities of the American case, the end cannot be its own means: either what is called "operative values" are not values at all, or they are second-order values that should be clearly distinguished from first-order values, or values proper.' ibid.
[16] ibid, 244–45.

Agamben poses the term (or syntagma) state of exception 'as the technical term for the consistent set of legal phenomena' that his study 'seeks to define'. Agamben notes that the choice of the term

> implies a position taken on both the nature of the phenomenon that we seek to investigate and the logic most suitable for understanding it ... the state of exception is not a special kind of law ... it defines law's threshold or limit concept.[17]

In tackling Møller's end of modernity thesis we have taken up a position on the nature of the phenomenon we face, whether it is described as neoliberalism or Empire, and the manner in which it totalises competition as the norm. We have also proposed that it is the logic and rationality of this new system that provides a more suitable method to understand what is at stake in the anti-doping apparatus. Thus, we have sought to describe implicitly throughout this study how the entire edifice of new forms of law (or quasi law) are carved out of spaces beyond State sovereignty, the administration and policing operations and its spectacular and arbitral adjudications – all backed by consent and contract – are, in one way or another, symptoms of Agamben's permanent state of exception. Furthermore, what is at stake is the law's threshold. The anti-doping apparatus straddles Law, law and governance. Although we are able to distinguish between different aspects – the Australian Sports Anti-Doping Authority (ASADA) act as public law, the WADC as private law, the Whereabouts and Biological Passport systems as governmental tools brought into being by private law, and the governmental mechanism of competition itself – they and the apparatus as a whole exist and operate to a large degree within a zone of indiscernibility. It is this zone of indiscernibility that defines 'law's threshold or limit concept'.[18]

In the end, it is an apparatus that seeks to 'conduct conduct', to establish the conditions for competition and pilot individual behaviour, from within and without, towards the 'pure performance' of each individual '100% Me'. In such a world, 'the rules of private law must prevail universally', they must govern the totality of existence to the extent that not only the individual, but also the State is subject to them.[19] The transformation of the Rule of Law under neoliberalism is what guarantees the order of this system – it is 'therefore not a rule of the law, but a rule concerning what the law ought to be, a meta-legal doctrine or political ideal'.[20] Below it, and constrained by it, sits the realm of public law and Government which, in turn, creates, maintains and contributes to the policing of the state of the market based on the totalising norm of competition.

---

[17] G Agamben, *The State of Exception* (University of Chicago Press, 2005) 4.
[18] ibid, 4.
[19] Dadot and Laval, *The New Way of the World* (n 1) 133.
[20] ibid, 135.

At its most basic, we can characterise our theory of sovereignty itself as a Permanent State of Exception; an exception to all law and social policy other than that based upon the economic relation of competition. Viewed through the lens of the history of human society, this 'consistent set of legal [and governmental] phenomena' that we have sought to investigate is an 'exceptional variant of the general model'; there is a hierarchy, but one that is contradicted or devoid of any value.[21] The exception here is founded by the privileging of economic relations based upon an individualism and a conversion of the public nature of society into a purely private manner that 'when seen against the background of the other great civilisations that the world has known, is an exceptional phenomenon'.[22]

What grounds this element of the exception, along with all others, is consent by contract. Contractual governance,[23] or government by private agreement, appears in our study as the juridical form which supports and finds its basis as a theory of sovereignty grounded in the exception. Here we can begin to uncover in more detail a response to our question: what is the juridical form and theory of sovereignty that is able to sustain and found the primacy of governance over law and sovereignty? Chapter 5 set out what appears to be, according to the logic of neoliberalism, a theory of sovereignty that is different in form to that which preceded it. The transformation of the State into just another economic actor has given rise to a theory of sovereignty which we might call *Homo Economicus* or the Society of Competition. It is no longer a question of the general will bringing forth the State and its system of sovereignty, but of individual ('sovereign') will consenting to the injunction of having to be an entrepreneur of the self. Throughout the history of the State, sovereignty has slowly but steadily moved from being vested in a transcendent God, to being vested in the figure of the monarch as God's representative, to being vested in the figure of the Law of the State, up to the contemporary context where, above all else, sovereignty appears vested in the economy. No longer do we move to the invisible hand of God as, within the new politico-theological structure of Empire, we are now moved and governed by the invisible hand of the economy and our own consent. It is at the most basic level that this theory of sovereignty performs the role of a single logic of rule that guides and governs the operations of everything else within its domain.

There is no value that sits outside the Rule of Law, public law, Government, private law, or the tools of administration and governance other than the value of

---

[21] Dumont, *Essays on Individualism* (n 14) 265: '[T]he modern model is an exceptional variant of the general model and remains encased, or encompassed within it. Hierarchy is universal; at the same time it is here partially but effectively contradicted.'

[22] ibid, 23.

[23] P Zumbanesen, 'Private Ordering in a Globalizing World: Still Searching for the Basis of Contract' (2007) 14(2) *Indiana Journal of Global Legal Studies* 181.

economic relations based upon competition. Everything is geared to the creation, maintenance and policing of that value.

Consent by contract, or consent otherwise, gives rise to the border crossing, or dissolving, assemblage of private arbitration; as with other hierarchies, this state of exception 'takes no account of the territorial factor, it ignores it and encompasses it'.[24] At the same time it also founds and justifies the panoply of governance tools we have encountered. Consent by itself also appears to not only justify the banishment of a violator but also their public pillory. Consent grounds the police; here the privatisation of the police is not the outsourcing of State policing functions to private corporations. It is our consent to have our body and its location monitored and assessed and, in the end, banished upon (exceptional) grounds that do not easily sit with the Rule of Law or the rational State of modernity. If any one thing marks the end of modernity, it is our consent to be governed by the economy. It is this consent which grounds the exception manifested by law's functionality.

In the world of the anti-doping apparatus any questioning of its operation, its mechanisms or its sanctions is often met by the glib response that the athlete consented to the rules when they made the choice to play sport. This response operates, of course, from the position that we are all individuals and islands ourselves with the inherent ability to be able to decide freely without the action of outside forces upon us. But is this consent itself illusory? For Dumont:

> ... the conception of man as individual entails the recognition of a wide freedom of choice. Some of the values, instead of emanating from the society, will be determined by the individual for his own use. ... The absence of prescription which makes choice possible is actually commanded by a superior prescription. ... value is embedded in the configuration of ideas itself.[25]

Where value is prescribed in the system itself and forms a governing function in the way that it does in neoliberalism, the logic of pure consent is tenuous at best. Frédéric Lordon and his analysis of consent in the context of neoliberalism is useful to us here. For Lordon, the total enlistment of the body under neoliberalism, the manner in which it makes the work of the subject their total vocation, means that there 'is no such thing as voluntary servitude. There is only passionate servitude'.[26] On his analysis, regimes of desire must be inscribed into individual psyches such that they consent to the total investment of their lives within the society of competition. In our example, the athlete performs a function of expressing desires and affects and provides the specific imaginary necessitated by the

---

[24] Dumont, *Homo Hierarchicus* (n 9) 83.
[25] Dumont, *Essays on Individualism* (n 14) 260.
[26] F Lordon, *Willing Slaves of Capital: Spinoza and Marx on Desire* (Verso, 2014) 17.

society of competition.[27] For us, the athlete in the society of competition operates on the playing fields where the social game converges and constitutes one of the very forces that drive the engagement with it.[28] Work and life itself in the society of competition 'must be reconstructed, but objectively and in the imagination, as a source of immediate joy. The desire to find employment should no longer be merely a mediated desire for the goods that wages circuitously permit buying, but an intrinsic desire for the activity for its own sake'.[29] Following Lordon, we can say that the athlete as an expert of the society of competition 'assumes the specific task of producing on a large scale desires that did not previously exist, or that existed only in a minority ... desires for happy labour, or, to borrow directly from its own vocabulary, desires for "fulfilment" and "self-realisation" in and through work'.[30] As a passionate economy, neoliberalism ultimately relies on free will as the surest way to obtain unreserved action from employees, that is, the surrender of their power of acting in full' but this free will – or, for Lordon, consent – is a form of involuntary servitude.[31] Consent is part and parcel of the art of neoliberal government; it surrounds the 'mystery of power as "actions on actions", as the art of making others do something ... the false transparency of consent is a symptom of the metaphysics of subjectivity ...' .[32]

But, from the Spinozist point of view, the governed body is incapable of being authentically individual such that 'if the act of giving consent is the authentic expression of a freely self-determined interiority, then consent does not exist'.[33] The authentic consent of the athlete becomes nothing more than the movements of desire motivated within the society of competition,[34] such that the athlete as expert is moved not by consent but by the effect of affects.[35] Neoliberalism's strength is this harnessing of the joyful affect provided by the athlete and the totalisation of the desire to be fully invested in one's life/work across society. The power of the athlete consists in a certain part of affecting and governing by directing the subjected bodies of neoliberalism to move towards the object of the norm of totalised competition.[36]

> [T]o be happy with one's chains is evidently not the same as to be saddened by them. 'Coercion' and 'consent' are simply the names of the respective effects of sadness and

[27] ibid, 49.
[28] ibid, 50.
[29] ibid, 52.
[30] ibid.
[31] ibid, 53.
[32] ibid, 54.
[33] ibid, 55.
[34] ibid, 58.
[35] ibid, 61.
[36] ibid.

of joy assumed inside institutional situations of power and normalisation. … Coercion and consent are forms of the lived experience (respectively sad and joyful) of determination. To be coerced is to have to been determined to do something but in a state of sadness. And to consent … is to live one's obedience, but with its intrinsic burden relieved by a joyful affect.[37]

The consent to take part in the society of competition requires a total investment that is always rationalised by those that love their activity in the manner of the athlete; it is always their choice and their vocation. Subjects are required 'to "fully invest themselves", but also to be fully invested – invaded – by' the society of competition. For Lordon, in this society

> it is the extreme nature of the whole claimed over individuals that is a hallmark of the neoliberal enterprises pursuit of total enlistment. To subordinate the entire life and being of employees … so that they serve its ends, in short, to refashion their singularity so that all their personal inclinations tend 'spontaneously' in its direction, such as the delirious vision of a total possession of individuals, in an almost shamanistic sense. It is therefore legitimate to call totalitarian an attempt to exercise control in a manner so profound, so complete, that it is no longer satisfied by external enslavement – obtaining the desirable behaviour – but demands a complete surrender of "interiority".[38]

Lordon's consent is the consent of the anti-doping apparatus. It is the consent of 'Just Do It!' of the 'pure performance' of '100% Me'. It is the consent that drives the subjection of the cyclists to the arbitration of the spectacle and the new forms of law beyond the Law. It is this consent that drives their subjection to the Whereabouts and Biological Passport systems and the ways in which their lives are governed, piloted and fashioned.

If we identify the juridical form that sustains this new sovereignty as consensual or contractual governance, we can also identify the institutional form as that of the police and the administration; possibly better described in this case as contractual policing. As we have attempted to highlight, the Law and the police are different animals – the former clearly a mechanism of sovereignty, the latter appearing on the governance side of the continuum. As we have seen in Chapter 4, Bauman's model of the administrative machinery of the Holocaust is one that fits comfortably with a description of the anti-doping apparatus. The machine, the professional and the bureaucracy combine in a policing operation in which the object is defined, identified and located, surveilled, monitored and assessed, segregated and eventually evicted, bringing us face to face with the world of Kafka. Everyone is potentially guilty and abnormal bodies are actively sought in all places and at all times.

---

[37] ibid, 63–64.
[38] ibid, 79–80.

≤UCI)

INTERNATIONAL CYCLING UNION

Riders' commitment to a new cycling

The Puerto affair highlighted the serious problem of doping in cycling. This, like all other doping cases, greatly harms my sport and me personally.

The uncertainty surrounding the identity of riders and other people who could be involved in the Puerto affair is also very harmful and will continue to be until the case is closed.

Currently, there is a climate of suspicion. It is undermining the credibility of my sport and is eroding the trust of the public, authorities, organisers and my colleagues.

For these reasons, I want to make a contribution to putting the situation right and making cycling clean by signing the statement below, to demonstrate that I fully adhere to the principles defended by the International Cycling Union (UCI).

«I do solemnly declare, to my team, my colleagues, the UCI, the cycling movement and the public that I am not involved in the Puerto affair nor in any other doping case and that I will not commit any infringement to the UCI anti-doping rules. As proof of my commitment, I accept, if it should happen that I violate the rules and am granted a standard sanction of a two-year suspension or more, in the Puerto affair or in any other anti-doping proceedings, to pay the UCI, in addition to the standard sanctions, an amount equal to my annual salary for 2008 as a contribution to the fight against doping.

At the same time, I declare to the Spanish Law, that my DNA is at its disposal, so that it can be compared with the blood samples seized in the Puerto affair. I appeal to the Spanish Law to organise this test as soon as possible or allow the UCI to organise it.

Finally, I accept the UCI's wish to make my statement public».

Done in.. on 2008

Surname and first name: ....

Signature: ....

CH 1860 Aigle / Switzerland
☎+41 24 468 58 11   fax +41 24 468 58 12
www.uci.ch

The rider's commitment to a new cycling

An open letter to McQuaid, Pedro Horrillo, Saturday 7 July 2007

Mr. McQuaid, I haven't had the pleasure of meeting you personally, although to make things clear from the start, I am not inclined to so in the slightest. However, it should not be so because, being the highest representative of our sport, you should be supported and welcomed by all those who are a part of it. But sadly this is not the case.

Maybe at this time you are congratulating yourself on the success of your latest initiative, the famous letter entitled 'Rider's Commitment to a New Cycling' that we have just been compelled to sign by you. And I am not mistaken in using the verb, compel, because many who have signed have done so under duress and threats: the fact is we simply sign, or don't ride. What seems not to matter is whether the riders are in agreement or not, whether we have a debate about the issues, and whether we work together for a common objective.

No, you have simply written the letter without consulting anyone. No, the only thing you care about is that we have signed our names – our 'agreement' – and that we have jumped through the hoops you have demanded. This is the substance of the issue, although you sell it as otherwise. Everyone will have their opinion, I've specifically signed the letter, but to me it seems to be the most absurd letter that has come from a thinking person. Though if I was to get to the bottom of the matter, I am in favour of tightening up the fight against doping – the scourge that is on track to finish our sport – and I commit myself as a rider to that. But I do not see why as proof of this I should refuse to get paid or give away my wages if I am somehow implicated in a doping scandal.

"¿Donde vas? Manzanas traigo" – where you're going? I bring apples – says the popular Spanish proverb. What is the reason? Where did you get such a brilliant idea? It seems to me that the reasoning was as simple as … 'we will hit you where it hurts most: money'. I assure you that you are wrong about me. What hurt me the most was that I had to swallow my pride to comply with your command, but I know that you do not care about that at all. The fact is that I signed. And by the way, I signed it knowing that this document is unlawful and undemocratic. That is to say, a useless piece of paper. You have a large collection of useless pieces of paper in a folder, but of course, all of them are signed just as you wanted. Anyway, my most sincere congratulations. And finally, a wish. I hope that with the departure of the first rider in this Tour de France 2007, your central role is over and from now on the attention will be drawn back to the rightful owners: the riders.

Sincerely, Pedro Horrillo.[39]

If the juridical form is contractual governance and the institutional form is the police, or contractual policing, are we are able to say that the legal basis is, in the end, a combination of adjudication or decision making (administrative, arbitral and spectacular), and functionality, both of which are given effect in the spectacle?

---

[39] Originally Published in *El Pais*, Translation by Martin Hardie.

Within the state of exception, Law and governance both receive their backing from their effect and functionality within the economy and its single logic of competition. The legal basis manifested by functionality and effect is important in order to found and sustain the system as a whole. Their operation is inextricably tied up with the theory of sovereignty itself and the way in which it founds and sustains the primacy of the permanent state of exception. The society of the spectacle here is used to describe the manner in which trial by media takes on an adjudicative function or form.

Guy Debord proposed in 1967 that in contemporary society the 'whole of life ... presents itself as an immense accumulation of spectacles' where images 'detached from every aspect of life emerge into a common stream, and the former unity of life is lost forever'. Here 'reality unfolds in a new generality as a pseudo-world apart ...'. For Debord, the spectacle appears at the very same time as society itself, as a part of society and as society's means of unification; it is 'where all attention, all consciousness, converges' it is 'not a collection of images; rather, it is a social relationship between people that is mediated by images'.[40] In this way the spectacle constitutes a 'world view transformed into an objective force' which when understood

> in its totality .... It is the very heart of society's unreality ... the spectacle epitomizes the prevailing model of social life ... the spectacle serves as a total justification for the conditions and aims of the existing system. It further ensures the permanent presence of that justification, for it governs almost all time ...[41]

The spectacle performs a totalising function as it expresses 'the total practice of one particular economic and social formation; it is, so to speak, the formations' agenda. It is also the historical moment by which we happen to be governed'. In performing this totalising function, the spectacle appears to have no value outside of itself, or of economic relations, echoing Dumont's moribund hierarchy. Debord wrote that the 'spectacle is essentially tautological, for the simple reason that its means and its ends are identical. It is the sun that never sets on the empire of modern passivity. It covers the entire globe, basking in the perpetual warmth of its own glory'. In this context

> as the perfect image of the ruling economic order, ends are nothing and development is all – although the only thing into which the spectacle plans to develop is itself. ... [it] is simply the economic realm developing for itself ...[42]

For Hardt and Negri, the spectacle is the 'glue that holds together the diverse functions and bodies of the hybrid constitution' that is Empire, 'an integrated and diffuse apparatus of images and ideas that produces and regulates public discourse and opinion'.[43] Here the public sphere evaporates, as all apparati of government form a zone of indiscernibility, and any sociality based upon the whole of society

---

[40] G Debord *Society of the Spectacle,* trans D Nicholson-Smith (Zone Books, 1995) 12.
[41] ibid, 13.
[42] ibid, 15–16.
[43] M Hardt and A Negri, *Empire* (Harvard University Press, 1999) 321–22.

is destroyed – everything is individualised, imposing a new kind of mass 'sociality', a 'new uniformity of action and thought'.[44] In the society of the spectacle, only what appears exists.

Agamben takes the view that Schmitt's notion of public opinion (as evinced by the Nazis' particular construction of modernity) and Debord's work on the society of the spectacle take on a new meaning and a new urgency today. Agamben's links Debord's analysis with Schmitt's thesis; a thesis which argued that public opinion is the modern form of the Imperial acclamation

> the entire problem, of the contemporary spectacle of media domination over all areas of social life assumes a new guise. What is in question is nothing less than a new and unheard of concentration, multiplication, and dissemination of the function of glory as the center of the political system.[45]

Agamben's point is that our current context – what he terms contemporary democracy – 'is a democracy that is entirely founded upon glory, that is, on the efficacy of acclamation, multiplied and disseminated by the media beyond all imagination' where we are 'once again caught, orientated, and manipulated in the forms and according to the strategies of spectacular power'. This allows us, according to Agamben, to 'better understand the sense of the contemporary definitions of democracy as "government by consent" or "consensus democracy" and the decisive transformation of the democratic institutions that is at stake in these terms'.[46]

Whether or not we describe this system as democratic, for our purposes what Agamben is exposing is the link between totalitarian notions of public opinion or acclamation through the global mechanism of the spectacle, in a situation where what founds the system is governance by consent. For us what has been important in order to ground the state of exception present, or presented by, the anti-doping apparatus is consensual or contractual governance. Furthermore, we have tried to describe how the spectacle of the athlete as expert of the society of competition itself goes to sustaining this new form of sovereignty. The glory associated with accomplishing the task of having to be an entrepreneur of the self radiates and sustains the mythology of the theory of sovereignty itself. Spectacular glory plus functionality in respect of the single logic of rule – the economy – founds and sustains the justification, deployment and operation of a myriad of governmental techniques all aimed at producing the paradigm of economic man we find embodied in the athlete. In the society of competition, the athlete is the paradigm of what we must be in order to 'Just Do It'.

The gloss of Foucault on the question we have posed is that the answer we have described gives rise to a form of sovereignty *typical* of the State. It is readily apparent by now that our system of law and governance is not one that is of the

---

[44] ibid.
[45] G Agamben, *The Kingdom and the Glory: For a Theological Genealogy of Economy and Government* (Stanford University Press, 2011) 255–56.
[46] ibid.

sovereignty of the State. That is, it is not a system that measures up to the image of law in modernity and the Rule of Law or the state of Law. The apparatus established or coordinated by the WADC appears 'increasingly to evince a will to sovereignty'[47] over the bare life of the athlete. As Hardt and Negri's *Empire* shows, identifying the holder of this sovereign power, in any one instance, may not be an easy task; it may be nowhere and everywhere simultaneously. Furthermore, whether sovereignty is an adequate term in this context is arguable and something that requires a complete investigation and consideration of its own. The definition of sovereignty provided by the Comaroffs as 'the exercise of control over the lives, deaths and conditions of existence of those who fall within its purview and the extension over them of the jurisdiction of some kind of law' provides us with some flexibility, but what we are facing is more than a kind of law. Furthermore, it is a modulating kind of law that appears to be able to be called forth whenever deemed necessary and despite the actions of what we might call competing sovereignties. The distinction drawn by the CAS in order to get around Valverde's double jeopardy arguments following his 'acquittal' by the Real Federación Española de Ciclismo (RFEC) and his 'conviction' by the Italian Olympic Committee (CONI) as to the nature of the violation exemplify the modulating and functional nature of this 'sovereignty'. Without ever clearly dealing with the facts that may have constituted a violation on the part of Valverde, the CAS was able to avoid arguments of double jeopardy by characterising the offence as being its discovery, manifested by a DNA 'match', not by the actual occurrence of extracting blood, adding Erythropoietin (EPO) and storing it for future use. This kind of modulating sovereignty potentially allows for cases to be brought successively until the right functional outcome can be achieved, so long as each modulating sovereign is able to make a discovery which they can, however flimsily, characterise as an asserted violation. What appear as an abundance of new forms of law and sovereignty manifest themselves as incidents of perpetual policing. Moving right away from cycling to recent events in Australia, possibly nothing bears this out more than the case of the players and support staff from the Essendon Football Club who were told that they were subject to an ongoing investigation without any apparent end. The fact is that the mechanisms of the anti-doping apparatus we have sought to describe are themselves systems of perpetual and continual surveillance, where no one is ever innocent but they are always a suspect.

Cycling in the Age of Empire

The anti-doping apparatus evinces all the characteristics or symptoms identified by Hardt and Negri as the principles of imperial administration. It is instrumental

---

[47] JL Comaroff and J Comaroff, 'Reflections on the Anthropology of Law, Governance and Sovereignty' in F von Benda-Beckmann, K von Benda-Beckmann and J Eckert (eds), *Rules of Law and Laws of Ruling* (Ashgate Publishing, 2009) 38.

in so far as the singularity and adequacy of actions to specific ends in the flexible management of difference are paramount. What is important is not unity and consistency but instrumental multi-functionality. One of Møller's criticisms of the WADA is that it does not practice what it preaches in its Code as it does not treat all athletes equally on a level anti-doping playing field. For example, the differences between the manner in which Davis was treated by the ASADA and the manner in which Valverde was dealt with by CONI, despite the findings of the RFEC, highlight the lack of any hypothetical level playing field and the equal application of the law. Rasmussen's Whereabouts case, extensively dealt with by Møller, is yet another example. The list could go on and would not be complete without reference to the difference between Armstrong and others. But with WADA apparently treating individuals, countries or sports differently at different times and in different places, can it really be said that it is not fulfilling the plain words of the WADC as argued by Møller? Does highlighting such a difference really point to some irrationality or even corruption in the organisation's behaviour?

It is evident that the WADC established a system that was not based upon right in the sense of generality, equality and rationality, as was understood by modernist conceptions of law and sovereignty. Instead, what the Code creates, and then seeks to administer and manage, is a system based upon the flexible management of difference. Thus, it creates the basis for modulating and hybrid networks of command, discipline and control. From this perspective we can say that the WADC establishes a praxis of governance based upon private agreement and contract. As Hardt and Negri tell us, this system of governance is composed of many sovereigns, none of whom are the 'centre' of this modulating system of governance based upon practice – an apparatus. This is apparent itself from the manner in which, for example, the UCI, WADA, RFEC, CONI, ASADA all compete in the exercise of modulating degrees of power or sovereignty. If we do not read the text of the WADC in this light, we will never be able to understand its operations on what might be argued as being a 'rational' basis. The WADC neither created nor even seeks to establish a legal level playing field and thus does not seek to create *ab initio* equality between all athletes on a global basis. This is abundantly clear from a careful and plain reading of the words of the text.

PURPOSE, SCOPE AND ORGANIZATION OF THE WORLD ANTI-DOPING PROGRAM AND THE CODE

The purposes of the World Anti-Doping Code and the World Anti-Doping Program which supports it are:

- To protect the Athletes' fundamental right to participate in doping-free sport and thus promote health, fairness and equality for Athletes worldwide, and
- To ensure harmonized, coordinated and effective anti-doping programs at the international and national level with regard to detection, deterrence and prevention of doping.

Beginning with the opening paragraph above, the purpose of the WADC is 'to protect the Athletes' fundamental right to participate in doping-free sport and

thus promote health, fairness and equality for Athletes worldwide'. We must separate these two phrases and thus their functions in this opening paragraph. One is
to 'protect a fundamental right to participate in doping-free sport'. The immediate
aim and purpose of the WADC is thus to create and protect this 'fundamental
right'. The granting of one right always involves the removal of another. The second
phrase of this first paragraph contains not an immediate purpose, but an aspirational goal, which is again evidenced by the plain words of the text and the use of
the words 'to promote'. The aspirational purpose is to 'thus promote health, fairness and equality for Athletes worldwide'. It is aspirational in the sense that this
is not an immediate goal, nor possibly even an achievable goal – but a stated and
ideal end point of the system. This is not a reality, not an actuality, but a potentiality. It must be read as such and in a similar manner to the aspirational goal of
the promotion of international peace and security in the United Nations Charter,
something that is clearly not a reality, but a goal of the UN system. In respect of
the level playing field, the second paragraph does, in fact, seek to ensure 'harmonized, coordinated and effective anti-doping programs at the international and
national level'. But even on a plain reading, this must be read in the context of
the qualification contained in the second paragraph, which also refers to which
programmes the WADC seeks to harmonise, that is, programmes 'with regard to
detection, deterrence and prevention of doping'. The purpose here is to focus upon
this question of flexibility rather than generality and its equal application: the 'level
playing field' approach.

It is the third paragraph, set out below, which is crucial to understanding
the meaning of harmonisation and coordination. It makes it abundantly clear
that under the system established by the Code what is regarded as an effective
programme at a national or international level does not depend upon each and
every programme being alike. The opening of this third paragraph makes it clear
that the 'purpose of the Code is to advance the anti-doping effort through universal harmonization of core anti-doping elements'. 'Core anti-doping elements' are
the (single) logic of the system and do not infer a mechanical application of the
same in each and every instance. The single logic of the system turns on concepts
of consent, competition, the level playing field, individual responsibility, policing
and strict liability. Importantly, it also includes the removal of the anti-doping
apparatus from the realm of State law. Although State bodies may play a role in the
administration of the anti-doping apparatus, in performing this function they are
subject to the law of the code, not that of the State. Here it is also clear that actual
harmonisation, in the sense of generality and all programmes being alike is, if
anything, again an aspiration. It is not a right, but it is something to be advanced,
and it is not a reality or an actuality now. We might even go so far as to state that
it is a myth or even a fantasy of the Real. Most importantly, the third paragraph
states that in the process of the advancement of that harmonisation, at any given
moment, and in any given place or situation, harmonisation must be both 'specific
enough to achieve complete harmonization on issues where uniformity is required,
yet general enough in other areas to permit flexibility on how agreed-upon

anti-doping principles are implemented'. That is, it is core anti-doping principles that must be implemented, the spirit and not the letter of the Code. Evidently, this is not a general and uniform harmonisation, but a flexible implementation of 'core principles' which recognise the actual differences that exist at national and international level, at different times, and between different sports.

To object to this analysis, as some might, on the grounds that this part of the Code is open to interpretation – that it is written in rubbery language and is thus a pragmatic solution to accommodate nations or sports which do not necessarily take anti-doping as seriously – is to both get, miss and deny the point all in one go. Harmonisation of anti-doping is not a one-size-fits-all affair, where each and every national anti-doping agency and each and every sport must act the same at all times so as to create an actual administrative level playing field. To then argue that what the Code requires is a level playing field where all countries, all sports and all athletes must be treated the same, or as if they were the same, and thus be treated equally on a level playing field of anti-doping law, is to seriously misread the plain and literal words of the document. It is a reading which also denies the political and institutional reality of the situation in search of a romantic, liberal and modernist notion of law and rights. As a form of critique, it simply replaces one fantasy with another, or the real with a bygone fantasy.

What all of this points to is that the Code is a part of a framework agreement which recognises difference. In doing so, it points to the creation of a new global system; it is a framework within which to construct a new form of law and governance, or if one is not convinced of that, at least a new global legal regime. The framework agreement recognises from the beginning the political realities of existing State power (whatever the changing nature of the role of the State may be) and the uneven development of this new system. It also recognises in this context that law, power and administrative governance are carried out by both State and non-State bodies. Hence, as explained above, harmonisation cannot be read as meaning that everything is the same – as imposing a generality that we might think of in terms of Law as it might have been. The instrumental role of anti-doping contributes to, and is aimed at, the construction of a new global system and, along with this instrumental flexibility, it is procedural, autocentric and always functional. It treats each case differently, always operating in a localised and contingent manner, in which the heterogeneity of actions is important – there is no longer a strategic plan, but actions are event and crisis driven. The unifying matrix of the imperial system arises from its local effectiveness and, through consent, to the single logic of rule of the economy.

Hardt and Negri tell us that Empire always comes or acts in the name of peace and justice. The logic of a Just War backs imperial action. In our case, the war against doping is a Just War and thus exceptional measures are required. In Empire, war is reduced to a police action and this power has an 'ethical' function. In pursuit of this Just War, the enemy is rendered banal and thus subject to routine policing; at the same time it is absolutized; an absolute threat to the ethical order in construction. In order to take control and dominate a completely fluid situation with no centre it is necessary for the intervening authority to have the capacity to define, every time, in an exceptional way, the demands of the intervention; and the capacity to set in motion the forces and instruments that can be variously applied to the diversity of the arrangements in crisis. The legitimacy of the Imperial order, brought about by its single logic, consent, functionality and glorification, supports the exercise of the global policing power; it is the activity of this global policy which demonstrates the real effectiveness of the Imperial order. Hardt and Negri argue that the two initial coordinates of the authority of Empire are the juridical power to rule over the exception and the supranational capacity to police. For them, Empire is a place where the exception has become the norm, where a decision-maker no longer orientates themselves according to a rule or a situation of fact, and no longer needs to decide whether a given fact falls within that rule. What is decided is at once a rule and a criterion – what becomes 'natural' is a rule that decides the fact and decides upon its own application without reference to any norm other than being functional within the construction of Empire. Empire and the exception are called into being based on their ability to resolve conflicts. Empire is formed and becomes juridically legitimate because of this functionality and because of our consent. Consent allows mechanisms of command to become more 'democratic' and more immanent to the social field. As we have seen, command and control are distributed through the brains and bodies of citizens. This biopolitical regulation of life from the inside can only be effective when it becomes an integral, vital function which every individual embraces and reactivates of their own accord. In Empire, as in the anti-doping apparatus, life has become the object of power.

The Athlete as a Paradigm of Life within Empire

In Chapter 5, we considered the figure, or paradigm of the athlete, as a privileged expert or ambassador of the society of competition. In *Empire*, Hardt and Negri proposed the Polybian constitutional model as being closer to our Imperial reality than the modern liberal tradition's transformation of it. Polybius recognised the Imperial structure of a monarchy, aristocracy and democracy. In today's genetic phase of power and its accumulation, functions are seen and rationalised primarily from the angle of relations and materiality of their force rather than from some equilibrium of power within a definite and stable sovereign State structure.[48] In this Polybian constitution, the figure of the athlete as an expert of the society of competition falls within and functions as a component of the middle tier of the aristocracy. The Imperial aristocracy plays its role in the definition of justice, measure

---

[48] Hardt and Negri, *Empire* (n 43) 316.

and virtue. Whereas the monarchy presents itself as a global police force,[49] the athlete here articulates justice, measure and virtue throughout the entire system, thereby contributing to the reproduction and circulation of the single logic of Imperial rule.[50] Within Empire, the command and ordering functions of the aristocratic athlete are deployed over the transnational processes of production and circulation[51] – in the creation of worlds.

As a paradigmatic member of the Imperial aristocracy the athlete appears as a privileged figure. At the same time, it is their position as 'governors' within Empire that opens them up to sanction. In a way, the athlete is always, in the words of Lazzarato, 'an indebted man', always the product of the 'techniques of fashioning the debtor subject'.[52] This athletic or aristocratic exposure to indebtedness is recognisable when we consider that for many, including themselves, the athlete occupies a privileged position within society. Accordingly, because of this privilege, they are in the first instance 'in debt' to that society and liable to repay this debt (which may, in fact, not be repayable) by fulfilling their function as good 'role models' and instilling the logic and fantasy of the individual as an enterprise or entrepreneur of the self within competition society. The athlete articulates or disseminates the specific Imperial conceptions of justice, measure and virtue throughout the system. As such, the athlete, always in debt, is in the second instance, in the moment of their transgression of the rules of the game, always open to being exposed to the threat of social insolvency – the ban. The ban applies if they fail in their governing role of instilling the ethos of pure competition. The governing function of the anti-doping apparatus in this context of debt regulates the allocation of the athlete's social or sporting insolvency. In so doing it delimits the field of pure competition and reinforces the myth or fantasy of natural competition on the level playing field of the economy.

> Q Do you think there's a myth … There's two things you hear in relation to the doping stuff. One is that professional athletes are privileged people and …
>
> A I think they are privileged people.
>
> Q Why do you reckon they're privileged?
>
> A I think they're privileged people because they're treated like kings and they go out and ride their bike for three or four hours and go home and sit home, have a massage, watch TV for a week, then go to a race and race a week and sign autographs and stay in hotels, get their food paid, get everything paid, get their wages paid, do a bit of travelling, you know, people are selling photos of them, they're in the front pages of the newspaper. That's a great lifestyle, but obviously there's a certain amount of sacrifice you have to be to be the [wind noise] … To keep a contract is massive. To get a good contract is even more massive. Do you know what I mean?

---

[49] ibid.

[50] ibid, 314.

[51] ibid, 318.

[52] M Lazzarato, *The Making of Indebted Man: An Essay on the Neoliberal Condition*, (Semiotext(e), 2011).

Q Yeah. [Wind noise] … because if you haven't invested anything. And at times it seems that the fact that it is a person's, somebody's total lifestyle and something they've invested in since they were fifteen [wind noise] …

A Yeah true. It doesn't seem to be taken into account. But it just comes back to a line. Everything comes back to that line in the same that you draw. And I mean fuck, you know, a woman has to spend fuckin' eight years and how many years [wind noise] … as a lawyer or how many years you did as a medical student and you had to pay back $150,000 of government fees …

Q I'm still fuckin' paying it back.

A Do you know what I mean it's like, you know, cyclists don't do that. They've got to buy a bike and everything's given to them, OK. But having said that, do you know a cyclist's career is fifteen years maximum. Do you know what? They wouldn't have time to pay something like that back. I mean they don't invest that. They're investing their time, which is money, fair enough. But when stop they're done. The cyclist, every cyclist, I guarantee you right now, every cyclist wants to win, right, every competition, every runner, every rower, they all want to win. That's number one right. But in cycling, right if you're the best fuckin' swimmer in the world, OK [wind noise] … you're going to have a huge endorsements. But like if you're in top thirty in the world, you're not going to get paid a contract unless you've got Speedo skin suit. That's fuckin' nothing. With cycling you can make half a million dollars a year and set yourself up for life in eight years and not have to work again. Do you know what I mean? And that's, I guarantee you, what cyclists think. OK I'll win two stages of the [name] I can sign three years with Kelme and they're going to pay me $600,000 a year. I can buy a house one year, put the rest away the year after, invest the year after and I'm fuckin' done. [Wind noise] … No it's reality.[53]

By supposing that the foundation of the privileged aristocratic expert of competition society is based upon the threat of debt insolvency,[54] we begin to see that what we have before us is a case of the close proximity between that of the sovereign or aristocrat and that of the outlaw or outcast. Within Empire, the athlete is not only the privileged expert member of the global aristocracy but at the same time they are exposed to and capable of constituting the bare life of *homo sacer*. Within our study the athlete has appeared in a variety of forms, but all exhibit a status outside of, beyond, and before the Law.

The athlete as participant in the society of competition is sovereign in the sense that they can consent and contract in order to allow them to play the game of the economy (which, after all, is everything). They are free as a bird (*vogel frei*) to play the game and to soar to the greatest heights – they can achieve the injunction of having to be, they are capable of just doing it. As entrepreneurs of the self, and as privileged experts, they can live the dream for themselves and for us all.

[53] M Hardie, D Shilbury, C Bozzi and I Ware, *I Wish I was Twenty One Now: Beyond Doping in the Australian Peloton* (Auskadi Samizdat, 2012) 34–35. The published version of the quote is incomplete. This quotes the passage in its entirety.
[54] M Hilgers, 'The Historicity of the Neoliberal State' (2012) 20(1) *Social Anthropology* 80, 90–91.

As ambassadors of *Homo Economicus*, or Imperial Aristocrats, they already hold ministerial or priestly positions of governance.[55] The aristocratic minister seeks, possesses and teaches the characteristics needed to get by in the new economy – hard work, dedication and resilience. The athlete may even appear as prince or sovereign of the economy in his or her own right. At the same time, the athlete is both governor and governed. This privileged status brings with it constant and perpetual policing of every aspect of their lives. They have to do it, but they are able to do it. The police, discipline and control are all internalised and defeat is overcome through resilience. But both privilege and exposure to governance give rise to the exposure to a ban. If one is to be free as a bird, one is just as free to be shot down. The governed and privileged athlete can quite quickly turn into the outcast, the outlaw or the wolf.

The Sovereign, the Kingdom and the Glory of the Wolf

The athlete as wolf moves beyond the description of the cyclist we opened with and beyond the becoming animal of the athletic experience we have discussed in our Excursus. The figure of *homo sacer* in Agamben serves to describe a situation whereby a life may be banished by anyone without recourse to the Law.[56] In our case it is a form of banishment that operates beyond the realm of the sovereign State of Law allowing the functional application of power, in whatever is the necessary form, on a modulating basis.

Agamben specifically links the figure of *homo sacer* with that of the wolf[57] and notes the coincidence of this form with that of the bandit and the outlaw. *Homo sacer* appeared as a man without peace – whom anyone was permitted to kill. Banishment itself was equated with death – it was considered to be a living death even before any legal process (if indeed there is any at all) takes its course. This status means that anyone may harm the banished, for he exists within a liminal world as a monstrous hybrid, not of a purely animal nature but within a threshold of indistinction, dwelling while belonging to nothing, or better, dwelling outside of the law.[58]

One of the points often overlooked in the work of Agamben is that there is a close proximity between the figure of *homo sacer* and that of the sovereign. Both exist outside the law. Both reside in this zone or threshold of indistinction that is constituted by the Permanent State of Exception. Furthermore, for sustenance, the sovereign requires to be fed by its association with the glory provided by our wolf; in the age in which we live, the power to be effective requires a connection

---

[55] See Agamben, *The Kingdom and the Glory* (n 45); G Agamben, *Opus Dei, Archaeology of Duty* (Stanford University Press, 2013).
[56] G Agamben, *Homo Sacer, Sovereign Power and Bare Life* (Stanford University Press, 1999) 86.
[57] ibid, 104.
[58] ibid, 104–05.

with glory for its continued survival. Agamben shows us that the roots of theological genealogy are still inscribed in the contemporary apparatus of governance. Of necessity, power must be sustained and maintained by liturgy, ceremonies and other forms of acclamation. These may be new forms of liturgy, but nevertheless, the theological dimension of both Government and governance persists. The validity of both is presented to us in contemporary capitalism, as glory, manifested in its ultimate form, in the immense accumulation of images in the spectacle.

In the achievement of this glory, and in the pursuit of a seat next to, or possibly as the sovereign, the 'personal' choice – to dope or not to dope – is inevitably determined by the confluence of influences (sporting, commercial, national, media) that find their focus on the sporting body. A liturgical society of competition is one that demands glory at all times and in which the athlete is never simply seeking an individual goal but is just another cog in the construction of a greater machine. Is not the lesson of the society of competition, its central fantasy, that the pursuit of self-interest is the best way in which to produce 'societal' outcomes? The promise of this fantasy is that everyone will win, that there will be no losers. Dean here refers to George, quoting Thatcher:

> Because competition is always a virtue, its results cannot be bad. For the neo-liberal, the market is so wise and so good that like God, the Invisible Hand can bring good out of apparent evil. Thus Thatcher once said in a speech, "It is our job to glory in inequality and see that talents and abilities are given vent and expression for the benefit of us all."[59]

The glory of inequality is what we must seek to overcome through the resilience taught to us by the paradigmatic figure of the athlete. But what, specifically, does Agamben have to say about this requirement for glory, and how does it relate to the needs of creating and sustaining the fantasy of a society where everybody wins? The goal of national high performance centres, such as the AIS in Australia, is to become a glorification factory, whose object is to produce glory machines.

This factory concept emerged from the combination of the Eastern European method of preparation training and the American model of management. In this glorification factory, the athlete is placed in the hands of one of the orders of new priests, such as the exercise physiologist, who like mechanics of beautiful cars, regulate them and make them fit for maximum performance. But another priestly order is also at play here, the one which manages, scripts and finesses the stories and images of the glorious achievements of these high-performance competitive machines. It is in respect of this priesthood that Agamben's approach became most relevant.

In another Kafkian turn, Agamben, in *The Kingdom and the Glory*, treats angels as being divided into those that perform the role of assistants and those that are administrators. The angelic assistants are the liturgical choristers of glory while the angelic administrators are the ministers of government. For Agamben, it is in

[59] J Dean, 'Enjoying Neoliberalism' (2008) 4(1) *Cultural Politics* 47, 55.

the tension between glory and governance that the articulation of the Kingdom (sovereignty) and the government (governance) attains its maximum opacity. The question he poses here is whether the opposition between the Kingdom and the Government – between sovereignty and governance; has become so effective that politics ceases to take the form of sovereign action and power but tends towards the pole of spectacular hymn and glory. He inscribes the ceremonial aspects of power and right provisionally under the heading of the 'archaeology of glory'.[60]

It is no coincidence that Australian athletes returning from the Olympic Games were greeted at the top of the aircraft stairs by the prime minister and the head of one of the countriy'sleading corporations and Olympic sponsors. There is more at play here than just simple old nationalistic fervour or the fact that sport is one of the contemporary opiates (or probably more accurately today, amphetamines) of the masses. Agamben's archaeology of glory is tied up with Schmitt's concept of public opinion, and the way in which power is consecrated through public accla-mation. In the context of the exchanges between Schmitt and Peterson, examined by Agamben, acclamation emerges as having both a legal and a political meaning.[61]

The acclamation as an exclamation of praise, triumph, of laudation or disap-proval, a gesture of the raising of the right hand (or the punching of the right fist in the victory salute of the athlete) was present in Roman times in both political and spectacular contexts – athletes, actors, magistrates and emperors – all were objects of the acclamation and the public's desire for victory, strength or salvation.[62] The juridical value of the acclamation was, for Peterson, the essential link which united law and liturgy and which expressed the people's consensus.[63] For Agamben, it is from this idea of consensus that the link between law and liturgy takes on both its political, but importantly and subsequently, its biopolitical significance. It is in this biopolitical context that the acclamation unites a people and the State (or beyond the State) in a way that individual secret voting can never achieve.[64] For Agamben, and for our purposes here, liturgy and governance are strictly intertwined. What is always promised in the glory of the athletic spectacle is a form of salvation that can only be provided to us by our partaking in the society of competition.

It is through the vehicle of the 'technico juridical meaning of acclamation that constitutes the "publicity" of liturgy' that the multitude takes on its constituted or political form. In our context, we must remember that our theory of sovereignty depends not upon the general will of the social contract but our individual wills as entrepreneurs of the self. It might be that through liturgical acclamation the multitude enter into and are accepted by the realm of biopolitical governance, or as functional players within the economy. At the same time, those who do not partake in this acclamation, who reject its tenets, are outside of it as outlaws. In this

---

[60] Agamben, *The Kingdom and the Glory* (n 45) 167–68.
[61] ibid, 168–73.
[62] ibid, 169.
[63] ibid, 170.
[64] ibid, 171–72.

society, acclamation of the expert of the society of competition politicises us in so much as we consent to and become part of its realm.

From this perspective, the need for the sovereign of Government to also take part in this acclamation might be explained. Not only do they derive and enhance their own support from the athletic expert but they too, just like the State in neoliberalism, become another player or citizen, another entrepreneur of the self, having to be in the society of competition. They too must bow before the new athletic sovereign at the start and finish of the race as the one who provides the system with its means of construction and its sustenance. It is in this context that Agamben refers to Paul and the manner in which the economy of glory is expressed in solely optical terms – glory irradiates, it emits luminous rays, it reflects upon those that bathe in its light.[65] Why else was the start of a stage of the *Tour Down Under* in Gawler, outside Adelaide, delayed to await the arrival of the prime minister so that he might shake the hand of Armstrong before the amassed throng.[66]

In this context, it is not without significance that in the pages following those referred to above, Agamben discussed the symbols, signs, or in his terms, signatures of power. Signatures 'inhere in other signs or objects in order to confer a particular efficacy upon them'.[67] He notes that the crown of laurel, which was, of course, the prize given to athletes in the Ancient Olympics, became, in Rome, a technical attribute of sovereignty.[68] He then goes on to refer to the legal significance of the colour purple as the insignia of sovereignty, and how at the beginning of the fourth century its production was nationalised.[69] Shortly, thereafter, we find a reference to the 'holy lance' which, of course in our context, is rendered with a capital L. This holy lance also reminds us of Sir Lancelot who was, after all, the right arm of the king. And, of course, particularly strong arms, carry with them a heraldic meaning. Is it then without significance that the symbol, sign or signature of Lance Armstrong was a colour that he took and made his own? It is the yellow of the *Tour de France* that he privatised and continues to bear as his signature in heraldic fashion even after he has been wiped from its records. The yellow wristband of Armstrong, that so many of his acolytes (those that acclaim him) wear (on their arms) is an amulet, a thing that renders him present, it is the thing without being the thing and yet it is the thing, identical with him and which confers upon them a certain efficacy.[70] By having the thing with them, they too are close to Lance and they too are made strong.

As we saw in Adelaide in January 2009, with the third coming of the American, this proximity is such, that it may be, that now it is not the wolf that licks the feet

---

[65] ibid, 203–04.
[66] Cyclingnews.com, January 20, Stage 2: Gawler–Hahndorf 133.5km, 2010.
[67] Agamben, *The Kingdom and the Glory* (n 45) 181.
[68] ibid, 177.
[69] ibid, 179.
[70] ibid, 71–73.

of the sovereign, but that, in some cases, it is the sovereign that comes to lick the feet of the wolf.[71]

If, as we have posited, our whereabouts is an exceptional one in human history – where the economic tends towards being sovereign and is one of a permanent state of exception – there is also something at stake here in relation to Agamben's analysis of the feast or fiesta.[72] The time of sport in modernity, and its precursors before that, was the time of the feast in many respects, the exceptional time away from work. It was at this time that competition was able to reign unlicensed. However, with the coming of the permanent state of exception, in the economic exception of the society of competition, the logic of sport spills over and serves as a model for the rest of society. No longer does sport mirror society, but rather in the society of competition, society itself must mirror the logic of sport.

---

[71] 'From Barthes to Foucault and Beyond – Cycling in the Age of Empire'. Paper delivered at *Foucault: 25 Years On*, Conference – University of South Australia, 25 June 2009, available at esodoweb.net/pdf/ agempire.pdf.

[72] Agamben, *The State of Exception* (n 17) 71–73.

Epilogue

'Deadline man is exposed to personal crashes.'[1]

We all now know the end of the Lance story. The multiple figures of Lance embody at their various times all the qualities that we have tried to attribute to the paradigmatic figure of the imperial athlete. Lance 1.0 was the young, driven pre-cancer version who seized the opportunity provided by the society of competition and played that game with verve and vigour. He was already a privileged expert and ambassador, already a minister or angel of the new order in construction. Being a player was the ticket to fortune and to a life free of the trailer park in which he was raised. Lance 2.0 was organised, disciplined and resilient; backed by a machine, he overcame death to enforce a form of victory and dominance that not only gave him the status of the sport's patron, but he also became an archetypical figure for us all: an inspiration. Lance 3.0 was the sovereign who returned to give us all hope. Even when he was pursued, Lance acted as a sovereign, as someone beyond the law, refusing right up until the end to recognise the law's power over him. But there is no post-confessional Lance 4.0. In the end, Lance as the outcast, as *homo sacer*, is simply the bare life, that is lance after he stops having to be Lance.

It may be that in this Imperial Age, cycling found its first Zane, not in Lance but in the figure of Floyd Landis.

A is for Armstrong

In the world of doping, A is certainly for Armstrong.[2] However, the problem is where to start. And, although in some ways we do start at the beginning, it might be useful to recall the words spoken in '*Rio Bravo*'[3] by John Wayne to Dean Martin who was at the time suffering a Homeric hangover: 'Don't set yourself up as being so special. Think you invented the hangover?' And surely, Lance Armstrong, would give the same answer as the plaintive Dean Martin: 'I could sure take out a patent for this one.'

Armstrong provides the figure with which to grasp both doping and sport in the neoliberal age. Armstrong didn't start doping in sport, but it might be said that

---

[1] P Dadot and C Laval, *The New Way of the World* (Verso Books, 2013) 291.

[2] G Deleuze, 'T is for Tennis' in *L'Abécédaire de Gilles Deleuze, avec Claire Parnet* [Gilles Deleuze's *ABC Primer*, with Claire Parnet] dir P-A Boutang (1996), overview prepared by CJ Stivale, Romance Languages & Literatures, Wayne State University, available at www.langlab.wayne.edu/cstivale/d-g/ABC3.html#anchor813836.

[3] Howard Hawkes (dir), *Rio Bravo*, 1959.

he and his entourage perfected a practice and machine that surpassed anything seen previously. In its own way, in its matter-of-fact naturalness, Armstrong was a sporting machine that surpassed in some ways the commonly accepted evil of the former East Germany. In the post-Cold War era, the Armstrong machine manifested the frightening force of the coming together of American and Eastern Bloc know-how, the coming together of American management, marketing and social control with the knowledge passed down from the former Eastern Bloc doping practices which surpassed anything seen in cycling before.[4]

Consistent with this age, the figure of Armstrong is multiple, each having its place as a paradigm of neoliberal man in the world of doping and anti-doping. Armstrong encompasses the figure of America, an America that has sought constantly to surpass its frontiers in order to extend across the globe. Armstrong was the figure that globalised cycling and shifted its center of power from Old Europe to the new Anglo world and economy. What has been called, euphemistically, the '*American Winning Years*' by British TV commentator Phil Liggett during the coverage of the 2013 *Tour de France*, was, in fact, the Armstrong Era, one which saw the rapid globalisation and Anglicisation of the sport. And just like a defrocked priest, in this context, Armstrong's evils are measured against his good works.

The Americanisation of cycling is not necessarily about 'opening up'; its process does and must contribute to a loss of tradition and respect. Not only did one person become bigger than the sport itself and, hence implicitly, the peloton, but old European solidarities that had dominated cycling from time immemorial were finally broken down. No longer was doping a manner in which to keep a band of workers in employment, a means of putting on a show, it became simply a means for the pursuit of individual interest, or the American Dream: Lance gave cycling America and beyond. Lance gave the sport and the corporate interests that pushed it – US clothing, bicycle manufacturers and television companies – everything they needed to establish their global dominions. But, just as America individualises everything – its heroes and its villains; when it came to the fall, systemic failure was never on the agenda. Failure is always personal, individual moral failure. The world that created Armstrong is the same world that brought him down; just as in Margaret Thatcher's world, there is no society; there are no systemic reasons why.[5]

Lance 1.0

Born in Plano Texas on 18 September 1971, Armstrong (or Lance Edward Gunderson) was destined to be anything but plain. The son of a broken marriage

---

[4] C Brissoneau, 'Doping in France (1960–2000): American and Eastern Bloc Influences' (2010) 27(2) *Journal of Physical Education and Sport* 33; C Arribas, 'El mismo dopaje, menor tolerancia' *El Pais*, 18 December 2010, available at elpais.com/diario/2010/12/18/sociedad/1292626801_850215.html.
[5] R Butt, 'Margaret Thatcher: Interview for the Sunday Times – The First Two Years' *Sunday Times* (3 May 1981) available at www.margaretthatcher.org/document/104475; and see also L Dumont, *Essays on Individualism: Modern Ideology in Anthropological Perspective* (University of Chicago Press, 1986).

and humble beginnings (possibly what they endearingly call in the United States 'trailer trash') Armstrong's only way up was to become a self-made man – he has, from the beginning, epitomized '*Just Do It*'. By the age of 12 he was excelling as a long-distance swimmer and at the age of 13 took up the quintessential neoliberal sport, with its total focus upon multiskilling and personal bests, of triathlon. At 16 he was a professional triathlete and aged 18, he became US sprint-course triathlon champion for the first time.

At the age of 21, Armstrong became a professional cyclist with the *Motorola* cycling team. In his first year as a pro he finished last in the *Clasica San Sebastian*. In his second year as a professional he won ten times. Included in these ten victories was Stage Eight of the *Tour de France* which finished in the fortress town of Verdun. Later that year he became the youngest-ever winner of the UCI Road World Championship held in the Norwegian capital of Oslo. The following year he placed second in both Liege–Bastion–Liege and the *Clásica San Sebastián*.

Already he was making his mark. In 1995, as a third-year pro, he won the stage of the *Tour de France* which finished in Limoges with his now-famous homage to his teammate Fabio Casartelli, who had crashed and died on the descent of *Col de Portet d'Aspet* three days earlier. The week following the Tour, he returned to the green hills of the Basque country, this time to take victory in the *Clásica San Sebastián*.

In 1996, his upward trajectory continued. He won the *Flèche Wallonne* Classic but had to withdraw from the *Tour de France* after only five days. Following the *Tour* he signed a contract valued at $4 million with the new French *Cofidis* cycling team. However, he was never to ride for *Cofidis* as he was diagnosed with testicular cancer in October 1996.

Lance 1.0, the young, driven pre-cancer version, seized the opportunity provided by the society of competition and played that game with verve and vigour. He was already a privileged expert and ambassador, already a minister or angel of the new order under construction. Being a player was the ticket to fortune and to a life free of the trailer park in which he was raised. His entry into professional cycling coincided with the entry into the professional peloton of new methods of artificial blood doping in the form of erythropoietin (EPO), the substance which had come to replace the blood transfusions of the 1980s. Armstrong was determined, and in order to live his particular dream he was determined not to turn up at the OK Corral with just a water pistol. He was not going to turn up at the shoot out without a gun.[6]

Lance 2.0

Without cancer, I never would have won a single Tour de France. Cancer taught me a plan for more purposeful living, and that in turn taught me how to train and to win more purposefully. It taught me that pain has a reason, and that sometimes the experience of

---

[6] M Hardie, D Shilbury, C Bozzi and I Ware, *I Wish I was Twenty One Now: Beyond Doping in the Australian Peloton* (Auskadi Samizdats, 2012) 63.

losing things – whether health or a car or an old sense of self – has its own value in the scheme of life. Pain and loss are great enhancers.[7]

This is my body, and I can do whatever I want to it. I can push it. Study it. Tweak it. Listen to it. Everybody wants to know what I'm on. What am I on? I'm on my bike busting my ass six hours a day. What are you on?[8]

The comeback commenced in Spain when Armstrong surpassed all his previous achievements and finished fourth in the 1998 *Vuelta a España*. Already things were different. The following year, in 1999, when Armstrong miraculously, or incredibly – in the fullest sense of the word – was first on the road in the *Tour de France*, his victory was heralded as the *Tour of Redemption*, a new clean start for pro cycling following the previous year's *Festina* tour which saw a number of riders arrested for doping by the French police. In 1999, the young Floyd Landis, who had only watched his first *Tour de France* four years earlier, was 'pretty convinced' that Lance was clean.[9]

In a post-*Festina* world, the figure of an American who had overcome death and was not tarnished by the old ways of Europe provided cycling's overlords with the perfect fodder to carry out their own dream: cycling as a global sport. On the back of the *Tour of Redemption* cycling began its journey from a European sport with a cult following elsewhere, to become the 'new golf'. As the American winning years progressed, more and more white, English-speaking, middle-aged men (and women) donned Lycra clothing and preferably the yellow amulet of Lance.

The yellow amulet of his foundation, Livestrong, rendered Armstrong present in their lives and conferred upon them a certain efficacy; by having the thing with them, they were close to Lance and they, too, were made strong. Lance 2.0 was organised, disciplined and resilient; backed by a machine, he had overcome death to enforce a form of victory and dominance that gave him the status not only of the sport's patron, but also as an archetypical figure for us all – an inspiration. He was driven. Driven by revenge against those who had not stood by him, against those who had dominated him, and against those in the UCI who had not properly administered their own health monitoring rules and not picked up the warning signs of his cancer. More importantly in the contemporary context, individualism can mean and emphasise both strength and suffering: Lance embodied both.

Armstrong not only changed the way we see cycling and cycling's nature as a product, but he also changed the way the game was played and the manner in which one prepared for it. Lance gave the sport and the corporate interests that pushed it – US clothing, bicycle manufacturers and television companies – everything they needed to establish their global dominions. Philosophers Deleuze and

---

[7] L Armstrong, 'Back in the Saddle, Lance Armstrong' *Forbes Magazine* (2001) available at www.forbes.com/asap/2001/1203/064_print.html.

[8] L Armstrong, Nike Television Commercial (2005), available at www.youtube.com/watch?v=MIl5RxhLZ5U.

[9] A Shen, *The Gospel According to Floyd: An Interview with Floyd Landis by Paul Kimmage* (31 January 2011), available at nyvelocity.com/content/interviews/2011/landiskimmage.

Guattari compare the royal or aristocratic approach with that of the nomadic.[10] The Armstrong of the 'American Winning Years' was definitely royal or aristocratic.

Armstrong both learned and appropriated the way the nomadic Italians and Spanish prepared and played the game. The Europeans had ridden like a journeymen's association, allowing each to survive and shine, at times allowing each to take their turn in putting on a show. They were nomadic bands who sought out and did what was necessary to obtain support from the outside (State and corporate) world. Lance 2.0 was fully immersed in both the world of the State and the corporation. With the coming of Lance 2.0, what was required was a search for constants. To enforce Anglo-American superiority, chance had to be tamed and in doing so Lance 2.0 assembled a team that reproduced himself. The royal approach was a homogenous approach in which science and technology were both autonomous and fully integrated. For Lance 2.0 there was only one race: the *Tour de France*. The way the team prepared and rode the race was scientifically calculated, planned, managed and executed. For all the hype around it, the model of racing developed by Lance 2.0, and which has since been adopted by the likes of *Team Sky*, was robotic. Lance 2.0 was a carpenter, albeit one with the most up-to-date technology, in contrast to the art displayed by some of his European rivals.[11] No one could challenge such domination and if they tried, they did not survive for long.

From the very beginning there were detractors; those who did not believe. They were dealt with. In the case of failed doping controls or suspicious results, the complicity of the International Cycling Union (ICU) ensured that Lance 2.0 was protected. Journalists who questioned either him or his success were ostracised and denied access.[12] Others were simply treated as being crazy or bitter. Teammates who sought to strike out on their own and take on Lance 2.0 all seemed to suffer a similar fate: Tyler Hamilton, Roberto Heras and Floyd Landis all tested positive after leaving the fold. And those who denied the strength of the peloton's *omerta* were the subjects of bullying and on-the-road enforcement.

The paradigm example is that of the Italian cyclist Filippo Simeoni, a former client of Dr Michele Ferrari, the same doctor who treated Armstrong and various other former and current cyclists. Ferrari was a disciple of Conconi who had been funded by both the International and Italian Olympic Committees to develop testing procedures for EPO. While undertaking that research, Conconi had been also testing the substance under real conditions by preparing various cyclists. The first great EPO victories were the result of these early experiments, notably the triple of the *Gewiss* team in the 1994 *Flèche Wallonne*.[13] In 2002, Ferrari faced trial in Italy for the crime of sporting fraud. He was convicted principally on the evidence of Simeoni, who testified that he had begun to be treated by him in 1993. By 1997,

---

[10] G Deleuze and F Guattari, *A Thousand Plateaus* (University of Minnesota Press, 1987) 362–73; and Deleuze, 'T is for Tennis' (n 2).

[11] L Armstrong, 'If I was the carpenter, Pantani was the artist' *Cyclingnews* (2014), available at www.cyclingnews.com/features/armstrong-if-i-was-the-carpenter-pantani-was-the-artist.

[12] J Whittle, Bad Blood: The Secret Life of the Tour de France (Random House, 2009).

[13] E Hood, 'The "Too Good to be True" Fleche: 1994' (2007), available at www.pezcyclingnews.com/page/latest-news/?id=87915#.UpKyI7ae4QI.

he was being supplied with and instructed on how to use EPO and human growth hormone by Ferrari. Ferrari's conviction was eventually overturned on appeal. In 2003, Armstrong called Simeoni a liar in the French newspaper *Le Monde*, to which the Italian responded with a defamation writ claiming €100,000 which he said he would donate to charity.

The following year, on Stage Eighteen of the *Tour de France*, Simeoni formed a part of a breakaway that posed no threat to the race's general classification. According to Armstrong, 'in the interests of the peloton'[14] he broke from his cover, where he was protected by his praetorian guard and under no threat at all, to chase down the breakaway group by himself. Armstrong's continued presence in the breakaway spelt the end of the move, as his rival in the General Classification, Jan Ullrich, could not risk having the Texan up the road with the potential of gaining more time on him. Without Armstrong, the seven riders would have been able to enjoy their day in the limelight and possibly even go on to contest the stage finale. Armstrong would have none of that; on reaching the group he called out 'Bravo' to Simeoni. The burly Navarran veteran, Jose 'Txente' Garcia Acosta, understanding their fate, pleaded with Lance 2.0 to return to the peloton, but the only condition under which Armstrong would do this was with Simeoni in tow. In a show of respect for the others in the group, the Italian dropped back to the peloton with Armstrong who set about handling him, gesticulating and giving him a lecture of sorts. Once back in the peloton, Simeoni was the subject of verbal abuse, he was spat upon and called a disgrace by the other riders and Lance 2.0 made his infamous 'zip the lips' gesture to emphasise that Simeoni had broken the *omerta* and should from now on refrain. Armstrong later said that Simeoni did not deserve to win or, it seems, even have the chance of winning. In the final stage, two days later, Simeoni interrupted the victory procession to the Champs-Élysées with constant attacks; each time he was chased by Armstrong's team and again insulted and spat at.[15]

By the end of the 'American Winning Years' Lance 2.0 was the patron and sovereign of cycling and more. Not only had he overcome cancer, he had won the *Tour de France* for seven consecutive years. Lance 2.0 was no ordinary cyclist, nor was he any ordinary doper. He had created a following who responded as he did to criticism. His was a business model that changed the face of professional cycling, perfecting techniques of racing, doping, media management and being the vehicle, even the pawn, through which cycling administrators globalised the sport.

Lance 2.0 left us with these words:

> Finally, the last thing I'll say to the people who don't believe in cycling, the cynics and the skeptics: I'm sorry for you. I'm sorry that you can't dream big. I'm sorry you don't believe in miracles. But this is one hell of a race. This is a great sporting event and you should stand around and believe it. You should believe in these athletes, and you should

---

[14] J Lindsay, 'Armstrong Hunts Down Rider, Personal disputes mar Armstrong's perfect Tour' (2004), available at www.bicycling.com/news/pro-cycling/armstrong-hunts-down-rider.

[15] M Beaudin, 'The wrath of Lance Armstrong: USADA outlines witness intimidation' *Velonews* (2012), available at velonews.competitor.com/2012/10/news/the-wrath-of-lance-armstrong-usada-outlines-witness-intimidation_256702#yJMTFQkCtcjOlCgu.99.

believe in these people. I'll be a fan of the Tour de France for as long as I live. And there are no secrets – this is a hard sporting event and hard work wins it. So *Vive le Tour* forever![16]

Lance 3.0

January 2009, the room was filled with television cameras, journalists from around the world, a contingent of Americans in the first row … This is Australia, the eve of the Tour Down Under, the first race of Lance Armstrong since his last Tour de France in 2005. Whispers, buzz, the anticipation. They bring in a bike, His Bike. A few times suddenly heard: "He's coming … False alarm … Do we have to stand when he enters?" It was like being in church. A dead silence accompanied His arrival. One British reporter commented that the reception was as if we were waiting for Jesus Christ after his resurrection and the Lance 3.0 quickly responds: "I don't think that Jesus Christ rode a bike."[17] And he surely didn't rise from cancer.

Armstrong tells the throng that the 'desire to succeed is different now'. Lance 3.0 has returned to promote the Livestrong Foundation. Good news for modern man: 'I have returned to bring the Livestrong message around the world and to discuss the burden of this disease.' On his bike are carved two figures: on the downpipe is inscribed '*1274*' – the number of days since his last appearance. The other '*27.5*', the millions of people who have died of cancer since he last spoke to us. 'A staggering number' he reminds us, 'more than the entire Australian population'.[18] Lance 3.0 appears in the guise of a privatised message of public health. Lance 3.0 is benevolent, he does not charge a fee to race, he will not accept prize money. He tells us:

> I am calm because I enjoy it, and I do this for free. I do it because I love it. During 2004 and 2005 cycling was just a job, but now I have regained the passion and that will help cycling and the Livestrong foundation.[19]

He omitted to say that he would receive around AUS$2 million every year for three years to come to Adelaide to preach the Livestrong message.[20] His annual fee was enough, in fact, to keep open two rural public hospitals which the State had recently closed down as a result of budgetary constraints. However, the economic value of Lance 3.0 was not forgotten. The then Premier of South Australia, Mike Rann, had already compared the race gaining *Pro Tour* status with the expansion of the world's largest uranium mine in that State. The Armstrong investment he said was 'the best investment the state could realise'.[21]

---

[16] Caroline Wyatt, 'Paris salutes its American hero' *BBC News* (24 July 2005), available at news.bbc.co.uk/2/hi/europe/4713283.stm.

[17] M Hardie, 'La nueva resurrección de Armstrong' *El Pais* (2009), available at elpais.com/diario/2009/01/18/deportes/1232233211_850215.html.

[18] ibid.

[19] ibid.

[20] ibid.

[21] ibid.

As a cyclist returning from retirement, Lance 3.0 should have been subject to the rules that would have required him to be tested for a period prior to his return to racing. But as Anne Gripper, the then UCI head of Anti-Doping, commented in a tête-à-tête with me: 'Lance is different', so the rules did not apply. Lance 3.0 *was* different and, importantly, his glory irradiated, it emitted luminous rays and it reflected upon those who sought to bathe in his light.

However, by the following year, in California during May 2010, things had started to change.

Floyd

Lance Armstrong: How bad do you want to win a stage in the Tour de France?

Floyd Landis: Real bad.

Armstrong: How fast can you go downhill?

Landis: I go downhill real fast. Can I do it?

Armstrong: Sure you can do it … run like you stole something Floyd.[22]

People are just looking out for themselves and I understand how business works and the connections that people like that have, [they] have very long tentacles. But some people do become nearly untouchable … It's hypocritical very, very hypocritical. I've come in contact with journalists with people who are supposed to be anti-doping journalists or people who are looking for the thing and there's stuff smack in their face. They still don't touch. Do you know what I mean? There's two very, very big standards that's been put out there and they still won't touch it. You're a joke, an absolute joke. What's the fastest guy in the world?[23]

When the Mennonite Floyd Landis first left his world to visit ours, so that he could compete in the World Junior Mountain Bike Championships, he felt as though he had gone to Mars. When he switched to road racing and joined the US *Mercury* team in 2001 he admitted to being 'still completely against' doping, 'it didn't represent what I felt cycling was to me'. He was 'really confused as to how people could just accept that that was the way it is'. He didn't know then that 'the people at the top could actually manipulate' the anti-doping system. He learnt soon enough that 'everyone with any power' was in on keeping the lid on the reality of what went on. He didn't expect that 'the guys publicly decrying the whole thing, and stating that they were the ones trying to fix it, were in fact making it happen'. He soon learnt the attitude of those governing the sport: 'We don't care what the rules are, this is how we do it.' And it was here that he first learnt to understand the story that Scorsese was telling in the film *Goodfellas*.[24]

[22] 'Score another for Armstrong' Velonews (2004), available at velonews.competitor.com/2004/07/news/score-another-for-armstrong_6638.

[23] Hardie et al, *I Wish I was Twenty One Now* (n 6) 134.

[24] Shen, *The Gospel According to Floyd* (n 9).

A year later, in 2002, Landis joined the *US Postal* team. He soon started to talk to Armstrong about doping and about how the Italian doctor Michele Ferrari worked. He also quickly learnt that in order to protect oneself at the top, one had to be able to call on favours from the sport's governors. In the course of this lesson he was told by Armstrong of the UCI's cover-up of the Texan's 2001 suspicious test result in the *Tour de Suisse*. Of his decision to begin to dope Landis is candid:

> I take responsibility for doing it. I made these decisions. I don't point fingers and no one forced me to do it but the circumstances were such that the decision was almost made for me … I just found out that things were not as simple as I thought they were.[25]

By 2004, Floyd's relationship with both Armstrong and Bruyneel was in tatters. He left *US Postal* and joined the Swiss-based *Phonak* team. Fast forward 18 months or so, the year after Lance 2.0 retired, and a few days after winning the *Tour de France* in 2006, Landis, of course, tested positive for testosterone. He still denies having used testosterone, raising doubts about the competence of the scientific procedures; however, he no longer denies doping.

Faced with the fact that the Holy Grail was being taken away from him, Floyd dug in. This was what the sport expected: deny doping, fight the case and, if necessary, take the ban. And after that, return to the fold. 'I was assured that, whatever I do I need to just not talk and I'll have a team'. The system demanded silence

> '… there is a parallel world where the fans see what's put in front of them and appreciate it for what they believe it to be and beside it is the peloton who know the real story … there are no secrets within the peloton, management, the UCI and anyone with a financial interest in cycling'.[26]

That's how Floyd justified the things he said in his defence.

The advice of the former *US Postal* rider and boss of the *Garmin* team, Jonathan Vaughters, was to 'tell the truth'. But Floyd and Vaughters had different conceptions of the truth: 'in my head the truth is more complex than in Vaughters' head'. The truth, for Vaughters, was only a truth about yourself; one must never say anything about anyone else. The *omerta* was and, as we shall see, remains strong

> … that's the problem I have with Jonathan's statement that I should just tell what I know about me. That's not the story at all. That's not the truth. There is more to it than just doping. And if you don't see the whole picture you don't know anything.[27]

The *omerta* entailed only talking about what you did as an individual. This importantly ensured that you did not 'spit in the soup',[28] that you never implicated another person who was not already implicated. It was this Floyd began to wrestle with as he began the journey to his coming out in the first half of 2010.

---

[25] ibid.
[26] ibid.
[27] ibid.
[28] P Kimmage, *Rough Ride, Behind the Wheel with a Pro Cyclist* (Yellow Jersey Press 1998), 229; V Møller, *The Doping Devil* (International Network of Humanistic Doping Research, 2010).

Floyd is unable to describe how he felt during his years of deceit. In his mind 'there was no difference between saying "I didn't do it" and telling a half-truth like David Millar did: "I did it once and was hoping to get caught" …'.[29] The trophy he had won in 2006 and which he later smashed had turned him into someone he was not. By 2010, faced with the reality that he was not going to return to the fold, to the security of the peloton, he had decided that was not who he wanted to be any longer.

In May 2010, Floyd became the Bartleby of the professional cycling world. Herman Melville's character Bartleby is a figure of dissent, a figure who decided he 'would prefer not to'. For Floyd, preferring not to meant rejecting the norms and customs of the world that he had found himself within. And in a world where cycling had seen the return of Lance 3.0, Floyd decided that he would prefer not to be bound by the truth of the peloton any longer. It would be the beginning of the unravelling of the myth, which Armstrong may have perfected, but which he had never invented.

It may be that the most decisive moment was not his revelations, his decision to speak a truth that went beyond himself, but was, in fact, his response to the legal threats of the former UCI President Hein Verbruggen and the then President Pat McQuaid. Both men took umbrage at Floyd's claim that the former had been involved in fixing suspicious test results for Lance 2.0. Faced with legal demands and threats of litigation in the Swiss Courts, Floyd decided not to play their game. He stepped outside the law and invented his own fake law firm, *Grey Manrod*, which claimed to be based in New York, Baghdad, and Djibouti, which specialised in vegetable rights abuse, advocacy and pronunciation mediation, to respond to their correspondence.[30] Floyd had not only rejected the peloton's norms, but in response to McQuaid and Verbruggen's legal threats he had also rejected the Law itself. It took a while for the sport's governors to cotton on.

In the end, it was neither evangelical anti-dopers nor investigative journalists who brought down Lance, but his own prodigy. Following his positive test result in the 2006 *Tour De France*, Floyd Landis had followed orders. He had stuck to the *omerta* and done what was expected of him: deny and fight. But even after serving his time, Floyd was still on the outer with no apparent prospect of ever entering the big time of pro cycling again. He had put together a small band of supporters and knocked around, riding the races he could, in the teams he could. With Lance 3.0 in full flight, Floyd sought support to have his team compete in the *Tour of California*, one of the events outside old Europe, like the *Tour Down Under* which had gained prominence in a global cycling world. That support was denied.

At the 2010 *Tour of California*, Lance 3.0, faced with Floyd rejecting the *omerta*, simply stated: 'We have our truth; we like our truth.'[31]

---

[29] Shen, *The Gospel According to Floyd* (n 9).

[30] 'The Landis Emails' *Velocity Nation* (2011), available at nyvelocity.com/content/features/2011/landis-emails.

[31] 'Landis pours more dirt on Armstrong' *The Scotsman* (2010), available at www.scotsman.com/sport/landis-pours-more-dirt-on-armstrong-1-1367256.

Novitsky and USADA

Initially, Floyd approached the US Anti-Doping Agency (USADA):

> There was nothing else for me in cycling. There was no team for me, no matter what I do it was going to get worse and worse until I leave, not that that's a deciding factor, but at least I didn't have to consider that any more. And then, the thought process was 'How do I do it? Who do I trust?' So I went to USADA ...[32]

Floyd's information was warmly received. The Agency jumped at the chance of getting involved taking such a high-profile scalp. But his advice was not taken: "'Look, everyone is immune – just tell us what the fuck is going on?" That's what I suggested to USADA and WADA that they just give everyone immunity and just get the facts but they won't do it.'[33]

Without such an approach, the best USADA would end up getting was testimony of the type of truth suggested by Vaughters to Floyd four years earlier.

Instead, the Landis revelations led to the case being taken up by US Federal Food and Drug Agency Investigator Jeff Novitsky. who had prosecuted the US athlete Marion Jones, baseball player Barry Bonds and had been at the centre of the *BALCO* case. He took control and began building a case. He initially enlisted Landis to go undercover in his pursuit of the US *Rock Racing* team, home to a number of exiled American and European pros including Landis himself and others such as Tyler Hamilton, Francisco Mancebo and Oscar Sevilla. Later, basing his case around allegations of perjury and defrauding the US Postal Service, Novitsky subpoenaed a number of current and former Armstrong teammates and staff to testify before the grand jury including Yaroslav Popovych, Tyler Hamilton, George Hincapie and Levi Leipheimer. Others did their best to avoid the jurisdiction so they would not be forced to give evidence. Unlike the baseball players Barry Bonds and Roger Clemens, who testified before a federal grand jury and were subsequently accused (but found not guilty) of lying under oath, Armstrong was not called to testify. Through cooperation with the Italian authorities and the WADA Novitsky had also gained access to Dr Ferrari's computer records.

However, following a 20-month long investigation and a secret grand jury process, in February 2012, Novitsky was stymied by what may have been political pressure which sought to ensure the Armstrong legacy remained untarnished. It was as if he, like the banks in the global financial crisis, was too big to fail. Speculation was rife that there had been political pressure exerted on the US Attorney General's Department to make the investigation go away. Armstrong, of course, was no stranger to the world of politics. His lawyer, Mark Fabiani, had been Bill Clinton's lawyer in the Whitewater scandal. Lance played golf with Clinton and went mountain biking with George W Bush. Lance 3.0 was chummy with politicians

---

[32] Shen, *The Gospel According to Floyd* (n 9).
[33] ibid.

around the world. He had even announced his own political aspirations.[34] At that point, it seemed as if the case against Armstrong was never to be.

Nevertheless, from the beginning, USADA had sat in on some of Novitsky's interrogations, allowing them to subsequently build upon his work. Throughout 2012, USADA built its case interviewing and collecting evidence. In his statement of October 2012, announcing the assertions against Armstrong, USADA CEO Travis T Tygart spoke of cyclists who had come forward to speak truthfully.[35] The reality was that a number of them had not come forward of their own accord, but had only done so when faced with the prospect of having their careers and reputations destroyed. One cyclist, who continued to race for the *Garmin* team, and who had spent the previous two years hoping that the whole thing would just go away, fearing that he would lose his million-dollar lifestyle and would spend the rest of his life delivering pizzas, had privately expressed his anger at Floyd and the situation he found himself in. In Tygart's world he had decided willingly to be a part of the solution by deciding to acknowledge the truth. However, Tygart's truth may well have been coloured by some of those informers seeking to only talk about what was already known and to lessen the sanctions they themselves faced.

In announcing the case against Armstrong, Tygart made the claim that the: '… evidence demonstrates that the "Code of Silence" of performance enhancing drug use in the sport of cycling has been shattered, but there is more to do'.[36] It was a big claim, as was his claim that the *US Postal* team's doping programme was 'the most sophisticated, professionalized and successful doping program the sport had ever seen'.[37] In respect of the latter claim, Tygart repeated similar words a year or so later when commenting on the case against baseball player Alex Rodriguez. In that case, Tygart's hyperbole was that it was 'probably the most potent and sophisticated drug program developed for an athlete that we've ever seen …'.[38]

In respect of the type of truth Landis attributes to Vaughters, Paul Kimmage has said:

> The law of silence: it exists not only in the Mafia but also in the peloton. Those who break the law, who talk to the press about the dope problems in the sport are despised. They are branded as having "crache dans la soupe", they have spat in the soup.[39]

[34] W Wallace, *Cycling Tips* (2012), available at cyclingtips.com.au/2012/02/too-big-to-fail/.
[35] USADA, US Postal Service Pro Cycling Team Investigation 2012, available at cyclinginvestigation.usada.org/.
[36] ibid.
[37] ibid.
[38] E Hilbert, 'Official: Alex Rodriguez's PED use "most potent we've ever seen' (2014), available at www.cbssports.com/mlb/eye-on-baseball/24410023/official-alex-rodriguezs-ped-use-most-potent-weve-ever-seen.
[39] Kimmage, *Rough Ride* (n 28) 229.

The themes of 'comradeship, loyalty and any instinctive human urge to protect oneself and one's family at any price' are what form the basis of the *omerta* and Hardie et al warned against seeing the

> closed nature of the peloton's community in isolation but as an aspect of the real dependencies that the peloton has formed as it has sought to maintain itself within the bounds of the physical and structural conditions of their sport. Thus, the *omerta* in cycling and the community which it has helped to sustain: 'was not something abstract, floating in the air so to speak, reinforcing or influencing actual behaviour. On the contrary ... it constituted a very concrete and real part of the behaviour of people who depended on each other in specific and fundamental ways'.

As Møller put it quoting the retired Danish cyclist, Jesper Skibby:

> They could just as well write about comradeship, loyalty and any instinctive human urge to protect oneself and one's family at any price. ... You just keep your secrets for yourself and avoid pointing a finger at others. It is no different from any other workplace. ...[40]

This 'code of silence' is the custom of not saying anything about anyone else, or at least not saying anything above and beyond what is already known. If one examines the affidavits of a number of those that gave evidence to USADA one can see that this particular characteristic of the *omerta* is still very much in place. Putting aside the fact that the form of the affidavits appears to have been written by the same person, in the main they are characterised as not adding anything new to the original statements of Landis. No facts, other than those already put out there by Floyd, are brought into play. Many appear to give a sanitised and incomplete, if not exactly untruthful version of their own involvement in doping. As Nietzsche reminds us, the past always governs the future and Tygart's shattering of the *omerta* appears only to be its eternal return in a new guise.

In coming forward, some appear to have engaged in the process of 'gilding the lily'. Compare the former *US Postal* team doctor Pedro Celaya's version of events with that given to USADA by Jonathan Vaughters. Vaughters' version of his early days in the team set out in his affidavit was that

> [a]t the beginning of the season Dr. Pedro Celaya, the U.S. Postal Service team physician and I had a frank conversation about my prior use of erythropoietin ... EPO use on the U.S. Postal Service Team in 1998 prior to the Festina doping scandal at the 1998 Tour de France was relatively open. Although a neo-pro such as Christian Vande Velde would be more shielded, for others who were already using drugs the communications about performance enhancing drugs were generally fairly open.[41]

[40] V Møller *The Ethics of Doping and Anti-Doping: Redeeming the Soul of Sport?* (Routledge, 2009) 58–59.
[41] USADA, US Postal Service Pro Cycling Team Investigation (n 35).

Celaya was widely regarded within cycling as always having the interests of the rider's health as his main concern. In 2012, when researching the Armstrong case, I was given a version of events that casts a different light on Vaughters' affidavit:

> Vaughters acted like an asshole. He insulted the doctor calling him soft and shit and telling him he had no idea how to use EPO. Vaughters thought himself wise in the matter. He was buying the EPO in Mexico or Andorra with Johnny Weltz, who was the team manager. And in the team he was proselytizing, telling everyone they had to use EPO … It was Vaughters who induced Vande Velde to start using EPO.[42]

Lance 4.0

> The penitent … falls raving to the ground, revealing her sins to the Lord, the pastor and the rest of the congregation. Then she is borne up, reinforced by other ex-sinners in a transport of therapeutic sharing. Forgiveness comes, not from authority, but from mutuality. The delight of confession prolongs the pleasure of sin.[43]

In the scheme of the World Anti-doping Council (WADC), the USADA Reasoned Decision (a term that comes from the UCI Anti-Doping Rules) was a series of untested, assertions that went unchallenged by Armstrong. In that sense it was not a judgment, nor did it contain any findings. It was, in the end, an assertion made in terms of the law and was not proof of anything in itself. Not until the case against Dr Celaya, Johan Bruyneel and Pepi Marti was heard in December 2013 were any of these assertions tested and challenged. But from Tygart's (and the WADC's) perspective the fact that Lance did not contest the charges was taken as an acceptance of the validity of the process. Armstrong had tried to challenge the USADA process unsuccessfully in the US Federal Court.[44] But, from another perspective, we might be assisted by Agamben to view Lance 3.0 as a sovereign standing naturally and necessarily outside the Law and refusing to recognise its power over him. 'There comes a point in every man's life when he has to say, "Enough is enough,"' Armstrong said. 'For me, that time is now.'[45]

In January 2013, Armstrong sought to begin his path to redemption. He confronted the 'institutional incitement to speak'[46] and headed to Hollywood's home of confessional TV,[47] Oprah Winfrey, to speak directly to the public; an

---

[42] Personal communication with the author.

[43] R Hughes, *Culture of Complaint, The Fraying of America* (The Harvill Press, 1995) 11.

[44] *Lance Armstrong v Travis Tygart, in his Official Capacity as Chief Executive Officer of The United States Anti-Doping Agency, and United States Anti-Doping Agency, United States District Court for the Western District of Texas Austin Division* Case No A-12-Ca-606-Ss, 2012.

[45] J Macur, 'Armstrong Drops Fight Against Doping Charges' *New York Times* (2012), available at www.nytimes.com/2012/08/24/sports/cycling/lance-armstrong-ends-fight-against-doping-charges-losing-his-7-tour-de-france-titles.html?pagewanted=all&_r=0.

[46] M Foucault, *The Will to Knowledge: The History of Sexuality*, vol 1 (Penguin, 1978) 18.

[47] Hughes, *Culture of Complaint* (n 43) 8.

explanation as much as a confession and a plea for the understanding of the world and the place Lance 2.0 had inhabited. Admitting that he was a flawed character who could neither control nor live up to the image of the myth he had created, Lance 4.0 responded to Oprah's questions saying 'I was used to controlling everything in my life. I controlled every outcome in my life'. Lance 4.0 admitted the myth had been 'so perfect for so long' that it was 'mythic perfect story' but 'it wasn't true'. He continued '[m]y ruthless desire to win at all costs served me well on the bike but the level it went to, for whatever reason, is a flaw. That desire, that attitude, that arrogance'.[48]

It could have been that there was no post-confessional Lance 4.0. In the end, he could have been like Pantani, like Rasmussen, and so many others, who continued to live, or die, as the outcast, as *homo sacer*, as bare life. Lance could have just been what was left of Lance Armstrong after he stopped having to be Lance. But it appears that Lance just cannot stop being Lance. He would not lie down, he still wanted to play his part and to redeem himself in whatever way he could, and of course to compete, no longer in cycling but as an Ironman. To this end, Lance 4.0 continued to be vocal, to be visible, and to be heard. He took on the role of continuing to call for a genuine process of truth and reconciliation for cycling and to advocate for what Floyd had suggested was the only option when he went to USADA.[49] USADA CEO Tygart had said in his statement announcing the case against Armstrong that 'no one wants to be chained to the past forever, and I would call on the UCI to act on its own recent suggestion for a meaningful Truth and Reconciliation program'.[50] But it is difficult to take this as more than lip service, for that same week Tygart said that such a process would never occur. It was not realistically on USADA's agenda.[51]

In 2014, the UCI announced an independent commission to look into the past; however, with threats of the ramifications of not coming forward being used to induce cyclists to come forward, its characteristics appeared to be no more than another police operation.[52] It was hardly the process suggested by Floyd. Nevertheless, Lance 4.0 continued to tell his truth to the world, at once confirming and putting into context the allegations of the cover up.

> The real problem was; the sport was on life support. And Hein [Verbruggen] just said, "This is a real problem for me, this is the knockout punch for our sport, the year after Festina, so we've got to come up with something".

---

[48] 'Lance Armstrong, The Worldwide Exclusive', *The Oprah Winfrey Show* (2012). Full transcript available at armchairspectator.wordpress.com/2013/01/23/full-transcript-lance-armstrong-on-oprah/.
[49] Shen, *The Gospel According to Floyd* (n 9).
[50] USADA, US Postal Service Pro Cycling Team Investigation (n 36).
[51] Personal communication with the author.
[52] UCI Cycling Independent Reform Commission, Terms of Reference (2014), available at www.uci.ch/Modules/BUILTIN/getObject.asp?MenuId=&ObjTypeCode=FILE&type=FILE&id=OTMwNzg&LangId=1.

He continued:

> 'Don't think I'm protecting any guys after the way they treated me, that is ludicrous,' he said, making clear that he won't hold back. 'I'm not protecting them at all. I have no loyalty towards them. In the proper forum I'll tell everyone what they want to know. I'm not going to lie to protect these guys. I hate them. They threw me under the bus. I'm done with them.'[53]

In the end, much has been said since the USADA case against Armstrong about how it set the stage for a new paradigm of anti-doping, based upon investigation rather than testing. The case against Armstrong was built upon investigation and policing and not the scientific testing that had dominated anti-doping discourse up until that time. The Armstrong case, in the end, is a police investigation. But it differs from the other two 'great' doping investigations of cycling, the *Festina* Tour and *Operacíon Puerto*, both of which resulted in chance findings. In the case of Armstrong, it might be said that the case illustrates the difference between the mafia's and cycling's versions of the *omerta*. They say of the mafia that it always looks after its own. Was it the failure to look after their own that finally caused the Armstrong myth to unravel? If Armstrong's case heralds a new method it is a clear that it requires two principal actors: a disaffected informer and a figure as abrasive and self-centred as Armstrong was in order to be able to provoke such disaffection. This is a rare combination and one whose importance anti-doping authorities do not appear to have grasped. It may also be that if Armstrong had understood the importance of gifts, and grasped their particular economy,[54] the wheels may not have fallen off in such a spectacular fashion.

---

[53] VeloNation Press, 'Armstrong implicates Verbruggen, Ferrari for first time over doping matters' (2013), available at Postal.
[54] Hardie et al, *I Wish I was Twenty One Now* (n 6) 136–37.

BIBLIOGRAPHY

Books and Articles

Abt, S, *Up the Road, Cycling's Modern Era from Lemond to Armstrong* (Boulder, Velopress, 2005).

Agamben, G *Homo Sacer, Sovereign Power and Bare Life* (Stanford, Stanford University Press, 1999).

Agamben, G, *Remnants of Auschwitz, The Witness and the Archive* (New York, Zone Books, 2002).

Agamben, G, *What is a Paradigm?* Lecture at European Graduate School. August 2002. Available at: www.egs.edu/faculty/giorgio-agamben/articles/what-is-a-paradigm/.

Agamben, G, *What is an Apparatus? and Other Essays* (New York, Meridian, 2009).

Agamben, G, *The State of Exception* (Chicago, University of Chicago Press, 2005).

Agamben, G, *The Time That Remains, A Commentary on the Letter to the Romans* (Stanford, Stanford University Press, 2005).

Agamben, G, *The Signature of All Things, on Method* (New York, Zone Books, 2009).

Agamben, G, *The Kingdom and the Glory: For a Theological Genealogy of Economy and Government* (Stanford, Stanford University Press, 2011).

Agamben, G, *Opus Dei, Archaeology of Duty* (Stanford, Stanford University Press, 2013).

Anderson, B, *Imagined Communities: Reflections on the Origin and Spread of Nationalism* (London, Verso, 1991).

Anderson, J, *Modern Sports Law: A Textbook* (Oxford, Hart Publishing, 2010).

Andrews, D, 'Desperately Seeking Michel: Foucault's Genealogy, The Body, and Critical Sport Sociology' (1993) 10(2) *Sociology of Sport Journal* 148.

Andrews, M and Silk, M (eds), *Sport and Neoliberalism, Politics, Consumption and Culture* (Philadelphia, Temple University Press, 2012).

Aristotle, *Ethics* (Harmondsworth, Penguin, 1981).

Armstrong, L with Jenkins, S, *It's Not About the Bike: My Journey Back to Life* (New York, Putnam, 2000).

Armstrong, L, 'Back in the Saddle, Lance Armstrong' *Forbes Magazine*, 2001 available at www.forbes.com/asap/2001/1203/064_print.html.

Armstrong, L with Jenkins, S, *Every Second Counts* (New York, Broadway Books, 2003).

Armstrong, L, *Comeback 2.0: Up Close and Personal* (New York, Touchstone, 2009).

Armstrong, L with Rodgers, J, *No Mountain High Enough: Raising Lance, Raising* (Broadway, 2002).

G Arrighi, *The Long Twentieth Century: Money, Power and the Origins of Our Times* (Verso, 2010).

M Ashenden, Open letter to Phil Liggett, 30 August 2012, published on Velocity Nation, available at nyvelocity.com/content/features/2012/filthy-business-indeed.

M Atkinson and K Young, *Deviance and Social Control in Sport, Human Kinetics* (Champaign, Human Kinetics, 2008).

ALRC *Australian Law Reform Commission Report* 'Essentially Yours'. Available at: www.austlii.edu.au/au/other/alrc/publications/reports/96/30_Genetic_Discrimination_in_Employment.doc.html#heading11, 2003.

Walsh, D and Ballester, P, LA Confidentiel: Les secrets de Lance Armstrong. (La Martiniere, Paris, 2003).

Barthes, R, 'The Tour de France as Myth' in Barthes, R, *Mythologies* (Editions du Seuil, France, 1957).

Barthes, R, *What is Sport?* (New Haven and London, Yale University Press, 2007).

Bastin, R 'Ritual Games for the Goddess Pattini' (2001) 45(2) *Social Analysis* 120.

Bauman, Z, *Modernity and the Holocaust* (Ithaca, Cornell University Press, 1989).

Benjamin, W, 'Critique of Violence' in Demetz, P (ed), *Reflections: Essays, Aphorisms, Autobiographical Writings* (New York, Schocken Books, 1978).

Berardi, F, *The Soul at Work, From Alienation to Autonomy* (Los Angeles, Semiotxet(e), 2009).

Berman, PS, 'From International Law to Law and Globalization' (2005) 43 *Columbia Journal of Transnational Law* 485.

Blok, A, *The Mafia of a Sicilian Village, 1860–1960: A Study of Violent Peasant Entrepreneurs* (New York, Harper Torchbooks, 1974).

Boardley, I D and Kavussanu, M, 'The Moral Disengagement in Sport Scale-short' (2008) 26(14) *Journal of Sports Sciences* 1507.

Boltanski, L and Chiapello, E, *The New Spirit of Capitalism* (London, Verso, 2005).

Boltanski, L and Chiapello, E, 'The New Spirit of Capitalism' (2005) 18 *International Journal of Politics, Culture, and Society* 161.

Bowrey, K, *Law and Internet Cultures* (Cambridge, Cambridge University Press, 2005).

Brissoneau, C, 'Doping in France (1960–2000): American and Eastern Bloc Influences' (2010) 27(2) *Journal of Physical Education and Sport* 33.

Brissoneau, C, Aubel, O and Ohl, F, *L'epreuve du dopage, Sociologie du cyclisme professionnel* (Paris, Presses Universitaires de France, Paris, 2008).

Browning, G, *Global Theory from Kant to Hardt and Negri* (Basingstoke, Palgrave Macmillan, 2011).

Bruyneel, J, *We Might as Well Win: On the Road to Success with the Mastermind Behind a Record-setting Eight Tour de France Victories* (New York, Mariner Books, 2009).

Bryson, L, 'Sport, Drugs and the Development of Modern Capitalism' (1990) 2 *Sporting Traditions* 135–36.

Callies, G-P and Renner, M, 'Between Law and Social Norms: The Evolution of Global Governance' (2009) 22(2) *Ratio Juris* 260.

Carstairs, C, 'The Wide World of Doping: Drug Scandals, Natural Bodies, and the Business of Sports Entertainment' (2013) 11(4) *Addiction Research & Theory*, 263.

Cassese, S et al, *Global Administrative Law: Cases, Materials, Issues*, 2nd edn (New York, Institute for International Justice and Law, 2008).

Casini, L, 'The Making of a Lex Sportiva – The Court of Arbitration for Sport "The Provider"', IILJ Working Paper 2010/5 *Global Administrative Law Series* (New York, New York University School of Law, 2010).

Casini, L, 'Global Hybrid Public-Private Bodies: The World Anti-Doping Agency (WADA)' (Draft paper for the Global Administrative Law Conference on Practical Legal Problems of International Organizations, Geneva, 20–21 March 2009).

Chesterman, S, *Just War or Just Peace? Humanitarian Intervention and International Law* (Oxford, Oxford University Press, 2001).

Coleman, JE and Levine, JL, 'The Burden of Proof in Endongenous Substance Cases: A Masking Agent for Junkscience' in M McNamee, and V Møller (eds), *Doping and Anti-doping Policy in Sport: Ethical and Legal Perspectives* (London, Routledge, 2011).

Collins, T, *Rugby League in Twentieth Century Britain, a Social and Cultural History* (London, Routledge, 2006).

Comaroff, JL and Comaroff, J, 'Reflections on the Anthropology of Law, Governance and Sovereignty' in F von Benda-Beckmann, K von Benda-Beckmann and J Eckert (eds), *Rules of Law and Laws of Ruling* (Ashford, Ashgate Publishing, 2009).

Cotterrell, R, 'Law's Community: Legal Theory and the Image of Legality' (1992) 19(4) *Journal of Law and Society* 405.

Dadot, P and Laval, C, *The New Way of the World* (London, Verso Books, 2013).

Dauncey, H and Hare, G 'The Tour de France: A Pre-Modern Contest in a Post-Modern Context' (2003) 20(2) *The International Journal of the History of Sport* 1.

Dean, J, 'Enjoying Neoliberalism' (2008) 4(1) *Cultural Politics* 47.

Debord, G, *The Society of the Spectacle* (New York, Zone Books, 1995).

Deleuze, G, 'Postscript on the Societies of Control' (1992) 59 October 3.

Deleuze, G, *Foucault* (Minneapolis, University of Minnesota Press, 2000).

Deleuze, G, 'Having an Idea in Cinema' in *New Mappings in Politics, Philosophy and Culture*, E Kaufman and KJ Heller (eds) (Minneapolis, University of Minnesota Press, 1998).

Deleuze, G, *T is for Tennis*, L'Abécédaire de Gilles Deleuze, avec Claire Parnet, Gilles Deleuze's ABC Primer with Claire Parnet, Directed by Pierre-André Boutang (1996), Overview prepared by Charles J Stivale, Romance Languages & Literatures, Wayne State University, www.langlab.wayne.edu/cstivale/d-g/ABC3.html#anchor813836.

Deleuze, G and Guattari, F, *Anti Oedipus, Capitalism and Schizophrenia* (Minneapolis, University of Minnesota Press, 1977).

Deleuze, G and Guattari, F, *Kafka: Toward a Minor Literature* (Minneapolis, University of Minnesota Press, 1986).

Deleuze, G and Guattari, F, *A Thousand Plateaus* (Minneapolis, University of Minnesota Press, 1987).

Desautels-Stein, 'The Market as a Legal Concept' (2012) 60 *Buffalo Law Review* 387.

Dicey, AV, *Introduction to the Study of the Law of the Constitution* (London, Macmillan and Co Limited, 1920).

Dimeo, P, *A History of Drug Use in Sport, 1876–1976, Beyond Good and Evil* (London, Routledge, 2007).

Dumont, L, *From Marx to Mandeville: The Genesis and Triumph of Economic Ideology* (Chicago, University of Chicago Press, 1977).

Dumont, L, *Essays on Individualism: Modern Ideology in Anthropological Perspective* (Chicago, University of Chicago Press, 1986).

Dumont, L, *Homo hierarchicus: The Caste System and its Implications* (Boulder, Paladin, 1972).

Ehrenberg, A, *The Weariness of the Self, Diagnosing the History of Depression in the Contemporary Age* (Montreal, McGill-Queen's University Press, 2010).

Henning, E, 'Three Dimensions of Playing the Game: About Mouth Pull, Tug-of-War and Sportization' in V Møller and J Nauright (eds), *The Essence of Sport* (University Press of Southern Denmark, 2003).

Elias, E, *The Civilizing Process* (Oxford, Blackwell, 1994).

Faber, N and Vandeginste, B, 'Flawed Science "Legalized" in the Fight against Doping: The Example of the Biological Passport' (2010) 15 *Accreditation and Quality Assurance* 373–374.

Fotheringham, N, *Put Me Back on My Bike, In Search of Tom Simpson* (London, Yellow Jersey Press, 2003).

Foucault, M, *The Birth of the Clinic* (London, Taylor & Francis, 1976).

Foucault, M, *The Will to Knowledge, The History of Sexuality, Volume 1* (London, Penguin, 1978).

Foucault, M, *Discipline and Punishment, The Birth of the Prison* (New York, Vintage Books, 1991).

Foucault, M, *The Birth of Biopolitics, Lectures at the College of France, 1978–1979* (Basingstoke, Palgrave Macmillan, 2008).

Foucault, M, *Society must be Defended, Lectures at the College of France, 1978–1979* (Basingstoke, Macmillan, 2008).

Foucault, M, *Security, Territory, Population: Lectures at the College of France 1977–1978* (London, Picador, 2007).

Foucault, M, 'The Confession of the Flesh' in M Foucault, *Power/Knowledge: Selected Interviews and Other Writings*, ed and trans C Gordon (New York, Vintage, 1980).

Galison, P, *Einstein's Clocks and Poincare's Maps, Empires of Time* (London, Hodder and Stoughton, 2003).

George, S, A Short History of Neo-liberalism, Twenty Years of Elite Economics and Emerging Opportunities for Structural Change. Paper presented at the *Conference on Economic Sovereignty in a Globalising World Bangkok*, 24–26 March 1999. www.globalexchange.org/resources/econ101/neoliberalismhist.

Goldman, DB, *Globalisation and the Western Legal Tradition, Recurring Patterns of Law and Authority, Law in Context* (Cambridge, Cambridge University Press, 2007).

Green, M and Houlihan, B, *Elite Sport Development: Policy Learning and Political Priorities* (London, Routledge, 2005).

Hacking, I, *The Taming of Chance* (Cambridge, Cambridge University Press, 1990).

Hamilton, T and Coyle, D, *The Secret Race, Inside the Hidden World of the Tour de France: Doping, Cover-ups, and Winning at All Costs* (New York, Bantam, 2012).

Hanstad, DV and Loland, S, 'Elite Athletes' Duty to Provide Information on their Whereabouts: Justifiable Anti-doping Work or an Indefensible Surveillance Regime? (2009) 9(1) *European Journal of Sport Science* 3.

Hanstad, DV, Smith, A and Waddington, I, 'The Establishment of the World Anti-Doping Agency: A Study of the Management of Organizational Change and Unplanned Outcome' (2008) 43 *International Review for the Sociology of Sport* 227.

Harcourt, B, *Illusions of Free Markets, Punishment and the Myth of Natural Order* (Cambridge MA, Harvard University Press, 2011).

Harden, I, *The Contracting State* (Maidenhead, Open University Press, 1992).

Hardie, M, 'Deleuze: Had I Not Done Philosophy I Would Have Done Law' (2007) 20 *International Journal for the Semiotics of Law* 81.

Hardie, M, From Barthes to Foucault and beyond – Cycling in the Age of Empire. Paper delivered at *Foucault: 25 Years On Conference*, University of South Australia, 25 June 2009, available at esodoweb. net/pdf/agempire.pdf.

Hardie, M, 'It's Not About the Blood, Operación Puerto and the End of Modernity' in *Doping and Anti-doping Policy in Sport: Ethical and Legal Perspectives*, M McNamee and V Møller (eds) (London, Routledge, 2011). Originally published as 'No va sobre la sangre, Operación Puerto n Puerto y el fin de la modernidad, Nó MADAS' (2010) 1 *Revista Crítica de Ciencias Sociales y Juridicas* 25.

Hardie, M, Cyclists, Health, Anti-doping and Medical Monitoring – A Better Approach? Available at: ph.au.dk/fileadmin/ph/Idraet/INHDR/Resources/Martin_Hardie_-_July_2011_-_INHDR_edito rial.pdf.

Hardie, M, Shilbury, D, Bozzi, C and Ware, I, *I Wish I was Twenty One Now: Beyond Doping in the Australian Peloton* (Geelong, Auskadi Samizdat, 2012).

Hardt, M and Negri, A, *Labor of Dionysus, A Critique of the State-Form* (Minneapolis, University of Minnesota Press, 2003).

Hardt, M and Negri, A, *Empire* (Cambridge MA, Harvard University Press, 1999).

Hardt, M and Negri, A, *Multitude, War and Democracy in the Age of Empire* (Cambridge MA, Harvard University Press, 2004).

Hardt, M and Negri, A, *Commonwealth* (Cambridge MA, Harvard University Press, 2009).

Harrington, J, *The Commonwealth of Oceana*, 1656.

Hayek, F, *Law Legislation and Liberty, A New Statement of the Liberal Principles of Justice and Political Economy*, Volumes 2 & 3 (London, Routledge & Kegan Paul, 1976).

Hegel, GWF, *Philosophy of Right* (Oxford, Oxford University Press, 2008).

Herlihy, DV, *Bicycle: The History* (New Haven, Yale University Press, 2004).

Hilgers, M, 'The Historicity of the Neoliberal State' (2012) 20(1) *Social Anthropology* 80.

Hoberman, J, *Mortal Engines: The Science of Performance and the Dehumanization of Sport* (Cambridge, The Free Press, 1992).

Hobsbawn, E, 'Mass-Producing Traditions: Europe, 1870–1914' in E Hobsbawn and T Ranger (eds), *The Invention of Tradition* (Cambridge, Cambridge University Press, 1983).

Horstman, DH, Gleser, M, Wolfe, D, Tryon, T and Delehunt, J, ' Effects of Hemoglobin Reduction on VO_2 Max and Related Hemodynamics in Exercising Dogs' (1974) 37(1) *Journal of Applied Physiology* 97.

Horstman, DH, Gleser, M and Delehunt, J, 'Effects of Altering O_2 Delivery on VO_2 of Isolated, Working Muscle' (1976) 230(2) *American Journal of Physiology* 327.

Houlihan, B, *Dying to Win: Doping in Sport and the Development of Anti-doping* (Strasbourg, Council of Europe Publishing, 1999).

Houlihan, B, 'Public Sector Sport Policy: Developing a Framework for Analysis' (2005) 40 *International Review for the Sociology of Sport* 163.

Hughes, R, *Culture of Complaint, The Fraying of America* (London, The Harvill Press, 1995).

Kafka, F, *The Complete Stories* (New York, Schocken Books, 1995).

Kafka, F, *The Penguin Complete Novels of Franz Kafka: The Trial, The Castle, America* (London, Penguin, 1983).

Kaufmann-Kohler, G and Rigozzi, A, 'Legal Opinion on Conformity of Article 10.6 of 2007 Draft World Anti-Doping Code with the Fundamental Rights of Athletes' (2007).

Kimmage, P, *Rough Ride, Behind the Wheel with a Pro Cyclist* (London, Yellow Jersey Press, 1998).

Kingsbury, B, Krisch, N and Stewart, B, 'The Emergence of Global Administrative Law' (2005) 68 *Law and Contemporary Problems* 15.

Koller, DL, 'Does the Constitution Apply to the Actions of the United States Anti-Doping Agency?' (2005–6) 50 *St Louis University Law Journal* 91–101.

Kolln, T, *The Peloton: Portrait of a Generation* (London, Rouleur Limited, 2010).

Konig, E, 'Criticism of Doping: The Nihilistic Side of Technological Sport and the Antiquated View of Sport Ethics' (1995) 30(3)–(4) *International Review for the Sociology of Sport* 247.

Kreft, L, The Elite Athlete: In a State of Exception? 31 *Sport, Ethics and Philosophy* 3.

Lacan, J, *The Seminar. Book VII:* The Ethics of Psychoanalysis, trans D. Porter (New York, WW Norton, 1992).

LaFeber, W, *Michael Jordan and the New Global Capitalism* (New York, WW Norton, 2002).

Latour, B, *The Making of Law, An Ethnography of the Conseil D'État* (Cambridge, Polity Press, 2011).

Lazzarato, M, 'From Capital-labour to Capital-life' (2004) 4(3) *Ephemera* 187.

Lazzarato, M, 'From Biopower to Biopolitics' (2002) 13 Pli: *The Warwick Journal of Philosophy* 100, available at www.warwick.ac.uk/philosophy/pli_journal/vol_13.html.

Lippi, G, Franchini, M and Cesare Guidi, G, 'Switch Off the Light on Cycling, Switch Off the Light on Doping' (2008) 42 *British Journal of Sports Medicine* 162.

Lippi, G, Franchini, M and Cesare Guidi, G, 'Tour de crisis: Doping in sport Should be Addressed by Prevention rather than Prosecution' (2007) 41 *British Journal of Sports Medicine* 625.

Londres, A, *Los forzados de la carretera Tour de Francia 1924,* Editorial Melusina SL, 2009.

Long, T, Pantaleon, N, Bruant, G and d'Arripe-Longueville, F, 'A Qualitative Study of Moral Reasoning of Young Elite Athletes' (2006) 20 *The Sport Psychologist* 330.

Lucidi, F, Zelli, A, Mallia, L, Grano,C, Russo, P and Violani, C, 'The Social-Cognitive Mechanisms Regulating Adolescents' Use of Doping Substances' (2008) 26(5) *Journal of Sports Sciences* 447.

MacAloon, J (ed), *Muscular Christianity in Colonial and Post-Colonial Worlds* (London, Routledge, 2008).

Madra, Y M and Özselçuk, C, 'Jouissance and Antagonism in the Forms of the Commune: A Critique of Biopolitical Subjectivity. Rethinking Marxism' 22(3) *Journal of Economics, Culture & Society* 481.

Marazzi, C, *Capital and Affects, The Politics of the Language Economy* (Los Angeles, Semiotext(e), 2011).

Martinez, JL, El Caso Valverde: Un complejo entresijo de decisions y actuaciones legales, Analisis del laudo TAS 2009/A/1879, 42 RJDE30 A310: 413, 2010.

Maso, B, *The Sweat of the Gods* (Norwich, Mousehold Press, 2005).

Mattei, U and Nader, L, *Plunder, When the Rule of Law is Illegal* (Oxford, Blackwell Publishing, 2008).

Mavromati, D, 'Indirect Detection Methods for Doping from A Legal Perspective: The Case of the Athlete Biological Passport, International 40. McLaren, R.H. CAS Doping Jurisprudence: What can we Learn?' (2006) 1 *International Sports Law Review* 4.

Mignion, P, 'The Tour de France and the Doping Issue' in H Dauncey and G Hare (eds), *The Tour de France, 1903–2003: A Century of Sporting Structures, Meanings, and Values* (London, Routledge, 2004).

Møller, V, 'The Anti-Doping Campaign – Farewell to the Ideals of Modernity?' in J Hoberman and V Møller (eds), *Doping and Public Policy* (Odense, University Press of Southern Denmark, 2004).

Møller, V, *The Doping Devil, International Network of Humanistic Doping Research* (Copenhagen, Books on Demand, 2008).

Møller, V, *The Ethics of Doping and Anti-Doping: Redeeming the Soul of Sport?* (London, Routledge, 2009).

Møller, V, 'One Step Too Far – About WADA's Whereabouts Rule' (2011) 3(2) *International Journal of Sport, Policy and Politics* 177.

Møller, V, *The Scapegoat, About the Expulsion of Michael Rasmussen from the 2007 Tour de France and Beyond* (Aarhus, Akaprint, 2011).

Negri, A, 'Postmodern Global Governance and the Critical Legal Project' (2001) 1(3) *Global Jurists Advances* Article 2.

Neocleous, N, *Fabrication of Social Order: A Critical Theory of Police Power* (London, Pluto Press, 2000).

Neocleous, N, Anxious Resilience, *Mute*, 18 August 2011.

Orwell, G, *Nineteen Eighty-Four. A novel* (London, Secker & Warburg, 1949).

Otlowski, M, *Implications of Genetic Testing for Australian Employment Law and Practice*, Centre for Law and Genetics, 2001.Occasional Paper No 1.

Paul, D, *A Guide to the World Anti-Doping Code: The Fight for the Spirit of Sport*, 2nd edn (Cambridge, Cambridge University Press, 2013).

A Peiper, *A Peiper's Tale (*Norwich, Mousehold Press, 2005).

Polanyi, K, *The Great Transformation: The Political and Economic Origins of Our Time* Paperback (Boston MA, Beacon Press, 2001).

Posner, EA, *Law and Social Norms* (Cambridge, MA, Harvard University Press, 2009).

Pottgiesser T, Umhau M, Ahlgrim C, Ruthardt S, Roecker K, Schumacher YO, 'Hb Mass Measurement Suitable to Screen for Illicit Autologous Blood Transfusions' (2007) 39(20) *Medicine & Science in Sports & Exercise,* 1748.

Read, J, *The Micro-politics of Capital, Marx and the Prehistory of the Present* (New York, State University of New York Press, 2003).

Rebeggiani, L and Tondani, D, 'Organizational Forms in Professional Cycling – Efficiency Issues of the UCI Pro Tour' (2008) 3(1) *International Journal of Sports Finance* 19–41. econpapers.repec.org/paper/handpaper/dp-345.htm.

Redmayne, M, 'Presenting Probabilities in Court: The DNA Experience' (1996–1997) 1 *The International Journal of Evidence and Proof* 187.

Rendell, M, *The Death of Marco Pantani: A Biography* (London, Weidenfeld & Nicolson 2006).

Robbins, L, *An Essay on the Nature and Significance of Economic Science* (London, Macmillan and Co, 1945).

Rosen, DM, *Dope: A History of Performance Enhancement in Sports from the Nineteenth Century to Today* (Wesport, CT, Praeger Publishers, 2008).

Sassen, S, *Territory – Authority – Rights. From Medieval to Global Assemblages* (Princeton NJ, Princeton University Press, 2006).

Scheuerman, WE, *Liberal Democracy and the Social Acceleration of Time* (Baltimore and London, The John Hopkins University Press, 2004).

Scheuerman, WE, *The Rule of Law under Siege, Selected Essays of F L Neumann and O Kirchheimer* (Berkeley, University of California Press. 1996).

Scheuerman, WE, 'Liberal Democracy and the Empire of Speed' (2001) 34(1) *Polity* 41.

Schneider, AJ, 'Cultural Nuances: Doping, Cycling and the Tour de France' (2006) 9(2) *Sport in Society* 212.

Smith, S, 'WADA as a Sporting Empire' *Proceedings: International Symposium for Olympic Research* (2008).

Soek, J, *The Strict Liability Principle and the Human Rights of Athletes in Doping Cases* (The Hague, Asser Press, 2006).

Sophocles, *The Three Thebian Plays* (London, Penguin Classics, 1984).

Sottas, P E, Robinson, N and Saugy, M, 'The Athlete's Biological Passport and Indirect Markers of Blood Doping, Doping in Sports: Biochemical Principles, Effects and Analysis' (2010) 195 *Handbook of Experimental Pharmacology* 305.

Straubel, MS, 'Lessons from USADA v. Jenkins: You Can't Win When You Beat a Monopoly' (2009) 10(1) *Pepperdine Dispute Resolution Law Journal* 119.

Strulik, H, Riding High – Success in Sports and the Rise of Doping Cultures; *Leibniz Universitat Hanover Discussion Paper No 372*, 1 January 2008. ssrn.com/abstract=1009826.

Thompson, EP, *Whigs and Hunters* (London, Penguin Books, 1975).

Turner, BS, *The Body and Society* (Oxford, Basil Blackwell, 1984).

Van Vaerenbergh, A, Regulatory Features and Administrative Law, Dimensions of the Olympic Movement's Anti-Doping Regime. IILJ Working Paper 2005/11, *Global Administrative Law Series* 9 New York, New York University School of Law, 2005).

Veblen, T, *The Theory of the Leisure Class* (New York, Mentor Books, 1953).

Voet, W, *Breaking the Chain, Drugs and Cycling – The True Story* (London, Yellow Jersey Press, 2001).

Waddington, I, 'Surveillance and Control in Sport: A Sociologist Looks at the WADA Whereabouts System' (2010) 2(3) *International Journal of Sport Policy and Politics* 255.

Wagner, U, 'The World Anti-Doping Agency, Power and Law Beyond the State' in U Wagner, RK Storm and J Hoberman (eds), (Birmingham AL, Hofmann, 2010).

Walsh, D, *From Lance to Landis, Inside the American Doping Controversy at the Tour de France* (New York, Ballantine Books, 2007).

Weber, M, *Economy and Society, Volume 2* (Stanford, University of California Press, 1978).

Wheatcroft, G, *Le Tour: A History of the Tour de France* (New York, Simon & Schuster, 2007).

Whittle, J, *Bad Blood: The Secret Life of the Tour de France* (New York, Random House, 2009).

Zumbansen, P, 'The Law of Society: Governance through Contract' (2007) 14 *Indiana Journal of Global Legal Studies* 191.

Zumbansen, P, 'Defining the Space of Transnational Law: Legal Theory, Global Governance and Legal Pluralism' in G Handl, J Zekoll, P Zumbansen (eds), *Beyond Territoriality: Transnational Legal Authority in an Age of Globalization* (Leiden, Martinus Nijhoff, 2012).

Zumbansen, P, 'Private Ordering in a Globalizing World: Still Searching for the Basis of Contract' (2007) 14(2) *Indiana Journal of Global Legal Studies* 181.

Zumbansen, P, 'Law after the Welfare State: Formalism, Functionalism, and the Ironic Turn of Reflexive Law' (2008) 56(3) *American Journal of Comparative Law* 769–805.

Žižek, S, *How to Read Lacan* (London, Granta Books, 2006).

Press, Media, Internet

Abarca Sports, *Comunicado de prensa de Abarca Sports en relación a las noticias que atañen a Alejandro Valverde*, 17 May 2007.

Abt, S, Pérez of Phonak is accused, *International Herald Tribune*, 1 November 2004, www.nytimes.com/2004/11/01/sports/01iht-phonak_ed3_.html.

L Armstrong, Nike Television Commercial available at www.youtube.com/watch?v=MIl5RxhLZ5U, 2005.

L Armstrong, The Worldwide Exclusive, *The Oprah Winfrey Show*. Full transcript available at armchairspectator.wordpress.com/2013/01/23/full-transcript-lance-armstrong-on-oprah/.

L Armstrong, 'If I was the carpenter, Pantani was the artist', *Cyclingnews*, 2013 www.cyclingnews.com/features/armstrong-if-i-was-the-carpenter-pantani-was-the-artist.

Arribas, C, Parad a los Galgos, *El Pais*, 19/12/2010, elpais.com/diario/2010/12/19/domingo/1292730388_850215.html.

Arribas, C, 'Queremos llegar al fondo de la trama', *El Pais*, 12/2/2009 elpais.com/diario/2009/02/12/deportes/1234393206_850215.html.

Arribas, C, Mancebo hace sufrir a Armstrong, *El Pais*, 17/2/2009, elpais.com/diario/2009/02/17/deportes/1234825207_850215.html.

Arribas, C, El mismo dopaje, menor tolerancia, *El Pais*, 18/12/2010 elpais.com/diario/2010/12/18/sociedad/1292626801_850215.html.

Arribas, C, Zapatero presiona a favor de Contador, *El Pais*, 10/2/2011 deportes.elpais.com/deportes/2011/02/10/actualidad/1297326128_850215.html.

Arribas, C and Hardie, M, 'En la Operación Puerto también había tenistas y futbolistas', *El Pais*, 18/1/2009 elpais.com/diario/2009/01/18/deportes/1232233212_850215.html.

AS Newspaper, *El lado oscuro del ciclismo: El escándalo destapado por Jesús Manzano y el Diario AS contado capítulo a capítulo*, 2004. www.as.com/misc/manzano/.

Bike Radar, Saiz and Belda fall out over Valverde, 2004. www.bikeradar.com/news/article/saiz-and-belda-fall-out-over-valverde-9981.

Bike Radar, Conspiracy of silence? 2006. www.bikeradar.com/blogs/article/conspiracy-of-silence-10980.

Bike Radar, Valverde; Sinkewitz implicates Bettini; Minister freezes funds, 2007. www.bikeradar.com/news/article/valverde-sinkewitz-implicates-bettini-minister-freezes-funds-12592.

Bose, M, Tour cyclist claims drug caused collapse, *The Telegraph*, 2004 www.telegraph.co.uk/sport/othersports/cycling/2375552/Tour-cyclist-claims-drug-caused-collapse.html.

Canadian Broadcasting Corporation, Cycle of denial implicated on the internet, 2006. www.cbc.ca/sports/indepth/landis/instantmessage.html.

CBS News, Feds close Lance Armstrong case; no charges, 3/2/2012. www.cbsnews.com/news/feds-close-lance-armstrong-doping-case-no-charges/.

The Consumerist, Judge Judy isn't real, consumerist.com/2007/12/17/judge-judys-tv-court-isnt-real/.

Cycling Archives, Henri Pélissier, www.cyclingarchives.com/coureurfiche.php?coureurid=3583.

Cyclingnews.com, Tour de France, Grand Tour 11 July–2 August 1998, Prologue, Dublin autobus. cyclingnews.com/results/1998/tour98/prol.html.

Cyclingnews.com, Tour de France, Grand Tour 11 July–2 August 1998, Stage 3, Roscoff–Lorient autobus.cyclingnews.com/results/1998/tour98/stage3.html.

Cyclingnews.com, Tour de France, Grand Tour 11 July–2 August 1998, Stage 4, Plouay–Cholet autobus. cyclingnews.com/results/1998/tour98/stage4.html.

Cyclingnews.com, Tour de France, Grand Tour 11 July–2 August 1998, Stage 5, Cholet – Chateauroux autobus.cyclingnews.com/results/1998/tour98/stage5.html.

Cyclingnews.com, Second Edition News 18 July 1998 Special Festina Roundup ftp.cyclingnews.com/results/1998/jul98/jul18a.html.

Cyclingnews.com, Tour de France, Grand Tour 11 July–2 August 1998, Stage 6, La Chatre–Brive-la-Gaillarde autobus.cyclingnews.com/results/1998.

Cyclingnews.com, Second Edition News for 19 July 1998, ftp.cyclingnews.com/results/1998/jul98/jul19a.html, News for 24 July 1998.

Cyclingnews.com, The drugs scandal widens autobus.cyclingnews.com/results/1998/jul98/jul24.shtml.

Cyclingnews.com, July 25, 1998, The drugs scandal update autobus.cyclingnews.com/results/1998/jul98/jul25.shtml.

Cyclingnews.com, Tour de France, Grand Tour 11 July–2 August 1998, Tarascon-sur-Ariège–Le Cap d'Agde autobus.cyclingnews.com/results/1998/tour98/stage12.html.

Cyclingnews.com, Tour de France, Grand Tour 11 July–2 August 1998, Stage 17, Albertville–Aix-les-Bains autobus.cyclingnews.com/results/1998/tour98/stage17.html.

Cyclingnews.com, 'Australian press report', 1998. autobus.cyclingnews.com/results/1998/sep98/sep2.shtml.

Cyclingnews.com, UCI Press Release May 2005. www.cyclingnews.com/news/the-uci-responds-to-the-spanish-affair.

Cyclingnews.com, Ullrich and Basso deny involvement with Fuentes, 2006. www.cyclingnews.com/news.php?id=news/2006/may06/may26news.

Cyclingnews.com, Beating the cheaters, 11 October 2006. www.cyclingnews.com/features/?id=2006/epo_protease.

Cyclingnews.com, Speculation catches fire over Tour de France positive test, 2006. www.cyclingnews.com/news.php?id=news/2006/jul06/jul27news2.

Cyclingnews.com, 51 witnesses for Operación Puerto, 2006. autobus.cyclingnews.com/news.php?id=news/2006/dec06/dec22news,

Cyclingnews.com, Spanish soccer clubs linked to Fuentes? 2006. www.cyclingnews.com/editions/first-edition-cycling-news-for-december-8-2006.

Cyclingnews.com, Valverde's defence optimistic, Davis fights to save World's spot, 2007. www.cyclingnews.com/editions/latest-cycling-news-for-september-21-2007.

Cyclingnews.com, Zabel, Valverde not welcome in Stuttgart, 2007. www.cyclingnews.com/news.php?id=news/2007/aug07/aug15news.

Cyclingnews.com, UCI says no Worlds for Valverde and initiates proceedings, 2007. www.cyclingnews.com/news.php?id=news/2007/aug07/aug30news.

Cyclingnews.com, Valverde cleared by CAS to ride world championships, 2007. www.cyclingnews.com/editions/cycling-news-flash-for-september-27-2007.

Cyclingnews.com, Complete coverage of 'Operación Puerto', 2009. autobus.cyclingnews.com/news.php?id=news/puerto_complete.

Cyclingnews, Anne Gripper breaks silence on blood passport, *Cyclingnews*, 2009. www.cyclingnews.com/features/exclusive-anne-gripper-breaks-silence-on-bloodpassport.

Cyclingnews.com, WADA frustrated by Spanish Courts in Operación Puerto case, 2009. www.cyclingnews.com/news/wada-frustrated-by-spanish-courts-in-operacion-puerto-case.

Cyclingnews.com, Operación Puerto: case closed, 2009. www.cyclingnews.com/news/operacion-puerto-case-closed.

Cyclingnews.com, 20 January, Stage 2: Gawler – Hahndorf 133.5km, 2010. www.cyclingnews.com/races/santos-tour-down-under-upt/stage-2/results.

El Mundo. Cronología del 'caso Alberto Contador'. *El Mundo Newspaper*, 2011 www.elmundo.es/elmundodeporte/2011/02/15/ciclismo/1297794357.html.

El Pais, Roberto Heras, positivo por EPO, 2005. deportes.elpais.com/deportes/2005/11/08/actualidad/1131438112_850215.html.

El Pais, Heras: 'Estoy completamente seguro de que soy inocente', 2005. www.elpais.com/articulo/deportes/Heras/Estoy/completamente/seguro/soy/inocente/elpepudep/20051108elpepudep_7/Tes.

Forbes, Back in the Saddle, Lance Armstrong, *Forbes Magazine*, 2001. www.forbes.com/asap/2001/1203/064_print.html.

Fuller, J, Is Spain is truly corrupt? watercooler.skins.net/2013/05/02/is-spain-truly-corrupt-we-cant-be-blamed-for-thinking-so/.

Guardian 2013 www.theguardian.com/sport/2013/apr/30/doping-doctor-eufemiano-fuentes-sentence-shock.

Grose, M, Cadel Evans is one tough hombre, one great role model, 2011. www.parentingideas.com.au/Blog/July-2011/Cadel-Evans-is-one-tough-hombre,-and-one-great-rol.

Hardie, M, Liberty trifecta, Cyclingnews.com, 2004. autobus.cyclingnews.com/road.php?id=road/2004/jun04/euskalbizikleta04/euskalbizikleta043.

Hardie, M, Belda takes aim, 2004 www.bike-zone.com/news.php?id=news/2004/sep04/sep25news2.

Hardie, M, Tyler starts the fight club on 11 September, *Cyclingnews*, 2004. autobus.cyclingnews.com/road/2004/vuelta04/?id=results/vuelta048.

Hardie, M, A Conversation with Pedro Delgado, Velonews, 2006 velonews.competitor.com/2006/11/news/road/a-conversation-with-pedro-delgado_11233 & velonews.competitor.com/2006/11/news/road/a-conversation-with-pedro-delgado-part-ii_11235.

Hardie, M, La nueva resurrección de Armstrong, *El Pais*, 2009.elpais.com/diario/2009/01/18/deportes/1232233211_850215.html.

M Hardie, No sólo resucitó Armstrong, *El Pais*, 26 January 2009, elpais.com/diario/2009/01/26/deportes/1232924427_850215.html.

Hardie, M, No es ya hora de actuar? *El Pais*, 27/4/2009, elpais.com/diario/2009/04/27/deportes/1240783228_850215.html. English version: An Open Letter, Velocity Nation, 12 April 2009. nyvelocity.com/content/features/2009/open-letter.

Hardie, M and Jones, J, Hamilton fails blood tests, 2004. www.cyclingnews.com/news.php?id=news/2004/sep04/sep21news3.

Hilbert, E, CBSSports.com, Official: Alex Rodriguez's PED use 'most potent we've ever seen', 2014. www.cbssports.com/mlb/eye-on-baseball/24410023/official-alex-rodriguezs-ped-use-most-potent-weve-ever-seen.

Hood, A, 'Liberty pulls plug on sponsorship' Velonews (25 May 2006). velonews.com/article/9913.

Hood, A, The scandal that just keeps on giving: Puerto investigation faces another delay, 2009.Velonews 16 October 2009. velonews.competitor.com/2009/10/news/the-scandal-that-just-keeps-on-giving-puerto-investigation-faces-another-delay_99302.

Hood, E, The 'Too Good To Be True' Flèche: 1994, 2007. www.pezcyclingnews.com/page/latest-news/?id=87915#.UpKyI7ae4QI.

Horrillo, P, An open letter to McQuaid, Original Published in *El Pais* in Spanish, Saturday 7 July 2007, elpais.com/diario/2007/07/07/deportes/1183759207_850215.html.

Horrillo, P, Mr. ADAMS, Original published in *El Pais* in Spanish, www.elpais.com/articulo/sociedad/senor/Adams/elpepisoc/20090210elpepisoc_2/Tes.

Shen, A, The Gospel According to Floyd Landis, Interview with Paul Kimmage, 2010, nyvelocity.com/content/interviews/2011/landiskimmage.

Le Monde, Des footballeurs ont été vus chez le docteur Fuentes, 2006. www.lemonde.fr/cgibin/ACHATS/acheter.cgi?offre=ARCHIVES&type_item=ART_ARCH_30J&objet_id=969121&clef=ARC-TRK-D_01.

Lindsay, J, Armstrong hunts down rider, Personal disputes mar Armstrong's perfect Tour, 2004. www.bicycling.com/news/pro-cycling/armstrong-hunts-down-rider.

Macur, J, Armstrong drops fight against doping charges, *New York Times*, 2012. www.nytimes.com/2012/08/24/sports/cycling/lance-armstrong-ends-fight-against-doping-charges-losing-his-7-tour-de-france-titles.html?pagewanted=all&_r=0.

Maloney, T, Six years, 11 doping scandals: The Phonak legacy, *Cycling News*, 2006 www.cyclingnews.com/news.php?id=features/2006/phonak_legacy.

Perth Now. 2011, www.perthnow.com.au/news/western-australia/dole-drug-tests-homeswestreform-proposed-at-wa-liberal-conference/story-e6frg13u-1226447842448.

Renee D, McQuaid: Spaniards are 'too lenient in their approach to doping', 2008. www.efluxmedia.com/news_McQuaid_Spaniards_Are_Too_Lenient_In_Their_Approach_To_Doping_21946.html.

Stokes, S, IPCT excludes discovery and Saiz and Rumpf: UCI to discuss reducing ProTour teams, *Cycling News*, 2006. www.cyclingnews.com/news.php?id=news/2006/dec06/dec10news.

Stokes, S, Operación Puerto delay scandalous, says McQuaid, *Cycling News*, 16 October 2009. www.cyclingnews.com/news/operacion-puerto-delay-scandalous-says-mcquaid.

Tan, A, 'Liberty Seguros terminate contract' *Cyclingnews* (2006) www.cyclingnews.com/news.php?id=news/2006/may06/may25news3.

The Scotsman, Landis pours more dirt on Armstrong, 2010. www.scotsman.com/sport/landis-pours-more-dirt-on-armstrong-1-1367256.

Thatcher, M, Interview for the *Sunday Times*: The first two years, 1981. www.margaretthatcher.org/document/104475.

Velocity Nation, Interview with Michael Ashenden, 2009. velocitynation.com/content/interviews/2009/michael-ashenden.

Velocity Nation, Open letter from Michael Ashenden to Phil Liggett, 30 August 2012. nyvelocity.com/content/features/2012/filthy-business-indeed.

Velocity Nation, The Landis emails, 2011. nyvelocity.com/content/features/2011/landis-emails.

VeloNation Press, Armstrong implicates Verbruggen, Ferrari for first time over doping matters 2013. www.velonation.com/News/ID/15836/Armstrong-implicates-Verbruggen-Ferrari-for-first-time-over-doping-matters.aspx#ixzz2tWJczY1v.

Velonews, Score another for Armstrong, 2004. velonews.competitor.com/2004/07/news/score-another-for-armstrong_6638.

Velonews, Beaudin, M, The wrath of Lance Armstrong: USADA outlines witness intimidation, 2012. velonews.competitor.com/2012/10/news/the-wrath-of-lance-armstrong-usada-outlines-witness-intimidation_256702#yJMTFQkCtcjOlCgu.99.

Wallace, W, Cycling tips, 2012. cyclingtips.com.au/2012/02/too-big-to-fail/.

Wikipedia, Judge Judy, en.wikipedia.org/wiki/Judge_Judy.

Wikipedia, Londres, Albert, en.wikipedia.org/wiki/Albert_Londres.

Wyatt, C, Paris salutes its American hero, *BBC News*, 2005. news.bbc.co.uk/2/hi/europe/4713283.stm.

RTVE Zapatero: 'No hay ninguna razón jurídica para sancionar a Contador' 2011. www.rtve.es/deportes/20110211/zapatero-no-hay-ninguna-razon-juridica-para-sancionar-contador/404359.shtml.

Police Reports

Guardia Civil, Seccion de Consumo y Medio Ambiente de Guardiia Civil, Dilegencia de Exposicion de Hechos, March 2004.

Guardia Civil, Jefatura Informacion y Policia Judicial, Unidad Central Operativa, Seccion de Consumo y Medio Ambiente. Dilegencia de Exposicion de Hechos, 23 May 2006.

Documents

UCI, International Cycling Union, Cycling Regulations, Part 13 Sporting Safety and Conditions, Chapter 1, Medical Monitoring.

UCI, Anti-Doping Rules of the UCI – Part 14 of the UCI Regulations www.uci.ch/includes/asp/getTarget.asp?type=FILE&id=NDc3MD.

UCI, Cycling Independent Reform Commission, Terms of Reference. 2014. www.uci.ch/Modules/BUILTIN/getObject.asp?MenuId=&ObjTypeCode=FILE&type=FILE&id=OTMwNzg&LangId=1.

UCI, Information on the biological passport 2007. www.uci.ch/Modules/ENews/ENewsDetails.asp?MenuId=&id=NTQzOA&LangId=1.

UCI, Whereabouts and location forms 2008. www.uci.ch/templates/UCI/UCI2/layout.asp?MenuId=MTI1Njk.

UCI, Riders' commitment to a new cycling, 2006. www.uci.ch/Modules/BUILTIN/getObject.asp?MenuId=MTI1NDg&ObjTypeCode=FILE&type=FILE&id=MzIwMzA&.

Union Cycliste Internationale, UCI ProTour: A label to promote the development of cycling. www.uciprotour.com/templates/UCI/UCI1/layout.asp?MenuId=MTcxw.

USADA, US Postal Service Pro Cycling Team Investigation 2012 cyclinginvestigation.usada.org/.

World Anti-Doping Code. www.wada-ama.org/en/world-anti-doping-program/sportsand-anti-doping-organizations/the-code/.

WADA International Standards. www.wada-ama.org/en/World-Anti-Doping-Program/Sportsand-Anti-Doping-Organizations/International-Standards/.

Cases

Australia

Briginshaw v Briginshaw (1938) 60 CLR 336.

Hammond v Commonwealth of Australia (1982) 152 CLR 188, 206, per Deane J.

Huddart, Parker and Co Pty Ltd v Moorehead (1909) 8 CLR 330, 379–80.

Melbourne Steamship Co Ltd v Moorehead (1912) 15 CLR 333, 346.

Plaintiff S157/2002 and The Commonwealth of Australia (2003) 211 CLR 476, 513.

XZTT and Anti-Doping Rule Violation Panel (2012) AATA 728. www.austlii.edu.au/au/cases/cth/AATA/2012/728.html.

Spain

Audienca Provincial de Madrid, Seccion no 5, Rollo 566/2007, Organo Procedencia: JDO Instruccion N 31 de Madrid, Proc. Origen: Diligencias Previas Proc. Abreviado no 4293/2006, Auto Numero 496/08, Ilmos Magistrados D Arturo Beltran Nunez, D Jesus Angel Guijarro Lopez, D Paz Redondo Gil, Dated 11 February 2008.

Audienca Provincial de Madrid, Seccion no 5, Rollo 702/2008, Organo Procedencia: JDO Instruccion N 31 de Madrid, Proc Origen: Diligencias Previas Proc Abreviado no 4293/2006, Auto Numero 63/09, Ilmos Magistrados D Arturo Beltran Nunez, D Jesus Angel Guijarro Lopez, D Paz Redondo Gil, Dated 11 January 2009.

Audienca Provincial de Madrid, Seccion no 5, Rollo 395/2009, Organo Procedencia: JDO Instruccion N 31 de Madrid, Proc Origen: Diligencias Previas Proc Abreviado no 4293/2006, Auto Numero 3734/09, Ilmos Magistrados D Arturo Beltran Nunez, Da Pascual Fabia Mir, D Paz Redondo Gil, Dated 26 November 2009.

Juzgado de Instruccion Num 31, Madrid, DPA 4293706 H, Autosobreseimiento, Dated 8 March 2007.

Juzgado De Lo Penal N° 21 De Madrid, Juicio Oral n° 52 de 2012., Doña Julia Patricia Santamaría Matesanz, Magistrada-Juez del Juzgado de lo Penal n° 21 de Madrid, SENTENCIA N° 144/13, procedimiento abreviado n° 4293/06: Eufemiano Claudio Fuentes Rodriguez, Jose Ignacio Labarta Barrera, Vicente Belda Vicedo, Manuel Saiz Balbas, Yolanda Fuentes Rodriguez. (**Sentencia Final**)

United States

Lance Armstrong v Travis Tygart, In His Official Capacity as Chief Executive Officer of the United States Anti- Doping Agency, and United States Anti-Doping Agency, United States District Court for the Western District of Texas Austin Division Case No A-12-Ca-606-Ss, 2012.

Sporting Arbitration

UCI v L and RFEC, CAS 2006/A/1119, 19 December 2006.

Alejandro Valverde Belmonte v Comitato Olimpico Nazionale Italiano (CONI) (2009/A/1879 CAS) decided 16 March 2010 (**Valverde 2**).

WADA & UCI v Alejandro Valverde & Royal Spanish Cycling Federation (RFEC) (CAS 2007/A/1396 & CAS 2007/A/1402) decided 10 July 2008 (**Valverde 1**).

WADA & UCI v RFEC & Alejandro Valverde (CAS 2007/A/1396 & CAS 2007/A/1402) decided 31 May 2010 (**Valverde 3**).

Films

Howard Hawkes, *Rio Bravo*, 1959.

John Ford, *The Man Who Shot Liberty Valance*, 1962.

Luchino Visconti, *Il Gatopardo, 1963.*

Steven Spielberg, *Minority Report*, 2002.

Songs

Edmund Kuepper, Chris Bailey, Swing for The Crime, Prehistoric Sounds, The Saints, 1978.

Other

Hardie, Shilbury, Bozzi and Ware unpublished interview 2010.

McQuaid, P, Personal Communication, UCI President Pat McQuaid 20 September 2007.

INDEX

Lightning Source UK Ltd.
Milton Keynes UK
UKHW010045291020
372362UK00003B/111

9 781509 936564